THE MOVING IMAGE

Also by Robert Gessner:

MASSACRE

BROKEN ARROW, a novel

UPSURGE, poems

SOME OF MY BEST FRIENDS ARE JEWS

HERE IS MY HOME, a novel

TREASON, a novel

YOUTH IS THE TIME, a novel

THE DEMOCRATIC MAN: THE WRITINGS OF EDWARD C. LINDEMAN (editor)

ROBERT GESSNER

The Moving Image

A GUIDE TO CINEMATIC LITERACY

New York   E. P. Dutton & Co., Inc.   1968

Published simultaneously in Canada by Clarke, Irwin & Company Limited, Toronto and Vancouver.

Library of Congress Card Catalog Number: 68–17287

Second Printing November 1969

for Peter and Stephen Gessner

Contents

9   Contents

Illustrations

Preface

Of all the ingredients that compose a motion picture, the shooting script is the least understood or appreciated by an audience. Yet it is the key that can unlock most of the secrets of cinema.

We are apt to be more mindful of acting, settings or locales, and physical movements of all sorts. A character can be fascinating for his expressions of love, hate, or indifference. A plot can be intriguing for its involvement, detachment, or puzzling dilemmas. The rhythm and acceleration of camera and editing may pace our concentration. Yet all these factors find their first life on paper, without which their final form on the screen could not exist. Even color and music have been indicated or suggested in some scripts. That there is a difference between the script page and the moving image is as obvious as the distinction between a printed play and a performance on a stage. Yet in the beginning there is the word.

Some films may appear to be scriptless, though this is an individual question of degree and style. All orchestra directors interpret musical scores differently, but they depend on printed notes. Federico Fellini and Michelangelo Antonioni have many versions of a shooting script before they direct their cameras. Fred Zinneman, on the other hand, sticks closely to his scripts, since he feels all else follows. David Lean says bluntly that the script is the most important element in the film. Akira Kurosawa goes further, believing one must be able to write a script in order to understand motion pictures fully. Avant-garde directors like Truffaut, Godard, Resnais, and Losey rely on cutting-room editing as much as the editing inherent in their scripts.

It is reasonable to conclude that no picture in cinema resembles exactly the mental image originally evoked in the language of words; conversely, no picture exists on the screen without first having had a prior form in the mind and usually on paper. As the writer is forced increasingly to think like a director, so the director correspondingly composes the final draft on celluloid. More often the writer-director is the same person, with both functions being enriched.

The aim of this book is to discover the unique patterns and structures that, through the visualization of ideas and emotions, make cinema an art. This may be called cinematic dramaturgy, the process in script form that inaugurates the creation of the product. Our major concern is not with production activity or studio problems as such, but more fundamentally in origins and motivations.

Changes from script to film can be valuable as a way of examining how ideas and emotions on paper do not always work on film. The translation of words into pictures can not be studied ideally without projecting a film with its script in hand, one eye on the paper, the other on the screen. Though such methods are impossible in book form, references are repeatedly made to the final screened version at appropriate points. Paper obviously has a different chemical composition and reaction than celluloid.

This new art form is numerically the ninth, whether it be called cinema, film, motion pictures, movies, or television; whether it is on celluloid or tape, projected toward a screen or upon a glass, transported in a circular can or over the air. For this book cinema has been chosen as the most generic word, similar to architecture, dance, drama, fiction, music, painting, poetry, and sculpture.

In discovering the essence of cinema we might recall E. M. Forster's observation that "the more the arts develop the more they depend on each other for definition." Similarly, by analyzing scripts of theatrical or storytelling films other forms of cinema, less narrative or dramatic, may be better understood. This book is intended for the spectator to whom cinema, contemporary and classical, has become as personal an experience as witnessing any of the performing arts. The book may guide the verbal-minded toward a cinematic literacy that can enhance enjoyment. A knowledge of process can permit curious persons to discover for themselves what they think and feel about cinema and why they like or dislike certain films more than others.

For over three decades this author has resisted temptations to academize motion pictures in book form, preferring the classroom swim through uncharted waters. The beach is now crowded, and the time has come to post lifeguards, label hidden holes, and plug in the public-address system. Textbooks lie just beyond the horizon.

The scripts selected have been from the exceptional stacks of the New York Public Library, a few from the Museum of Modern Art Film Library, and from my personal collection. The examples chosen are illustrative of concepts, and not necessarily salutory models. They differ in style according to studio, country, and period.

Dates of films have been a complex confusion, since script, production, copyright, and release (world premiere) dates hardly ever coincide in a single year; some foreign films have no copyright dates available. The dates stated (with a minimum of human error) are the copyright dates in the country of origin; an *R* prefixed to the date is the release date when no copyright year is known.

These scripts, even as excerpts, comprise a cross section or anthology of screen writing during the past forty years. It is fascinating to observe how the formal plot patterns of the thirties and forties begin to loosen during the fifties and sixties. Ideas and dramatic situations evolve toward experiments and freedoms comparable to those of other arts.

Scripts are challenging to read since the reader is obliged to imagine in his mind's eye how the action unfolds in terms of actor and camera movements as well as dialogue. Nor does he have the advantages of the novel's more extensive descriptions of place, mood, character motivations, and facial expressions.

The extraordinary variety in form, style, and punctuation should indicate that it is a highly individual mode of composition. At their best, scripts can be literature in the same sense as plays; in their baldest form they resemble what blueprints are to architecture. The continuity script is a nonliterary record kept by an editor, based on the final print of the film, and includes footage lengths. The word "scenario," incidentally, has become meaningless in films, though it has acquired a startling political usage. In his biography *Kennedy,* Theodore Sorensen referred to the "cover story" during the Cuban crisis as the State Department's "scenario" that proceeded to lay a smoke-screen according to schedule. The public was to be fooled while diplomats maneuvered, the means of doing so labeled with a bit of movie jargon. Finally, to facilitate reader comprehension the physical form of continuity and double-column scripts have been modified toward the more common playscript style.

Cinema, in its variety of types and lengths, is a many-fingered fan whose leaves overlap, but all are anchored to a common base, the script.

Earlier versions of certain passages appeared in *American Heritage, Art Journal, Film Culture, The Journal* of The Society of Cinematologists, *The New York Times Book Review* and *Theatre Arts*. I am indebted, first of all, to my students who with varying patience tolerated my explorations. I am obliged especially to Erwin Panofsky for encouraging my formulations in what he generously calls "the *Grundbegriffen* of cinema," to the Ford Foundation for supporting experimental productions at Harvard University in association with I. A. Richards. In particular, I am indebted to Monroe C. Beardsley of Swarthmore College, Carmen Blacker of Clare Hall, Cambridge; Anne Paolucci of the City College of New York, George Rylands of Kings College, Cambridge; and Robert Steele of Boston University for reading the manuscript with helpful eyes. For their encouragement in this work I am obligated to E. M. Forster, Howard Mumford Jones, Ernest Lindgren, Sig Moglen, and Gerald Noxon.

For facilitating scripts I bow to George Freedley and Paul Myers of the New York Public Library, Sidney Schrieber of the Motion Picture Association, Eileen Bowser of the Museum of Modern Art Film Library, and to Lewis Allen, Joseph Hazen, Harold Ober Associates, Abby Mann, Princeton University Library, Tony Richardson, and Audrey Wood.

To the archives of the British Film Institute, the Museum of Modern Art; to Ramona Javitz of the New York Public Library Picture Collection, and to the motion-picture distribution companies for facilitating photos. To the Arts and Science Faculty Research Fund of New York University for support in preparing the manuscript, and to student assistants Florence Wallach who tenaciously checked dates, Philip di Franco who assisted on the glossary, and to James Graham and Al Roman for photographing certain stills from screening prints.

I am obliged for the sheltering hospitality of the Frederick Lewis Allen Room in the Main Branch of the New York Public Library, to Yaddo, and to the MacDowell Colony. Finally, I am indebted to my two sons in cinema, Peter David and Stephen Lindeman, who kept a sharp lookout, as descendants of three generations of professors, for any academic double-talk.

Introduction

"Hundreds of people can talk for one who can see," Ralph Waldo Emerson observed in his study of mankind. The most revealing discovery about cinema is that we remember so little of what we have looked at.

"We see only what we are ready to see," said a pioneer in hypnosis, Jean Martin Charcot (1825–93). Cinema obliges us to look in a very special way. An artistic pace, as designed by the creators, is fed into a projection machine that gives us no personal control over the time allotted to perceive, accept, or reject. In the arts of architecture, fiction, painting, poetry, and sculpture the recipient determines his own rate of reception. Whereas the four performing arts, cinema, dance, drama, and music, are presented in a predetermined rhythm.

Cinematic movements need a means of interpretation so that, regardless of projection speed or artistic pacing, we are able to explore our reactions and enlarge our emotional responses. By now cinema should be in the stage of literature, drama, and fine arts wherein textual and iconographical analyses are the basis for judgment. But the exciting plastic surface makes objectivity difficult, since cinema in its movements and lights, its sense of presence and immediacy, is similar to a dream experience or a stream-of-consciousness. The dreamer is both the writer of the script and the director of the production who, at will, changes settings, fades time away, flashes bits of memory, develops drama, brings objects into foreground view, flies through the air, emphasizes minute elements, enlarges on meaning, and coats the whole with feeling. This omnipotence is both the creator and his own audience. Such duality is what makes cinema unique as a personal art to be experienced in public, even in the living room.

A rational approach to so idiosyncratic an art may appear to contradict its essential emotional appeal. Yet without some rationality cinema stammers amid gibberish and chaos or remains mediocre. Witness how exceptional are the lucid moments. What makes order and meaning are the uses of a grammar. Grammatical fluidity consists of connected units of expression, each the result of a single camera operation, its length determined by editing, and is called a shot. Shot-awareness is the fundamental means of becoming "ready to see" what we are looking at. Shots are like sentences in writing or melodic phrases in music. Scripts are written in the form of shots; films are photographed and edited in accordance with shot designs. Shot-consciousness is the essential tool for measuring any film.

The acceleration of shots over the years is a clue to style in contemporary cinema. In *Citizen Kane* (1941), the rapid, revolutionary film of pioneering fame, the shots average one every 14.5 seconds. In the action movie *The Guns of Navarone* (1961), the shots average one every 11.5 seconds. *A Hard Day's Night* (1964) approximates ten seconds per shot average. In current cinema there is also more image alteration by compositional changes within shots, done by actor movements, camera movements, and lighting shifts. In a fifteen-second commercial we may see four, six, or eight shots. Our exposure to rapid perception has been intensified, thanks ironically to commercial television, but how many shots do we remember? We are more inclined to recall scenes, actor performances, and occasional dialogue. A second viewing often surprises us with what is really on the screen. Even the projection of certain classics twenty-five to thirty times discloses on each occasion some element or object not taken cognizance of before.

For those teethed on TV and fed on its pabulum, the capacity to perceive shots and recall them should be considerably greater. Overexposure more often leads to pneumonia of the cerebrum. Strong minds have been lulled into a semicomatose state by a persistent flow of uninteresting images, not unlike the verbal massage administered by a verbose preacher or the drone of a lecturer. The rising generation is television prone but visually illiterate, which is ironic, since cinema has become the private art form of younger people throughout the world.

Cinematic illiteracy is an affliction that affects the educated and uneducated alike by reducing their capacity for judgment, their ability to discriminate, and by dulling their senses. Violence may become normal, indifference natural. As art critic and novelist, André Malraux warned that tasteless films and bad TV are greater threats to civilization than atomic or hydrogen bombs, and consequently ordered, as the Cultural Minister of France, tens of millions of francs to be spent in training the talents of cinema students. "Television is a vast, phosphorescent Mississippi of the senses, on the banks of which one can soon lose one's judgment and eventually lose one's mind," wrote *The New Yorker* critic Jonathan Miller.

To become visually literate is not easy. We need consciously see through the eyes of the writer-director into whose hands we have placed ourselves the moment we sit down and watch his pictures. Though he may be single or several persons, the composite talent is in charge of directing our eyes at objects and actors, and in the patterns of motion and light with which he wishes us to see them. Since he has mastery over the stimuli sent to us, we need to become conscious of the thinking behind the camera. "The task I'm trying to achieve is above all to make you see," confessed D. W. Griffith, the pioneer director. The veteran John Ford was more specific, believing the viewer should "see through the eyes of a character." The original of this obligation was expressed by Joseph Conrad in his 1897 preface to *The Nigger of 'The Narcissus'*: "My task which I am trying to achieve is, by the power of the written word to make you hear, to make you feel—it is, before all, to make you *see*. That—and no more, and it is everything." Behind the image lies a design.

No guide exists. This is a curious phenomenon, unprecedented in the history of man and his major arts. Our most persuasive and influential source of entertainment and enlightenment lacks a tradition of critical guidelines. Much meaning and beauty are missed or ignored in both the making and the receiving of emotions and ideas. It is as though the fast rotary presses were invented in the fifteenth century and mankind was deluged under a flood of cheap comic books, sexy paperbacks in sign language, illustrated crime tales, westerns, and sports books. A few semiliterates might discern a word here, a phrase there. What would have happened to the Renaissance? In the twentieth century verbal literacy at least permits taste to operate; sex and violence have become literary and less salacious, whereas their sensational depiction in vulgar films and on tasteless TV has stimulated a broader response.

Seeing is an optical capacity, while perception is awareness, involving visual intelligence and visual sensitivity. Grammar in cinema is the means of evolving seeing into perceiving. Taste can be acquired through learning and practice. A shot-awareness of what is going on behind the camera can empower a viewer to resist or enjoy a purely sensory seduction. The eye being the subtle thief of all other senses, the optic nerve the shortcut to the brain, we often become annoyed at ourselves for being seduced by the easy allures of face and figure, ordinary acting, or insipid narrative.

Our habits of viewing cinema require reorganization if there are to be new standards of judgment and taste. Word-oriented people have been writing the scripts, on the whole, and directing them. Sight-oriented writers and viewers are more shot-conscious. A revolution in visual perception is now occurring, mostly without our knowing it, especially in the plastic arts and in advertising.

The new audience for quality films expands every year as storytelling television lowers its common denominator. The eye becomes bored with visual forms as simple as cartoons (except in commercials), and the mind is dulled by being fed cues (through stock casting and music) instead of characterizations. The artistic growth of cinema depends on our capacity to absorb new experiences. As we move toward an expert discernment, we acquire a more refined visual sensitivity. Great cinema will grow as we become a great audience.

THE MOVING IMAGE

CHAPTER ONE ✖️⑤⑨

Conflict in Cinema

1. THE NATURE OF CINEMATIC CONFLICT

In an age of acceleration, when more people have been killed and born than in any previous century, a new art has been created uniquely capable of depicting conflict. The sharp mirror of cinema reflects the speed, compression, complexity, and fragmentation of our experiences in a way that makes it the art form of the twentieth century. Both the depiction of conflict and an avoidance or involvement with conflict explain cinema as an appeal and a gratification, as educator and escapist.

In contemporary cinema the two general approaches to storytelling might be called the impromptu and the plotted. Both deal differently with conflict. In the impromptu, which is less common, the shooting script serves as an elaborate outline. Artistically successful examples are Fellini's *8½* (1963), Antonioni's *L'Avventura* (1959), Truffaut in *400 Blows* (1958) and *Shoot the Piano Player* (1960), Godard's *Breathless* (1959), Resnais in *Hiroshima Mon Amour* (1959) and *Last Year at Marienbad* (1961), and others. Cassavetes' *Shadows* (1959) is an early American example of the impromptu approach. Richardson's *Tom Jones* (1962) was composed more on an editing table than at a typing desk.

What characterizes such motion pictures is their low-key drama, based on slack character conflicts, though there may be high-key activity as in *Tom Jones* and *Shoot the Piano Player*. The disengaged personality—the dissolution of character as a dramatic force—tends to render certain films unreal or abstract. Such passages are evident in Fellini's *La Dolce Vita* (1960), Antonioni's *Eclipse* (1962), *Red Desert* (1964) and *Blow-Up* (1966), Robert Rossen's *Lilith* (1964), Arthur Penn's *Mickey One* (1965), Losey's *Accident* (1967), and others. Lucid moments of exceptional realism and beauty evolve from the impromptu method, and often original experiments.

The plotted approach is more commonly employed because character conflicts can be more readily related and intensified. Since cinema is expensive to prepare and produce, though scripts by themselves don't make budgets, the plotted story is preferred by producers, actors and their agents, and by most directors. Writers who envision character motivations and interplay write plotted scripts. Fred Zinneman's *A Man for All Seasons* (1966), David Lean's *Doctor Zhivago* (1966), Truffaut's *Fahrenheit 451* (1966), John Huston's *The Bible* (1966), Resnais' *La Guerre Est Finie* (1966), Strick's *Ulysses* (1967), Howard Hawks' *El Dorado* (1967), and Arthur Penn's *Bonnie and Clyde* (1967) are various examples of plotted pictures.

Conflict to some degree exists in both low-key and high-geared stories. There is a biological basis for the universality of conflict. Our bodies are products of evolutionary warfare. "Wherever there is life, there is conflict," wrote Eduard C. Lindeman, the social philosopher. "Where there is no conflict, there is death." The principles of the Yang and the Yin encompass the positive and negative in the world, a basic duality, such as time and space, process and form—all inseparable.

Depiction of conflict in cinema, as we shall see, involves more than presentation of theme or characters. Actions that can be photographed and intensifications that can be mounted are qualities that affect the storytelling. There is more conflict per minute, seen or implied, witnessed or sensed, in cinema than in dramatic or narrative forms. This basic and fundamental difference begins in the creator's initial attitude toward the form of the contest.

Though the very nature of conflict is perpetual, the storyteller shapes a beginning and an end to his material. He needs to place his hands on it, more so in shaping it for cinema. This measurement of conflict is his attitude toward it, even in contemporary scripts wherein plot is not treated in traditional patterns. At the Cannes Festival of 1966, during a public debate among writers and directors as to whether plot is essential to motion pictures, the veteran Henri Clouzot asked, "But surely you agree, Monsieur Godard, that films should have a beginning, a middle part, and an end?" Jean-Luc Godard answered, "Yes, but not necessarily in that order."

2.   CONTEMPORARY CONFLICTS: RACIAL

The predominant friction in America today revolves around the color of skin, a problem also at the University of Moscow.

One Potato, Two Potato (1964) is the first contemporary film to deal with miscegenation. A white woman falls in love with a Negro, marries him, and consequently loses custody of her daughter by a former white husband. The external or action conflicts are handled better than the internal or psychological, such as the shy and touching courtship, the going to live with the Negro in-laws, the custody fight in court, the separation of the daughter from her mother. The internal conflicts are skimmed over, such as the divorcée's doubts about her colored suitor—her reactions to the intimacy—and the implied potency problem of the weak, white ex-husband and the unmotivated rejection by former white friends and the inner doubts and joys of the Negro as husband and father of a half-white infant. Conflict in *One Potato, Two Potato* is skin deep.

Nothing But a Man (1965) deals with a young man's natural ego, complicated by his being colored and a lowly worker. At first he is content to avoid trouble by accepting second-class status. When he marries a colored girl from a higher class, a schoolteacher and the daughter of an Uncle Tom preacher, he is forced to face his inner dilemma. This internal conflict humanizes him as a character, and makes the core of the film honest. His emotional involvement is real. Unfortunately, the preacher's daughter is not so clearly motivated. Whatever scruples and doubts she had to overcome in marrying a man less educated than she, with little money, and divorced with a loaned-out child, are not portrayed. Her defiance of her father is not portrayed. A sexual attraction is implied, but no inner struggle is enacted. The external frictions with white men as police, racists, and employers are real.

What these two films demonstrate is not only basic in terms of character motivations, since the avoidance of inner conflicts is obviously a narrative deficiency. The camera magnifies the script. It is a major characteristic of cinema that the presence or absence, emphasis or deemphasis of conflict is rendered more evident by the photographing of action. Indeed, the camera is a magnifying glass scanning the lines of a script for flaws or fireworks.

Equally revealing would be a comparison between dramatic and film-script versions of common material. The change in representation of conflict as a character moves from one medium to another would provide a different comparison. *One Potato, Two Potato* and *Nothing But a Man* were written expressly as films.

Eugene O'Neill's *The Emperor Jones* was the first work to treat the color problem primarily as an internal battle; a play in 1920, it became a film in 1933. The story line is simple:

A former Pullman porter and ex-convict, Brutus Jones (Paul Robeson), becomes emperor of an island in the West Indies "as yet not self determined by White Marines," in the words of O'Neill. When the inevitable rebellion begins he plans to head for France, where he has banked a looted fortune. He has supplies hidden in the forest, and these he seeks as the means of leaving the country. While in flight through the forest, a metamorphosis occurs. Inner fears accelerate. A series of brief symbolic scenes, expressionistic in form, show Jones's mental return to earlier stages of his life and of his race's history. During this retrogression to a primitive character, he is killed by silver bullets of rebel tribesmen.

The turning point in the emperor's character occurs when the inner contest begins to assert itself, stimulated by both the scenic conflict of the forest itself and by the pursuing natives.

In the play version this is in Scene Four:

Scene Four: *In the forest. A wide dirt road runs diagonally from right, front, to left, rear. Rising sheer on both sides the forest walls it in. The moon is now up. Under its light the road glimmers ghastly and unreal. It is as if the forest had stood aside momentarily to let the road pass through and accomplish its veiled purpose. This done, the forest will fold in upon itself again and the road will be no more.* JONES *stumbles in from the forest on the right. His uniform is ragged and torn, his eyes blinking in the bright moonlight. He flops down exhaustedly and pants heavily for a while. Then with sudden anger.*

I'm meltin' wid heat! Runnin' an' runnin' an' runnin'! Damn dis heah coat! Like a strait jacket! (*He tears off his coat and flings it away from him, revealing himself stripped to the waist.*) Dere! Dat's better! Now I kin breathe! (*Looking down at his feet, the spurs catch his eye.*) And to hell wid dese high-fangled spurs. Dey're what's been a-trippin' me up an' breakin' my neck. (*He unstraps them and flings them away disgustedly.*) Dere! I gits ride o' dem frippety Emperor trappin's an' I travels lighter. Lawd! I'se tired! (*After a pause, listening to the insistent beat of the tom-tom in the distance.*) I must 'a put some distance between myself an' dem—runnin' like dat—and yit—dat damn drum sound jes' de same—nearer, even. Well, I guess I a'most holds my lead anyhow. Dey won't never catch up. (*With a sigh.*) If on'y my fool legs stands up. Oh, I've sorry I evah went in for dis. Dat Emperor job is sho' hard to shake. (*He looks around him suspiciously.*) How'd dis road evah git heah? Good level road, too. I never remembers seein' it befo'. (*Shaking his head apprehensively.*) Dese woods is sho' full o' de queerest things at night. . . .

How does this inner conflict appear in the corresponding scene, numbered 175 in the script version? Is it more accelerated? What verbal indulgences of O'Neill have been omitted?

SCENE 175: FADE IN

on the forest. A wide dirt road runs diagonally from right front to left rear. JONES *stumbles in from the forest on the right. He flops down exhausted, then with sudden anger.*

JONES

I'm meltin' wid heat! Runnin' an' runnin' an' runnin'! Dis heah coat! Like a straight jacket! (*He tears off his coat and flings it away from him, revealing himself stripped to the waist.*) Dere! Dat's better! Now I kin breathe! (*Looking down at his feet, the spurs catch his eye.*) An' dese high-fangled spurs! Dey're what's been a trippin' me up an' breakin' my neck. (*He unstraps them and flings them away disgustedly.*) Dere! I gits rid o' dem frippety Emperor trappin's an' I travels lighter. Lawd! I'se tired!

After a pause, listening to the insistent beat of the tom-tom in the distance, he looks around him suspiciously.

How'd dis road evah git heah? Good level road, too. I never remembers seein' it befo'. (*Shaking his head apprehensively.*) Dese woods is sho full o' de queerest things at night.

The Dubose Heyward adaptation has not altered plot or character content, but what has happened is a considerable compression and intensification. These two cinematic characteristics are clearly evident, even though the above scene is not written in the shot-by-shot form that is the method of the modern shooting script.

The words are so arranged, nevertheless, as to evoke in the mind's eye a series of images of external actions that express internal conflict. In the play version one continuous image and action convey both surface information and psychic feeling. In the script this stage image is fragmented into six parts, which are really shots that

Emperor Jones. Courtesy of the New York Public Library.

concentrate on specific elements of the action and emphasize specific moments of emotion.

The shots are: (1) Jones flops down on the road and becomes angry; (2) he tears off his coat and feels relieved; (3) he looks down at his feet and protests against his spurs; (4) he removes them and feels he can travel lighter, though he is tired; (5) he hears distant tom-toms and becomes suspicious of the road he sees; and (6) he shakes his head with apprehension, and expresses fear.

This fragmentation of an action via shots is a distinguishing characteristic of cinema that permits an enlargement of conflict through visual intensification. We identify more intensely with Jones's predicament by seeing so many physical parts of himself from his point-of-view. Stated conversely, it is the employment of shots that adds voltage and energy to the visualization of ideas and emotions.

For Sir Laurence Olivier to play the Moor in extreme blackface is to give *Othello* (1965) a visual dimension, in stunning close-up shots, that adds a special power to the characterization and motivation. For writer-director Guy Green to conceive of a lonely, blind white girl (Elizabeth Hartman) placing her hands on the face of a kind, befriending Negro (Sidney Poitier) is to vitalize, again in close shots, the theme of *A Patch of Blue* (1965) .

An exceptionally ingratiating and emotionally evocative examination of intermarriage between colored and white—a truly American film—is Stanley Kramer's *Guess Who's Coming to Dinner* (1967) . The title betrays a clever mixture of genuine sentiment and forced humor, applied to a controversial subject. Though the burden of conviction rests mainly on freighted dialogue—"Well, I'll be a son-of-a-bitch," moans Spencer Tracy when he learns to what extent his only daughter loves Sidney Poitier—the characterizations are so human and natural that we enjoy the excessive close-ups of Katharine Hepburn being weepy and Spencer Tracy being taciturn. It is a mature leap forward by a courageous producer-director from the days, four decades earlier, of *Emperor Jones'* initial expression of Black Power. "I don't think of myself as a colored man," Poitier tells his retired mail-carrier father, "but as a man." The conflict generated by that point of view will be reflected in films for years to come.

3. WAR

Another major contemporary conflict is our concern over war. A look at examples from World War I and II, both adaptations from novels, can be revealing since the novel, more than the play, is closer to cinema in fluidity and flexibility. The novel can shift views and sizes of images from sentence to sentence.

Erich Maria Remarque's *All Quiet on the Western Front* became the first film (1930) to treat former enemies with an international humanity. The eighteen-year old hero, Paul Baumer (Lew Ayres) , outlives his comrades until the unexpected death of the veteran Stanislaus Katczinsky (Louis Wolheim) . To stay alive in the face of impending death is the struggle. Told in the first person and present tense, the novel approaches its conclusion when Paul, having carried Kat on his back with a shin wound, discovers he is dead:

On the way without my having noticed it, Kat had caught a splinter in the head. There is just one little hole, it must have been a very tiny, stray splinter. But it has sufficed. Kat is dead.

Slowly I get up.

"Would you like to take his pay-book and his things?" the lance-corporal asks me.

I nod, and he gives them to me.

The orderly is mystified. "You are not related, are you?"

No, we are not related. No, we are not related.

Do I walk? Have I feet still? I raise my eyes, I let them move around, and turn myself with them, one circle, one circle, and I stand in the midst. All is as usual. Only the Militiaman Stanislaus Katczinsky has died.

Then I know nothing more.

How is the simple but eternal conflict between life and death so visualized that we come to see what Paul experiences? In transposing Paul from the novel to the screen for this climax what would bring his own death "to life"? The novel merely implies it: "Then I know nothing more." In cinema, seeing is believing.

Director Lewis Milestone and his writers Maxwell Anderson and George Abbott, assisted by Del Andrews, depict Paul's death in two general shots, labeled Scene 23-J and Scene 24-J. The final sentence of the novel is visualized by means of a sentimental daydream:

SCENE 22-J:

ORDERLY
You two related, are you?

PAUL *shakes his head. He rises. He looks down at* KAT, *a last farewell look and then walks away, half stumbling like a drunken man.*

SCENE 23-J: SHOT OF THE FRENCH SNIPER ADJUSTING TELESCOPE SIGHTER

PAUL *has walked out into an open space, oblivious to his surroundings. He pauses. Across his face comes a vision of marching troops. They are German soldiers marching to* "Die Wacht am Rhein." *Another shadowy column comes from another angle, a column of French marching to* "The Marseillaise."

Other columns march, and other anthems are merged into the music. The troops march toward a single point on the horizon and disappear into a common grave. PAUL *is agitated in his dream. He calls out to stop the passing troops and finally leaps to his feet.*

PAUL
No, stop. No more! No more!

He stops abruptly and sinks down.

SCENE 24-J: SHOT FROM ABOVE

As he rolls over, a trickle of blood runs down his forehead. There is a smile of peace and calm on his face.

DISSOLVE TO:

Scene 25-J

The sound of a typewriter and the printed report "ALL QUIET ON THE WESTERN FRONT," *double-exposed across* PAUL'S *face.*

FADE OUT.

What evolved in the final shooting version was an action less verbal, intended more to be seen than read. Paul, back at the front

All Quiet on the Western Front. Courtesy of Universal Pictures.

and during a lull, reaches carefully over the trench sandbags for a butterfly. A French sniper adjusts his telescope. We see a close-up view of the hand reaching for the butterfly; then follows a medium-sized close-up of the French sniper squinting behind his sights and rifle, then the hand—the *zing* of the bullet on the sound track—the hand jumps and gradually relaxes.

The death of Paul has been personalized through an intensification of related images, creating one of the most poignant endings in cinema, quite different from the verbal "Then I know nothing more."

Another poignant scene in an antiwar film is not in the novel upon which the script is based, but is needed to focus the underlying conflict. James Jones' *From Here to Eternity* represents the struggle between individuality and the army. This friction is discursively treated in an oververbalized novel.

In Daniel Tardash's script (1955) the hero, Prewitt (Montgomery Clift), replaces the regular bugler and blows Taps in respect and affection for Angelo (Frank Sinatra). Angelo has been murdered by Fatso (Ernest Borgnine), but in the novel Prewitt is in the stockade with Angelo and thus unable to play Taps.

By having Prewitt play Taps in the script he becomes the hub of a wheel to whom others might relate, particularly Warden (Burt Lancaster). Warden's inner conflict is his preference to remain a staff clerk rather than take on officer responsibility. His admiration for Prewitt's independence of spirit, personified in part by the bugle blowing, reinforces his decision to remain a sergeant.

Here is that scene:

EXTERIOR: QUADRANGLE (H) —NIGHT

272. LONG SHOT— (H)
Framed in the moonlight the Quadrangle and Barracks area look like a college campus. Silence. No movement.

273. LONG SHOT—ANOTHER ANGLE   (H)
A figure can be seen far in b.g. [background], at the Bugler's post beside the megaphone. Another figure stands near him. The silence continues, then is broken by the sound of the bugle beginning Taps. The first note is incredibly clear and loud and certain. It is held longer than most buglers hold it. The second note is daringly short, abrupt. The last note of the first phrase rises, peals out, heartfelt. TWO MEN *come into the shot, smoking. They stop, turn toward the* BUGLER, *listen attentively. One of them flips away his cigarette. The Taps continues through the following.*

INTERIOR: SQUAD ROOM—NIGHT

274. FULL SHOT
Most of the men turn in their beds toward the sound of the bugle.
Some prop up on their elbows.

275. CLOSE SHOT—BUCKLEY
as he listens.

276. MEDIUM SHOT—TREADWELL AND ANDERSON
listening. Their bunks are next to each other.

> TREADWELL
> *(a reverent whisper)*
> I bet you it's Prewitt . . .

EXTERIOR: QUADRANGLE (H)—NIGHT

277. MEDIUM CLOSE SHOT—PREW
at the Bugler's post. Behind him stands FRIDAY CLARK, *motionless.*

278. MEDIUM SHOT—SECOND FLOOR PORCH   (H)
THREE MEN *come out of the squad room, lean over the porch rail,*
listening. Their faces are thoughtful, sad.

INTERIOR: ORDERLY ROOM—NIGHT

279. MEDIUM SHOT—WARDEN
The office lit only by a light over his desk. He is working late, a sheaf
of papers spread out before him. He listens to the bugle call, moved,
sorrowful. He snaps off the light, listens in the darkness.

What is occurring is a sort of catharsis for each man. No explanation is needed. Knowing Warden's dilemma—the woman he loves (Deborah Kerr) also wishes he would go to officers' school—we need only read his face while Taps continues. This is cinema in a pure form, without narrative explanation or dialogue; the images convey everything:

289. MEDIUM CLOSE SHOT—WARDEN   (H)
He comes out of the Orderly Room, stops and listens on the walk
outside.

290. CLOSE SHOT—PREW   (H)
coming to the end of the Taps. CAMERA MOVES IN *to a* CLOSE-UP.
There are tears in PREW's *eyes now. He blows the final notes.*

291. MEDIUM CLOSE SHOT—AT BUGLER'S POST—SHOOTING IN THE DIREC-
TION OF ORDERLY ROOM   (H)

PREW *lowers the bugle slowly and lets the megaphone rest in its swivel. He withdraws the mouthpiece, puts it in his pocket. He hands the bugle to* CLARK. CLARK *looks at the instrument as if it has become hallowed.* PREW *walks off. He passes* WARDEN, *who is still standing near the Orderly Room, and disappears into the darkness.*

292. CLOSE SHOT—WARDEN (H)
looking after PREW.

FADE OUT.

Prewitt remains an individualist until his death, caused by his refusal to heed a sentry's challenge during the Pearl Harbor raid. The irony of his senseless death (he went AWOL) is a comment on anarchistic individuality in time of war. Personification of ideas and emotions through characters and the actors who play the roles is another basic factor in screen writing and directing.

4. SEX ATTITUDES

Love as essentially a sexual hunger violates love as a romantic adventure. The clash of values in such films involves a revolution in attitude, which is in part reflected in censorship or the lack of it. Unhampered cinema, free of restrictions that hinder true characterizations, can remind us of the inherent power in this art for heightening conflict, especially between the sexes.

An important early example from the thirties, when strict censorship ruled Hollywood, is *The Postman Always Rings Twice* (1934), adapted from a novel by James M. Cain, a pioneer exponent of contemporary tough sex. A drifter without ambition, Frank Chambers, arrives dead-broke at a roadside joint, operated by Nick Papadakis, whose wife is not Greek. Frank, who narrates his story in the first person, describes her:

Then I saw her. She had been out back, in the kitchen, but she came in to gather up my dishes. Except for the shape, she really wasn't any raving beauty, but she had a sulky look to her, and her lips stuck out in a way that made me want to mash them in for her.

Later:

She came over and began helping me with the wind wing. She was so close I could smell her. I shot it right close to her ear, almost in a whisper, "How come you married this Greek, anyway?"

She jumped like I had cut her with a whip. "Is that any of your business?"

"Yeah. Plenty."

"Here's your wind wing."

"Thanks."

I went out. I had what I wanted. I had socked one in under her guard, and socked it in deep, so it hurt. From now on, it would be business between her and me. She might not say yes, but she wouldn't stall me. She knew what I meant, and she knew I had her number.

Husband Nick accepts Frank's suggestion to get a new sign, and goes to town. Frank locks the door of the roadside café.

She looked at me, and got pale. She went to the swinging door, and peeped through. Then she went into the lunchroom, but in a minute she was back.

"They went away."

"I don't know why I locked it."

"I forgot to unlock it."

She started for the lunchroom again, but I stopped her. "Let's—leave it locked."

"Nobody can get in if it's locked. I got some cooking to do. I'll wash up this plate."

I took her in my arms and mashed my mouth up against hers. . . .

"Bite me! Bite me!"

I bit her. I sunk my teeth into her lips so deep I could feel the blood spurt into my mouth. It was running down her neck when I carried her upstairs.

Their mutual antagonism, an initial conflict that culminates in the first kiss, is handled differently in the screenplay (1946). The realism is reduced by the former Motion Picture Producers Production Code (1927), so tyrannical for decades, but which no longer intimidates Hollywood, economic pressures at the box office being what they are. As unrealistic as the Code is the script's unnatural dependence on dialogue to convey the imagerial impact—a basic contradiction of verbal and visual languages. Dialogue is the least cinematic element in films.

Instead of washing dishes in the kitchen, Frank (John Garfield) and Cora (Lana Turner) are involved in painting the furniture, a literal whitewash. The new talkiness of the characters changes them into domesticated animals. The conflict is watered down to a kitchen quarrel.

Here is the parallel passage in script form:

SHOT 56A. CLOSE SHOT—FRANK

He takes can of paint from under counter. CAMERA PANS *him left and* TRUCKS *back with him to* CORA. *He speaks.* FRANK *places paint on table, starts to open paint can with end of paint brush.* CORA *reacts to* FRANK. FRANK *stirs paint, drops brush and turns to* CORA. CAMERA TRUCKS *in as he steps closer to her.* CAMERA TRUCKS *in to* MEDIUM CLOSE-UP *of them as they look at each other. She reacts to* FRANK *as he takes her in his arms—kisses her—they break. She takes compact from pocket, wipes lipstick off with handkerchief, looks at* FRANK, *takes lipstick from pocket and paints lips.* CAMERA PANS *left on* FRANK *as he watches her exit door at center background.*

> FRANK
>
> Why didn't you start this campaign of rehabilitation before I came—or were you waiting for me?

> CORA
>
> Nick was saving that paint.

> FRANK
>
> Nick saves a lot of things.

> CORA
>
> It's none of your business what he saves.

> FRANK
>
> I didn't say it was. Only when I have something, I don't save it. Why do you want to paint those chairs for? They look all right to me.

> CORA
>
> Because I want to make something of this place, I want to make it into an honest-to-goodness—

> FRANK
>
> Well! Aren't we ambitious. We want to make a lot of money, so we can buy lots of pretty clothes. Or maybe we want to put a little aside for our husband and us, in our old age?

LAP DISSOLVE TO:

57A. MEDIUM LONG SHOT—EXTERIOR: TWIN OAKS
Couple seen coming out of Lunch Room and climbing into parked car as FRANK *enters right foreground.*

> FRANK'S VOICE
>
> For a couple of weeks then, she wouldn't look at me—or say a word to me if she could help it.

LAP DISSOLVE TO:

58A. LONG SHOT—EXTERIOR: TWIN OAKS
FRANK *in background pacing back and forth. It is a dark and windy*
night and Sign on post at left swings back and forth. Lettering on
Sign reads: TWIN OAKS.

FRANK'S VOICE
I begin to feel like a cheap nobody, making a play for a
girl that had no use for me. Oh, I disturbed her.

Frank's Voice on the soundtrack is a pale substitute for the fleshy
tones of the novel. The Production Code and the excessive dialogue
have emasculated Frank Chambers. It is a weak, unrealistic film
based on a strong, truthful novel. Conflict is alive, or it ceases to be
conflict, first in script and then on camera.

Since that period of scriptwriting, cinema has depicted sex differently. John Garfield has been replaced by Jean Paul Belmondo,
whose corruption is without conscience. Not only does the Belmondo
type look out for himself; he is also capable of any act of nihilism. In
the opening scene of *Breathless* the antihero glares into the camera
and informs the audience where it can go. He has no conflicts that
are visual. He steals from girl friends; he is totally indifferent when
his mistress becomes pregnant. Their bed is a trampoline, a place on
which to perform with the greatest of ease and without resistance.

In writer-director Jean-Luc Godard's subsequent study of the
antihero wife, *The Married Woman* (1964), extramarital and marital sex are identical. Charlotte (Macha Méril) is a hedonistic female
with no feeling for the past (she is ignorant of Auschwitz as a name)
and whose future is a void. Her pilot husband Pierre (Philippe
Leroy) senses the marriage is not solid, and her actor-lover Robert
(Bernard Noël) is aware of imminent death (he carries a cyanide
pill). The film begins with a close view of an unrelated hand sliding
forward over a white sheet. A woman's voice says, "I don't know." A
man responds, "You don't know if you love me?" The voice answers,
"Why do you talk all the time? This is so nice."

The film continues in this manner, all impact and little content.
Though the female form is fragmented into intimate angles, showing
a hand, a leg, a torso, a head, the whole is never felt; the film is
passionless, clinical, and unerotic. Printed words, half-words, and
pages are flashed on the screen for significance. Though the narrative
presents the eternal triangle of two men and a woman, the conflict is
in the mind of the viewer when he beholds the juxtaposition of flesh

and materialism (underwear, phonograph records, modern apartment). The film concludes with Charlotte's hand withdrawing slowly, leaving a blank white sheet.

Nonetheless, the degree of conflict, slight or exaggerated, appears to be more self-evident in cinema than in other forms of drama or narrative.

5. SCRIPTLESS AND IMPROMPTU CONFLICT

Beginning with Robert Flaherty's *Nanook of the North* (1922), photographed in 1919–20 as a pioneer documentary about Eskimo life, there have been a variety of documentary films "shot off the cuff" in natural settings. Conflict in such films is implied or improvised. The sources of conflict, more expository than narrative and more intellectual than emotional, are rooted in environment, color, poverty, war, adjustment or rejection, and in similar non-narrative soil.

Flaherty's diary served as his script. Here is his description of Nanook's attack on a bull walrus: "Never had I such filming as that on Walrus Island. . . . With harpoon set and a stout seal line carefully coiled, and my motion picture camera and film retorts in hand, off we crawled for the walrus ground. The herd lay sleeping. . . . Now only a dozen feet intervened; quickly Nanook closed in. As I signalled he rose upon his feet, and with his harpoon held high, like lightning he struck down at the nearest bull. . . . By night all my stock of film was exposed. . . . At last I thought I had shot enough scenes to make the film, and we prepared to go home." Such is the script of the first documentary.

Plotless conflict has a tradition older than generally realized. Mack Sennett, the father of American comedy, devised vaudeville bits, slapstick actions, chases, and comic situations in the early 1900's. Stock characters like the henpecked husband, the shrewish wife, the darling daughter, the foppish suitor, the clod, the flatfoot cop—all were varied or refurbished on sets and locations. Improvisation became the routine procedure, and the golden opportunity for the genius of Chaplin. Trite situations such as mistaken identity, Cinderella-before-and-after-the-ball, Jack the Giant-Killer wins again, the pursuit of the pretty girl, the chase of the cops, and the reverse, the rescue of the damsel in distress—these were conflicts so obvious and inconsequential that they were virtually plotless actions. There was no suspense over who won. Sheer joy was in the improvisation, both in the making and in the viewing.

David W. Griffith, the godfather of cinematic language, experimented constantly while he shot. His direction consisted of "writing the shots" as they were photographed, even when he extended his short subjects to feature and epic lengths. Though the narrative source might be a short story, a play, or novel, Griffith's adaptation to the screen was characterized by an improvisation of ideas, images, and their sequential order. More than any pioneering director, Griffith created cinematic plot. His cameraman, G. W. Bitzer, recounted to me how frequently Griffith composed actions around a central idea, such as sentimental romance or a threat of rape. Though he might have sheaves of paper bound in script form to consult on the set, Griffith transcended plot in the traditional sense by shooting as though he were creating a scriptless film. His major influence on Erich von Stroheim, Eisenstein, Pudovkin, John Ford, and others was precisely in this fluidity that overflowed the edges of pages.

Grigori Kozintsev, director of *Hamlet* (1964), describes a similar approach in the Leningrad studios during the relatively free twenties: "The masters of cinema . . . enjoyed giving generalized instruction . . . about scenarios that were written on a cuff during a gay supper. . . ." In his own production of *Hamlet*, photographed in Esthonia on the Baltic Sea and in the Crimea on the Black Sea, Kozintsev created shots neither indicated nor suggested in Shakespeare's scenes, nor written in Pasternak's free translation. Such actions include the marching of Fortinbras' army along the seashore, Queen Gertrude riding on horse outside the castle walls en route to Hamlet's duel with Laertes, and additional activities by Guildenstern and Rosenkrantz.

In general, the escape from theatrical inheritance, the closely knitted plays of Ibsen toward the looser weaves of Bernard Shaw and Eugene O'Neill, has been more evident in the films of the fifties, beginning with the so-called Italian Neorealism, the French *nouvelle vague,* the British Free Cinema, the New American Cinema, and above all the growth of the documentary or informational film.

What is germane for us at this stage is a recognition that the degree of plot in storytelling scripts is usually in direct proportion to the amount of conflict implied or presented. We shall see how this relationship functions in certain European and American films of the more loosely plotted varieties. In the documentary, the degree of thematic juxtaposition often assures a potentially equal amount of conflict.

Obviously another principle is at work, already indicated in Griffith and Kozintsev and others, namely, that once the basic conflict and its plot situation have been established solidly and dynamically, improvisation becomes easier and is more tempting. Much of the charm and ingenuity to be found in *Lolita* (1961) and *Dr. Strangelove* (1963) is the result of Stanley Kubrick's improvisation, following the initial establishment of plot.

One of the most free-flowing of the plot-diluted scripts and films is *Tom Jones,* in which episodes are so loosely connected they almost stand by themselves.

Here is the opening scene in the novel as printed in 1773:

Mr. Allworthy had been absent a full Quarter of a Year in London, on some very particular Business, though I know not what it was. . . . He came to his house very late in the evening, and after a short Supper with his Sister, retired much fatigued to his Chamber. Here, having spent some Minutes on his Knees, a Custom which he never broke through on any Account, he was preparing to step into Bed, when, upon opening the Cloaths, to his great Surprize, he beheld an Infant, wrapt up in some coarse Linen, in a Sweet and profound Sleep, between his Sheets. He stood some Time lost in Astonishment at this Sight; but, as Good-nature had always the Ascendant in his Mind, he soon began to be touched with Sentiments of Compassion for the little Wretch before him. He then rang his Bell, and ordered an elderly Woman Servant to rise immediately and come to him. . . . She therefore no sooner opened the Door, and saw her Master standing by the Bed-side in his Shirt, with a Candle in his Hand, than she started back in a most terrible Fright, and might perhaps have swooned away, had he not now recollected his being undressed, and put an End to her Terrors, by desiring her to stay without the Door, till he had thrown some Cloaths over his Back. . . .

When Mrs. Deborah [Wilkins] returned into the Room, and was acquainted by her Master with the finding the little Infant, her Consternation was rather greater than his had been; nor could she refrain from crying out, with great Horror of Accent as well as Look, "My Good Sir! what's to be done?"

The John Osborne screenplay differs as much from Henry Fielding's novel as Tony Richardson's freewheeling direction emancipated drawing-room comedy. Here follows Osborne's opening scene (dated 1962) :

TOM JONES

PRE-CREDIT SEQUENCE:

1. EXTERIOR: ALLWORTHY'S HOUSE—DUSK
SQUIRE ALLWORTHY, *a simple, kindly, middle-aged widower, is return-*
ing home. He looks out of the carriage window at the rolling park
land of his Somerset estate.

2. EXTERIOR: ALLWORTHY'S HOUSE—DUSK
ALLWORTHY'*s carriage draws up outside his house. He is greeted with*
great affection and excitement by his sister BRIDGET *and the servants.*
They all go in together.

3. EXTERIOR: ALLWORTHY HOUSE—NIGHT
The house is glowing with the lick of swaying candle light, the glint
and rattle of warming pans being rushed along corridors, the laugh-
ter of MR. ALLWORTHY *and his sister as they finish their dinner and*
the pleasure of the servants in having their master home.

4. INTERIOR: ALLWORTHY HOUSE—STAIRCASE—NIGHT
ALLWORTHY *bids good night to his sister and walks gratefully and*
happily upstairs to bed.

5. INTERIOR: ALLWORTHY'S BEDROOM—NIGHT
ALLWORTHY *kneels to say his prayers. Then he turns back the bed-*
clothes happily and is about to get into bed but something stops him
short in amazement. Recovering himself, he rings the bell for his
elderly servant, MRS. WILKINS.

6. INTERIOR: ALLWORTHY HOUSE—STAIRCASE—NIGHT
MRS. WILKINS *thunders down the stairs like a routed goose. She opens*
the bedroom door and is shocked to find her master only in his night-
shirt. She closes the door immediately but ALLWORTHY *calls her back.*
She stands inside the doorway and ALLWORTHY *points to the bed.*

7. INTERIOR: ALLWORTHY'S BEDROOM—NIGHT
A small baby lies fast asleep on the bed.

8. INTERIOR: ALLWORTHY'S BEDROOM—NIGHT

MRS. WILKINS
What's to be done, Sir?

ALLWORTHY
I hardly know, Mrs. Wilkins. We must look after it until we
discover more.

MRS. WILKINS
Who can its mother be? (*She gasps indignantly.*)

On celluloid this scene has a special vitality, achieved through camera tricks of stop motion of momentarily frozen frames and jerky motions achieved via acceleration. Since tempo is not ordinarily indicated in scripts, the final film, in terms of its rhythm, is partially scriptless. There is much "winging of shots" in *Tom Jones,* based on maturity rather than on chance.

A certain chemistry is possible when actors, director and staff, cameramen and crews are assembled on a set or in a location. This confluence of talent and energies and setting tempts directors to try actions, angles, and compositions not previously conceived and written. Though spontaneity may evoke rewarding values, the risks run high. Self-indulgence can result in shooting for shooting's sake, like writing words more for sound than meaning.

The challenge is there, first in the mind of the scriptwriter intrigued with the unique possibilities inherent in the composing and executing of shots, and in their fluidity, and aesthetic excitement that might be called *the mystique of the plastic.* All creative processes are wrought with risks—and should be—but cinema demands more discipline than other art forms principally because its technical complexity is so interlocked with its humanistic values. How, when, and where the image moves, internally with its actors and externally in the form of its frame, affects the why and what of emotions and ideas. This is style and meaning inseparable, discipline and design inseparable.

Beginning in the late twenties the plotless script became associated with and was stimulated by two current art movements, surrealism and the linguistic revolt. The renowned Spanish artist of cinema Luis Buñuel created his first film in *An Andalusian Dog* (1928), assisted in part by Salvador Dali. They conceived of a scenario, written in three days, consisting of vaguely related gags associated with dreams. None of it was meant to be explicit or rational. Buñuel filmed the script in two weeks in Paris; it was finally reviewed in June, 1929. The version of the script, which he approved, was published on December 15, 1929. It reads:

PROLOGUE

Once upon a time. . . .

A balcony at night. A man is sharpening a razor near the balcony. The man looks through the window at the sky and sees. . . .

A small cloud advancing toward the moon, which is at the full.

Then the head of a young girl, her eyes open wide. The razor blade advances toward one of the eyes.

The small cloud passes in front of the moon.
The razor blade passes over the young girl's eyeball, sectioning it.

The exotic writer Henry Miller wrote a "scenario directly inspired by a phantasy called 'The House of Incest' by Anaïs Nin," *Scenario (A Film with Sound)*, (1937), is verbalized surrealism, lacking in any rational or explicit plot or conflict. Images are evoked, nonetheless, and are intended to startle in the manner of Buñuel. Selecting almost at random, here is the orgiastic climax of Chapter III.

. . . Dancing to the frenzied beating of drums, a continuous roll of deep drums that makes the hair stand on end. They [savages] dance in the shadow of a great fire, and as the din increases the animals which were hidden in the depths of the forest are seen rising from their lairs and bounding through the flames. Lions, wolves, panthers, jackals, hyaenas, boars—leaping through the flames as if they had gone mad. The screen is filled with terrified beasts: they leap through the bamboo walls of the huts, through the sides of circus tents, through glass windows, through furnaces of molten steel. They rush in troupes over the sides of precipices—deer, chamois, antelopes, yaks. Troupes of wild horses rushing madly over burning pampas, hurling themselves into craters. Monkeys, gorillas, chimpanzees scrambling from the limbs of burning trees. The earth is aflame and the beasts of the earth are running mad.

Meanwhile, amidst the pandemonium, Alraune continues her orgiastic dance. She is surrounded by a cluster of naked savages who clasp an enormous bracelet about her body. The bracelet tightens about her body like a vise. A boy is lying on the ground; they are bending over him with sharp instruments, tattooing eyes all over his body. He lies very quiet, terrified. The voodoo men have long, matted hair, dirty nails, disfigured faces, and their bodies are smeared with ashes and excrement. Their bodies are grotesquely emaciated. As they tattoo the young man's beautiful strong body the eyes are seen to open, one after the other; they wink, blink, twitch, roll from side to side.

The bracelet round Alraune's squirming body is unloosed; she recommences her obscene movements, the drums beat again, and the rhythm of the drums works up to an even more tremendous climax than before. The young man's body writhes and squirms; it is fastened to the ground by heavy stakes. The tatooed eyes open convulsively; they shudder and twitch. We see the eyes up very close, the veins stand out taut. Alraune's body flashes more convulsively; her vulva looks like a tattooed eye. The boy squirms and twists, the veins so taut and swollen that finally they burst. As they burst Alraune flashes in her most obscene pose, the vulva twitching, the eyes bursting. This keeps on and on until there gushes from her body a flood of blood, whereupon suddenly, abruptly, we see the huge bowl in the garden, the water calm, the glass intact, and goldfish swimming lazily.

Although Henry Miller titles his compositions *Scenario* (*A Film with Sound*), it is neither a silent nor a sound shooting script. He does indicate, in part, the size of the image he describes, and a sudden juxtaposition of images, like two shots in the conclusion. His *Scenario* is an impromptu form of writing in which tensions of a sort are indicated as substitutes for conflict.

Federico Fellini has a conclusive word on improvisation, and in saying it he discloses his dependence on planned and instinctive conflict. Speaking of *Juliet of the Spirits* (1964), he says: "People always think I improvise my films—that something—some scene, some moment, some idea just flies into my head, and I then and there put it in. The fact is, it's all intentional. I appear to be improvising only so as not to suffocate the flow of a scene. I call it 'attentive passivity.' I *allow* for things to happen."

Actually, how scriptless can a script be? "Impromptu" is not synonymous with "instantaneous." Jazz, that other indigenous American art form, is both plotted and impromptu, and appropriately for us Duke Ellington has made an observation. "I never heard anybody play anything I wanted to hear," said the Duke, "without any prethought—whether it's a week or a half-beat ahead. It's like everything—if it doesn't come out of the mind, it doesn't have any personality, it has no father, no mother, it's nothing."

Applying the principle to cinema, David Lean, in talking about his *Doctor Zhivago* (1965), puts the point simply: "The script is the most important thing in the film. If you haven't got a good script, you cannot make a good film. You can mess up a good script and make a bad film, but I don't think you can make a good film out of a bad script."

Akira Kurosawa, whose Japanese films are superior art for their disciplined style and humanistic meaning, goes further than Lean, whom he admires. The writer-director of *Rashomon* (1950), *Ikiru* (*Living*, 1952), and *The Magnificent Seven* (1954), among others, believes that the capability for understanding cinema is rooted in the script: "To understand motion pictures fully, one must be able to write a script." Not actually compose one, Kurosawa intimates, but an ability to do so.

Stuart Rosenberg, the young and adventurous director of *Cool Hand Luke* (1967), advises apprentice film-makers "to learn to read."

Conversely, an ignorance of script requirements combined with a disregard for the nature of cinematic conflict result in the sort of underground footage that too often leaves us with a feeling of embarrassment for the ineptness, boredom with its substance, or both. This is cinematic aphasia. Examples of adolescent voyeur-narcissism, boyish glee in the discovery of frame and zoom-lens movements, prolonged navel gazing, homosexual homilies, and off-focus, limp pornography can be seen in the work of Andy Warhol, the popular patron saint of the New American Cinema.

Warhol's marathon effort, *The Chelsea Girls* (1966), typifies the average scriptless and conflictless work that aims, among its serious practitioners, to express freedom from form and content, but in the end is victimized by its tyrannical compulsion to be different. This is done more often at the expense of the viewer than over any violation of the creator's creed, should one be discernible. Warhol, as the Truman Capote of a later generation, aims to be original at all costs. So in *The Chelsea Girls* (photographed in a New York hotel that does not exclude children) he has exposed eight hours of cool happenings on warm celluloid: dull needles are jabbed through dirty dungarees, Lesbians talk incessantly, male homosexuals talk incessantly, LSD turns on pinkish colors, and everyone talks mean and nasty to everyone else. Since editing (the manipulation of meaning) is not a Warhol consideration, the marketing problem was solved by dividing the product, returned from the developing tanks, into two equal parts for simultaneous screening on adjacent projectors. Is this "a whole new dimension" or plain laziness?

An energetic breakthrough is marked by Kenneth Anger in his scriptless but structured *Scorpio Rising* (1963), wherein homosexual aggression acquires an unusual significance with and relationship to the comprehensible world. Similarly, a poetic reality is captured aesthetically in Stan Brakhage's *Window Water Baby Moving* (1959) in which the physical beauties of childbirth are depicted without romanticism.

Stan VanDerBeek controls his images by exerting a deliberate manipulation of meaning, a control achieved through cinematic collage, a juxtaposition of still photos and newsreels, both sources fragmented in parts and in length. His mind, being lively and political, can lapse, unfortunately, into repetition and redundancy. The totality of impact denotes a planned approach and a designed execution—aside from the multiple-screen gimmicks and the novelties of multimedia executions (cartooning and screening simultaneously) — all of which marks a disciplined spirit seeking new forms. Awareness of script does not preclude, but can facilitate, experimentation.

CHAPTER TWO ✗✗

Focusing Conflict

1. IDEA AS INSTIGATOR

Since behind every conflict there lies a clash of wills, ambitions, emotions, concepts, themes, or whatever motivates characters, the most difficult task is a correct identification of the feeling or thought at work. Cinema poses a special challenge because the very terms that ordinarily relate to emotional response and ideas become antiquated when applied to the unique language of the Ninth Art.

The convenient labels used for drama since the Greeks will hardly describe the emotions and thoughts evoked in the films of Fellini, Antonioni, Kurosawa, Bergman, Resnais, Truffaut, Lumet, or Kubrick. These and other creators evolve new forms of perception and feeling in their personal projection of experiences, observations, and attitudes. The problem in storytelling cinema is to adapt dramaturgy to the forms of visualization that have special movements. It is no simple problem.

Nonetheless, a start needs to be made if conflict is to be utilized for the purpose of telling a story or structuring a documentary film. Let us consider *idea* as a tool for using the energies released by a clash of human atoms. Webster's *Dictionary of Synonyms* says:

Idea is the most comprehensive and widely applicable of these terms (concept, conception, thought, notion, impression) : it may be used of an image of something at one time or another actually perceived through the senses, or of something never perceived but visualized from bits of information.

This elasticity of idea permits us the latitude needed to comprehend the complexities of cinematic writing. Indeed, idea and image are linked—"it may be used of an image of something at one time or other actually perceived through the senses." And so we have one's idea of a penthouse, his idea of heaven, her idea of sexual intimacy, et cetera.

By associating idea with image for the purpose of exploring cinematic creativity, we acquire an instrument for testing the correct identification of whatever motivation is at work. What idea, we may ask of a series of related shots or of a single shot, lies behind these images? What feeling or thought is being conveyed in the surface features of the shot, such as its scenic views? Or its plot activity? Or in the facial expressions and gestures of a performer?

In expounding idea in cinematic drama, intellectual intention must not be confused with artistic presentation. One may succeed or fail independently of the other. Not to explore idea every moment along the way would ignore the very nature of drama in general and of cinema in particular.

2.   CINEMATIC IDEA

Different kinds of ideas exist in story content and in types of writing. Ideas may be abstract, expository, descriptive, narrative, dramatic, and cinematic. By briefly defining them we may better understand cinematic idea.

First, idea without a representational image is abstract. Abstract films of dots, dashes, lines, and forms began in Europe in the twenties as the scriptless works of creators influenced by cubist painters and sculptors. Though abstract cinema can be revolutionary in concept, it is limited, since motion and light require, for any prolonged viewing, some sort of self-sustaining design. On the whole, abstract cinema carries little or no intellectual freight. It is wholly impressionistic in impact, but uniquely capable of evoking feelings and other responses.

Idea existing in an informational image is expository. Documentary scripts—anthropological, educational, industrial, instructional, scientific, sociological (including TV news features) —present information that flows from the fundamental idea that first created that documentary.

Idea embodied in a surface image is descriptive. Having the

surface image as vehicle, the idea is carried by the plastic aspects of persons, their faces and bodies, and of inanimate objects, all of which are evoked by light and shadow and by varieties of movements. When idea is exemplified by an image of a concrete object, the matter may become a symbol. The Cross is the symbol of the idea of Christianity.

Idea when conveyed by a sequence of events, internally connected by character motivations, is narrative. A segment of a plot can carry an idea. Images, though accompanied by descriptive elements, are vehicles for an idea when they are predominantly concerned with story.

When narrative events are staged we have dramatic idea. It is the intensification and compression of plot and characterization with actors, dialogue, and setting that distinguish dramatic idea.

Idea when dependent uniquely on the flow of movements and light is cinematic. Though other ideas are present—abstract, expository, descriptive, narrative, dramatic in combinations or singly—the cinematic idea dominates the image whenever motion and light are the primary means of expression. Here the emphasis is on fluid visuality—even though initially expressed in words. Cinematic writing is the visual molding of emotions and thoughts and objects—with or without characters and plots—through an interplay of movements, lights, and shadows.

Cinematic idea plays a special role because of the demands of the medium. Effective films are rich in cinematic ideas, while failures are poor in such examples. Artistic punishment is swifter when cinematic idea is uncertain or absent. On the other hand, artistic rewards are greater when idea—no matter what category—is especially suitable to the plastic advantages of cinema. For example, *Ben Hur* (1927 and 1959) was successful twice at the box office primarily because of its extraordinary chariot race with genuine crack-ups. This cinematic passage demonstrated perfectly the glory and cruelty of Ancient Rome. No such clear idea existed behind *The Fall of the Roman Empire* (1964), an artistic and commercial failure. The tribulations of Marcus Aurelius in the face of decadence, an excellent narrative idea, was not developed. An excitedly photographed chariot race was isolated and irrelevant—the opposite of the *Ben Hur* chariot race, which was germane. Cinematic ideas, to be effective, need to relate to more than physical action. Behind the flow of movements and lights is the energetic substance of dramatic, narrative, descriptive, and expository ideas.

3.   MAJOR IDEA AND MAJOR IMAGE

Since idea and image should be ideally inseparable in effective cinema, a combination of shots may very well culminate in a key shot, like a punch word in a line of poetry. When this occurs it is a sudden climax or summary, and might be called the major image of that particular idea. Often it is the shot best remembered.

The Odessa Steps scene in Eisenstein's *The Battleship Potemkin* (1925) is climaxed by the close-up of the elderly lady whose face and pince-nez glasses have been smashed by a saber-wielding Cossack on horseback. This is one possible major image among the many shots showing the slaughter of civilians. The ruthless tyranny of the czar's soldiers is the idea of that passage. According to personal preference, other major images could be the shooting of the civilians as they pleaded for their lives, arms outstretched, or the precarious journey of the baby carriage down the steps.

In a broad sense every film has a basic idea or more likely a combination of several general ideas and their major images. A viewer can always select or recall some feature that stands out prominently in the film he has just seen, though it might not dominate a loosely organized and disunited film.

In every artistically effective film there are memorable major images that promote ultimate unity and impact. The master idea of a prolonged passage, for example, might need several major images for complete expression or may evoke individual responses and choices. Personal taste is involved. Often the major idea is never quite adequately summed up in a particular image, even though it seeps through many images.

A major image is what the exploitation department of a studio might choose for advertising purposes, though that picture may not be in the film. A major image might be conjured in your mind when you hear of an about-to-be released picture, starring a favorite actor or actress.

For Eisenstein, in his *Word and Image* essay, it is the "initial general image which originally hovered before the creative artist." It is the matrix, the mold that stirs the mind and imagination of spectators.

Such richly endowed films as Fellini's *8½* and Welles's *Citizen Kane* are studded with the jewels of major images that embody major ideas. Guido trapped in his car in an underpass during a traffic jam is a major image epitomizing his frustration. Also, Guido imagining himself being served the spa water by the hand of his ideal maiden in white. The urge to escape in reverie is expressed in that major image. In *Citizen Kane,* Kane is the savior of the downtrodden when he stands on a political platform, arms outstretched for applause, his campaign poster enormous behind him. Another: Kane is a beaten man in a wheelchair being propelled over the grounds of his estate. Obviously, these choices are personal.

What is useful about the concept of major idea and major image is the emphasis it places on the visualization of content. What is implied is the capacity for a clearly conceived idea to evolve ideally into an equally clear image. This is the inestimable value of a script. Fred Zinneman said, "You make a picture before you shoot it; once you start shooting, it is merely a matter of putting it on film."

As may be seen, major ideas and major images give a thumbnail synopsis of a film. As analytical tools they should be viewed as Aristotelian aids for understanding the creative process and for the evaluation of works. They are not rules for the making of art, any more than Aristotle's "four causes" and "three unities" are dicta for dramatists. Especially is there a certain mysterious, unknowable-in-advance quality in cinema, evolving from a very special amalgamation of script and production.

4. EVALUATION

Attitudes toward conflict so alter in successive generations that the mirror held to life becomes a two-way glass. We see the values the creator intends in terms of "only what we are ready to see," as Charcot indicated. The artist may be our educator as well as entertainer if he be the necessary thorn in the body politic.

When Nora slammed the door on husband and child, Ibsen fired a suffragette shot heard round the world. A sharp historical turn in nineteenth-century family life was depicted in *A Doll's House.* Albee performs a similar service in both stage and film versions of *Who's Afraid of Virginia Woolf?* (1965), but with a vengeance. Few married people can emerge from that experience without some hidden scar exposed. Louis Malle's *The Lovers* (1958) is a modern French treatment of a wife walking out on a stolid husband and a lovely child for a younger lover and all the consequences.

In *Monsieur Verdoux* (1947), Chaplin turns the moral table

completely about, making wife-killing more sportive than criminal. The ironic comedy has a morality: "numbers sanctify." The generals, the munition manufacturers are decorated for their deeds of mass murder. Only Charlie, the lone operator, gets the guillotine. In *Major Barbara* (1941), Bernard Shaw keeps the morality bitterly humorous.

In contemporary cinema, nineteenth-century values have been replaced by their opposites. What was once a plus virtue is now a negative fault. In *Divorce—Italian Style* (R 1963), murder and adultery have become substitutes for divorce. The major idea in the exquisitely photographed French film *The Girl with the Golden Eyes* (R 1964) is the beauty and the tragedy of lesbianism. The heroine in *Irma La Douce* (1963) is a prostitute who enjoys her work. Fellini's *Cabiria* (1956) has a similar idea, touched with pathos. The heroines in *A Taste of Honey* (R 1962) and *The L-Shaped Room* (1963) have out-of-wedlock pregnancies and are befriended, incidentally in each instance, by a gentle homosexual. In *Hiroshima Mon Amour* the romance is with wartime enemies, Japanese and German; guilt is a Caucasian burden in the first case; humanity is the plea in the second.

The sexual roles of women in a frustrated film director's life, *8½*, is depicted in a master image of Guido in black hat and white sheet, snapping a whip at all his girls from boyhood through marriage into his adulteries. The idea is psychologically astute: the relation between sexual dissatisfaction and artistic impotence. Guido's promiscuity not only suggests his inability to give himself fully to one woman, but implies—in Fellini's brilliant juxtaposition—a creative impasse, a writer-director's block.

Ingmar Bergman's concern with sex is in its moral, human, and religious consequences. To name only his later films, his major ideas have been incest in *Through a Glass Darkly* (1961), rape in *The Virgin Spring* (1959), a clergyman's love affair in *Winter Light* (1962), and physical releases (masturbation and fornication) in *The Silence* (1963). *Persona* (1967) implies latent lesbianism.

A hero's habitual promiscuity becomes a source of comedy in the films of Operator 007, Cary Grant, Rock Hudson, and others. That statutory rape can be enjoyed by a nymphet and an older man is a comic idea in *Lolita*. Drug addiction gets its treatment in the film adaptations of *The Man with the Golden Arm* (1955), *The Connection* (1961), and *Long Day's Journey into Night* (1962).

The revolution in values isn't being fought exclusively on the ramparts of sex. National leaders, presidents, senators, and military brass are no longer sacrosanct, nor are they above the law of dramatic license. *Dr. Strangelove* deals with stupidity and insanity on the highest levels of military and political administration. *Advise and Consent* (1962) depicts McCarthyism, *The Best Man* (1964), the homosexual background of a candidate for his party's presidential nomination. *Seven Days in May* (1964) exposes a right-wing conspiracy in the Pentagon to execute a *Putsch* and take over the government. In *In Cold Blood* (1967) murderers are examined as members of society. *Bonnie and Clyde* romanticizes the amoral glee of young, attractive thieves and killers (their bloody end doesn't erase the total impression of fun with guns). *The Graduate* (1967) is funny in depicting the generation gap and the enjoyment of Oedipus sex.

Apparently no idea is impossible any longer. Codes have been replaced by the First Amendment to the Constitution, which guarantees free expression. Television, on the other hand, adheres to the commercial as well as the moral codes of the thirties, or as a Hollywood wit puts it, "The bland leading the bland."

In England and Italy cinema approaches the thematic freedom enjoyed by the novel and drama in America. Sharp social analysis of the classes at play and at work can be seen in John Schlesinger's *Darling* (1965), a keen satire on promiscuity, inspired probably by the Profumo Affair, and reminiscent of Fellini's *La Dolce Vita*. Other English critiques of the Establishment and *status quo* are almost too numerous to list: *Look Back in Anger* (1959), *Room at the Top* (1958), *The Loneliness of the Long Distance Runner* (1962), *Saturday Night and Sunday Morning* (1960), *This Sporting Life* (1963), *The Servant* (1964), *Privilege* (1967), and others—an unmatched collection of mirrors.

The fundamental ideas are universal. It is the treatment of them, or the taboo against them, that differs. Basic plots remain; it is the twist that changes from time to time. The number of plots is not significant—Plotto's hundreds, Polti's 39, or Mark Twain's handful. The human equation, for its pluses, minuses, and neutrals, produces plots.

Sime Silverman, the illustrious founder of the bible of show business, *Variety*, once thought that three main motivations in man, money, power, and sex, should be sufficient. They could be called rewards, influence, and love. Money has many faces: gold, jewels, oil, cattle, water. Power has many faces: social dominance, political suppression, psychological supremacy, economic control. Sex has many faces: hetero, homo, suppressed, sublimated, familial, religious, and platonic.

The varieties of relations between persons for ideas for plot purposes are limited only by a writer-director's imagination. The imagination of certain creators functions within an attitude of nonconflict. There is a perverse faith in being disengaged as the secret for instant salvation. To be against any interpretation is to be against any meaning, a flat postponement of emotional involvement. Commitment is an embarrassing word. What is preferred—not even sought— is detachment and distance. In reaction against the synchronized, company product of big studio operations, independent film writer-directors have conceived of the personal film. Emphasis is on style, the relation between audience and the surface texture of the image. Stanley Kauffmann's description of this tendency in the theatre applies to the parallel current in cinema. Writing in *The New York Times* of "a view much in vogue" (referring to Edward Albee's *Tiny Alice* and *Malcolm*), he says: "This view reduces ideas to decoration, character to pageant symbol, and theme to a conveyor belt for effects. It is to shrink art to no more than sensual response— one kind or another of 'happening.' To some of us, this modish view is nihilistic, not progressive. It can be seen as a theory of the socially eccentric using their undoubted gifts to attack vindictively the main body of society through its culture."

The so-called Theatre of the Absurd, as fathered by Cocteau, Ionesco, Genet, and Beckett, is alleged to be spawned by cinema since those writers are avid fans. All of them, including Sartre, have written screen plays. Antonin Artaud, who founded the so-called Theatre of Cruelty, composed surrealistic essays on the Marx Brothers and their significance. Artaud also acted in films, Carl Dreyer's *The Passion of Joan of Arc* (1928), G. W. Pabst's *Three-penny Opera* (1931), and Abel Gance's *Napoléon* (1926).

The withdrawal from life can be a fascinating idea, as Alain Jessua demonstrates in his first film, *Life Upside Down* (1964). What characterizes its strength and sensitivity is a sympathetic dramatization of a man's conversion from the mundane spiritless world to a euphoric bliss in a private prison. It is a horror film in its unreasoning depiction of an inner death. Landru (Charles Denner) stares at objects and people, and by willing them invisible they disappear, thanks to camera tricks. He appears healthy. It is his vision that is ill. The visual contrast creates the conflict. Jessua's imagination makes a quiet, seductive impact out of the urge to avoid conflict.

CHAPTER THREE 🕊

Conflict and Character

1. THE CINEMATIC DIALECTIC

The juxtaposition between idea and counteridea, which is the essence of drama, is concentrated in cinema, where speed and complexity make for economical storytelling and swift transitions. Though poetry, painting, and other arts may become concentrated by juxtaposing ideas, it is camera and editing that make the dialectic cinematic.

The camera makes for a charged reality that may go deep into psychosensuality through unique combinations of external motion and altering light. Editing makes for a charged time sequence through the juggling of movements affecting space and objects. Internal motion, of course, depends on a clear dialectic within a character. Without this internal movement of will, the external movements of photographed actions lack validity and feeling. There are films that sail downhill at splendid speed through attractive camera work and clever editing, but carry no human feelings or thoughts on board.

Aristotle defined dialectic as the method for arguing. In cinema, the dialectic becomes the means of putting argument on wheels. Hegel said, "Contradiction is the power that moves things." Movement, being accelerated in cinema, means that contradiction can be more intense because perception has been quickened.

Opposites appear to attract and repel more decisively in those films that are highly visual in camera work and in their editing. The hero, or protagonist, is effective in cinema in proportion to how clearly his motivation is in conflict with obstacles, competition, or resistance.

In launching *Hamlet* (1948) Sir Laurence Olivier utters these words against an imageless screen: "This is the tragedy of a man who could not make up his mind." A dialectic is implied, which Olivier then proceeds to render cinematic, but didn't he trust his images to make the point?

In the Soviet version of *Hamlet* the dialectic of activity versus inactivity revolves around evil and corruption in a court setting (the Russian Hamlet feels at home only with the soldiers and peasants). Kozintsev's camera fluidity, more than his editing rhythm, makes his dialectic cinematic. Olivier's *Hamlet* was done rather slowly, whereas Shakespeare's melodrama does run at a terrific pace.

The question for us, in understanding the nature of a cinematic dialectic with regard to *Hamlet,* is what prevents a Renaissance man of action from taking action. In other words, can inactivity be photographed so that it has movement? How does the sharpening of idea and counteridea give *Hamlet* more possibilities in cinematic terms?

In casting a hasty eye over Olivier's version, what bald outline appears? A murdered father charges his son to revenge the treasonous killing; the emphasis is on Hamlet stalling. He stalls by substituting actions other than the one he was charged to do, the execution of Claudius.

Olivier's Hamlet stalls because there is a force in him as powerful as his urge to act, and in conflict they battle back and forth, giving us the drama. Revenge is obviously the one idea in this version. The opposing idea might be called compassion—Hamlet can not kill Claudius in cold blood when he has the opportunity. The opposing idea also might be guilt, the Freudian interpretation emphasized by Olivier—Hamlet can not kill his stepfather when he subconsciously longs to possess Gertrude. Still another opposing idea might be intellectuality—Hamlet, the rationalizer, the nose-in-the-book man, the director of plays, can not act until he realizes he is about to die himself. Perhaps a combination of these possibilities might explain the force Olivier emphasizes that acts in opposition to revenge.

As a character on film Olivier's Hamlet is more clearly seen in opposites, and is motivated in actions that excuse himself. Like the Russian *Hamlet,* it is designed to be seen more than heard. They are but two versions of Shakespeare's play.

The short story of Ring Lardner called *Champion* was later a screenplay, written by Carl Foreman and produced by Stanley Kramer (1949). "Midge Kelly scored his first knockout when he was

Hamlet (Sir Laurence Olivier). Courtesy of J. Arthur Rank.

Hamlet (USSR). Courtesy of Artkino.

seventeen," begins Lardner's account. "The knockee was his brother Connie, three years his junior and a cripple." But Midge got the half-dollar and lied to his mother about it, and knocked her down as well. In the sequence of his actions he became a sponger of free drinks, a welsher of debts, a crooked fighter, a wife-beater on his wedding night, a wife-deserter, an ingrate who fires the manager who made him, the thief of his new manager's wife and in turn fires that manager, a squanderer of money on women but refuses to give a cent to wife and child, mother, and crippled brother. "Suppose you can prove it," says Lardner's Sporting Editor on the *News*. "It wouldn't get us anywhere but abuse to print it. The people don't want to see him knocked. He's champion."

In this narrative form Midge lacks a dialectic; he has no inner conflict based on remorse or conscience. He is one-dimensional and totally predictable. Lardner's story reads like an object lesson, meant to shock.

In writing the screenplay, Carl Foreman and Stanley Kramer developed a morality play by giving Midge (Kirk Douglas) motivation and a cinematic dialectic. Midge is protective of his crippled brother Connie (Arthur Kennedy). Midge is robbed, beaten, and thrown off a freight train by three hoboes. The brothers hitch a ride with a wealthy prizefighter, and his doll Grace, to Kansas City, where Midge again protects Connie from insult, and is beaten by thugs, slaughtered in the ring by a veteran fighter, laughed at by Grace sitting ringside, but puts up a valiant fight only to be cheated of his earnings by a crooked manager.

Now Midge commands our sympathy and understanding in the scene with the crooked ring operator, Hammond, who had hired him to fill a vacancy. The fight is over, Midge has been brutally beaten:

SHOT 47. INTERIOR: HAMMOND'S OFFICE

HAMMOND *is sitting carelessly on his desk, looking on as two hard-faced* TICKET-SELLERS *check the night's receipts, as* MIDGE *enters the office.* MIDGE'*s face has been worked on, and his puffed eye had gone down somewhat.*

HAMMOND *looks at him coldly.*

MIDGE

(*expectantly*)

Got my money now?

HAMMOND
(calmly)

Sure— (He takes out his wallet, removes a bill and hands it to MIDGE.) Here you are.

He rises and goes around his desk to rummage in a drawer for a fresh cigar. MIDGE stares at the bill, his smile disappearing.

MIDGE
(blankly)

Ten bucks? Where's the rest? Where's my thirty-five?

HAMMOND
(coolly)

That's it. Ten bucks for your second, five for dressing room facilities, ten dollars for manager's fee. . . .

MIDGE stares at him, outraged.

MIDGE

I haven't got any manager!

HAMMOND
(harshly)

In this club I'm the manager for unattached fighters. Go on, hit the road, bum—

Raging, MIDGE starts for him. Simultaneously, the TICKET-SELLERS rise menacingly. MIDGE stops short, seeing what he is up against. He looks at HAMMOND bitterly, and his shoulders sag.

MIDGE
(defeated)

Okay—

He turns as if to go, then whirls suddenly and before HAMMOND or the two toughs can move he plants his fist in HAMMOND's stomach. As HAMMOND crumples with an agonized grunt, MIDGE whirls toward the door.

DISSOLVE TO:

SHOT 48. INTERIOR: MOVING TRUCK—NIGHT (PROCESS)

MIDGE and CONNIE are at the rear of the truck as it wheezes along the road. CONNIE is asleep, his body swaying with the motion of the truck, but MIDGE, leaning against a rail that divides the interior of the vehicle, is staring bitterly into the darkness. There is the sound of movement in the b.g., and then a sheep presses its head against the barred railing and looks at MIDGE sadly. It bleats.

FADE OUT.

Now we have the story of a decent-tough boy who becomes spoiled and corrupt. It becomes a morality play, a battle between means and ends that is its dialectic. Though Midge aims to do good in the script version, his means become increasingly bad, and in the conclusion the means corrupt the ends. No doubt Lardner could have written his short story with a dialectic had he chosen to do so. Nor is dialectical conflict by itself inherently narrative or cinematic, but must be rendered so by the writer.

In both the narrative and cinematic treatment of *The Red Badge of Courage* (1951) the Youth's dialectic is identical. Here is a classic study of a young soldier fighting an inner battle of fear in the face of death at the same time that he is joyous at being alive. They are different sides of the same coin, but they are opposites. How is the fear-joy dialectic to be visualized?

Though the Youth had "dreamed of battles all his life" and he "had burned several times to enlist," as Stephen Crane describes him, it "had suddenly appeared to him that perhaps in battle he might run. He was forced to admit that as far as war was concerned he knew nothing of himself." So Crane states the dialectic in literary terms.

In the John Huston–M-G-M script the fear is stated as the first climax, with dialogue and description—which is the basic weakness in this noncinematic script and its subsequent production. The dialectic remains narrative; it is not visualized:

YOUTH

Lots of good-a-'nough men have thought they was goin' to do great things before the fight, but when the time come, they skedaddled.

LOUD SOLDIER

Oh, that's all true, I s'pose, but I'm goin' t' do my share of the fighting. The man that bets on my runnin' will lose his money, that's all.

YOUTH

Oh, shucks! You ain't the bravest man in the world, are you?

LOUD SOLDIER
(*indignantly*)

No, I ain't, and I didn't say I was the bravest man in the world. I said I was goin' to do my share of fightin'—that's what I said. And I am, too. Who are you anyhow? You talk as if you thought you was Napoleon Bonaparte!

He glares at the YOUTH *for a moment, then strides away.*

YOUTH
(in a savage voice)
Well, you needn't git mad about it!

But the other is gone and the YOUTH *is left alone.*

MEDIUM LONG SHOT—THE YOUTH

In the gathering darkness, he feels a thousand-tongued fears. He hears low, desultory sentences behind him in the distance.

VOICE
(off shot)
I'll bid five.
Make it six.
Seven.
Seven goes.

DISSOLVE TO:

The above half of the dialectic is not demonstrated as an action that speaks for itself. Here the lens of the camera only magnifies words. This passage resembles a radio drama. We are told the Youth is frightened and we may see fear registered on the face of Audie Murphy, but our degree of involvement is limited by the absence of any enactment or visual action of that fear beyond facial expressions and words. It is primarily a literary-dramatic scene; it is cinematically ineffectual.

In presenting the other half of the dialectic following the battle, John Huston is cinematic:

CLOSE SHOT—THE YOUTH

He looks off to his right.

MEDIUM SHOT—NEW ANGLE—PART OF THE LINE

A few ghostly forms lie motionless on the ground; arms are bent and heads are turned in incredible ways. It seems that the dead must have dropped out of the sky onto the ground to have gotten into such positions.

MEDIUM SHOT—ANOTHER PART OF THE LINE

Among the wounded and the dead, a man, holding onto a tree, is yelling for assistance.

SOLDIER
A ball's knocked off my kneecap! Somebody come 'round here! Help, somebody! I can't leggo this tree! A ball's knocked off my kneecap!

In the distance are the dark lines of other troops. The sound of BAT-
TERIES *goes on uninterruptedly.*

CLOSE SHOT—THE YOUTH

*The haze of battle dissipates and shafts of sunlight strike trees
around him. He looks up, at a sound above him.*

CLOSE SHOT—A TREE

The blue, pure sky is revealed, and A BIRD IS SINGING.

CLOSE SHOT—THE YOUTH

He smiles at the sound, turns back to his fellows, radiating good will.

YOUTH

Gee! Ain't it hot, hey!

Thus ends the second climax with the dialectic established. Compare the above passage to Stephen Crane's climax at the end of
Chapter Five:

As he gazed around him the youth felt a flash of astonishment at the
blue, pure sky and the sun gleaming on the trees and fields. It was sur-
prising that Nature had gone tranquilly on with her golden process in
the midst of so much devilment.

Narrative is generally evolutionary, scenes growing out of one into
another; whereas cinema should be dialectic in its presentations,
images becoming dynamic, even explosive by their juxtaposition.
Without understanding this principle, people will say—not necessarily through laziness—that they would prefer to wait till the novel
is made into a picture.

2. CONFLICTING SYMBOLISM

Objective images, such as items, signs, tokens, emblems, figures,
make the dialectic more comprehensible because they can be photographed. When placed in dramatic juxtaposition they illustrate the
idea of the plot.

The most ancient symbol of contrasts, dating to the eighth century
B.C., is the Yang and the Yin circle with its curved inner division
between the orange and azure halves (also the Northern Pacific Railroad trademark!) . Yang and Yin are names for the positive and negative principles, for male and female, penetration and absorption,

light and dark, sun and moon, odd and even numbers, mountains and valleys, waxing and waning. All the rhythms in life are represented in perpetually complementary forms. Contrast implies an underlying unity, like a synthesis, for every pair of opposites.

Not all artistically accomplished creations have or need symbols, but when effectively selected they help sharpen the dialectic. Selection is the clue and the key. One man's symbol may be another's ash can. The intelligence of a creator can be judged by the symbols he keeps.

Is not the skull in the reflective hand of Hamlet a symbol, as well as the sword a symbol of action and revenge?

In Ring Lardner's *Champion* there are no symbols. Objects might become symbols through attitudes toward them. In the Foreman-Kramer *Champion* the radio microphone in the hand of the sports announcer becomes a symbol of the public image, publicity, illusion, false front. Boxing gloves became the money-prestige symbol of immigrant youngsters clamoring for success, first the Irish and Jewish, then the Italian. Now the contenders are mainly Negro and Puerto Rican. For Midge the gloves meant fame and fortune. There is no conflicting symbol within him, only the counteridea of Connie's cane, a symbol of humanity handicapped.

When the conflicting symbolism exists within the breast of the main character, then the dialectic might have higher voltage. Compare Joe Bonaparte in *Golden Boy* by Clifford Odets (1937) to Midge Kelly. Joe explains himself in the play version to his father, an Italian immigrant who loves music:

Poppa, I have to tell you—I don't like myself, past, present and future. Do you know there are men who have wonderful things from life? Do you think they're better than me? Do you think I like this feeling of no possessions? . . . You don't know what it means to sit around here and watch the months go ticking by! Do you think that's a life for a boy my age? Tomorrow's my birthday! I change my life!

To Moody, a decent fight manager, Joe first appears in one light:

I don't want you calling me Tom. You're brash, you're fresh, you're callow—and you're cock-eyed! In fact, you're an insult to my whole nature! Now get out!

Later, Joe has had five fights, but is unsuccessful as an attraction. His defense is brilliant, but he won't fight. According to his father, "My boy'sa besta violin' in New York!" Now the secret is out—Joe is saving his hands. This is his dialectic: to be a good violin:st or a great fighter, he can't be both. Opposite values are rather blatantly at stake, even for 1937. When he plays the violin, Joe's face "turns soft and tender." But greed is more dominant, and Joe Bonaparte goes to his Waterloo death with the manager's girl.

Dialectic symbols exist more than we may realize. Cross and sword clash in both the *Becket* (1964) of Richard Burton–Peter O'Toole and in the T. S. Eliot–George Hoellering (1952) film version of the verse play *Murder in the Cathedral*. Seldom do symbols clash so visually. In the Peter Glenville production and direction the Cross is physically present in the hands of John, Becket's attendant; also, Becket makes the sign of the Cross. The other clergy are hardly visible, the four murderous barons are in the foreground. One of them, Moreville, calls Becket a "dog." In the following shots note how the symbols become props, part of the action that can be photographed; they are highly cinematic:

215. *At this* JOHN *turns in blind rage, raising the Metropolitan Cross now as a lethal weapon and charges towards them. The* MONKS *in the background stop singing. There is a tense silence. As* JOHN *rushes towards them* FITZNURSE *runs him through. He falls, and as the Metropolitan Cross crashes out of* JOHN's *hands his body rolls to the foot of the steps.*

BECKET *looks sorrowfully down and whispers.*

BECKET
Oh Lord, how heavy your honour is to bear.

He descends the steps quietly and kneels over JOHN's *body, making the sign of the Cross in Absolution as he does so.* MOREVILLE *slips his mail and noseguard from his head and steps towards* BECKET. BECKET *looks up at him and starts to rise.* MOREVILLE *strikes the first blow and* BECKET *staggers under the impact.*

(*softly*) Poor Henry.

(*He turns to the altar and staggers up a couple of steps, uttering a prayer.*)

Et exultavit spiritus
meus in Deo Salutare meo

As he prays the rest of the knights close in on him.

Paratus sum pro Domino mori
pacem et libertatem per sanguinem
meam gaudeat Ecclesia.

(These were actually his last words. English translation is "I am ready to die for my Lord. May the Lord's Church obtain peace and liberty through my blood.")

216. HIGH SHOT—LONG SHOT

From above we see the BARONS *aim two more great blows at* BECKET's *prostrate figure.*

217. CLOSE-UP

BECKET's *head lying on the stone floor. Blood streams down one side of the face. As the music changes to the* MONKS' *intoning of the Dies* Irae *the face* DISSOLVES *into a face of stone. The miter is still on the head, which is in almost the same position. It is the stone effigy shown in the first scene.*

Face dissolving into stone is cinematic and symbolical.

In other examples of symbols they are more often indirectly present but photographable. In *The Informer* (1935) Gypo Nolan, played powerfully by Victor MacLaglen, acquires £20 for informing on his closest friend, Francis McPhillip. The money is squandered on drink and women. We see it disappear. The boat fare to America in steerage is also £20—the dream of escape—in the shape of a miniature ocean vessel in the window of a travel agency.

In *Executive Suite* (1954) the power struggle for control of the giant company focuses, during the climactic scene, on a cheap but profitable line of furniture. Don, the protagonist, demonstrates how cheap it is at a boardmeeting:

> DON
> (*continuing*)
> That's when we started doing things like *this!* (*He picks up the table; the papers on it scatter to the floor.*) The K-F Line! (*He moves toward* DUDLEY *with the table.*) Walt . . . are your boys *proud* when they go out and sell this stuff— when they know the finish is going to crack and the veneer split off and the legs come loose?

DUDLEY *begins to smile.*

> SHAW
> (*interrupting*)
> Now wait a minute! That's price merchandise! It serves a definite purpose in the profit structure of this company! We're not cheating anyone—

DON

Ourselves!

SHAW

At that price the customer knows exactly what he's going to get!

DON *yanks mightily on the table-legs and rips off one, shouting:*

DON

This!

(he raises the table above his head and smashes it against the floor)

This is what Tredway has come to mean!

Symbols can be props for actors as well.

Bridges can symbolize different ideas. The bridge in *The Bridge on the River Kwai* (1957), for an example, has three progressive meanings: first, as a symbol of British prisoner-of-war resistance to the Japs, since the bridge they are ordered to build is constantly caving in; second, as a symbol of personal and national pride in accomplishment as they build the bridge seriously; and, finally, as the enemy target of a raiding party.

For Whom the Bell Tolls (1943) centers around a bridge that is a symbol of war and death. Since Robert Jordan (Gary Cooper) is never tempted to desert his bridge-blowing duty for a prolonged sojourn in the double sleeping bag with María (Ingrid Bergman), suspense is not in personal drama. The suspense is whether the messenger Andres can get through the lines in time to have General Golz halt the offense, which had been the signal for Robert Jordan to blow the bridge. No dialectic exists within the breast of Jordan, which may explain why the picture fails to involve us beyond the image appeal of actors, scenery, and action. From the very beginning we expect the bridge to play a more important personal role. The first view of the bridge through Jordan's binoculars fixes the symbol in our minds for the whole of the story.

In the Dudley Nichols script (1943), perception is accelerated:

A-16. MOUNTAIN LEDGE—DAY

SHOOTING BACK (*from parallel*) ACROSS A SHELF OF ROCK *that juts out over a valley we see a lovely vista of high rolling country terminated by snow-capped sierras. No one visible though we hear* ANSELMO's *voice very near, cautiously lowered.*

VOICE

From here you can see the bridge.

Binocular lenses push across the edge of rock SO CLOSE TO CAMERA *that they look like siege guns. Then as* CAMERA RISES SLIGHTLY *we see* JORDAN's *head lift stealthily behind the binoculars. Another head,* ANSELMO's, *is raised and they peer down into space behind* CAMERA. *The old man points off left and down, and* JORDAN *props himself on his elbows and focusses the binoculars that direction at:*

A-17. BRIDGE—AS SEEN THROUGH BINOCULARS

First it is a blur and then it comes into clear focus where it spans the deep gorge in solid-flung metal grace. The road swings left across the bridge and passes out of sight in a long curve. On the near side the road passes out of sight below the ledge where the two men are lying concealed. A white sentry box at each end of the bridge.

JORDAN'S VOICE
(very low)

Are those sentry boxes?

ANSELMO'S VOICE

At each end, Roberto. Always two sentries on guard.

When a symbol is so visually implanted upon the beginning of a story, involving the life or death of the main character, it is natural to anticipate a more personal relationship toward that symbol. In the course of his love for María not once does Jordan question the necessity of blowing the bridge. Not even after Fascist reinforcements have crossed the bridge, a maneuver he was to prevent by destroying the bridge, does he question the necessity. Symbols, in other words, may reveal more than ideas; they may expose character and structural weaknesses in the writing and not necessarily in the film form.

The Bridge of San Luis Rey (1929), as a final example, offers a symbol of Judgment Day. In a reverse *deus ex machina,* occurring at the beginning rather than at the customary conclusion, an ancient rope bridge falls, and thus exposes—instead of resolving—a set of characters at dramatic moments in their lives: the Marquesa de Montemayor, Pepita, Esteban, Uncle Pio, and Jaimé. Of the three stories forming the novel by Thornton Wilder, the symbols of life—in apposition to the bridge as a symbol of death—are letters in two stories, those of the Marquesa to her spoiled daughter Clara and those of the actress La Périchole written by her adoring scribe Manuel. In the third story the conflicting symbol is the mirror of the vain La Périchole.

How does Wilder introduce the bridge catastrophe? Here, through the eyes of Brother Juniper, we see:

It was a very hot noon, that fatal noon, and coming around the shoulder of a hill Brother Juniper stopped to wipe his forehead and to gaze upon the screen of snowy peaks in the distance, then into the gorge below him filled with the dark plumage of green trees and green birds and traversed by its ladder of osier. Joy was in him; things were not going badly. He had opened several little abandoned churches and the Indians were crawling in to early Mass and groaning at the moment of miracle as though their hearts would break. Perhaps it was the pure air from the snows before him; perhaps it was the memory that brushed him for a moment of the poem that bade him raise his eyes to the helpful hills. At all events he felt at peace. Then his glance fell upon the bridge, and at that moment a twanging noise filled the air, as when the string of some musical instrument snaps in a disused room, and he saw the bridge divide and fling five gesticulating ants into the valley below.

Here are twelve shots from the editor's continuity script, which merely lists the action on the basis of what was photographed and edited. For our purposes, we see the symbol in action:

SHOT 17. MEDIUM SHOT
FATHER JUNIPER *blessing peasants.*

18. CLOSE-UP
People's feet going across bridge. Bridge starts to sag.

19. LONG SHOT
Entrance of bridge. Dust starts to rise.

20. MEDIUM SHOT
FATHER JUNIPER *and peasants looking off scene.*

21. LONG SHOT
Bridge sagging.

22. MEDIUM SHOT
FATHER JUNIPER *looking off scene, reacting to what he sees.*

23. LONG SHOT
Entrance to bridge. People running toward entrance.

24. LONG SHOT
Bridge breaks.

25. MEDIUM SHOT
Man and boy falling through scene.

26. MEDIUM SHOT
Lady falling through scene.

27. MEDIUM CLOSE-UP
FATHER JUNIPER *looking off scene, peasants running by him.*

28. LONG SHOT
Street in town. Man rides in on mule yelling:

29. TITLE
"The Bridge has fallen—the Bridge of San Luis Rey! God help us!"

The title is intended to convey the castastrophic meaning of the collapse: the sky has fallen; God help us. The symbol is ever present in the background while the lives of its victims are being probed. By fragmenting the collapse of the bridge into many shots, the script—through varied and repeated views—emphasizes the symbolism more than the novel. The bridge of life is indeed suspended over death, and it collapses upon a certain step.

Ingmar Bergman is highly cinematic while somberly portraying the unrefined minerals below facial surfaces. In *Silence* a troop of dwarfs suggests with irony, in juxtaposition to a fatherless boy, the idea that the child is father to the man. At crucial times in the intercharacter conflicts of the warring sisters, Bergman reintroduces the performing dwarfs as though to nudge us.

One of the more esoteric selections of Bergman's symbolism, used to depict the dialectic in a character, is the repulsive black spider as seen by the tortured, schizophrenic wife in *Through a Glass Darkly*. In her mind the spider represents God. The symbols flow fast and furiously in *The Seventh Seal* (1956), ranging from the traditional statue on the Cross to the innocent girl accused of having intercourse with the devil and about to be executed on a cross. The Virgin Mother and Child stroll in a sort of Garden of Eden as seen by Adam and Eve. There are the obvious chess game and the tree of life being sawed by Death. When elementary symbols are seen on repeated viewings, their power, unfortunately, is diminished. Since there is no God in *The Seventh Seal* Bergman may imply that Death is the devil.

This is a Fellini fault. Performers in circuses, in the streets, in cabarets are Fellini's recurrent symbols for life being a parade, a joy, a pathetic circus. In *8½* Fellini concludes with all the players and persons in Guido's life holding hands as they jog around the white parapet of a circus ring. Less clearly defined characters, functioning as types or symbols, are evident in *La Dolce Vita* wherein clowns, fools, and performers wear evening gowns and tuxedos while indulging in the dance of decadence and death.

Potemkin stimulated the use of symbolism in cinema. To portray the *status quo* against which the sailors were rebelling, Sergei Eisenstein presents rapid shots of a priest's Cross held high, then a bugle, followed by the imperial crest on the prow of the ship. To depict the spirit and force of the rebellion he flashes swift glimpses of stone lions, first prone, then rising. From that time forward the employment of symbols in cinema became a challenge to the artistry of the writer-director.

3. CONTEMPORARY VARIATIONS

TV viewing with its constant interruptions for commercials, its shock techniques to keep hands off the switching dial, its unnatural size—smaller than life—has affected a reduction of narrative idea. People are not expected to believe what they see on storytelling TV. Shocks are expected.

Of all the consequences of this revolution in viewing—altering social and psychological points of view as well as visual perspective—is the emergence of a TV-conditioned writer-director who aims primarily to please his generation, its rhythm and its values. "We didn't try to tell a story in the two Beatles films or in *The Knack* (1965)," says their director Richard Lester. "What we were trying to do was say something about people, about youth, about communication, about attitudes. The first Beatle film was about communication without speech. *The Knack* was about speech without communication. These were contemporary films. The styles and lives were contemporary. Plot was simply not important in any of them."

In Lester's *A Funny Thing Happened on the Way to the Forum* (1966) he does deal with a carefully constructed comic plot, but the emphasis is on sight gags and improvisations. Frenetic style is the key to Lester's determination to amuse his generation. On the other hand, Michael Winner, the writer-director of *The Jokers* (1967), is amusingly hilarious and original as well as frenetic.

An older generation of writers-directors appears more interested in making personal statements. Few in number, these self-elected, serious artists have exerted ironically an enormous impact in their protest against the beliefs and values of the majority. Bergman revolts against conventional church and conventional sex. Antonioni creates essays on loneliness in the materialistic world. Fellini is disgusted with decadence. Truffaut, Resnais, and Godard, divergent as they are in subject matter and technique, reduce solid narrative and dramatic ideas in favor of exciting cinematic ideas. Characters and plots become secondary to the means employed to make the personal statement. Though the result is not always salutary or artistically effective, this is the cinema that extends the frontiers of a new art.

The presentations of sensations without motivating explanations is a sort of illogic that has become the contemporary logic. "All men by nature wish to know" is Aristotle's observation, but know motivations in action, in the give-and-take of winning and losing, in the dynamics of contact. The inclination behind many personal statements of writers-directors is to zero-out winner and loser by avoiding motivation and the consequence—conclusion. Nobody wins, not even the audience, who may be left frustrated and dissatisfied.

An Italian version of *The Postman Always Rings Twice* is credited with the inauguration of the new cinema in Europe. The Hollywood characterizations of Cora and Frank were hedonistic on a one-dimensional level. They could have enacted their passion in northern New Jersey as well as southern California. In contrast, contemporary cinema depends more on where the story is being told and in what period. It is rather revolutionary to accept the power of place—setting, lighting, texture, mood—as a major determinant.

The first feature film of Luchino Visconti, *Ossessione* (1943), was based on James M. Cain's novel; but having been produced without copyright permission, it was never publicly shown in the United States. In Visconti's version, photographed in the northern countryside around Ferrara with its harsh light, the emphasis is not on two sensualists determined to achieve their future by the murder of an obstacle, Cora's Greek husband. Rather, the mundane setting, the roadside café, is their prison in which the lovers are drawn together like irresistible magnets. Outside is the world of freedom, illustrated in shots of long, straight roads, the countryside, the sunshine illuminating the village. This contrast between their prison and the landscape becomes the external force that drives the two lovers to desperate acts. No such setting in highway-littered southern California, one of the most crass areas in American culture, was so utilized as a dramatic or cinematic factor. Tony Richardson in *The Loved One* (1965) might have exploited that environmental banality as well as the freaks. Sex as a dialectic should never be isolated. On the other hand, environment by itself might be fascinating as plastic impact, but can hardly serve as a substitute for the more fundamental functions of characters in dramatic conflicts. Space alone, even with the *sui generis* flavors of motion, texture, lighting, and all the visually decorative powers of composition, cannot sustain cinematic acceleration. The eye wearies of pictures for picture's sake.

The avowed objectives of the impromptu approach are nonetheless important in that they reflect an effort to escape from both literary and theatrical inheritances.

Professor Umberto Barbaro of the Centro Sperimentale di Cinemagrafica, the film-training academy in Rome, wrote a manifesto in 1943 calling for an end to conventional approaches, and he used the term Neorealism. Barbaro attacked both historical and fictional adaptations, rhetoric of "noble sentiments," including "naïve and mannered clichés" and all "those fantastic and grotesque fabrications which exclude human problems and the human point-of-view." Barbaro was calling for a return to the humanism that Fascistic culture had outlawed.

A French critic, Alexandre Astruc, issued in 1948 his manifesto that eventually unloosened the new wave upon the banks of the Seine. *Le Camera Stylo* called for the camera as "a means of writing as supple and as subtle as that of written language . . . through which an artist can express his thoughts, however abstract they may be, or translate his obsessions, just as in an essay or a novel. . . ." In claiming "no area must be barred," Astruc proceeded to identify areas charged with conflict—"psychology, metaphysics, ideas, passions are very precisely its province. Indeed, these ideas and visions of the world are such that today the cinema alone is capable of giving them full realization."

These objectives, for all their clarion calls for fresh attacks, are unavoidably involved in the nature of conflict within human relations, regardless of whether productions are based on a one-page outline or a fully composed shooting script. Whether nonprofessional actors and natural locations are used, humans and their environment are involved. Rossellini's *Open City* (R1945) recounted the resistance actions of the Romans and the cruel Gestapo reprisals—conflict intensified by the pavements, houses, and rooftops of Rome, and by that superb actress Anna Magnani forcing her aroused and enraged body through the Roman streets. Was there a script? The question seems rhetorical, since conflicts were constantly present.

A script of a sort had been written by Ernest Hemingway for *The*

Spanish Earth (1937). It, too, has the conflict of war, and appears more detailed than whatever writing may have charted the Rossellini film, but it lacks personal involvement; it is primarily expository. Here is part of the commentary and narration from reel six:

> The Rebels attack the Madrid-Valencia road again. They have crossed the Jarama River and try to take the Arganda bridge.
> Troops are rushed from the North for the counter-attack.
> The village works to bring the water.
> They arrive at the Valencia road.
> The infantry in the assault where cameras need much luck to go. The slow, heavy-laden, undramatic movement forwards. The men in echelon in columns of six. . . .

Hemingway's words appear to have been written after he had viewed the Joris Ivens footage. In Italian and French productions, with rare exceptions, voice, music, and sound effects are added after filming. This adds to the freedom. Fellini reiterates, "I direct on the basis of a script which is in reality an outline on which I elaborate—or not—on the spur of the moment." *8½* is, nonetheless a finely chiseled film, a masterpiece of balance and detail, based on solid characterizations in conflict. Antonioni, who describes his films as "novels told with images," rewrites his scripts five or six times, and then improvises each scene during shooting.

Antonioni depicts his objective behind *La Notte* (1960) and all his films as an aim to suppress "outward physical action within the narrative of the film and, where possible, eliminate dialogue. . . . My only objective is to relate human experiences. If they are tragic it's because I believe the tragic sentiment dominates all of contemporary life. . . . Scientific man lives in a different world from that of pre-scientific man. . . . We are frightened because we can't create a life out of old longings."

Here from *Il Grido* (1957) is a typical and rather revealing excerpt from Antonioni. The setting is poetically lovely, the characters intelligent, sensitive, sensual:

BEACH AT THE MOUTH OF THE PO: EXTERIOR—EARLY AFTERNOON

450. ALDO AND ANDREINA

are sitting on the sand on the bit of beach that lies between the sea, the Po, and the fishing village. The scenery, transfigured by the faint light, is softly melancholy.

ANDREINA *watches the sea waves mingle with the river water and stir the reeds along the banks. She points this out to* ALDO *with all the wonderment of a child.*

> ANDREINA

Look how beautiful it is.

ALDO *looks and agrees with a nod.* ANDREINA *observes him for a moment and says:*

> Listen, I've known all kinds of guys, but one who enjoys life less than you. . . .

451. ALDO
smiles. His tone is almost affectionate when he speaks.

> ALDO

I wasn't always like this, you know; (*Then suddenly rousing himself.*) I remember once, we were setting up a mill near Ferrara. . . . You ever been to Ferrara?

> ANDREINA

I was supposed to go there once.

> ALDO

Well, anyway, one Sunday, my friends came to pick me up. . . .

> ANDREINA

All men?

> ALDO

There were girls too; what a question! So, in the end, the thing is, the others decided to go dancing. The girl with me was called Irma, and she said, "Why do you want to go to the dance hall? We're always dancing. Let's go in here instead." And so we went into the museum.

452. ALDO *stops.* ANDREINA *turns around to look at him. Seeing that the man is not going to continue, she says:*

> ANDREINA

And then?

> ALDO

Nothing. We saw the museum.

ANDREINA *shifts her position abruptly, almost with irritation.*

> ANDREINA

What kind of a story is that? It doesn't have an ending!

453. ALDO *does not answer. He takes a handful of sand and lets it*

pour slowly through his fingers. ANDREINA *makes another abrupt movement.*

ANDREINA

Now, there, that's the kind of thing that drives me crazy. You start talking and then you stop. Always just as you please. . . .

The ironic point to this sort of Antonioni conflict is its irritating tendency to be pointless. Andreina, as a self-respecting prostitute, is driven "crazy" by an aimless character doing just as he pleases.

Disregard for character motivation is reflected in Antonioni's treatment of his actors. Speaking of *The Eclipse,* Ingmar Bergman complains of Antonioni's "limited interest in his actors, in their instruction and guidance." Antonioni defended himself by stating that actors are "not always the most important element [of a shot]."

In *Red Desert* Antonioni is intrigued with color as the means of expressing idea. For mood purposes he colors water, repaints grass, varnishes wood, alters wall colors as a scene unfolds. Color becomes the master image, a substitute for plot. Repeatedly in this beautifully composed and visually arresting film, Antonioni will present an image of the industrial desert—the lifeless, monotonous expanse of oil storage tanks, a factory dump, huge ships, a harbor in fog—and into this composition, often in close-ups, comes the neurotically detached face of the modern young wife and mother, Giuliana, played by Monica Vitti. The juxtaposition, via this cinematic idea, is intended to convey the expository idea that the overwhelmingly oppressive character of the industrial world causes women to be neurotic. In the words of Antonioni, there is "a need for truth stronger than all industrial calculations."

This contemporary preference for idea, as illustrated—not dramatized—by character, appears to be a major substitute for conflict. Luis Buñuel, in *Viridiana* and *The Exterminating Angel* (1962) and *The Diary of a Chambermaid* (1964), is more interested in satirizing and attacking middle-class morals and mores than in depicting the humanity within such characters, their hypocrisy and frustration. Examples of Buñuel's ideas being illustrated are such scenes as Viridiana playing cards in a *ménage à trois* finale, the double suicide in *The Exterminating Angel,* and the marriage to the retired captain who lives next door in *The Diary of a Chambermaid.* Fascinating as they may be as expository ideas, such scenes are not rendered dramatic or cinematic merely by photographing actors. In his earlier masterpiece *The Young and the Damned* (1950), Buñuel as a writer-director brilliantly demonstrated that he could dramatize expository ideas.

The uses of time as a means of relating character and ideas are a particular contribution of Alain Resnais. In *Hiroshima Mon Amour* (1960), scenario and dialogue by the sensitive French novelist Marguerite Duras, the director Resnais has as his major idea man's inhumanity to man, and what the unselfish love of a woman might mean in counterpoint. In the wars of survival she is her enemy's keeper (German and Japanese).

SCENARIO, PART I, begins:

As the film opens, two pairs of bare shoulders appear, little by little. All we see are these shoulders—cut off from the body at the height of the head and hips—in an embrace, and as if drenched with ashes, rain, dew, or sweat, whichever is preferred. The main thing is that we get the feeling that this dew, this perspiration, has been deposited by the atomic "mushroom" as it moves away and evaporates. It should produce a violent, conflicting feeling of freshness and desire. The shoulders are of different colors, one dark, one light. Fusco's music accompanies this almost shocking embrace. The difference between the hands is also very marked. The woman's hand lies on the darker shoulder: "lies" is perhaps not the word; "grips" would be closer to it. A man's voice, flat and calm, as if reciting, says:

HE

You saw nothing in Hiroshima. Nothing.

To be used as often as desired. A woman's voice, also flat, muffled, monotonous, the voice of someone reciting, replies:

SHE

I saw everything. Everything.

The literary elusiveness of the opening is translated through compositional lighting and the editing of shots into concrete cinematic idea.

SHE (Emmanuelle Riva) "saw it," though the bomb deflowered Hiroshima twelve years earlier, when she was a young girl in her native Nevers in Occupied France, and at a time when she was in love with a young German soldier who was later killed at the Liberation. The juxtaposition of Nevers, where her head was shaved as cruel punishment, and Hiroshima, leveled to the ground, provides the dramatic and cinematic power of this masterpiece. Lying with her Japanese lover, appropriately an architect (Eiji Okada), she is asked if the man she loved during the war was French. Her reply is negative:

Nevers. A shot of love at Nevers. Bicycles racing. The forest, etc.

SHE
At first we met in barns. Then among the ruins. And then in rooms. Like anywhere else.

Hiroshima. In the room, the light has faded even more. Their bodies in a peaceful embrace.

And then he was dead.

Nevers. Shots of Nevers. Rivers. Quays. Poplar trees in the wind, etc. The quay deserted. The garden. Then at Hiroshima again.

I was eighteen and he was twenty-three.

Nevers. In a "hut" at night. The "marriage" at Nevers. During the shots of Nevers SHE *answers the questions that* HE *is presumed to have asked, but doesn't out loud. The sequence of shots of Nevers continues. Then:*

(*Calmly*) Why talk of him rather than the others?

HE
Why not?

SHE
No. Why?

HE
Because of Nevers, I can only begin to know you, and among the many thousands of things in your life, I'm choosing Nevers.

The cinematic idea of juxtaposing Hiroshima and Nevers, Japanese lover and German lover, projects visually the basic universality of man, whether he be conqueror or victim.

In *Last Year at Marienbad* Resnais greatly extended the juxtaposition of time while maintaining the same place. Though baffling on occasions when narrative idea is abandoned or ignored, the film is a unique experience. While the neglect of conflict as a motivating force confuses and puzzles the mind, the eye is entranced by surface textures of rare precision and beauty. *Marienbad* is a sensual experience that stirs the imagination and moves the spirit. It has more cinematic than expository, narrative, or dramatic ideas.

Time, like environment, can be a unifying force, but hardly a substitute for the inevitable interplay between characters. The play's indeed the thing, regardless of place and period, but not of people. Resnais in *La Guerre Est Finie* (1966) did concentrate on characterization in a way he hadn't done in his previous films. A middle-aged revolutionary, active for twenty-odd years, functions against the background of the continuing struggle of Communist revolutionaries in today's Franco Spain. Neat in clothes, precise in manner and speech, unmarried but sensuous, rational and realistic, the main character (Yves Montand) is three-dimensional. His lovemaking with both an immature nineteen-year-old Marxist and a middle-aged, mature career woman (Ingrid Thulin) is exquisitely handled for their semiromantic but thoroughly sensual passages. Resnais has the gift of portraying the feeling of a moment, the touch of it, its shape and texture in visual terms. The body of the young girl is so fragmented in its lovely parts, treated so tenderly for its freshness, that we readily understand how an older man responds and why she, in her youthful hero-worship, adores the seasoned revolutionary. The fragmentation of the older woman's body is done differently. There are maturity and understanding, a great compassion, a different tenderness that is expressed in her desire for a child. This is superb cinema, rare in the contemporary depiction of sex as sexuality.

The mind of the trained Communist—his sensibilities and apprehensions, fears and phobias—distinguishes *La Guerre Est Finie* in another manner. This texture of the film is more mental. For example, when the garage mechanic dies of a heart attack (so we are told), and we know him to be a plain, run-of-the-mill worker in the cause, his funeral is imagined in the mind of our seasoned comrade. Resnais does this without dissolves or fade-ins or any technical traffic signals. The burial scene comes right on after the information announcing the death. For a moment, it might appear that the hero is actually attending the funeral, but we know he must hurry back to Spain. He sees it all in his eyes, and we see it with him. Similarly— and there are dozens of such little excursions—our hero imagines himself missing a train when he is driven from Spain across the border, and although he does not miss a train but arrives in Paris rather rapidly from southern France, we do see him hurry up the railway-station steps to see a train pulling out. Such might be confusing to the average viewer if he were unprepared for the technical brilliance of Alain Resnais. Such adventurous explorations help push the frontiers of cinema into the twenty-first century.

CHAPTER FOUR ✗⅘

Idea into Action Through Character

1. CHOOSING THE PROTAGONIST

Must we take sides? We often do, unconsciously. When we are prevented from doing so, we are left unsatisfied, aesthetically and narratively. If there is no purging of emotional frustrations, we are bewildered.

Was it Bernard Shaw's male effigy that cast Professor Higgins as the aggressor? Suppose Eliza Doolittle in *My Fair Lady* (1964) were not a Hollywood Cinderella and instead was the activator using Higgins for her purpose. If she aimed to make herself into a great lady of fashion, the shift in roles would have made a different film.

The Shavian Cinderella is described in Shaw's afterword:

The rest of the story need not be shown in action, and indeed, would hardly need telling if our imaginations were not so enfeebled by their lazy dependence on the ready-mades and reach-me-downs of the ragshop in which Romance keeps its stock of "happy endings" to misfit all stories. . . . Eliza, in telling Higgins she would not marry him if he asked her, was not coquetting. . . .

Eliza is being realistic, Higgins is an inveterate bachelor. His sense of beauty, idealism, and affections are disengaged from "his specifically sexual impulses," according to Shaw:

This makes him a standing puzzle to the huge number of uncultivated people who have been brought up in tasteless homes by commonplace or disagreeable parents, and to whom, consequently, literature, painting, sculpture, music, and affectionate personal relations come as modes of sex if they come at all.

In Shaw's afterlife for Eliza she marries Mr. Frederick Eynsford Hill, who would make an ideal errand boy for her flower shop. She only daydreams of getting Higgins alone on a desert island to "drag him off his pedestal and see him making love like any common man. . . ." There is no such Shavian protagonist in *My Fair Lady,* nor does Higgins make love to Eliza in either the play or the film. *Pygmalion Revisited* with Eliza as protagonist would be indeed different from *My Fair Lady.*

Since the term "protagonist," quite simply, means the one who takes the decisive action, his selection is determined by the writer's attitude toward all his main characters. There can be no choice if there is no competition in the mind of the writer-director over who dominates the action. Much of the dramatic dullness in *Camelot* (1967) can be attributed to Lancelot being too obviously a protagonist, a weight which imposed a pictorial static on the production and reduces the impact of King Arthur.

Unfortunately, in commercial productions this problem of choice is solved exclusively by the producer, or by the star who accepts or rejects roles offered. The star system is often self-defeating because a popular performer will wish to protect his public image by choosing a role similar to his previous success. Or a role is expanded out of proportion to the whole, as in *My Fair Lady* when Jack L. Warner chose Audrey Hepburn over Julie Andrews, and consequently added scenes to demonstrate Miss Hepburn's ability to portray a cockney flower girl.

Any character can be the protagonist if he be complex enough to have conflicting aspirations churning in his chest. As a matter of observation, the richer the characters are, the more active will be their interplay. Fortunate is the writer who is so blessed with such prospects that he is tempted to unfold his story from any one of several points of view. In *Rashomon* we have four different stories from four divergent views, though the material is common to all, the bandit, the wife, the husband, and the woodchopper.

2. EXPOSITION, ENVIRONMENT, ACTION

Much has been written about the physiognomy of a character: Napoleon was short, which reputedly made him dynamic; Lincoln was tall and hence awkward. Similarly, there have been thoughts about the pressures of poverty, climate, and other environmental

factors. Important as all these may be, varying in individual circumstances, colorations are not to be confused with motivations.

Not all poor boys wish to be wealthy when they grow up. Many
short persons are fat and lazy, and many tall ones are smooth lawyers.
Hot climates tend to decelerate energetic people, but the point,
dramaturgically speaking, is what a character does about it when he
realizes he is at a decisive turn: he either gets lazier or he leaves. The
color of skin, for instance, precipitates drama only when a confrontation is pertinent.

The expository and the environmental do not exist apart from
dramatic action, except for sociologists and political scientists. For
the cinematic dramatist they may be implied in what characters do.
They are coloration. A man may be known to certain eyes by the
company he keeps, but in cinema all eyes judge by what is seen in
terms of what is done.

Exposition and environment are most helpful when, like small
children, they are seen and not heard. A skillful writer knows how to
weave whatever is pertinent into natural setting and actions and
dialogue. His skill may be tested by the pattern of his threads. In *All
About Eve* (1950) Joseph L. Mankiewicz concludes the story with
exposition, a reversal of the usual ending. The environment is the
special jungle of the world of the theatre. Eve Harrington is the
actress who has arrived, after a bit of clawing, at the top. Phoebe
from Brooklyn arrives to take her turn at flexing her claws:

132: *A young* GIRL, *asleep in a chair, wakes up with a jump. She
stares at* EVE, *horror-stricken.*

> EVE
>
> Who are you?

> GIRL
>
> Miss Harrington . . .

> EVE
>
> What are you doing here?

> GIRL
>
> I—I guess I fell asleep.

EVE *starts for the phone. The* GIRL *rises in panic.*

> Please don't have me arrested. Please! I didn't steal any-
> thing—you can search me!

EVE
(*pauses*)
How did you get in here?

GIRL
I hid outside the hall till the maid came to turn down your bed. She must've forgot something and when she went to get it, she left the door open. I sneaked in and hid till she finished. Then I just looked around—and pretty soon I was afraid somebody'd notice the lights were on so I turned them off—and then I guess, I fell asleep. . . .

EVE
You were just looking around.

GIRL
That's all.

EVE
What for?

GIRL
You probably won't believe me.

EVE
Probably not.

GIRL
It was for my report.

EVE
What report? To whom?

GIRL
About how you live, what kind of clothes you wear—what kind of perfume and books—things like that. You know the Eve Harrington Clubs—that they've got in most of the girls' High Schools?

EVE
I've heard of them.

GIRL
Ours was one of the first. Erasmus Hall. I'm the president.

EVE
Erasmus Hall. That's in Brooklyn, isn't it?

GIRL
Lots of actresses came from Brooklyn. Barbara Stanwyck, Susan Hayward—of course, they're just movie stars.

EVE *makes no comment. She lies wearily on a couch.*

You're going to Hollywood—aren't you?

EVE *murmurs "uh-huh."*

From the trunks you're packing, you must be going to stay a long time.

EVE

I might.

·GIRL

That spilled drink is going to ruin your carpet.

After ingratiating herself with Eve, the girl Phoebe manages to stay on, and Eve retires to bed. The "lucky break" occurs with the appearance of Addison deWitt, the producer. Though the weight of all this exposition and environmental attitudes is carried by dialogue, which is contrary to the essence of cinema, the weaving is worth watching:

132:

ADDISON

Hello, there. Who are you?

GIRL
(*shyly*)

Miss Harrington's resting, Mr. deWitt. She asked me to see who it is.

ADDISON

We won't disturb her rest. It seems she left her award in the taxicab. Will you give it to her?

She holds it as if it were the Promised Land. ADDISON *smiles faintly. He knows that look.*

How do you know my name?

GIRL

It's a very famous name, Mr. deWitt.

ADDISON

And what is your name?

GIRL

Phoebe.

ADDISON

Phoebe?

GIRL
(*stubbornly*)

I call myself Phoebe.

ADDISON

Why not? Tell me, Phoebe, do you want someday to have an award like that of your own?

PHOEBE *lifts her eyes to him.*

PHOEBE

More than anything else in the world.

ADDISON *pats her shoulder lightly.*

ADDISON

Then you must ask Miss Harrington how to get one. Miss Harrington knows all about it.

PHOEBE *smiles shyly.* ADDISON *closes the door.* PHOEBE *stares down at the award for an instant.*

EVE'S VOICE
(*sleepy—from the living room*)

Who was it?

PHOEBE

Just a taxi driver, Miss Harrington. You left the award in his cab and he brought it back.

EVE'S VOICE

Oh. Put it on one of the trunks, will you? I want to pack it.

PHOEBE

Sure, Miss Harrington.

She takes the award into the bedroom, sets it on a trunk. As she starts out, she sees EVE's *fabulous wrap on the bed. She listens. Then, quietly, she puts on the wrap and picks up the award.*

Slowly, she walks to a large three-mirrored cheval. With grace and infinite dignity she holds the award to her, and bows again and again . . . as if to the applause of a multitude.

FADE OUT

We have come to know all we need to know about Phoebe at this stage of her career-to-be, and curiously, without being familiar with the whole of the plot, we have an insight into Eve via Phoebe.

Whenever a characterization presents a problem in motivation or attitude, there are useful procedures to explore. As truth has many faces, depending on who is listening to whom, so are there various approaches to an analysis of experience. Dumas the Younger advises: "Before every situation that a dramatist creates, he should ask himself three questions. In this situation, what should I do? What would other people do? What ought to be done?"

"For those who become enamoured of the practice of the art," Leonardo Da Vinci observed, "without having previously applied to the diligent study of the scientific part of it, may be compared to mariners, who put to sea in a ship without rudder or compass, and therefore cannot be certain of arriving at the wished-for port."

With idea and character in mind, action awaits, but from what port does the mariner set forth?

3. THE POINT OF ATTACK

In *As You Like It* Shakespeare neatly divided threescore and ten by seven:

All the world's a stage,
And all the men and women merely players.
They have their exits and their entrances;
And one man in his time plays many parts,
His acts being seven ages. At first the infant . . .
And then the whining school-boy . . . the lover . . .
Then a soldier . . . the justice . . . the lean and slipper'd pantaloon
. . . second childishness, and mere oblivion. . . .

With the exception of infancy and second childhood, protagonists have come from adolescence through advanced age, and often have spanned more than one period. Dramatic impact and biographical narrative, however, make difficult mixtures. Compression is one of the characteristics of drama, and even more so of cinema. Such exceptions as Noel Coward's *Cavalcade* (1933), the parade of the British Empire at its zenith, or *The Winning of the West* (1953), have had biographical or historical ideas behind them. Their point of attack is determined more by dates than by a character's dialectic.

Once the conflict is poised, ready for action based on the protagonist's dialectic, the point of attack should evolve most naturally from this initial stage. It is not unlike seeing a posed still picture of actors in a stopped frame during projection, and then with the flick of a switch the actors perform, the scenery moves, and life has begun.

The internal struggle in the heart and mind of the protagonist must make an initial movement. He goes either toward good or evil, love or hate, fear or faith, superego or ego, or whatever the dialectic might be. In other words, he moves toward another character; he advances to make contact. Since the conflict already exists within him, he must demonstrate one side of it. He cannot sit on dead center, and expect us to be intrigued by his movements.

If the protagonist is not put on a spot at the beginning, or if he fails to make a move toward a character who personifies one part of his dialectic, then it can be deduced that the dialectic is weak or non-existent or that the main character is one-dimensional and therefore not a protagonist. One-dimensional characters may act and react, whereas the protagonist begins the action by making an initial selection between his alternatives.

The first five minutes on a screen are a precious gift placed tenderly in the hands of the writer-director. What he does with those golden moments may well determine the success, artistically and commercially, of the entire production, whether it run an hour or four. This gift of the gods is based on a friendly anticipation, buttressed by a payment of box-office coins or a searching exercise of the wrist. The viewer is anxious not to have wasted his money and time; he is apperceptively willing to give the writer-director the most eager greeting and the benefit of any doubt. Actually, the batting averages of Hollywood feature films rank very high on the point of attack; the strikeouts come more frequently at the point of finish. TV producers have been under extraordinary commercial-rating pressures to concoct a hook, a gimmick attention-grabber so that viewers won't exercise their wrists. Such points of attack usually center upon some extremity of violence, brutality, sex, or personal relations. Opening on such mountain peaks often means that all paths thereafter lead downward. It is not only unsavory but indigestible to follow very rare steak with canapés and soup.

Another common ailment that weakens points of attack is the belief that information must precede conflict, or that setting is a prelude to drama. This is the novelist approach. John Steinbeck's *Of Mice and Men* (1940) offers contrasts between narrative, dramatic, and cinematic points of attack.

From the novel, here is a straight descriptive opening:

A few miles south of Soledad, the Salinas River drops in close to the hillside bank and runs deep and green. The water is warm too, for it has slipped twinkling over the yellow sands in the sunlight before reaching the narrow pool. On one side of the river the golden foothill slopes curve up to the strong and rocky Gabilan mountains, but on the valley side the water is lined with trees—willows fresh and green with every spring, carrying in their lower leaf junctures the debris of the winter's flooding; and sycamores with mottled, white, recumbent limbs and branches that arch over the pool. . . .

Description continues for several pages. Two men appear and are described. The huge one drinks from the pool. The small man, George, shakes him to stop, but Lennie dips his "whole head under, hat and all. . . ." George isn't sure it is good water. Lennie is fascinated by the ripples his fingers make. George is annoyed because the bus driver let them off four miles short, and is angry when Lennie forgets where they are going, and so recounts how they got work cards and bus tickets from an employment agency. Lennie thinks he's lost his card, but George wouldn't trust him to keep it. Lennie is hiding a dead mouse in his pocket. Again, he can't recall where they are going. George reminds him he is not to talk; if the boss "finds out what a crazy bastard you are, we won't get no job. . . ." George also reminds him not to repeat what he did in Weed, where they had to run from town.

From the play, written by John Steinbeck and staged by George S. Kaufman:

ACT ONE, SCENE 1:

Thursday night.

A sandy bank of the Salinas River sheltered with willows—one giant sycamore right, upstage.

The stage is covered with dry leaves. The feeling of the stage is sheltered and quiet.

Stage is lit by a setting sun.

Curtain rises on an empty stage. A sparrow is singing. There is a distant sound of ranch dogs barking aimlessly and one clear quail call. The quail call turns to a warning call and there is a beat of the flock's wings. Two figures are seen entering the stage in single file, with GEORGE, *the short man, coming in ahead of* LENNIE. *Both men are carrying blanket rolls. They approach the water. The small man throws down his blanket roll, the large man follows and then falls down and drinks from the river, snorting as he drinks.*

GEORGE
(*irritably*)
Lennie, for God's sake, don't drink so much. (*Leans over and shakes* LENNIE.) Lennie, you hear me! You gonna be sick like you was last night.

LENNIE
(*dips his whole head under, hat and all. As he sits upon the bank, his hat drips down the back.*) That's good. You drink some, George. You drink some too.

As may be seen, the play follows the novel closely, one may see the play as you read the novel. The dialectic of George is soon established. Though Lennie is no relative, George feels he is his brother's keeper, whereas "if I was alone I could live so easy. . . . Why, I could stay in a cat house all night. I could eat any place I want, hotel or any place, and order any damn thing I could think of. . . ."

In the play version the dialogue is sharper, the exposition more indirect:

GEORGE
(*shouts*)
. . . You crazy son-of-a-bitch, you keep me in hot water all the time.

LENNIE *is trying to stop* GEORGE's *flow of words with his hands. Sarcastically.*

You just wanta feel that girl's dress. Just wanta pet it like it was a mouse. Well, how the hell'd she know you just wanta feel her dress? How'd she know you'd just hold onto it like it was a mouse?

LENNIE
(*in panic*)
I didn't mean to, George!

GEORGE
Sure you didn't mean to. You didn't mean for her to yell bloody hell, either. You didn't mean for us to hide in the irrigation ditch all day with guys out lookin' for us with guns. Alla time it's something you didn't mean.

George's tirade is triggered by his discovery that Lennie is hiding a dead mouse, one he had meant to pet but had clumsily killed. Lennie retrieves it from the brush after George has thrown it away. The point of attack in the play is the action over the dead mouse. In the motion picture script the point of attack is the posse pursuing George and Lennie through the fruit orchard, following Lennie's encounter with "that girl's dress." For plastic impact of flight and chase this opening is more arresting and stimulating; it is an effective cinematic start to the story. For dramatic impact a posse in pursuit visually demonstrates the danger inherent in George's dialectic. As his brother's keeper he is in danger of getting himself lynched.

FADE-IN:

1. WIDE SHOT—SKY—DAY

A hot California sun is being threatened by an approaching bank of black clouds which have already overcast a large section of the sky. A streak of lightning. The rumble of distant thunder.

1A: FULL SHOT—SECTION OF FRUIT ORCHARD

SHOOTING THROUGH *lanes between the trees. The distant rumble of thunder carries over from preceding shot. In f.g. [foreground] a rabbit nibbling a blade of grass. Birds close by digging for worms and insects in the newly cultivated ground. A crashing of heavy feet out of scene suddenly sends the rabbit and the birds flying. In the b.g. [background] two men suddenly appear, dodging between the trees, running for dear life. They run straight toward the* CAMERA. *As they come closer, we are able to distinguish them—the first is* GEORGE— LENNIE *is at his heels. In the distance can be heard the shouts and shots of a pursuing posse.* GEORGE *and* LENNIE *run to the edge of the orchard, one row of trees separating them from the* CAMERA, *make an abrupt turn and start running up the row at right angles.* CAMERA *trucking with them parallel to orchard—always keeping one row of trees between the fugitives and the lens.* CAMERA HOLDS, *allowing* GEORGE *and* LENNIE *to run out of scene.*

2. FULL SHOT—SECTION OF FRUIT ORCHARD

SHOOTING *through lanes between the trees. The shouts of the pursuing posse are heard. In a moment they come crashing through the orchard spread out fan-wise—sheriff, deputies and workers, armed with shot-guns and other implements. They comb through the orchard,* CAMERA MOVING ALONG *with them parallel to the pursuit.* CAMERA HOLDS, *allowing posse to run out of scene.*

3. WIDE SHOT—IRRIGATION DITCH

SHOOTING *toward orchard.* GEORGE *and* LENNIE *come running out of orchard at full speed. The shouts of the pursuers can be heard in the distance coming toward them.* GEORGE *stops suddenly, looks up and down the irrigation ditch for a cover, then motioning to* LENNIE, *jumps into the ditch.* LENNIE *follows. . . .*

Having aroused curiosity, the explanation follows in Aunt Clara's house via dialogue. To see Lennie stroke the girl's dress and be misunderstood, to see the posse being formed and the chase begun, would have constituted a different point of attack. It would have been Lennie's story, his dialectic about his inner conflict: to stroke and yet to kill the things you like. With Lennie as protagonist, *Of Mice and Men* would have been less meaningful; Lennie is one-dimensional, not the appealing character that George is.

The following scene in Aunt Clara's house visualizes George's dialectic by having Aunt Clara serve as his conscience:

19. CLOSE SHOT—AUNT CLARA

In rocking chair. GEORGE *enters, stands in front of her for a fraction of a second, then crosses over to window alongside of* AUNT CLARA. *Looking out of window he suddenly blurts out . . .*

> GEORGE
> *(angrily)*
> I ain't gonna take him no more!

20. CLOSE-UP—LENNIE

Mouth full—stops chewing—stares at GEORGE.

21. CLOSE-UP—AUNT CLARA

rocking.

> AUNT CLARA
> *(smiling wisely)*
> Think you can, hey?

22. CLOSE SHOT—GEORGE

Pie still in hand at his side.

> GEORGE
> I ain't thinkin' it—I'm doin' it. *(Pleadingly)* Look, ma'am—
> I can't stand it no more. *(Angrily)* Keeps me in hot water
> all the time. Can't keep no job. Gettin' in trouble—all the
> time trouble.

23. CLOSE-UP—LENNIE

Looking at GEORGE *then at* AUNT CLARA *as she starts to speak.*

24. CLOSE SHOT—AUNT CLARA

> AUNT CLARA
>
> You brang him back before.

CAMERA PULLS BACK *to include* GEORGE *and* LENNIE *in picture.*

> GEORGE
>
> This here time I'm leavin' him.

> AUNT CLARA
>
> What's he done this time?

In dialogue with Aunt Clara—not the preferable method in cinematic writing—George recounts the action prior to the chase. George aims now to get a job alone on a ranch. Aunt Clara states George's dialectic for him:

> AUNT CLARA
>
> He ain't no kin of yours—you can leave him—and there won't be a soul that can say you ain't done everythin' for him. You can leave him—if you can.

> GEORGE
> (*quickly*)
>
> I ain't goin' to talk no more. I'm gittin' out. He ain't no kin of mine. Goodbye, ma'am.

GEORGE *exits.* AUNT CLARA *looks after him.*

Lennie follows George out of the house, and George orders him to sit on the front porch (Shot 27). In the subsequent shots, 28–33, the argument raging inside George is visually conveyed by the short tempo and the cross-reference of the shots, coming to a climax in the close-up of Shot 34. Then tension is heightened in the crosscuts between George and Lennie, shots 37–44, when Lennie runs to catch the freight, so that we become involved visually in wanting Lennie to make the train. From George's point of view we see and want Lennie; we join George in being our brother's keeper.

First, Shot 27:

> GEORGE
>
> And stay here!

> LENNIE
>
> How long?

GEORGE

Till I give you a call.

GEORGE *exits quickly.* LENNIE *sits there looking after him—waiting —watching like a dog ready to spring up and follow.*

28. CLOSE TRUCK SHOT—GEORGE

walking up street. Use foot tempo and CLOSE-UP *to show first determination—then indecision—then reluctance.*

29. CLOSE-UP—LENNIE

watching, gathering his muscles to follow.

30. CLOSE SHOT—GEORGE

as he reaches corner. He stops. The train whistles out of scene. GEORGE, *torn between two temptations (the approaching train which offers freedom and the compassion he feels for helpless* LENNIE), *suddenly makes up his mind, and dashes out of scene toward train.*

31. MEDIUM SHOT—TRAIN OF BOX CARS

GEORGE *enters from* BACK OF CAMERA, *and starts climbing the iron ladder heavily with one hand to top of slowly moving box car.*

32. LONG SHOT—FREIGHT TRAIN

SHOOTING FROM *center of street toward railroad track. The box car upon which* GEORGE *is sitting enters scene.* GEORGE *looks up street toward* LENNIE.

33. LONG MOVING SHOT—LENNIE (FROM GEORGE'S ANGLE)

MOVING CAMERA *giving effect of the moving box car.* LENNIE *is still sitting on porch waiting for the word from* GEORGE. *His head follows the progress of the box car, across the street and out of sight.* CAMERA PASSES LENNIE *until he is lost from view.*

34. CLOSE SHOT—GEORGE

Looking back sadly . . . then reversal—he suddenly breaks—jumps to his feet and runs back on top of box car out of scene.

35. MEDIUM LONG SHOT—FREIGHT TRAIN

SHOOTING *from street toward tracks.* GEORGE *enters and is forced to keep moving as on a tread-mill along the top of the moving car in order to keep* LENNIE *in view. He puts his fingers in his mouth and whistles. Train whistle blows simultaneously, drowning out* GEORGE's *signal.* GEORGE *starts running, waiting for the whistle to stop so he can make himself heard. He turns his head from* LENNIE *to look in front of him.*

36. LONG SHOT—FREIGHT TRAIN (FROM GEORGE'S ANGLE)

SHOWING *only four box cars left.*

37. MEDIUM LONG SHOT—GEORGE

Running across top of box cars. He begins to wave frantically to LENNIE.

38. CLOSE SHOT—LENNIE

waving back but still not moving.

39. LONG SHOT—GEORGE (FROM LENNIE'S ANGLE)

as the train picks up speed, forcing GEORGE *to speed up to keep* LENNIE *in sight. The train whistle suddenly stops.* GEORGE *lets out a piercing whistle through his fingers.*

40. CLOSE SHOT—LENNIE

He stiffens, listens—then leaps to his feet and plunges up the street in direction of train.

41. LONG SHOT—LENNIE

running from BACK OF CAMERA—*speeding toward train. In b.g. we can see* GEORGE *running on top of box car to keep even with street.*

42. CLOSE SHOT—GEORGE

He sits down, relieved. He looks down.

43. CLOSE SHOT—LENNIE (FROM GEORGE'S ANGLE)

as he catches train and climbs ladder.

44. CLOSE-UP—GEORGE

sitting on top of box car. LENNIE *climbs up into scene, sits down beside* GEORGE. GEORGE *has a resigned sneer on his face. He is still holding his untouched piece of pie in his hand.* LENNIE'S *eyes focus on the pie.* GEORGE *follows his glance—breaks the hunk of pie into two equal pieces—giving one of them to* LENNIE. *They both begin to eat.*
FADE OUT

Our eyes have been kept active; the language of motion has been fluent. George's dialectic has been the key to the point of attack. In a shoot-first world, brotherly love is a dangerous doctrine to live by, a posse hot on the heels of the hero as we start the story, but a philosophy worth practicing according to John Steinbeck. George fights what should be called the good fight until, in the end, Lennie unwittingly murders, and George is forced to kill him to save Lennie from a lynching.

Though the narrative and dramatic versions are altered and improved, the transfer from novel and play into a shooting script does not automatically render the story cinematic. It is inherently characteristic of cinema that motion conveys meaning, and most often it is physical motion. The alternating views of George on the moving train and of Lennie on the porch and then on the street are unique in parallel time and place, and hence cinematic. Ideas and emotions are portrayed in an exceptional style.

Another instructive example of novel-play-film versions of a protagonist's dialectic may be seen in *The Heiress* (1949), based on *Washington Square* by Henry James. The triangle is classic: a plain girl torn between a domineering father and a fortune-seeking suitor. First published in 1881, James ruled that Catherine Sloper chooses principle over passion; she prefers spinsterhood in her prime of life to fruitful companionship all her life.

"During a portion of the first half of the present century, and more particularly during the latter part of it," the novel begins, "there flourished and practised in the city of New York a physician who enjoyed perhaps an exceptional share of the consideration which, in the United States, has always been bestowed upon distinguished members of the medical profession." The novel, continuing in this self-conscious style, states that the doctor had married an heiress for love. His wife's connections helped his practice. Their first child was a boy, but he died at three years of age. The second was a girl, her sex a disappointment to the good doctor, and a week later his wife expired.

Catherine was raised the first ten crucial, psyche-forming years by nurses and maids. Henry James, a bachelor and never a father, only says, "She grew up a very robust and healthy child, and her father . . . at least need have no fear of losing her." At ten, Father asked his sister "to come and stay with him." At twelve, he ordered sister Lavinia to make "a clever woman" of Catherine. It took Catherine some years to realize that her plain face and lack of wit disappointed her father. "He smoked a good many cigars over his disappointment. . . . 'I expect nothing,' he said to himself, 'so that if she gives me a surprise, it will be all clear again. If she doesn't, it will be no loss.'"

The surprise arrives when Catherine is twenty, and Aunt Lavinia encourages Morris Townsend to call. Catherine is overjoyed and falls in love and accepts Townsend's proposal and dutifully seeks her father's consent. Father refuses, having investigated Morris to discover him penniless, even poorer than Father was when he married Catherine's mother.

The play version, *The Heiress*—a more explicit title, opens with Dr. Sloper's arrival, having delivered a male infant, which permits him to advise the maid, Maria, "to have a lot of children. That way you won't put all your hopes on one." When Catherine enters "she is dressed in an over-elaborate red satin gown with gold trimmings"—intended to indicate a passionate potential in spite of being in her late twenties and socially inexperienced. Morris arrives and plays French songs on the spinet. On the third visit (Act One, Scene 2) he proposes and is accepted, although Catherine can see that Father is hostile. Morris instructs her to defy the doctor. Aunt Lavinia advises her brother to be thankful that Catherine has a suitor. What is more important to Sloper than love at first sight, or his daughter's happiness, is Morris' selfishness; Sloper expects perfection, the older woman says. When tested, Catherine tells her father not to abuse Morris, they shall marry quite soon. She has the will. Act One ends with Morris letting her down by advising Catherine to go to Europe with the doctor for six months to test their love and Morris' intentions. First love, not taken in the flood, is doomed to wallow in low tide.

In the motion-picture script, also written by Ruth and Augustus Goetz (1948), Catherine is introduced buying a fish. Presumably, this new scene serves several chores: Catherine (Olivia DeHaviland) is independent-minded, she selects her own fish and doesn't believe what she's told (is the mackerel a symbol of Morris?) and she is devoted to her father—a cod for the chowder he likes.

A-11. CLOSER SHOT

As we come closer to the fish vendor we get a good look at CATHERINE SLOPER. *She is in a simple dress protected by an apron. She is a healthy, quiet girl in her middle twenties. Her bearing is matter-of-fact and deliberate.*

Three cats are meowing impatiently near the fish cart, and MR. RYAN *is waiting for a decision from* CATHERINE, *who is staring at a fish,* CATHERINE, *in order to make up her mind, feels the fish.*

MR. RYAN

It's a mackerel, Miss Sloper.

CATHERINE

I know it is—and a very dead one.

MR. RYAN
(*with emphasis*)

They *live* in the water.

CATHERINE
(*patiently and not to be ruffled*)

Yes, Mr. Ryan, I am trying to decide how long ago this one
was *in* the water.

MR. RYAN
(*indignant*)

Miss Sloper, that's last night's catch.

CATHERINE
(*pointing into the cart*)

I'll take the cod.

*She turns her head away slightly and raises one hand to shield her
eyes as he slaps the fish on his cutting board and deftly cuts the head
off and throws it to the cats. The cats scramble for the head.*

MR. RYAN

Four cents a pound—that'll be twenty-one cents, miss.

*She puts the money on his wagon. He places the fish on her kitchen
plate and hands it to her. He picks up the money, takes hold of the
handles of his cart, and starts to wheel it away.* CATHERINE *turns back
toward her house, carrying the plate.*

A-12. EXTERIOR GARDEN—LOOKING TOWARD THE HOUSE

CATHERINE'*s back is toward us as she starts along the path. We hear
the fish vendor hawking his wares in the mews and the* SOUND *of
his little horn.*

FISH VENDOR'S VOICE

Fresh fish . . .

SOUND *of horn.*

Here comes the fishman; bring out your dishpan. . . .
Porgies at five cents a pound!

SOUND *of horn again.*

Eels . . . halibut . . . who likes halibut . . .

As CATHERINE *gets closer to the house we see the* DOCTOR *coming down the exterior stairs from the winter garden. He is now wearing his hat and carrying his medical bag.*

CATHERINE
(*smiling at him*)
Good morning, Father.

DR. SLOPER
(*removing his hat*)
Good morning, Catherine.

CATHERINE
(*with pleasure*)
I've bought a fine fish—for the chowder you like.

DR. SLOPER
That's very thoughtful. . . . Next time let the man carry it in for you.

CATHERINE
Yes, Father.

DR. SLOPER
(*looks up at the sky*)
It's a lovely morning. . . . Why don't you invite your Aunt Lavinia or a friend to take lunch with you, and then perhaps go to one of the Park concerts?

CATHERINE
I can't, Father. I have some embroidery I would like to attend to.

DR. SLOPER
(*politely*)
I see. . . . Well, good day, my dear.

She meets Morris (Montgomery Clift) at a dance, at which she is a wallflower. Their dance is a visual enactment of their characters in juxtaposition:

A-40. ON THE DANCE FLOOR

CATHERINE *is silent, concentrating hard on keeping in time with the music. For no apparent reason,* MORRIS *stops.*

MORRIS
We must make an arrangement, Miss Sloper. I will not kick you, if you do not kick me.

CATHERINE
(*distressed*)
Oh, dear . . . I am so clumsy. . . .

MORRIS
(*correcting her*)
No, Miss Sloper, it's only that I am wearing Arthur's boots, and he's a very bad dancer.

He takes her in his arms and they start to dance again.

(*Counting.*) One—two—three—
One—two—three—

A-41. TWO SHOT—CATHERINE AND MORRIS

CATHERINE *is very conscious of her feet, and she, too, is counting under her breath. We see her lips move as she does so.* MORRIS *looks down at her.*

MORRIS
You are looking at your feet.

CATHERINE
Yes, I am.

He smiles reassuringly, and she smiles back at him. Now she stops counting and they start to dance off together with assurance and in perfect time.

These discursive beginnings are no substitute for a clearly projected point of attack. The delay in confrontation hinders dynamic movement. Actually, the dramaturgy in the stage play is more compelling than in the film script. For example, the first master climax, comparable to the end of Act One in the play, does not come, inexplicably, until Sequence D, page 100 of the 174-page script:

D-14.
DR. SLOPER
He is a selfish idler.

MORRIS
My sister never said that.

DR. SLOPER
I say it.

CATHERINE
But, Father, I know he loves me.

DR. SLOPER

I know that he does not!

CATHERINE

In Heaven's name, Father, tell me what makes you so sure!

The DOCTOR *finds himself unable to tell* CATHERINE *that she is undesirable and unloved. . . . He looks for a kinder way to stop her. Finally, giving up, he says:*

DR. SLOPER

My poor child, I can't tell you. You must simply take my word for it.

CATHERINE

Father, I can't! I can't! I love him! (*despairing*) I have promised to marry him, to stay by him, no matter what comes.

DR. SLOPER

So he forearmed himself by getting a promise like that, did he? (*to* MORRIS) You are beneath contempt!

CATHERINE
(*stolidly*)
Don't abuse him, Father! (*after a pause*) I think we shall marry quite soon.

DR. SLOPER *turns away and starts for his study.*

DR. SLOPER

Then it is no further concern of mine.

CATHERINE

I'm sorry.

Catherine has won. It is Morris, at this point, who says they cannot marry without Dr. Sloper's approval. "It would bring unhappiness to all of us." In the end, unhappiness comes to all of them because he failed to take Catherine on her terms. Had the point of attack been less expository in its introductory material and presented Catherine's dialectic earlier, the motion picture might have been as compelling as the play.

When characters act out a historical situation against semidocumentary background, such characters are generally secondary to idea, their dialectics being representational rather than personally rooted conflicts. It is a separate type from the other forms we have examined, its backgrounds social, political, military, or scientific. *Exodus*

(1960), *Advise and Consent, The Best Man, Seven Days in May, Dr. Strangelove* are examples of this genre.

In *Judgment at Nuremberg* (1961) Stanley Kramer and Abby Mann were concerned with the trial of the Nazi war criminals as an American problem, since America was rapidly reconstructing Germany economically as an ally against Soviet Russia. West Germany was not permitted by the American military and policy-makers to resolve its own guilt problem through a search of moral standards. So the Nuremberg trials were more than an embarrassment; they were considered a brake to a rejuvenated Germany. Abby Mann's *Judgment at Nuremberg* was seen on TV in April, 1959, only after what Mr. Mann describes as "a series of crises involving threats, cajolery and intrigue of which I knew only a part."

Integrity juxtaposed to expediency. How to project that dialectic, and how to dramatize it as an American dilemma—that was the challenge. A federal judge from the granite rocks of Maine was chosen as the protagonist.

Judge Haywood (Spencer Tracy) is introduced sitting in the rear of a large black Mercedes-Benz as he is being driven in 1948 through devastated Nuremberg. The German driver Schmidt annoys him by constantly sounding the horn in a gross insensitivity to his fellow citizens. The issue of responsibility within the law is the crux of the conflict as centered in Minister of Justice Ernst Janning (Burt Lancaster). Not until the end of the picture do Haywood and Janning, the American and German judges, have their personal confrontation. The bulk of the drama is a review of certain Nazi atrocities, sterilization and blood-purity decrees, enforced by the judges on trial, so that we are instructed in the nature of the beast beneath the Nazi skin.

By default, the dynamics of the protagonist are assumed by the defense attorney, Herr Rolfe (Maximilian Schell). A judge on the bench can not, occupationally, be an active protagonist in court:

HAYWOOD

Herr Rolfe will make the opening statement for the defense.

ROLFE *rises slowly and goes to the microphone in the centre of the room. He is a vital-looking young man in his late twenties. He stands before the Tribunal. He looks at the judges on the bench with piercing, arresting eyes. Not allowing their attention to waver for an instant. A word about* ROLFE's *background. He was once a Hitler youth leader. His studies as a law student were interrupted when*

*he had to join the Army at a very early age. His manner is of de-
corum and politeness before the Tribunal. Underneath, one sees
his scorn of the trials. His conviction that they are unfair, that
they are no more than the trial of the vanquished by the victors,
covered by hypocritical, high-sounding verbiage. Very much appearing in his action, too, is his intention of taking the game at its own
price, to hoist the trials up by their own petard. But he is even
more deeply involved than that. He is, himself, on trial although he
is not fully aware of it.*

ROLFE

May it please the Tribunal. (*Waits until he has the attention of the judges completely.*) It is not only a great honour
but also a great challenge for an advocate to aid this Tribunal in its task. For this is not an ordinary trial by any
means of the accepted parochial sense. The avowed purpose
of this Tribunal is broader than the visiting of retribution
on a few men. It is dedicated to the reconsecration of the
Temple of Justice. (*Pauses a moment.*)

Camera moves to HAYWOOD's *face.*

30. FULL SHOT—THE COURTROOM

ROLFE
(continuing)

It is dedicated to find a code of justice the whole world will
be responsible to. (*Pause.*) How will this code be established? (*He looks over at* COLONEL LAWSON.) It will be
established (*Pause.*) in a clear, honest evaluation of the
responsibility for the crimes in the indictment stated by the
prosecution. In the words of the great American jurist,
Oliver Wendell Holmes, "This responsibility will not be
found only in documents that no one contests or denies. It
will be found in considerations of a political or social nature. It will be found, most of all, in the character of men."
(*Pause.*) What is the character of Ernst Janning? Let us
examine his life for a moment. (*Pause.*)

Camera moves to ERNST JANNING's *face.*

ROLFE'S VOICE

He was born in 1895. Received the degree of Doctor of Law
in 1917. Became a judge in East Prussia in 1924. Following
World War One, he became one of the leaders of the
Weimar Republic and was one of the framers of its democratic constitution. In subsequent years, he achieved international fame. Not only for his work as a great jurist, but

also as the author of legal text-books which are still used in universities all over the world. He became Minister of Justice in Germany in 1935. A position the equivalent of the Attorney-General of the United States. Finally, in a Reichstag speech of 26 April 1942, Hitler attacked Janning and forced him to resign. (*Pause.*)

Camera returns to ROLFE. *He waits until he has the complete attention of the judges, arresting them with his eyes.*

ROLFE
(continuing)

If Ernst Janning is to be found guilty, certain implications must arise. (*Pause; sharply*) A judge does not make the law. He carries out the laws of his country. (*Pause; with emphasis*) He carries out the laws of his country. (*Pause; with emphasis*) The statement, "My country right or wrong," was expressed by a great American patriot. It is no less true for a German patriot. (*His eyes pierce the judges; then he looks at* COLONEL LAWSON *sitting at the prosecution table.*) Should Ernst Janning have carried out the laws of his country? Or should he have refused to carry them out and become a traitor? This is the crux of the issue at the bottom of this Trial. (*Pause; smiles a little at the judges*) The defense is as dedicated to finding responsibility as is the prosecution. For it is not only Ernst Janning who is on trial here. It is the German people.

(ROLFE *bows politely and goes back to his seat in front of the dock.*)

As an umpire ruling on the prosecution's objections to the defense's tactics, Haywood is basically passive. The main battle is between the lawyers, not the judges. When Rolfe cleverly gets a prosecution witness to admit he took the Loyalty Oath of 1934 as proof that he failed to fight Hitler—the same procedure of Janning, whom Rolfe is defending—prosecution objects. There is a violent clash:

COLONEL LAWSON
(coming to the stand)

Your Honor, I object to the entire line of questioning and ask that it be stricken from the record!

ROLFE
(as though innocently)

I thought prosecuting counsel was dedicated to finding responsibility.

> COLONEL LAWSON
> (*impatiently*)
> Your Honor, I made an objection.

> ROLFE
> (*as though innocently*)
> Prosecution is not interested in finding responsibility?

> COLONEL LAWSON
> (*turning to* ROLFE)
> There is responsibility for more here than swearing to a
> Loyalty Oath and you know it!

Haywood speaks against emotional outbursts; only justice is to be served. The objection is overruled, and Court is adjourned. Colonel Lawson stands staring at Haywood; Rolfe smiles sardonically at Lawson. What is new, at this point, is the reaction of the white Nazi Janning in a close-up: "He is looking at Rolfe. He is not smiling."

A courtroom is a tested launching pad for a point of attack, but hardly a visually arresting site.

4.   THE IAC: WHO CARRIES THE BALL?

From the above it should be evident that a motivation, emotional and/or intellectual, needs to be enacted by the character or the protagonist if we are to believe what we see, and see something to believe in. The key is enactment. Visualization implies movements that are dramatic and cinematic, narrative and plastic, and expository and plastic.

The concept might be called THE IAC: IDEA INTO ACTION THROUGH CHARACTER.

It is a simple means of inducing plot movement on one hand, and, deductively on the other hand, of testing character truth and image fidelity. All should blend so rationally and naturally that idea, action, and character are inseparable within the image.

In every shot, scene, and sequence there should be an idea in motion that is enacted by the character who dominates that image. He may be the protagonist or a secondary figure, but if the moment belongs to him—for whatever dramaturgical reason—his action as a character, not as an actor, will largely determine the effectiveness of that moment.

CHAPTER FIVE

Intercharacter Relations

1. THE NATURE OF THE TRIANGLE

The conflict that is depicted when an idea goes into action through a character's feelings or deeds is generally seen in connection with a choice. A protagonist may have more than one target to shoot at. This factor of choice creates what is called the triangle.

Such patterns may appear to be formal, but they can evolve, if used creatively, since natural patterns carry within themselves anti-formal potentials. The leaf with its veins becomes a mold that nourishes, as altered matter, new leaves. The triangular plot of the thirties and forties has looser forms of interplay in the fifties and sixties. The hero evolves into a no-hero or antihero, the triangle into quadrangle or circle. Social and sexual freedoms have repainted character relations; the triangle appears less rigid.

In its visual shape, the triangle is a figure with three sides, a number that has an extraordinary variety of associations, ranging from a symbol of the Trinity, Father, Son, and Holy Ghost, to the triangle in art with its apex down representing female genitalia, and is also considered a symbol of life.

Why three? Triangles are not absolutely obligatory in drama, but it is rewarding to realize how many effective dramas revolve around the triangle. Adam and Eve were confronted with no dramatic intrigue until the arrival of the snake, who gave Eve a choice. In John Huston's *The Bible* the third presence is the other man up a tree, with unctuous wiles and voice. Would there still be a paradise if Eve had resisted? Two in a canoe may be a romantic picture, but three can rock the boat.

Three is biologically rooted in life: sperm and egg reproduce offspring. In Greek myth the Three Fates are the *moira*—Clotho who spins the thread of life, Lachesis who determines its length, Atropos who cuts it off—the image used by D. W. Griffith in his epic masterpiece *Intolerance* (1916). The three Fates of Latin poetry are the *Parcae;* the Christian virtues are faith, hope, and charity. Terrestrial space is in three dimensions of heighth, width, and depth. There are Three Musketeers; three circles advertise a beer. The three primary pigments are red, yellow, and blue; the three primary colors in the additive process are blue, green, red. Out of all the numbers, only seven has a similar mythology and application.

The triangle in general is a useful device: as a means of identifying and sorting out the characters, it lines up the teams before the game commences; it can organize conflict; it can aid in character development.

Because the fact film deals primarily with expository or narrative equations that are not dramatized in terms of character conflicts, their stories do not require the dynamics of the triangle. In the contemporary trend of using the streets of New York, London, Paris, Rome, and Tokyo, fiction films with fact backgrounds do employ the triangle.

As a device by itself the triangle is not cinematic, nor does its existence automatically guarantee a cinematic application. Since cinema, through its multimovements and light alterations, can intensify and compress any fragment of the human experience, the triangle becomes cinematic when it contributes specifically in this process. The cinematic triangle, in other words, has sharper points.

2.   TRIANGLES AT WORK IN SCRIPTS

There is a triangle buried under the Dreiser linguistic labyrinth and structural grillwork in *An American Tragedy* that is liberated when the novel is transformed into a screenplay. The film version, called *A Place in the Sun* (1951), reinterprets and redefines the original triangle by sharpening the conflict and compressing character interplay.

Because of its constant visualization, cinema demands a more immediate impact than a novel. Whenever this innate quality is exploited, the resultant film risks being too obvious or banal or too faithful to the novel. The visualization of narrative in adaptations need not produce trite situations (assuming they were not trite in the novel), if the characters remain truthful within their respective realities.

What could be more potentially banal than a story about a poor boy who meets a beautiful, rich girl, and they fall in love, but he is not free to marry her since he is involved with a poor girl who is pregnant. Would not intensification run the risk of rendering the story boringly obvious?

By emphasizing the conflict within the breast of Clyde Griffiths, now renamed George Eastman, the film version presents an appealing inner turmoil, more implied than seen in Dreiser's socioreligious tapestry. George (Montgomery Clift) appears torn between conscience and ambition, and to equate these two forces the two women in his life must appear equally human and attractive. The poor girl, Roberta Alden in the novel, is a likable person, renamed Alice Tripp (Shelley Winters). The rich girl, Angela Vickers (Elizabeth Taylor), is a genuine character. Pregnant Alice personifies George's conscience, while debutante Angela embodies all he ever dreamed of. What renders the tragedy so poignant is the understandable nature of George's love for Angela (not a spoiled rich bitch), while his attachment to Alice is not sordid. In the film the story is a tragedy for all three; in the novel it is primarily Clyde Griffith's tragic rise and fall.

Another characteristic of an effective triangle in cinema is the opportunity it provides for a running conflict. The roles of both Alice and Angela are enlarged in order to accommodate an opposite appeal for George, thus sharpening the horns of his dilemma. If one horn is shorter than the other, it is an uneven and less engrossing contest. The outcome is predictable.

Executive Suite (1954), located in Tredway Tower, Millburgh, Pennsylvania, presents a naked fight for power. The comptroller, Loren Shaw (Frederic March), and the treasurer, Frederick Alderson (Walter Pidgeon), are at war; the savior of the company, Don Walling (William Holden), is appropriately in Design and Development. In the novel by Cameron Hawley, Don Walling is not introduced until the fourth chapter in a book totaling thirteen chapters. The spark of ambition does not glow in him until the tenth chapter, and throughout the novel he is half submerged in the murky waters churned by the contentious dramatis personae. There is actually no triangle in the novel; the concentration is on the fight itself against a racing clock.

The triangle in *Executive Suite* as a film is effective because Don Walling, occupying the apex from the start, relates to the conflict, even during his period of indecision. With Shaw in the negative corner of the triangle are Stockbroker Caswell and Dudley in Sales. Julia Treadway (Barbara Stanwyck) and Grim in Manufacturing are not committed at the beginning of the contest. A change in plot does not assure by itself a more cinematic film.

Once the new plot is under way the triangle looks like this:

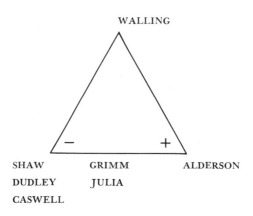

Being predominantly a power-fight drama, there is only a minor struggle in the breast of Walling as to his ambition to become president. The dialectic of the main character is overshadowed by the dynamics of the triangle, the negative versus the positive men, with the neutrals swinging the balance. In the chapter "Structuring Conflict" we shall see how this basic triangle alters and evolves as we move from climax to climax.

Sunset Boulevard (1950) is an excellent example of sharp triangular corners, but of unequal balance. How does this affect the film, if at all?

Joe Gillis (William Holden) is an unhappy scriptwriter whose hocked car is about to be repossessed by the finance company when the picture opens. Joe is willing enough to sell body and soul to the Devil, embodied in a psychotic ex-silent-film star, Norma Desmond (Gloria Swanson). This Faustian deal has as its goal for Joe the Hollywood fame-and-fortune mirage. He will write Norma's comeback picture, though it is obvious that Norma's histrionic talent is dated beyond recall. Joe is partner to the deception; that is his dialectic. His conflict is shaped into a triangle by the existence of a girl in the Script Department at Paramount, Betty Schaefer (Nancy Olson), who believes Joe has genuine talent. The triangle avoids triteness by the cool cynicism of Joe. He is an American Jean Sorel from Stendhal's *The Red and the Black;* he is a native existentialist, a forerunner of a Norman Mailer hipster. We feel he is basically decent; we expect him to cease being a gigolo at some point. Actually, Joe leans on women. With Norma he is dishonest, having no faith in her script project. With Betty he finds moral and professional support in writing, at night, an original script. He can't have both simultaneously and be a whole person.

So far we have been using the plane equilateral triangle with three sides of identical dimension, indicating that all three characters exercise equal power. Though this may be theoretical perfection, no such character alignment exists, either in life or art. In *Sunset Boulevard* Betty is unevenly matched against Norma and her resources, an unbalanced conflict. The triangle should be obtusely angled:

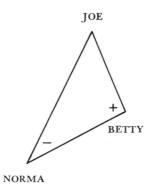

Is it an uneven fight because Betty is hardly more than a symbolical figure? Actually, Joe is en route to Ohio for a newspaper job—deserting both women—when he is shot in the back by Norma. An obtusely angled triangle can be effective. After all, the picture is dominated by Norma and her relationship with Joe; it is her triangle, although not her choice of action. It is Joe's decision that lands him in the swimming pool, floating face down—the opening and closing scenes of the film.

3. THE LOVE TRIANGLE

So many effective love stories are based on the Cinderella idea, a case might be argued for poor girls making the most appealing heroines. Seldom does Cinderella occupy the apex of the triangle, however, since she prefers to marry her Prince Charming rather than return to her swain in the cowbarn.

Bernard Shaw avoids clichés in his Cinderella story by concentrating on Higgins. A comparison between the play and the script version of the opening scene, which introduces the professorial Higgins and the cockney flower girl Liza Doolittle—opposites have box office appeal—discloses Higgins in both versions as the dominant character.

Here in *Pygmalion* Higgins' sense of professional challenge toward Liza is planted early in Act One:

> THE FLOWER GIRL
> (*with feeble defiance*)
> I've a right to be here if I like, same as you.

> THE NOTE TAKER
> A woman who utters such depressing and disgusting sounds has no right to be anywhere—no right to live. Remember that you are a human being with a soul and the divine gift of articulate speech: that your native language is the language of Shakespeare and Milton and The Bible: and don't sit there crooning like a bilious pigeon. . . .

> THE FLOWER GIRL
> (*rising in desperation*)
> You ought to be stuffed with nails, you ought. (*flinging the basket at his feet*) Take the whole blooming basket for sixpence.

> *The church clock strikes the second quarter.*

> HIGGINS
> (*hearing in it the voice of God, rebuking him for his Pharisaic want of charity to the poor girl*) A reminder. (*he raises his hat solemnly; then throws a handful of money into basket and follows* PICKERING)

> THE FLOWER GIRL
> (*picking up a half-crown*)
> Ah-ow-ooh! (*picking up a couple of florins*) Aaah-ow-ooh!

(*picking up several coins*) Aaaaaaah-ow-ooh! (*picking up a half-sovereign*) Aaaaaaaaaaaah-ow-ooh!!!

In the screen adaptation of *Pygmalion* (1938), Bernard Shaw is credited for the screen play and dialogue; the scenario is awarded to W. P. Lipscombe and Cecil Lewis. The comparable passage, from above, is now expanded in substance. In particular, the visualization of the conflict renders the characters more intense in their quarrel, and hence sharpens their corners of the triangle (Pickering is in the third corner as a skeptical friend). Note the effect of close-up shots, close two-shots (two persons), the rapid change of composition through editing, a frame movement of the camera through panning, and a voice heard off—out of view. All this cinematic fluidity affects the triangle through character intensification:

MEDIUM CLOSE SHOT—ELIZA

HIGGINS *enters shot making* MEDIUM CLOSE TWO SHOT.

ELIZA
(*muttering to herself*)
Let him mind his own business . . . and leave a pore girl to mind her own business . . .

CLOSE TWO SHOT—HIGGINS AND ELIZA

HIGGINS
Woman, cease this detestable boo-booing instantly.

ELIZA
I've a right to be here if I like, same as you.

HIGGINS
A woman who utters such depressing and disgusting sounds has no right to be anywhere.

ELIZA
Ooer!

HIGGINS
Remember that you are a human being with a soul, the divine gift of articulate speech, and that your language is the language of Milton, Shakespeare, and the Bible, and don't sit there crooning like a bilious pigeon.

ELIZA
A . . . ah . . . awou!

My Fair Lady. Courtesy of Warner Brothers.

HIGGINS

    A . . . ah . . . awou!

MEDIUM THREE SHOT

as HIGGINS *walks over to* PICKERING.

HIGGINS

    Heavens, what a sound . . .

CAMERA PANS *with* HIGGINS *to a* TWO SHOT *of* PICKERING *and* HIGGINS.

    . . . you see this creature with her kerbstone English . . .

This fragmentation into visual movements, the essence of cinema, accelerates character interplay, and can sharpen conflict. A silent close-up of Eliza, for example, is more effective as an insight into her ambition while she listens to Higgins's voice doom her to the gutter than if we saw her with Higgins in view. His presence would reduce her impact. Similarly, she listens alone when Higgins describes job opportunities. Such fragmenting enhances identification in a manner unique to cinema.

Further along, corresponding to Act Two, Higgins responds in the script more intensely to the challenge. Occupying the opposite (at the moment neutral) corner of the triangle are Colonel Pickering, the linguist from India, and Mrs. Pearce, the housekeeper. The scene is when Eliza calls on the professor for private instruction:

CLOSE-UP—ELIZA
listening.

> HIGGINS
> (*off*)

. . . the English that will keep her in the gutter until the end of her days . . .

MEDIUM CLOSE TWO SHOT—HIGGINS AND PICKERING

> HIGGINS

Well, sir, in three months I could pass her off as a Duchess at an Ambassador's Reception.

> PICKERING

Ah ha ha!

CLOSE-UP—ELIZA

listening.

> HIGGINS
> (*off*)

Yes . . . I could even get her a job as a lady's maid or shop assistant, which requires better English.

> ELIZA

You mean you could make me . . .

MEDIUM TWO SHOT—HIGGINS AND ELIZA

as ELIZA *sits.*

> HIGGINS

How much do you propose to pay me for the lessons?

> ELIZA

Oh, I know what's right. A lady friend of mine, she gets French lessons at h'eighteen-pence an hour from a real French gentleman . . .

CLOSE SHOT—ELIZA

ELIZA

. . . well you wouldn't have the nerve to ask the same for teaching me my own language as what you would for French, so I won't give you more than a shillin'. Take it or leave it.

CLOSE SHOT—HIGGINS

HIGGINS

I . . . m'm . . . I'll take it . . .

CAMERA PANS *with him as he starts to move.*

. . . You know, Pickering . . .

CLOSE SHOT—ELIZA

looking pleased.

MEDIUM TWO SHOT—HIGGINS AND ELIZA

CAMERA PANS *to a* TWO SHOT *of* HIGGINS *and* PICKERING.

HIGGINS

. . . a shilling to this girl is worth sixty or seventy pounds to a millionaire. It's handsome . . . it's enormous . . . It's the biggest offer . . .

CLOSE SHOT—ELIZA

ELIZA

Sixty pounds, what are you talking about? I never offered you sixty pounds.

MEDIUM SHOT—ELIZA

MRS. PEARCE *enters making* MEDIUM TWO SHOT.

HIGGINS
(*off*)

Hold your tongue.

ELIZA

I ain't got sixty pounds.

MRS. PEARCE

You foolish girl, nobody's going to touch your money.

HIGGINS *enters shot from right.*

HIGGINS

Somebody's going to touch you with a broomstick if you don't stop snivelling. Sit down, will you.

He exits shot.

ELIZA

A–ah–ahoau! Anyone would think you was my father.

CLOSE SHOT—PICKERING

PICKERING

Higgins . . .

HIGGINS *enters shot from camera left, making* CLOSE TWO SHOT.

. . . I'm interested. What about that boast of your's that you could pass her off at the Ambassador's Reception?

HIGGINS

Well, what about it?

CLOSE TWO SHOT—ELIZA AND MRS. PEARCE

PICKERING
(*off*)
. . . I'd say that you were the greatest teacher alive . . .

CLOSE TWO SHOT—HIGGINS AND PICKERING

PICKERING
(*off*)
. . . I'll bet you all the expenses of the experiment you can't do it. And I'll pay for the lessons.

ELIZA

Oh, you're real good . . .

CAMERA TRACKS BACK *and* PANS *with her as she walks over to* HIGGINS *and* PICKERING, *making* MEDIUM THREE SHOT.

HIGGINS

Come here.

ELIZA

. . . Oh! Thank you, Captain.

HIGGINS

Come here, sit down.

She starts to sit.

MEDIUM CLOSE TWO SHOT—HIGGINS AND ELIZA

as ELIZA *sits.*

HIGGINS

This is almost irresistible . . . She's so deliciously low . . . so horribly dirty.

CLOSE SHOT—ELIZA

ELIZA

A–ah–ahaou! I ain't dirty. I washed my face and hands afore I come, I did.

HIGGINS
(*off*)

I shall make a . . .

CLOSE TWO SHOT

favoring HIGGINS.

HIGGINS

. . . duchess of this draggle-tailed guttersnipe.

ELIZA

A–ah–ahaou!

HIGGINS

In six months . . . in three, if she has a good ear and a quick tongue . . . I'll take her anywhere and pass her off as anything. We'll start today . . . now . . . this minute. *He walks out of shot, leaving* EIZA *open-mouthed.*

HIGGINS
(*off*)

Mrs. Pearce . . .

MEDIUM TWO SHOT—MRS. PEARCE

as HIGGINS *moves into shot.*

HIGGINS
(*off*)

. . . take her away and clean her. Take off all her clothes and burn them. Ring up and order some new ones. Wrap her up in brown paper till they come.

More clearly than before, it should be seen how cinematic movements, achieved through rapid alterations of pictorial composition and the intensification of many close shots, render the conflict within its triangle more incisive. Note that the number of movements almost equal the number of speeches—an extraordinary fluidity—and three years before *Citizen Kane,* the most fluid film between *Intolerance* and *8½.*

Higgins roars like a lion from his apex. It is Pickering and Mrs. Pearce who raise protesting voices from their corner, protests strangely muted by producers Gabriel Pascal and Jack L. Warner in their film versions. Were their heroes (Leslie Howard and Rex Harrison) not to have feet of human clay for box office reasons? This is a weakness in the structure, apparent when the triangle fails—for that scene—to continue as a triangle. However, in Shaw's play (Act Two) Mrs. Pearce and Pickering function as Higgins's conscience; they are the voices of society, saying it is improper to install a young lady under your roof for a linguistic lark.

Here is Pickering: "Oh, come, Higgins! be reasonable."

> MRS. PEARCE
> (*resolutely*)
> You must be reasonable, Mr. Higgins: really you must. You
> can't walk over everybody like this. You can't take a girl like
> that as if you were picking up a pebble on the beach. . . .
> Stop, Mr. Higgins, I won't allow it. It's you that are wicked.

The absence of these countervoices weakens the dynamics of both film versions. Shaw remains consistent to the end. In his epilogue to the play the cantankerous bachelor-at-heart concludes, "Galatea never does quite like Pygmalion: his relation to her is too godlike to be altogether agreeable."

My Fair Lady is Americanized. The triangle is more evident; Cinderella gets Prince Charming. Galatea falls in love with her Pygmalion, and he in turn has feet of putty. As every American college girl knows, young professors often marry their prize pupils and live happily ever after. The Hollywood Higgins falls in love with Eliza, in spite of his English eccentricities. The lad Freddy is no longer an object of amusing contempt to Higgins, but a competitor! Shaw on Olympus is not laughing. In this Warner film version, written by Alan Jay Lerner, the triangle is a cliché and a box-office smash. It is a lopsided triangle, since Pickering and Mrs. Pearce never interfere with Higgins' lark, nor is Freddy a real threat. Nor is there an inner qualm rippling through the breast of the egotistical drillmaster.

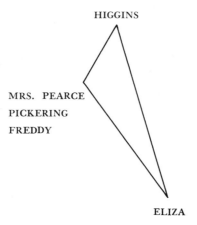

What was rewarding in *My Fair Lady* were music and songs and color, which, as we may see later, can add or detract from character and conflict.

The career girl's dialectic is cleverly treated in *Kitty Foyle*. As a novel, Christopher Morley thickens a thin story with a faint triangle by telling it through the heroine's eyes in the first person, with feminine touches and observations, sometimes naughty or earthy, on every other page. It is a Cinderella story, set in Philadelphia, about an Irish girl who meets a Main Line prince, Wynnewood Strafford VI, who in turn loves her. But railroad tracks make dangerous crossings, especially in Philly, so there is another waiting on the sidewalk, Mark Eisen, a Jewish New York doctor. Kitty's father, Pop Foyle, advises independence. Kitty has a ready-made symbol in the novel, which Morley described as "the toy snowstorm. That was the glass ball that stood on a bracket ever since I remember. It was full of clear water and a figure inside, a little girl on a sled coasting down a hillside with a red scarf flying round her neck and a castle in the background. When you shook the ball she was surrounded by a whirling blizzard, then gradually it would settle down and was clear and peaceful. I took that with me and have it yet. The castle came to mean Wyn and the Main Line, and I say 'Hello, little girl on a sleighride.' "

The glass ball is reminiscent of the one Charles Foster Kane held in his hand when he expired, except that it contained a boy and his sled—known only to Citizen Kane and the flames as "Rosebud." At appropriate moments in the film version (1940) Ginger Rogers shakes her glass ball, while staring at herself in the seeing-all mirror, and we get a flashback into her past relations with either one of the two men in her life. Kitty must decide between romantic adventure with Wyn and affectionate security with Mark. Being an All-American career girl, Pop's vote for independence carries topical appeal. Kitty's dialectic involves three directions, as envisaged by Dalton Trumbo whose screenplay was subtitled "The Natural History of a Woman." The arrows indicate the direction of her choices, all positive:

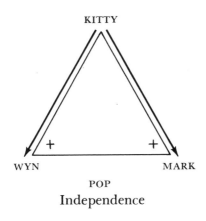

KITTY

WYN   MARK

POP

Independence

In the TV version, written by Whitfield Cook, the triangle resembles the more elementary form of the novel in that Mark is quite secondary, never an equal choice. In the closing moments of that version Kitty confesses to her roommate Molly that she doesn't want to date Mark:

KITTY

I can't go on giving Mark the runaround. He keeps looking at me as though the Hour of Decision is just around the corner.

MOLLY

What's wrong with Mark?

KITTY

Nothing. It's what's wrong with me. . . .

MOLLY *goes.* CAMERA MOVES *up on* KITTY.

KITTY'S VOICE

Wyn—Wyn—Maybe I should have fought for you and taken you away from the Paper Dolls . . . But I guess you're doing what you were meant to. And I just hope you can forget me easier than I can forget you . . . Wyn, are you all right?

Door buzzer over shot. KITTY *doesn't move. Buzzer again.* MOLLY *sticks her head in from the kitchenette.*

MOLLY

That must be Mark.

KITTY

Yes.

MOLLY

Aren't you going to open the door?

KITTY
(turning)
Mark's always hurt if you don't say "darling." He says, "You don't greet me, darling? Is it an argument?"

MOLLY

Well, my gosh, you can say "darling" without committing yourself to anything. Darling is only politeness nowadays.

KITTY
(nodding rather numbly)
Dearest is what I couldn't say—unless by accident.

MOLLY *disappears.* KITTY *goes to hall door. She opens it.* MARK *stands there with a tiny bunch of flowers.*

MARK

Hello, Kitty.

KITTY

Hello—darling.

MARK *comes in.*

FADE OUT

END OF ACT THREE

It is so overwhelmingly Kitty's and Wyn's story, with all the interaction between those two, that Mark with his security is never a serious contender for Cinderella's crown. The result is an inverted triangle; Mark is a standby while Kitty and Wyn run the race. On the whole, TV triangles are more transparent, since they are designed to hold the gaze, between commercials, of a lower common denominator than films.

Ladies in distress have an apparent advantage, seated in their lofty apexes, for determining the credibility of what we see.

Henrik Ibsen, writing of his play *Hedda Gabler* in 1890, said, "My intention in giving it this name was to indicate that Hedda, as a personality, is to be regarded rather as her father's daughter than as her husband's wife." As such, Hedda destroys the work and the life of her former lover, Lövborg, and rejects her husband, simple Tesman, and ruins the devoted intentions of Thea Elvsted toward Lövborg. All that remains for Hedda, in her psychopathic logic, is suicide.

In contrast, the boredom of a provincial French wife and mother— bored even with her Parisian polo-player lover—is a modern Madame Bovary who never once contemplates suicide but escapes with her young student lover. The bored wife (Jeanne Moreau) in *The Lovers* (1958) deserts husband, child, and security for the romantic adventure of being alive with a younger man (Jean-Marc Bory). It is precisely the cinematic elements—the rhythmic movements of compositions and lights—by director-writer Louis Malle that translates an old triangle into a fresh film.

This quality of visual reality, or plastic plausibility, enhances the triangle in *Anna Karénina* (1935). The suicide is never doubted. On the narrative level, Anna's dilemma is real because she is a conventional woman at heart, caught in a nonconventional affair. In Tolstoi's novel Anna at first covertly manages the affair with Count Vronsky, then openly defies the established institution of marriage. The mores of the society Tolstoi depicted prevented conventional persons like Vronsky and Anna from sustaining themselves with their overwhelming love for each other. Anna's suicide was determined from within her and from outside social pressures, especially from her husband Karenin and his cruel alienation of her son Sergei.

This scene between father and son, following the ecstasy and premonition-of-punishment scene between Anna and Vronsky, depicts the coldhearted sadism of Karenin. The juxtaposition is cinematic (Shots 42/43). The sadism is rendered cinematically: in Shot 4 "the camera moves up on them," thus emphasizing Karenin's approach to the terror-stricken boy. The defenseless son is a helpless stand-in for his mother, as the husband (Basil Rathbone) behaves as though he were condemning Anna (Garbo) to death *in absentia*. Here the film version excels in its language of movement, light, and

Anna Karénina. Courtesy of Metro-Goldwyn-Mayer.

composition, comparable to the excellence of Tolstoi's prose. Here are both the fatalism and pressure seen and witnessed, with the result that that corner of the triangle is strengthened, making the suicide all the more inevitable. The scene has five compositions (shots) taken from the editor's continuity script, a skeletal form with numbers indicating the length of each shot in feet and frames (interesting for rhythmic studies) :

SHOT 42

> VRONSKY
> You're trembling. Are you cold?

> ANNA
> We'll be punished.

> VRONSKY
> Punished?

> ANNA
> For being so happy!

43. MEDIUM CLOSE SHOT   INTERIOR—SERGEI'S ROOM

Night light swinging by wall. CAMERA PANS *to right to* SERGEI *in bed. He sits up—calls.*

> SERGEI
> Mother!

Music "Nur Wer Die Sehnsucht Kennt" *by Tchaikovsky—scenes 43 to 52.*

44. MEDIUM LONG SHOT—KARENIN ENTERS SERGEI'S ROOM

CAMERA PANS *him to right to* SERGEI. *He sits on edge of bed.* CAMERA MOVES *up on them.*

> KARENIN
>
> Sergei! Sergei, what is it?

> SERGEI
>
> I dreamed—I thought—

> KARENIN
>
> Yes.

> SERGEI
>
> That—that mother came in and kissed me good night. But when I woke up I found she wasn't here. Was she here?

> KARENIN
>
> No, Sergei.

> SERGEI
>
> But—but I'm sure she kissed me good night.

> KARENIN
>
> Sergei, you might as well know, once and for all—

> SERGEI
>
> What?

> KARENIN
>
> That your mother—is dead.

45. CLOSE-UP—SERGEI *reacts—speaks.*

> SERGEI
>
> D-dead?

> KARENIN
> (*off shot*)
>
> Yes.

> SERGEI
>
> That means that—that I won't see her again? That—that—I'll never see her again?

46. CLOSE-UP—KARENIN

looks down off shot—speaks.

> KARENIN
>
> Yes.

The scene is climaxed by close-up shots of Sergei and Karenin, which are like double blows. The power in the scene, coming from that corner of the triangle, seals the fate of Anna. Her only acceptable relations with society are via husband and son, but Vronsky's cold departure crushes her ego. The dynamic forces that run against her are too powerful. Suicide is inevitable.

4. THE INVERTED TRIANGLE

As seen in the TV version of *Kitty Foyle,* the triangle becomes inverted when two of the three main characters are teamed against the third, or its representatives. Lovers-against-the-world, for example, place them as equal partners on a shared plateau. Juliet teaches Romeo to have faith in love. In the play, Act Two, Scene 1, Juliet's dialectic is clearly expounded:

> JULIET: My bounty is as boundless as the sea,
> My love as deep—the more I give to thee
> The more I have, for both are infinite.

It was Romeo who faltered at the end, upsetting their united front against the multitudes. In the Irving G. Thalberg production (1936), "arranged for the screen by Talbot Jennings," the triangle is identical with the play. Inversions in screenplays pose no special problem. The inverted triangle in its basic form:

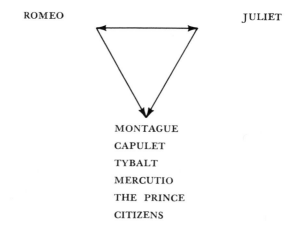

ROMEO

JULIET

MONTAGUE
CAPULET
TYBALT
MERCUTIO
THE PRINCE
CITIZENS

In *Wuthering Heights* (1939) the lovers are similarly paired against a hostile world. In the novel by Emily Brontë these are no simple romanticists whose major problems stem from their family names. Theirs is a masochistic frustration, a rare portrayal of the love that hates, and hatred that feeds on love.

Baldly recounted, Heathcliff, a gypsy bastard off the streets of Liverpool, is reared by Earnshaw as his own child along with daughter Catherine and son Hindley. After Earnshaw's death Hindley reduces Heathcliff to a stableboy, and bullies him. Catherine and Heathcliff, however, fall passionately in love. Pride forces him to flee when he overhears Cathy say it would degrade her to marry him. Returning wealthy, Heathcliff finds Cathy married to an insignificent neighbor, Edgar Linton. In spite he marries Isabella, Linton's sister. The violence of Heathcliff's love for Cathy and her own irrevocable involvement cause her death following the birth of her daughter, Cathy. The remainder of the novel concentrates on the following generation.

The inverted triangle is similar in pattern to *Romeo and Juliet*. The screenplay was by Ben Hecht and Charles McArthur:

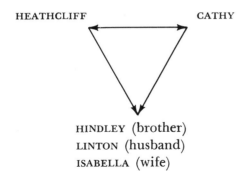

HEATHCLIFF   CATHY

HINDLEY (brother)
LINTON (husband)
ISABELLA (wife)

In Paddy Chayefsky's screenplay of *Marty* (1955) the lovers against the world are plain, family-ridden, and reside in the North Bronx. Marty (Ernest Borgnine) is a good-humored butcher; Clara is a college graduate and a schoolteacher. They have their problems in common, and chief of these is loneliness.

For the establishment of a lovers' plateau Chayefsky resorts almost exclusively to dialogue, the antithesis of the cinematic, and a TV inheritance from radio dramas:

123.

MARTY

Well, I'll tell you, Clara. I think you're kidding yourself.
I used to think about moving out, you know? And that's

what I used to say. "My mother needs me." But when you really get down to it, that ain't it at all. We're just afraid to go out on our own.

That's a big step when you go out on your own. And I think you're kidding yourself about how much your father needs you. Actually, you need your father. You know what I mean?

CLARA *regards* MARTY *for a moment, a little surprised at the simplicity of the insight.*

(*continuing*) You know what I mean? You're living at home, and you got your father and mother there, and you can go on like that being a little girl all your life. But people like you and me, we got to grow up sometimes.

CLARA

I went away for one term to Ohio State University. I couldn't stand it.

MARTY

Sure. I know. I was in the army. I was miserable.

CLARA

I'm afraid of being lonely.

MARTY

Oh, you won't be so lonely. You'll make friends right away.

CLARA

Actually, I don't make friends easily.

Arranged against them are Marty's mother, Mrs. Pilletti, Marty's relatives, Marty's bachelor friends—Angie, Ralph, Leo, Joe, George. The realism of the Bronx dialogue and setting gives authenticity, but with no cinematic assistance in the writing.

The triangle:

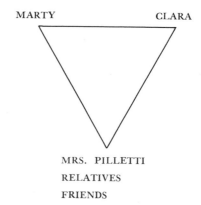

MARTY   CLARA

MRS. PILLETTI
RELATIVES
FRIENDS

Jules et Jim. Courtesy of Janus Films.

5. THE CIRCLE

   To conclude with a contemporary variation, François Truffaut has
done two eternal triangles concerning marriage among the dearest of
friends, or three-in-the-house, *ménage à trois*. The first of these, *Jules
et Jim* (1962) circles around two men and a woman: Jules, the German (Oskar Werner) ; Jim (Henri Serré) and Catherine, Jules's wife,

(Jeanne Moreau). Since all three interact upon one another, arrows of action run in all directions. An inversion of the triangle is inadequate; a circle would be more appropriate.

The subtle motivation in all these characters goes beyond adultery by the wife as idea. Sex as an answer to boredom, or as a novelty, is also erroneous. *Jules et Jim* is a highly moral film rooted in love; there is no hate, only love that flows and overflows. The dialectic in all three is identical: the endless circle of the deepest love.

The circular triangle:

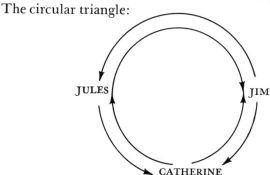

There is a French saying to the effect that the bonds of matrimony are so heavy it takes three to carry them. Aside from the psychological aspects of this *bon-bon,* the observation makes for respectable dramaturgy.

In *Soft Skin* (*La Peau Douce*) (1963) Truffaut reverses the players: two women and one man. It is a bourgeois husband's dilemma to be torn between the love of both women, the banality of adultery made realistic, or, as Truffaut says, "a sort of polemic response to *Jules et Jim*—a nonpoetic view of love."

The *Soft Skin* triangle:

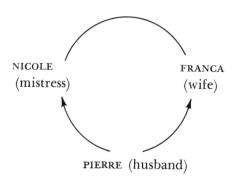

In summary, one character does not make for dramatic conflict; two don't offer dramatic alternatives; but three, fortunately, is a crowd. The triangle is not a dictum; it is a device. It exists; it is three to be used in all the infinite varieties that emotions and ideas can devise. Its usefulness as an illuminating instrument should not be flawed by too rigid an application. For cinema, the triangle can be a focusing lens on the corners from which the conflict springs.

CHAPTER SIX 🖎

Structuring Conflict

Languages and certain crafts have units of expression that serve to distinguish and measure their passages. In literature, they are the word, phrase, clause, sentence, paragraph, and chapter; in music, notes, bars, octaves, and the chromatic scale. In the craft of drama, the beat, the scene, the act. Units are useful devices for comparisons and evaluations.

In cinema, the units of expression center upon degrees or amounts of movement and light, such as *frame:* a separate composition; *shot:* a single unit of cinematic expression; *scene:* a minor dramatic or expository unit; *sequence:* a major dramatic or expository climax of scenes; and *phase:* a coordinated combination of sequences.

A knowledge of the expressive entities is essential for a fuller understanding of the art as well as the craft. The failure to employ them has hindered a serious study of the moving image. As a prerequisite for a common discourse there need be common definitions.

The cinematic units are:

1. *Frame:* a single composition within a shot wherein space has been shaped and motion is implied. In a strict photographic sense *frame* is a still picture, but a cinematic frame is a frozen extract from a unit of motion. As such, its sole value lies in being an evaluation of composition and light as those factors relate to action or acting. A frame may be selected for study from any part of a shot, the beginning, middle, or end. The frame is what the writer-director first sees

in his mind's eye when he envisages a setting, a face, or a scene. By itself a frame goes nowhere, but without it a shot cannot begin. The master image, already noted, is a frame, sometimes similar to an illustration in an advertisement. Frames are what animated cartoonists draw and which in turn are photographed frame by frame. Also, frames are sketched by production designers for the director and cameraman. Historically, the frame has its origins in aboriginal drawings on cave surfaces as illustrations of hunting lessons, on Oriental scrolls that unfold stories, on pyramids, vases, the walls of pharaohs, on medievel tapestries and Renaissance frescoes, and in photography.

2. *Shot* is composed of frames, the result of a single camera operation, its length determined by editing. A shot may consist of the fewest number of frames capable of making a physiological impact on the brain—approximately eight (⅓ of a second) —or a shot may run for minutes and contain several thousands of frames. Thus a shot may have a beginning that differs from its middle or end. Such are the cases in traveling shots—trucks, pans, and zooms. Also, alteration of size within a shot gives the equivalent of an *inside-edit;* that is, compositional alterations in a shot of long duration are, in effect, several shots. A shot is not unlike a sentence. It may be as simple as a subject and predicate, or may consist of modifiers, phrases, and a variety of associated clauses. Ideally, a shot should aim to express a single cinematic emotion or idea.

3. *Scene.* In cinema the scene is composed of shots so arranged as to express a minor dramatic climax or an expository statement. A scene is constructed by joining shots in a continuous flow through editing or cutting, the *cut* being the "curtains" within the scene. The concluding curtain at the end of a scene is called a *dissolve,* which can be optically noted. However, in the tempo of contemporary cinema most scenes are connected by ordinary cuts. Several emotions or thoughts might be involved within one scene, but they should be so related that they constitute a unified idea. Thus there might be changes of scenery within a cinematic scene, and an alteration of time by clock or climate, and a manipulation of action. The old unities of Grecian time-place-action, which Elizabethan drama did so much to dissolve, has been further fragmented by cinema. What Shakespeare did to Aristotle, D. W. Griffith did to Shakespeare. Subsequently, Resnais in *Last Year in Marienbad* and Fellini in *8½* have dated Griffith as though he were Shakespeare. The unity within a scene may be a combination of narrative, dramatic, cinematic, and

psychological elements. In this respect, the scene in contemporary cinema has most in common with modern poetry.

4. *Sequence.* The sequence is composed of scenes, and constitutes a major dramatic climax or a major expository statement, and as such corresponds to an act in the theatre. Whereas there are generally three acts to a play, the feature film has anywhere from five to ten sequences, with eight as an average. Such is the degree of dramatic compression in cinema. If a plot dialectic is in operation, a sequence should not have less than three scenes—a plus scene, a minus scene, and a synthesis—but there are no patterns in dramaturgy that are sacred or unbreakable. More often, a sequence in contemporary cinema is identified by its unifying rhythm or mood or idea. Technically, a sequence is marked by a *fade-in* at the beginning and a *fade-out* at its end, the traditional sequence curtain. Current directorial fashion has been to eliminate fades as well as dissolves in favor of a jump-ahead cut that marks a sharp break.

5. *Phase.* The phase is composed of several sequences unified by a period in time or history, or by a place such as a country. Phase is a grand unit employed in longer productions, usually in spectacles where much material is presented so that a larger unit than sequence is required. Phase is a helpful means of grouping together a series of sequences under a common identity.

These units, it may be seen, comprise a natural progression: the frame is to the shot what the shot is to the scene, what the scene is to the sequence, and what the sequence is to the phase.

The master image, as a frame, should exist somewhere within some shot—or the idea of it, if not an exact photographic symbol. That particular shot, then, might well become the master shot of a scene, which in turn could render that scene the master scene of a sequence. Such aesthetical logic is more common than realized, though artistic cinema is constantly variable. In common terminology the master shot is considered the establishing shot, a long shot that establishes locale or setting, and to which the editor frequently returns after close-ups and medium shots. However, the master shot should contain the master idea rather than furniture or landscape. The master sequence should be the major climax of the story and of the production. More often than otherwise, the units function in progression, not necessarily in neat order, and irrespective of our cognizance. Like phenomenon in nature, form exists, even when we are not looking.

Here are the units as seen in one motion picture, *The Greatest Story Ever Told* (1965):

Christ on the Cross is the master image and a *frame*. However, there are a number of such frames in a corresponding variety of such *shots* from different perspectives and sizes, angles and lighting. Individual preferences are not essential. Together the *shots* constitute the *scene* of the crucifixion, which in turn is part of the *sequence* of Golgotha. That sequence has the crucifixion as its climax, and also includes Christ bearing the Cross to Calvary, all that occurred attendant to the actual crucifixion, the time on the Cross, and the death. In turn, the sequence of Golgotha follows the sequence of the trial. Before that is the sequence of the Apostles and the betrayal. Following Calvary is the sequence of the resurrection. These four sequences comprise the *phase* of Saint John—as seen by Author Oursler and Director Stevens.

2.   SEQUENCE CLIMAXES AS PLOT OUTLINES

The critic Eric Bentley said, "It is easier to renounce the 'well-made' structure than to create a satisfactory alternative." For our purpose, the writer-director who avoids plot and character alteration does not stand in the need of instruction or prayer. He may suffer from a horror of being understood.

Once the fundamentals of cinematic dramaturgy are understood, a writer-director has a solid base from which he can experiment with assurances that he will not unwittingly wander into unintelligible fields. He knows when he is taking a fresh path, instead of thrashing about in the underbrush. The avant-guardist must know what it is he is rejecting. For exploration, a compass is a necessity.

As we may recall, the master triangle for *Hamlet* involves his conscience, which renders him a procrastinator. In Sir Laurence Olivier's version the major actions, having to do with the hero's delay, mark the sequence climaxes because of the kinetic demands of cinema as an art and the high commercial penalty for failure. The sequence climaxes follow the act climaxes of the play with one exception. Only the climax of Sequence D differs from that of Act IV.

Sequence A ends with Hamlet charged by his father's ghost to revenge the murder by killing Claudius, a charge so terribly weighty to Hamlet that he repeatedly pledges his friend Horatio and the guards, Marcellus and Bernardo, to secrecy. He curses his fate; that is Hamlet's dialectic. The fatherly charge may be considered positive, for our purposes, and substitute actions as negative.

Here is the climax concluding in Shot 116, the fade-out of Sequence A which coincides with the curtain of Act I:

SCENE 116

HAMLET

Go in,
And still your fingers on your lips I pray.

MARCELLUS *and* BERNARDO *go out of picture* LEFT.
    (*To* HORATIO.) The time is out of joint.
    O, cursed spite,
    That ever I was born to set it right:
    Come let us go together.

HORATIO *goes out of picture* CAMERA RIGHT—HAMLET *turns to look at*

High Tor in the b.g. then follows him. CAMERA CENTRES *on High Tor.*

FADE OUT: MUSIC STARTS

The triangle for Sequence A:

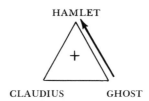

HAMLET

CLAUDIUS   GHOST

The arrow indicates the action, its motivating character, and the target.

Although Hamlet feigns madness with Polonius and mercilessly teases Ophelia and bemoans his conscience in soliliquy, the act against Claudius in Sequence B is to embarrass him with the Players. Not a very murderous revenge:

SCENE 181: VERY LONG SHOT—PLAYERS FOLLOWING POLONIUS

SCENE 182: MEDIUM CLOSE SHOT—HAMLET

SCENE 183: LONG SHOT—STAGE

from HAMLET'*s eyeline.*

SCENE 184: MEDIUM CLOSE SHOT—HAMLET

He walks past CAMERA LEFT *to* RIGHT *and* CAMERA PANS *with him as he runs into* LONG SHOT *onto the stage.*

HAMLET

The play's the thing,
Wherein I'll catch the conscience of the king.

FADE OUT: MUSIC FADES OUT

The triangle for Sequence B:

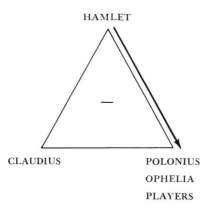

HAMLET

CLAUDIUS   POLONIUS
                        OPHELIA
                        PLAYERS

In Sequence C, Hamlet continues to tease Polonius, taunt Ophelia, observe the King react to the Players, refuses to kill the King while at prayer, abuses his Queen Mother, but does act in killing Polonius as a psychological stand-in for Claudius.

SCENE 266: CAMERA PANS ONTO POLONIUS

then back to include the QUEEN *and* HAMLET.

HAMLET
(*to* QUEEN)

Indeed this counsellor
Is now most still, most secret and most grave,
That was in life a foolish, prating knave—

CAMERA TRACKS *and* PANS *with* HAMLET *as he picks up* POLONIUS's *body by his feet and pulls him from the room.*

Come sir, to draw toward an end with you.
Goodnight, mother.

CAMERA TRACKS BACK *in front of* HAMLET *who goes out of picture* LEFT *leaving the* QUEEN *in the background.*

FADE OUT:

Sequence C triangle:

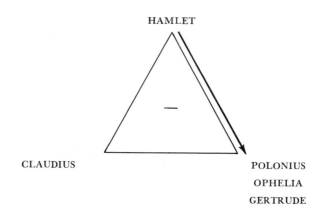

HAMLET

CLAUDIUS

POLONIUS
OPHELIA
GERTRUDE

In Sequence D, Hamlet leaves town and so becomes inactive, but upon returning to discover himself the cause of Ophelia's suicide (negative), Hamlet declares his will to act—he will fight Laertes to the death to prove he loved Ophelia—a substitution since he does not fight Claudius. This corresponds to Act V, Scene 1 in the play, and marks the cinematic climax of Olivier's sequence:

SCENE 323: LONG SHOT—LAERTES

jumping into the grave.

HAMLET
Now pile your dust upon the quick and dead,

HAMLET *comes into picture and* LAERTES *runs towards him.*

Till of this flat a mountain you have made,
What is he whose grief bears such an emphasis? It is I,
Hamlet the Dane!

They fight.

LAERTES
(*to* HAMLET)
The devil take thy soul.

> HAMLET
> (*to* LAERTES)
>
> Thou prayest not well.
> I prithee take thy fingers from my throat.
> Hold off thy hands.

SCENE 324: MEDIUM SHOT—KING

> KING
> (*to the soldiers*)
>
> Pluck them asunder.

CAMERA TRACKS *back and* PANS *to include the* MOURNERS, HAMLET, LAERTES, *and the* QUEEN.

> HAMLET
>
> I will fight with him upon this theme
> Until my eyelids will no longer wag.

Sequence D triangle:

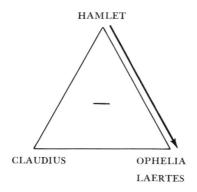

In Sequence E, Hamlet kills Claudius after discovering his Queen Mother is poisoned, Laertes finished, and he has only moments himself:

SCENE 406: LONG SHOT—HAMLET

jumping from the gallery onto the KING *who is in f.g.*

> HAMLET
>
> Then, venom to thy end!

SCENE 407: CLOSE SHOT—HAMLET

falling onto the KING. CAMERA PANS *down with them as they fall to the floor.*

SCENE 408: MEDIUM SHOT—HAMLET

standing over the KING *and thrusting his sword into him.*

SCENE 409: MEDIUM SHOT—KING

HAMLET'*s sword is once more thrust into the* KING'*s bosom.*

SCENE 410: MEDIUM SHOT—HAMLET

SCENE 411: MEDIUM SHOT—KING

dragging himself across the floor towards his crown which has fallen off.

SCENE 412: CAMERA SHOOTING

from a high angle onto the entire scene, the KING *is in the centre of the room, surrounded by* SOLDIERS.

SCENE 413: MEDIUM LONG SHOT—QUEEN

the KING *tries to crawl towards her, but dies before he can do so.*

Sequence E triangle:

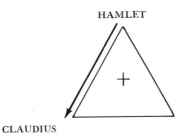

HAMLET

CLAUDIUS

With Hamlet's fatal act against Claudius the charge of the Ghost is concluded. It is the dramatic conclusion of the plot, and its cinematic climax. Shots 406 through 410 are rapid, energetic, and plastically exciting. Hamlet twice thrusts his sword into the body, having first fallen upon the King and rolled to the floor with him. It is the moment we have been awaiting since Sequence A when the Ghost ordered him to do it.

Sequence climaxes, we have seen, are visually evident and determined by major actions.

In *A Place in the Sun* George Eastman's tragedy is first poised in the climax of Sequence A by his enthrallment with Angela, the wealthy, glamorous rich girl. In the Dreiser novel she is called Sondra Finchley, and here is the moment of first encounter as seen by Clyde, the poor cousin from the West:

To Clyde's eyes she was the most adorable feminine thing he had seen in all his days. Indeed her effect on him was electric—thrilling—arousing in him a curiously stinging sense of what it was to want and not to have—to wish to win and yet to feel, almost agonizingly, that he was destined not even to win a glance from her. It tortured and flustered him. At one moment he had a keen desire to close his eyes and shut her out—at another to look only at her constantly—so truly was he captivated.

This first meeting occurs in Book Two, Chapter X, which is almost halfway into the novel. In the screenplay, written by Michael Wilson and Harry Brown, Dreiser's collar factory now manufactures bathing suits.

The sequence climax comes at their initial encounter in the Eastman mansion, a love-at-first-sight made more credible by planting the opening glimpse of glamorous Angela. The butler and maid bring wraps, George sees Angela:

59. CLOSE-UP—ANGELA

ANGELA
(*music*)
Men are so disgustingly prompt.

60. MEDIUM CLOSE SHOT—GEORGE

fascinated by ANGELA, *off shot*

ANGELA
(*off*)
I think they do it just to put us women in a bad light, don't you think so, Mrs. Eastman?

61. CLOSE SHOT—ANGELA AND MRS. EASTMAN

f.g. GEORGE *b.g. gazes at* ANGELA. (EARL *and* TOM *are tipped in behind* ANGELA) ["tipped in" means angle, and describes composition in relation to an actor].

MRS. EASTMAN
(*music, off*)
I hear your place at the Lake is coming along fine.

ANGELA

Oh, did Marcia tell you? It's a dream palace. I'm going to end my days there.

MRS. EASTMAN

Will it be ready for summer?

ANGELA

Even if I have to stand over everyone with a whip.

EARL

All right, Simon Legree, let's go.

ANGELA *laughs.*

ANGELA *and* TOM (*tipped in*) *exit.*

(EARL *turns to* GEORGE.)

Good night, Eastman.

MUSIC.

62. MEDIUM SHOT—GEORGE

spellbound.

GEORGE

Oh, good night.

MUSIC.

63. VERY LONG SHOT—ANGELA

EARL *and* TOM *at door.*

ANGELA

Bye-bye.

MRS. EASTMAN
(*off*)

'Bye.

Music stops.

Sequence A triangle:

GEORGE

+

ANGELA

One corner of the triangle is established in the climax of Sequence A. Since Angela is a more powerful motivating force acting upon George than Alice, the poor girl who works under him in the bathing-suit factory, it is natural that the introductory sequence climax be hers. More often, Sequence A climaxes establish all three corners of the triangle.

In order to balance, if possible, the opposing corners—or, at least, to make it appear to be a suspenseful struggle—Alice is made more than a sexual attraction. There is rare poignancy in her devotion to George, and decency in him.

Here is that moment in the novel that becomes in turn the climax of Sequence B. The passage is from Book Two, Chapter XVII (George is Clyde Griffiths and Alice is Roberta Alden) :

There was a sob—half of misery, half of delight—in her voice and Clyde caught that. He was so touched by her honesty and simplicity that tears sprang to his own eyes. "It's all right, Roberta. It's all right. Please don't cry. Oh, I think you're so sweet. I do. I do, Roberta."

. . . It seemed at the moment as though life had given him all—all—that he could possibly ask of it. . . . They had found love.

Now he is truly trapped, not between a rich girl and a poor one, but between two types of love, and his conscience is involved. If Roberta (Alice) were a passing fancy, there would be no dramatic suspense.

Like Sequence A triangle, Sequence B is also positive.

Here is the climax of Sequence B:

EXTERIOR: ALICE'S ROOMING HOUSE

2. MEDIUM SHOT—ALICE AND GEORGE

huddled on porch steps under eaves. (CAMERA BOOMS BACK.) *He kisses her.* (RAIN.)

ALICE

Oh . . .

3. CLOSE SHOT—GEORGE AND ALICE

He reaches inside window and turns on radio. (RAIN.)

ALICE

Gee, I wish I could ask you in.

RADIO MUSIC.

But Mrs. Roberts is so strict.

A Place in the Sun. Courtesy of Paramount Pictures.

GEORGE

I don't want to make things difficult for you.

Music grows louder. ALICE *tries to turn down radio.*

ALICE

Oh!

GEORGE *exits.*

INTERIOR: ALICE'S ROOM (RADIO MUSIC)

4. MEDIUM LONG SHOT—ALICE

outside, trying to turn radio down. GEORGE *enters room and crosses to radio. He lowers volume.*

ALICE

Yeah, I wish I could ask you in. But we'd have to keep the music awful low.

She looks around doubtfully, then quietly exits up steps. She comes into room and they dance. GEORGE *closes door.* CAMERA BOOMS FOR-WARD. DOOR CLOSES.

> GEORGE
>
> This is nice.

> ALICE
> *(whispers)*
> Mrs. Roberts is right next door.

> GEORGE
>
> This is the way it should have been.

> ALICE
>
> Yes, this is the way . . .

They dance out of scene. CAMERA BOOMS FORWARD *and* HOLDS *on radio at window.* GEORGE's *car b.g. on street.*

> *(off)* Oh, George . . . George . . .

LIGHT CHANGES *to dawn.* RADIO MUSIC STOPS. STATIC. ROOSTER CROWS. DOOR OPENS—CLOSES—OFF.

GEORGE *enters and goes down steps.*

Sequence B triangle:

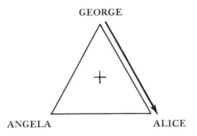

The sincerity of George's tender passion for Alice—which Dreiser called love—rates a positive. Now with two opening sequences positive, George is truly impaled on the horns of a dilemma. Alice is equated with Angela, so that the climax of Sequence B completes the triangle. Now we have conflict and plot with cinematic significance.

In Sequence C, Angela and George fall quickly in love. The climax comes when they are dancing at a party in the Eastman house. That Angela is of the upper class and admires him, that she is beautiful and they are dancing so intimately, that he is with her in his wealthy uncle's house—these are visually and cinematically projected; their reality and effectivity appear credible.

Here the camera helps sell the plot:

11. VERY CLOSE-UP—GEORGE AND ANGELA *tipping in, dancing.* (MUSIC.)

12. VERY CLOSE-UP—ANGELA AND GEORGE *tipped in.* (MUSIC.)

13. CLOSE-UP—ANGELA AND GEORGE *as they stop dancing.* (*Couples b.g.*) (MUSIC.)

ANGELA

Aren't you happy with me?

GEORGE

Happy? The trouble is I'm too happy tonight.

ANGELA

You seem so strange. So deep and far away. As though you were holding something back.

GEORGE

I am.

ANGELA

Don't.

(MUSIC.)

GEORGE

I'd better.

They resume dancing.

ANGELA

Why?

GEORGE

This is nice. I don't want to spoil it.

They pause again.

ANGELA

You'd better tell me.

GEORGE

I love you! I've loved you since the first moment I saw you . . . I guess maybe I even loved you before I saw you.

ANGELA

And you're the fellow that wondered why I invited you here tonight. I'll tell you why. I love . . . (ANGELA *looks off, startled*) are they watching us?

14. CLOSE-UP—ANGELA (MUSIC)

CAMERA PANS SWIFTLY *as she rushes toward balcony.*

EXTERIOR: BALCONY

15. MEDIUM CLOSE SHOT—ANGELA (MUSIC)

comes out on balcony. GEORGE *follows. They come f.g., past musicians and face each other.*

ANGELA

I love you, too! It scares me! . . .

MUSIC.

(*Later*) . . . *He kisses her hands.*

GEORGE

Oh, Angela, if I could only tell you how much I love you! If I could only tell you all.

ANGELA

Tell mama.

MUSIC.

Tell mama all.

26. VERY CLOSE-UP—ANGELA AND GEORGE

tipped in. They kiss and embrace.

FADE OUT

The triangle of Sequence E:

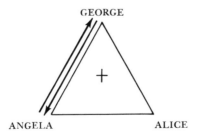

The structure moves in parallel. Sequence C, we note, is an extension of Sequence A. Now Alice becomes pregnant; George understands he must marry her. Accordingly, Sequence D becomes an extension of Sequence B:

EXTERIOR: SUBURBAN STREET. IN GEORGE'S CAR—NIGHT

1. CLOSE SHOT—ALICE AND GEORGE

tipped in, seated in car.

> ALICE
>
> You just got to marry me! Family or no family—this future of yours or no future.

> GEORGE
>
> Just lookin' at it that way, settles everything. But we haven't got any money . . . and if this thing comes out I'm through . . . I won't even have the little job I got now.

> ALICE
>
> You're just stalling.

> GEORGE
>
> I'm not! . . . I'm tryin' to think . . . I want to figure out some way, maybe. I was thinking maybe when I get my vacation, first week in September . . .

> ALICE
>
> All right, that's when we'll do it. When you get your vacation, we'll go some place way out of town and get married! You understand?

GEORGE *lights cigarette, starts car.*

> GEORGE
>
> Yeah, I understand.

SOUND OF MOTOR.

Sequence D triangle:

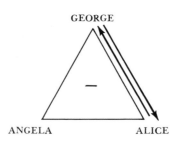

The arrows run in both directions, Alice demanding marriage, George acquiescing to Alice.

In Sequence E Angela promises to marry George:

EXTERIOR: BEACH—LOON LAKE (MUSIC)

1. CLOSE-UP—ANGELA

> ANGELA
>
> Are you worried about my family?

2. CLOSE SHOT—ANGELA

seated on ground and GEORGE, *with his head in her lap.*

> GEORGE
>
> Yes, I suppose I am.

> ANGELA
>
> Don't. I've known them intimately for several years and they're quite nice. (*she strokes his hair*) Perhaps they are a little unused to you, but that'll come in time.

> GEORGE
>
> Suppose it doesn't?

> ANGELA
>
> I'd go anywhere with you.

MUSIC.

3. CLOSE-UP—GEORGE

looking up at ANGELA, *tipped in.*

> GEORGE
>
> You really mean that? You'd marry me?

4. CLOSE-UP—ANGELA

> ANGELA
>
> Haven't I told you?

MUSIC.

> I intend to.

5. MEDIUM SHOT—ANGELA AND GEORGE

She kisses him and jumps to her feet, exits. (MUSIC.) GEORGE *sits up* (*back to* CAMERA). (LOON CALL.) *He gazes out at lake.*

DISSOLVE

Ironically, in terms of the subsequent sequence, it is the lake George gazes upon, the lake where Alice will drown.

Now the horns of the dilemma sink deeper; the parallel structure deepens. Triangle E repeats Triangle C:

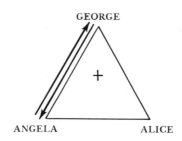

The climax of Sequence F is the accidental drowning from a boat:

55. CLOSE-UP—ALICE

MUSIC.

> ALICE
>
> George?

56. CLOSE-UP—GEORGE

with hand to face. (MUSIC.)

57. CLOSE-UP—ALICE

> ALICE
> What did you think of when you saw the star?

58. CLOSE-UP—GEORGE

staring off. (MUSIC.)

59. CLOSE-UP—ALICE

> ANGELA
> You wished that you weren't here with me, didn't you? You wished that I was some place else where you'd never have to see me again . . . didn't you?

60. CLOSE-UP—GEORGE

MUSIC.

61. CLOSE-UP—ALICE

> ALICE
> Or maybe you wished that I was dead. Is that it? Do you wish that I was dead?

MUSIC.

62. MEDIUM SHOT—GEORGE AND ALICE

favoring him. He stands up in boat.

> GEORGE
> No, I didn't! Now, just . . . leave me alone. (*He sits down again*)

> ALICE
> Oh, poor George!

63. CLOSE-UP—ALICE

MUSIC

> ALICE
> I know it isn't easy for you. I shouldn't have said that . . .
> I . . . (*she rises*)

64. MEDIUM CLOSE SHOT—GEORGE

f.g. and ALICE, *coming toward him.* (MUSIC.)

> GEORGE
> Stay where you are!

Boat rocks. ALICE *screams. He tries to catch her.*

65. MEDIUM LONG SHOT—ALICE AND GEORGE (MUSIC)

Boat capsizes and they are flung into water. (SPLASH.)

66. EXTREME LONG SHOT

(*Shooting down*) *capsized boat.* (MUSIC.) (LOON CALL.)

DISSOLVE

Triangle F:

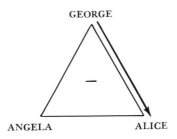

GEORGE

ANGELA   ALICE

In the above sequence George is psychologically guilty, since he brought Alice onto the lake with intent to drown her, but couldn't enact the deed. Nonetheless, he did not swim toward her to save her while knowing she was unable to swim. This guilt emerges when he is arrested at the climax of Sequence G:

41. MEDIUM LONG SHOT—GEORGE AND MARLOWE

f.g.; KELLY, DEPUTY *and* OFFICERS *b.g.*

GEORGE

No . . .

MARLOWE

I suppose you don't know anything about the murder of Alice Tripp.

GEORGE

Well, I'm not guilty.

MARLOWE

Oh, come on, son, we have the evidence. You're not going to deny it, are you?

GEORGE

Yes, I deny it.

MARLOWE

Well, in that case, there's nothing to do but take you over to the Vickers house.

OFFICER *comes forward.*

and see what your friends have to say about you.

He snaps handcuffs on GEORGE's *wrist. Another officer enters, searches him and exits.* (CAMERA MOVES IN.)

GEORGE

Please . . . don't take me back there! I'll tell you all I can, but don't take me back there!

MARLOWE *removes glasses.*

MAURER

I didn't intend to, son. I just wanted to see what you'd have to say. Take him to Warsaw, boys, and lock him up.

GEORGE *is lead b.g. to jeep.* MARLOWE *rises.* (SOUND OF MOTOR.)

42. MEDIUM CLOSE SHOT—(SIREN) (SOUND OF MOTOR) MARLOWE

and KELLY *f.g. watch* GEORGE *being driven away in jeep.* MARLOWE *turns to* KELLY.

> MARLOWE
> Now, we'll go over to the Vickers place and see what they
> have to say about him.

> DISSOLVE

It was George's love for Angela that motivated him to act against Alice, and that very love now terrifies him with the thought that she would see him in handcuffs. If he were psychologically innocent in heart and mind, he would want to see Angela on his side as a character witness. Hence the triangle is a fascinating reversal: a negative against Angela.

Triangle G:

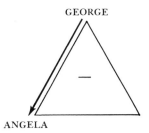

The concluding Sequence H is actually anticlimactic, since the drama has been resolved and the end foredoomed. Angela visits George in his cell where he awaits the electric chair; their love will go on after the fade-out:

INTERIOR: CELL

19. MEDIUM SHOT—ANGELA

past GEORGE (*back to* CAMERA).

> ANGELA
> Well . . . I . . . guess there's nothing more to say.

20. CLOSE-UP—GEORGE

> GEORGE
> I know something now that I didn't know before. I am
> guilty of a lot of things—most of what they say about me.

21. CLOSE-UP—ANGELA

ANGELA

All the same . . . I'll go on loving you . . . as long as I live.

22. CLOSE SHOT—GEORGE

He crosses to ANGELA.

GEORGE

Love me for the . . . time I have left.

23. CLOSE-UP —TWO

favoring ANGELA. *She kisses* GEORGE.

GEORGE

Then . . . forget me.

MUSIC.

Angela leaves, smiling. George never speaks again. The chaplin comes and recites. As they move down the corridor the prisoners unroll their clichés: "So long, kid . . . God bless you, son. . . . You're going to a better world than this."

Triangle H has the concluding arrows: Angela loves George; George loves Angela; and Alice's death is punished.

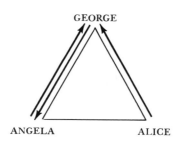

There are eight sequences in *Sunset Boulevard*. Here is an over-structured plot that makes for a superficial story, but cinematically exciting with natural settings and performances. Sequence A sets the basic triangle. Joe Gillis, a bankrupt scriptwriter, meets Betty Schaefer, a studio scriptreader, who rejects one of his corny stories but recalls his name as a man who could once write well. Fleeing from finance-officer repossessors of his mortgaged car, Joe takes refuge in the estate of Norma Desmond, who gives him her script to read. Her butler-chauffeur is her former director, Max (Erich von Stroheim). The climax of the sequence:

EXTERIOR: GARAGE (MUSIC)

12. MEDIUM LONG SHOT—MAX

enters, followed by GILLIS *(carrying scripts) and leads him to room above garage.*

> GILLIS' VOICE
> I felt kind of pleased with the way I'd handled the situation. I dropped the hook and she snapped at it. Now, my car would be safe down below while I did a patch-up job on the script.

INTERIOR: BEDROOM OVER GARAGE (MUSIC)

13. LONG SHOT

Door opens and MAX *followed by* GILLIS, *enters.*

> GILLIS' VOICE
> And there should be plenty of money.

MAX *twists light bulb on wall fixture which dimly illuminates room.* MUSIC STOPS.

> MAX
> This room hasn't been used for a long time.

GILLIS *looks room over.*

> GILLIS
> Well, it'll never make House Beautiful, but I guess it's okay for one night.

SOUND OF SCRIPTS. *He tosses scripts on bed.*

> MAX
> I made your bed this afternoon.

> GILLIS
> Thanks. How did you know I was going to stay this afternoon?

> MAX
> The bathroom is over there. I put in some towels, soap, and a toothbrush.

Sequence A triangle:

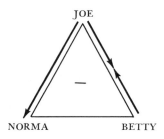

Sequence B depicts Joe's submission. With the loss of his car, which the finance company repossesses, it is Joe—not Norma—who is hooked:

EXTERIOR: TERRACE (SOUND OF MOTOR—OFF)

27. MEDIUM SHOT—GILLIS

staring off sorrowfully. NORMA *comes out of house b.g. and joins him just as car lights sweep over his face.*

> NORMA
>
> Now what is it? Where's the fire?

> GILLIS
>
> I've lost my car.

> NORMA
>
> Oh! (*she looks off, casually*) And I thought it was a matter of life and death.

> GILLIS
>
> It is to me. That's why I came to this house. That's why I took this job . . . ghost writing.

> NORMA
>
> Now you're being silly. We don't need two cars. We have a car. And not one of those cheap new things made of chromium and spit. An Isotta-Fraschini.

The B triangle is obtuse inasmuch as Betty has faded into the background, and Joe shelves his independence for the privileges of being a gigolo.

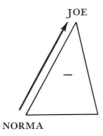

Joe rebels in Sequence C. He begins to resent her complete possessiveness:

15a. MEDIUM CLOSE SHOT—GILLIS

> GILLIS
> Has it ever occurred to you that I may have a life of my own . . . that there . . . there may be some girl that I'm crazy about?

16. CLOSE SHOT—NORMA

(*over* GILLIS' *shoulder*). (MUSIC.)

> NORMA
> Who? Some car hop or a dress extra?

> GILLIS
> What I'm trying to say is that I'm all wrong for you. You want a Valentino . . . somebody with polo ponies . . . a big shot.

> NORMA
> What you're trying to say is you don't want me to love you. Say it! Say it! SLAP.

She slaps him viciously. She exits and he faces CAMERA, *looks after her.*

Sequence C triangle:

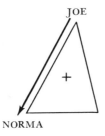

Joe visits a friend who offers to put him up for several weeks, and meeting Betty confirms his urge to leave Norma. But upon learning that Norma has attempted suicide, Joe "is dazedly clutching the phone." Joe leaves without a word to Betty. He tells Norma: "You've been good to me. You're the only person in this stinking town that *has* been good to me." Sequence D ends:

INTERIOR: NORMA'S BEDROOM

1. MEDIUM SHOT—NORMA

lying on bed f.g. tipped in, raises her other bandaged arm and puts it over her face. GILLIS *stands at foot of bed b.g., gazing at her. He crosses to chaise lounge and sits down.* (*Orchestra off shot is playing* "Auld Lang Syne.")

NORMA

I'll do it again.

SOBS. MUSIC. SOBS.

2. LONG SHOT—NORMA

lying on bed, sobbing. GILLIS *rises into scene f.g. and goes to her.* CAMERA BOOMS FORWARD. *He sits on bed and takes her bandaged arms from her face.* (MUSIC STOPS.)

GILLIS

Happy New Year, Norma.

She slowly turns to him. She reaches up and clutches his coat collar, drawing him down to her.

NORMA

Happy New Year, darling.

MUSIC.

FADE OUT

Sequence D triangle:

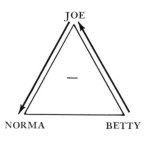

Norma visits Cecil B. De Mille at Paramount to plan her come-back picture, which is a delusion, and Joe drops in on Betty in the Story Department. They decide to collaborate nights on a script, and Joe sneaks off evenings to be with Betty. The climax of E:

> GILLIS
>
> All right, I drove to the beach. (*he slams book shut*) Norma, you don't want me to feel that I'm locked up in this house?

31. CLOSE-UP—NORMA (MUSIC)

> NORMA
>
> Of course not, Joe. It's just that I don't want to be left alone. Not while I'm under the terrible strain. My nerves are being torn to shreds. All I ask is for you to be a little patient and a little kind.

MUSIC.

32. CLOSE-UP—GILLIS

> GILLIS
>
> Norma, I haven't done anything.

33. MEDIUM CLOSE SHOT—NORMA AND GILLIS

She strokes his hair. She pulls it. (MUSIC.)

> NORMA
>
> Of course you haven't. I wouldn't let you. Goodnight, darling.

She goes b.g. to doors, exits, closing them. GILLIS *looks at his wristwatch, then at gouged-out keyholes in* NORMA's *door.* CAMERA TRUCKS UP *to them. Lights go out behind them.*

> DISSOLVE INTO:

EXTERIOR: GARAGE (MUSIC)

34. LONG SHOT—GILLIS

coming forward from house. CAMERA PANS *with him into garage. He gets into Isotta and starts motor.*

> GILLIS' VOICE
>
> Yes, I was playing hookey every evening along in there. It made me think of when I was twelve and used to sneak out on the folks to see a gangster picture.

He drives forward. CAMERA PANS *with him up driveway.*

This time, it wasn't to see a picture. It was to try and write one.

SOUND OF MOTOR

That story of mine Betty Schaefer had . . .

The E triangle:

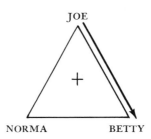

In Sequence F Betty admits she loves Joe, an admission precipitated by an offer of marriage from her friend Artie:

She exits out on porch. CAMERA PANS *with* GILLIS *as he follows, reveals her standing at top of her stairs.*

GILLIS

Betty, there's no use running out on it. Let's face it, whatever it is.

BETTY

I got a telegram from Artie.

GILLIS

From Artie? What's wrong?

BETTY

He wants me to come on to Arizona. He says it only costs two dollars to get married there. It would kind of save us a honeymoon.

GILLIS

Well, why don't you? We can finish the script by Thursday.

She puts her hand to her face, weeping.

Stop crying, will you? You're getting married. That's what you wanted.

BETTY

I don't want it *now*.

GILLIS

Why not? Don't you love Artie?

She puts her hand down. She turns to GILLIS.

BETTY

Of course I love him. I always will. I . . . I'm not in love with him anymore, that's all.

GILLIS

What happened?

BETTY

You did.

They go into each other's arms and he kisses her.

The F triangle:

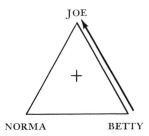

Betty comes to rescue Joe in Sequence G, but he refuses to leave Norma and his easy life:

21. CLOSE SHOT—BETTY (MUSIC STOPS)

BETTY

No! I haven't heard any of this. I never got those telephone calls and I've never been in this house! Now get your things together and let's get out of here.

22. CLOSE SHOT—GILLIS (MUSIC)

GILLIS

All my things? All my eighteen suits, all my custom-made shoes and the six dozen shirts and the cuff links and (OFF)

23. CLOSE SHOT—BETTY

the platinum key chains and the cigarette cases?

BETTY

Come on, Joe.

MUSIC.

24. MEDIUM CLOSE SHOT—GILLIS

as he crosses room. (CAMERA PANS.)

GILLIS

Come on where? Back to a one-room apartment I can't pay
for? Back to a story that may sell and very possibly will not?

BETTY

If you love me, Joe.

He moves forward, continuing his role. He pauses. BETTY *turns her head away in anguish.*

GILLIS

Look, sweetie, be practical. I've got a good deal here. A
long-term contract with no options. I like it that way.
Maybe it's not very admirable. (*he goes back to* BETTY)
Well, you and Artie can be admirable.

He tilts up her chin, but she puts her hand to her face and turns away.

BETTY

I can't look at you any more, Joe.

GILLIS

How about looking for the exit? This way, Betty.

He takes her arm and leads her out into hall.

The G triangle:

JOE

BETTY

Sunset Boulevard. Courtesy of Paramount Pictures.

H, the concluding sequence, has Joe deciding to head for a copy desk in Dayton, Ohio, and he returns Norma's gifts. He packs his bag; he tells her that De Mille wanted only to rent her car and that Max sends the daily fan mail.

> GILLIS
>
> Norma, you're a woman of fifty. Now, grow up! There's nothing tragic about being fifty . . . not unless you try to be twenty-five.
>
> NORMA
>
> I'm the greatest star of them all.

He picks up typewriter case.

> GILLIS
>
> Goodbye, Norma.

He exits. She gazes after him insanely.

> NORMA
>
> No one ever leaves a star. That's what makes one a star.

INTERIOR: STAIRCASE (MUSIC)
8. LONG SHOT—GILLIS

as he enters and descends stairs.

INTERIOR: UPPER LANDING AND STAIRCASE (MUSIC)
9. LONG SHOT—NORMA

enters (carrying gun) .

                         NORMA

Joe!

(She comes f.g. to railing. She crosses to stairs.)

Joe!

10. LONG SHOT *(Shooting down)* — (MUSIC)
GILLIS *going down steps.*

                         NORMA
                          (off)

Joe!

He reaches bottom and exits through door.

EXTERIOR: NORMA'S HOUSE (MUSIC)
11. VERY LONG SHOT—GILLIS

comes out of house (carrying typewriter) .

                         NORMA

Joe!

As he moves forward, NORMA *rushes out. He continues toward pool. She fires and bullet hits him in back. He keeps on going.* (MUSIC STOPS.) CAMERA *excludes* NORMA. *He is shot again in the back. He staggers toward pool, dropping typewriter.* (MUSIC.) *He turns to pick it up and is shot in stomach. He falls into pool.* (SPLASH) (CAMERA PANS.)

H triangle:

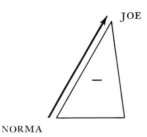

The story comes full circle with Joe's voice as the narrator, talking about his body being fished out of the pool by the police. Norma at last has her comeback scene, descending the stairs to the newsreel cameras, Max directing. "All right, Mr. De Mille," she concludes, "I'm ready for my close-up."

Structuring conflict for a gigolo suffering from the American dream of a Hollywood success—on the surface a trite story—is fascinating for being an inside-movieland struggle as seen through the eyes of Joe and Betty, the little people in the business. The structure reveals value weaknesses in the character of Joe that doomed him to death. Twice he deserted Betty, his savior. Though the plot was given a dialectic push on each occasion, the motivation was never clear in psychological terms. The question is raised, then, whether the necessity for structure may not often force character actions that are unnatural and hence unbelievable. A mechanistic structure is suspect at all times, but in the case of *Sunset Boulevard* the first two sequences are negative. We have a desperate young-man-on-the-make, the sort of character that for its cynicism makes fascinating structuring. The English like this sort of character in *Room at the Top* and *Nothing But the Best* (1964). The opportunists stay alive with their loot. Joe ends in the drink. Because he wanted a quiet life in Ohio? Because he has seen the light and has reformed? We never know. We suspect the Producers Code of yesteryear, when connivers must be punished. At any rate, it provides a cinematic conclusion for Gloria Swanson descending the stairs.

Structuring conflict for villainy involves more than plotting, more than going from positives to negatives in a chase. The nature of villainy is psychologically more intriguing than heroism. Why does an attractive personality indulge in crimes against himself? For money, sex, power? The motivation must be individualistic to be believed, typical of a sort and yet atypical to be original.

An examination of *The Informer* reveals to what extent structure may develop character, rather than plot. The plot in this classic is rather stark. A simple-minded giant, Gypo Nolan, informs to the Black and Tan on his revolutionary friend Francis McPhillip (Frankie) for the reward of £20. Frankie is ambushed and killed. Gypo's conscience is half shelved while he enjoys the money, but he is hunted by Commander Gallagher, and eventually destroyed. What is fascinating is the revelation of the black side of Gypo's character.

The novel by Liam O'Flaherty has eighteen chapters, and contains seven major climaxes. Gypo's compulsion to spend the money is an expression of his guilt for having acquired it as an informer. The novel's climaxes are noted by chapters:

1. Chapter I: Gypo informs. Negative.
2. Chapter IV: Gypo gives guilt money to Frankie's mother, Mrs. Mc-Phillip. Positive.
3. Chapter VII: Gypo accuses Mulligan (a harmless little man) of being the informer. Negative.
4. Chapter IX: Gypo gives money to an English prostitute who wishes to return to London. Positive.
5. Chapter XI: At the Court of Inquiry Gypo confesses he didn't know what he was doing when he informed. Positive.
6. Chapter XIV: Gypo escapes from his cell. Negative.
7. Chapter XVIII: Gypo is cornered and shot by boys from the Independent Republican Army, and, dying in church, he is forgiven by Frankie's mother. Positive.

It is curious to note how the positive values outnumber the negative, four to three. For all its depiction of a dark deed, *The Informer* is a highly moralistic novel. Numerically, at least, good outweighs bad. O'Flaherty has delved into what one of his Irish critics called "the melodrama of the soul."

In the motion-picture version (John Ford directed, Dudley Nichols wrote the screenplay) the structure is simplified; there are five sequences. The visuality, however, is greatly expanded. For example, Chapter I ends with the following two paragraphs:

He walked up the steps, steadily, one at a time, making a loud noise. He kicked the swing door open with his foot without taking his hands out of his pockets. In the hallway, a constable in a black, cone-shaped, night helmet stood facing him, pulling on his gloves. Gypo halted and stared at the constable.
"I have come to claim the twenty pounds reward offered by the Farmers' Union for information concerning Francis Joseph McPhillip," he said in a deep, low voice.

Chapter II consists of two paragraphs:

At thirty-five minutes past seven Francis Joseph McPhillip shot himself dead while trying to escape from No. 44 Titt Street, his father's house. The house had been surrounded by Detective-Sergeant McCartney and ten men. Hanging by his left hand from the sill of the back-bedroom window on the second floor, McPhillip put two bullets into McCartney's left shoulder. While he was trying to fire again, his left hand slipped and lost its hold. The pistol muzzle struck the edge of the sill.

The bullet shot upwards and entered McPhillip's brain through the right temple.

When they picked him out of the orange box in the back garden where he fell, he was quite dead.

In the picture version, Frankie is eating with his mother and sister Mary attending him when the Tans arrive in their lorries: Note how the conflict is structured through actions, highly photographable, and climaxed with a return to Gypo at headquarters with Shot 32:

Through the fog we see the neat house as the lorries come rolling in and stop with a screech and the Tans begin piling out and jumping off swiftly. A squad of them run up the alley to cover the rear while the other squad goes towards the front door.

CUT TO

27. INTERIOR: KITCHEN

FRANKIE *is drinking coffee when the noise grows louder and he sets down* (SOUND) *the cup hard. Then there is a heavy knocking at the front door, the sound carrying through the hallway to the kitchen at rear.* FRANKIE *jumps up like a shot and* MARY *puts her hand over her mouth to suppress a scream, while* MRS. MCPHILLIP *turns from the stove in terror.*

MRS. MCPHILLIP
(*hoarsely*)

My boy!

FRANKIE

Ssssh.

And he motions them to be still. Now he is tense and quiet—a cool head in a pinch. He had thrown off his raincoat on the floor near the door before he sat down, and now he pulls out his automatic and steps swiftly to the hall door. The knocking is loud and ominous now and we hear voices clamoring. FRANKIE *turns sharply to his mother and sister, his voice low and commanding.*

Stay where ye are! Ye'll be safest!

And he shuts the door behind him as he steps into the dark hall. MRS. MCPHILLIP *makes as if to scream out but* MARY *seizes her arm and quiets her.*

CUT TO

28. INTERIOR—HALLWAY

CAMERA SHOOTING *from rear end of hall towards the front door where a gas jet burns. A stairway runs up to the second floor from that front end of the hall.* FRANKIE *takes a swift look towards* CAMERA. *No escape there. Then he tiptoes swiftly towards the front door, where the Tans* (SOUND) *are pounding now and shouting for the door to be opened.* FRANKIE *stands just inside that resounding door for a moment, gun in hand. Then the door begins to split and, thinking fast, he turns and starts up the stairway. Now he is facing towards* CAMERA *again, though rising above it, and as he vanishes upstairs, the door gives way with a crash and Tans pile into the hallway with drawn guns. As they do so the kitchen door at left foreground flies open and* MARY *comes running out recklessly followed by her mother, and they run and confront the Tans at the foot of the stairway.*

CUT TO

29. INTERIOR—HALLWAY

MEDIUM SHOT GROUP *as* MARY *and her mother face the Tans.*

TAN SERGEANT

Where's McPhillip?

MARY
(*fiercely*)

He's not here! Get out!

Several Tans simply block the way of the two women while the others start up the stairway with their guns. MRS. MCPHILLIP *cries out in terrible fear and* MARY *screams at the top of her voice.*

FRANKIE WATCH OUT! THEY'RE COMING UP!

But the Tans have leaped up the stairs and now (SOUND) *we hear a quick fusillade of shots and* MARY *screams with pain as if the bullets were tearing through her own heart.*

FRANKIE! FRANKIE!

MRS. MCPHILLIP *drops to her knees to pray, clutching her rosary, and the shots continue as we*

CUT TO

30. EXTERIOR—REAR UPSTAIRS WINDOW

CAMERA ON PARALLEL SHOOTING *at window in* MEDIUM SHOT. *Through the open window we see into the upstairs hallway. We see* FRANKIE *backing towards window and* CAMERA *and several Tans go down* as he shoots. Then FRANKIE *reaches the window, throws a leg over the sill, and swings out to drop to the ground. He is hanging now to the sill with his left hand, his automatic in his right. A Tan comes running down hall towards him, and leans out window to shoot him, but* FRANKIE *shoots first and the Tan crumples out of sight on the floor inside the window.*

CUT TO

31. INTERIOR—HALLWAY.

CAMERA SHOOTING DOWNWARD THROUGH WINDOW *where* FRANKIE *is hanging. Right in front of* CAMERA *is* FRANKIE'S *clinging left hand. Downward beyond him we see what* FRANKIE *does not—the dim figures of half a dozen Tans moving in, their guns upraised. We see the flashing points as their guns all seem to fire at once, and* FRANKIE'S *hand twitches and slips from the sill.*

LAP DISSOLVES OUT

LAP DISSOLVES IN

32. INTERIOR—INNER OFFICE AT R.I.C. HQ.

MEDIUM SHOT—GYPO *as before, sitting with hunched muscles, sweat on his face,* (SOUND) *staring at the loud ticking clock. The three officers are still in the same pose, their heads together.* (SOUND.) *The clock is ticking very rapidly now, and louder. . . . A telephone bell rings sharply. The seated officer takes up the receiver and speaks into the phone.*

OFFICER

Headquarters! . . . Yes?
The officer hangs up the receiver and the clock suddenly stops ticking and all is deathly still as the officer turns curtly on GYPO.

You may go now. I will let you out the back way.

GYPO, *his face covered with sweat, rises mechanically, as with an immense effort, and instinctively he lifts his hands and looks down at his upturned palms, like a man in a trance, not conscious of what he is looking for.*

MOVE IN CAMERA ON CLOSE-UP *of his big hands.*

LAP DISSOLVE

32a. INTERIOR—INNER OFFICE AT R.I.C. HQ.

GYPO—*as a riding crop pushes the money across a table to him.*

VOICE
(icily)
Twenty pounds! You might count it.

GYPO *takes it up without counting, crushes the notes into a roll
and mechanically stuffs them into his right pants pocket.*

LAP DISSOLVE

The shooting of Frankie—witnessed by us on the stairs (Shot 28) —
sharpens the structure by emphasizing the horrible consequences of
Gypo's deed, an important counterpoint since Gypo's character can
be devilishly attractive at times. Here is Sequence A triangle:

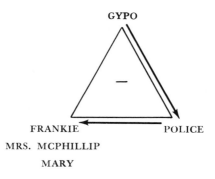

Remorse is the idea behind Sequence B. Gypo attends the wake for
Frankie in the McPhillip house. Words catch in his throat; he
manages to shout with all his might, "I'm sorry for yer trouble, Mrs.
McPhillip!" The assembly is shocked. Gypo jumps to his feet, and
four silver crowns jingle upon the hard floor. In guilt, he shouts, "I
swear before Almighty God that I warned him to keep away from
this house!"

For the purposes of constructing triangle B we must recall the role
of Katie, the girl-friend-prostitute, first introduced in Sequence A.
She is hungry and can't pay her rent. Together they had stood before
the window of a travel bureau with a model ship and a poster advertising steerage rates to America for £ 20. "Twenty pounds—and the
world is ours!" Katie had said, and Gypo answered, "What are ye
sayin' that fer? What are ye drivin' at?" Now, in Sequence B, Katie
meets Gypo in a bar, tells him she loves him, and he cries, "I've got
it! I did it for *you!*" He explains he robbed a sailor off an American

ship. Katie wants him to come home with her, but he must be off to the McPhillips—"They'll be wonderin' why I'm not there already!" Katie has replaced the Police in Sequence A triangle as the embodiment of his greed:

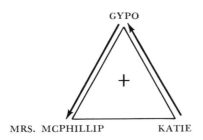

In the subsequent sequence Gypo is conducted to Commandant Dan Gallagher, and Gypo expects confidently to be taken back into the organization. He accuses little tailor Mulligan of being the informer on Frankie. Katie is not present in Sequence C. It is Mulligan who is the object, indirectly, of his greed, and Gallagher the custodian of his conscience.

Triangle C:

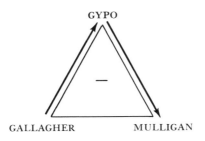

In Sequence D Gypo is called King Gypo by Terry the Snug, a leech, and together they go to Aunt Betty's where the girls wear hats so the American censor can't identify it as a whorehouse. Katie is not in this sequence. Mulligan is tried and vindicated. Gypo is brought to the ammunition dump for the Court of Inquiry. Dan Gallagher recounts where he spent £20, and asks him to tell where he got the money:

80.

> GYPO
> (*in agony*)
> I can't remember. I'm drunk, I tell ye! I can't remember nothin'!

DAN *cries out at him as if the tension were almost unbearable even to himself.*

> DAN
> Confess, man—and ease your soul! Who is the informer?

GYPO *rises with an awful effort and sways there in agony and reaches out trembling hands towards* DAN *as he cries out.*

> GYPO
> I didn't know what I was doin'! I didn't know what I was doin'! Can't ye see what I mean?

Eyes of hatred look at him from all sides as he stretches out his hands on either side, panting as his voice shudders.

> Is there no man here to tell him why I did it? Me head is sore! I can't tell him!

MARY *is sobbing, her body trembling. The four or five young men behind* GYPO *have drawn their guns, pointing them at* GYPO'S *back.* DAN *raps the table sharply with the muzzle of his gun and they all stop rigidly as in a tableau.* DAN *is thinking of the presence of* MARY.

> DAN
> No! . . . Lock him up!

They seize GYPO *and he resists for a moment. But they fling themselves upon him and in a moment he gives up and is like a child in their hands. They move across the room, unbolt the heavy oaken door, thrust him inside roughly and lock the door again, standing guard outside it grimly.*

> CUT TO

This self-sentencing on the part of Gypo is the high point in his conscience struggle. His positive expression of goodwill toward the English prostitute who wishes money to return to London does not constitute a major climax. We are no longer narratively involved in Gypo's escapades; we are seeing his problem on a grander scale, more heightened, more dynamic.

The triangle D:

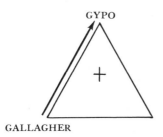

In the final sequence Gypo escapes, goes to Katie's room, and asks for the £20 he gave her—"I sold out me own pal for ye!" Katie puts him to sleep and seeks out Gallagher, begs that he spare Gypo, and discloses that Gypo is asleep in her room. The Boys go off to shoot him. Katie kneels to pray with Mary. Gypo manages to stagger into church with considerable lead in him.

107. INTERIOR: CHURCH—DAY

TRUCK ON GYPO *as he stands there swaying in the dim mysterious interior of the simple little church. He tries to think where he is. Then he sees a kneeling figure in a black dress, alone in the church and on the aisle about halfway up, on the side. He staggers on with that stiff slow walk.*

TRUCK HIM *to the kneeling figure. It is* MRS. MCPHILLIP *praying for her dead son.* GYPO *swallows the blood in his mouth and stands there weaving before her, and his voice is a thick whisper.*

> GYPO
> Twas I informed on your son, Mrs. McPhillip. . . . Forgive me. . . .

> MRS. MCPHILLIP
> *(tears are running down her worn, kindly face)*
>
> I forgive you, Gypo. You didn't know what you were doing.

GYPO *shivers from head to foot. A great joy fills his heart. Mercy and pity and peace are upon him at last. He turns towards the front of the church and cries out in a loud voice of joy.*

> GYPO
> Frankie! Frankie! Your mother forgives me!

The Informer. Courtesy of RKO.

And then he moves on stiffly and CAMERA TRUCKS ON HIM *until he comes to the foot of a great carved Christ, and with a gurgling sound he falls at the foot of it, dead.*

FADE OUT

Triangle E:

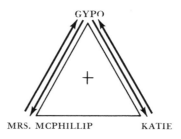

The dying Gypo begs forgiveness from Mrs. McPhillip, which is his final action on behalf of his conscience. So he dies a better man than when he informed. In forgiving him, Mrs. McPhillip demonstrates the perfection of Christian faith. Even Katie redeems herself by begging for the life of the man she loves. Frankie had promised forgiveness in an hallucination of Gypo's if his mother would forgive Gypo. The sentimentality of the ending flaws the reality of John Ford's otherwise masterpiece. As the arrows indicate, everybody loves everybody, in spite of all the shooting.

To conclude this examination of sequence structure of conflict, the inverted love triangle offers a different insight. It has been noted in *Wuthering Heights* that the joint protagonists, Heathcliff and Cathy, enacting a hateful, irrevocable love, were paired against a hostile world. As children growing up together, Cathy sided with the orphan Heathcliff and against her own brother, Hindley. Upon the father's death the doctor tells the three young people that they "may come up now and pray beside him"—the deceased father Earnshaw. Here is the climax of Sequence A:

C8. CLOSE-UP—DOOR OF MR. EARNSHAW'S DEATH ROOM

It is opened by DR. KENNETH. ELLEN *enters, holding* CATHY. JOSEPH *enters. The* DOCTOR *follows.* HINDLEY *stands barring* HEATHCLIFF'S *way.*

HINDLEY

(alone outside the door with HEATHCLIFF)

You are not wanted here.

HEATHCLIFF
(hotly)

He loved me more than he did you!

HINDLEY
(pushing him)

My father is past your wheedling. . . . Go and help the stable boys harness the horse for the parson. . . .

As HEATHCLIFF *hesitates.*

Do as you're told. I'm master here, now.

He closes the door on HEATHCLIFF. HEATHCLIFF *stands staring at the closed door. He digs his fists into his eyes to keep from weeping. He turns slowly and walks away.*

FADE OUT

Here, then, is triangle A:

HEATHCLIFF   CATHY

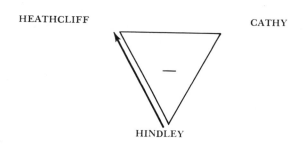

HINDLEY

In Sequence B, Heathcliff is reduced to rags and the work of a stableboy. He secretly meets with Cathy on the moors at their "castle" rock. Cathy begs him to run away and "come back to me rich and take me away! Why aren't you my prince like we said long ago . . . Why can't you rescue me?" Returning through the moors they peek in the window of the Linton Georgian mansion where a fancy dancing party is under way. The dogs attack them; Cathy is bitten. She pleads to Heathcliff to run, but he follows her when she is carried indoors. Sequence B climax:

16. THREE SERVANTS *spring on* HEATHCLIFF *and start to drag him away. For a moment he does not resist, but then one of the servants cuffs him savagely on the side of the head. With a cry he wrenches himself free. His ragged, dirty figure for a moment dominates the elegantly dressed merry-makers who only stand staring at him.*

HEATHCLIFF
(*addressing them all—his voice vibrant with rage*)

I'm going—I'm going from here and this cursed country both!

17. CLOSE SHOT—CATHY

As she reacts to this last—a sudden gleam of excitement in her eyes.

18. BACK TO FORMER SCENE

HEATHCLIFF
(*his voice is low, intense*)

But I'll be back in this house one day, Judge Linton, and pay you out! I'll bring this house down in ruins around your heads! That's my curse on you! (*Suddenly he spits on the floor*) On *all* of you!

Then he turns and goes.
There is a moment of horrified silence, followed by a babble of
voices:

AD LIB

The scoundrel! After him! Get the dogs! Impertinent
creature! Throw him out!

As this goes on the CAMERA MOVES UP TO CATHY *who has half raised*
herself and is looking after him, a wondering expression on her face.

CATHY
(excitedly)

Good-bye, Heathcliff! Good-bye—I'll be waiting. . . .

FADE OUT

Judge Linton and his son Edgar have replaced Hindley as per-
sonifiers of the hostile world. Triangle B:

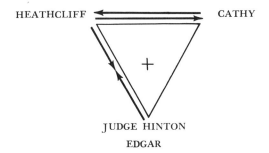

Although Heathcliff suffers, the sequence may be rated positive
because he takes an action on behalf of his love for Cathy. He will
pay them all back one day when he becomes rich and powerful.

Sequence C demonstrates the tortured ties between the lovers.
Though Edgar is attentive during Cathy's convalescence, she will not
permit him to speak ill of Heathcliff; she loves Heathcliff and hates
the look of Edgar's "milk-white face." Once again she and Heathcliff
meet at their "castle" on the moors. We see visual evidence of their
strangely magnetic affinity, which constitutes an essential passage in
the structure. In order to feel keenly the pathos of their tortured love
we must see, in dialectic contrast, the positive side of their love in
action (Heathcliff has jumped his ship at Liverpool, unable to leave
Cathy) :

CATHY

You're strong, Heathcliff, you're so strong. Make the world stop right here—make everything stop—and stand still—and never move again—the moors never change—and you and me never change.

HEATHCLIFF

The moors and I will never change—don't you, Cathy. . . .

She touches him gently with her hand, in answer, then looks into his eyes. All the passion she feels toward him, but does not comprehend, surges up within her.

CATHY
(filling her lungs)

Smell the heather, Heathcliff, fill my arms with heather—all they can hold.

HEATHCLIFF *hastily snatches a large bunch, thrusts the heather into her arms. She closes her eyes.*

HEATHCLIFF

Cathy, you're not thinking of that other world now?

CATHY
(breathlessly)

Don't talk, Heathcliff—all this might disappear.

He piles more heather into her arms.

FADE OUT

Triangle C continues the positive:

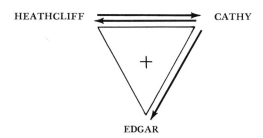

Heathcliff becomes possessive, demanding, and jealous of Edgar's calls. The frustrated love intensifies and turns Cathy resentful. "And I'm to take orders from you—a dirty stable boy. . . . You had your chance to be something else. Now let me alone!"

If he has become "a pair of dirty hands" on her pretty dress then she can have them where they belong—he slaps her face. It is the turning point—a visual demonstration of love turned to hate for a flashing moment. He flees to his place over the stable, where he drives his hands in the same motion as when he struck Cathy—into the windowpane and slashes his flesh.

Cathy confides to Ellen, the housekeeper, that she will marry Edgar, for Heathcliff "gets worse every day. It would degrade me to marry him—I wish he hadn't come back!" Heathcliff, listening to Cathy, runs away on horseback. Cathy pathetically pursues him in the storm. Edgar finds her half dead on the moors:

CAMERA DOLLIES AHEAD OF THE GROUP *as* EDGAR *carries* CATHY *to a large couch before the blazing fire in the study.*

> DR. KENNETH
>
> . . . And a lot of dry towels . . . hurry.

> ISABELLA
>
> Where was she?

> EDGAR
>
> Crumpled in front of the big rock on the moor, with life nearly out of her.

DR. KENNETH *holds a glass of brandy to* CATHY's *lips, forces a few drops between them, then turns away to put the glass down.* CAMERA MOVES TO A CLOSE-UP OF CATHY. *Her lips form the word:* "HEATHCLIFF."

> FADE OUT

Triangle D:

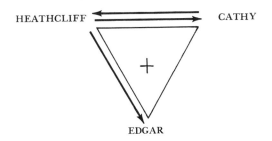

By pursuing Heathcliff to the brink of death, Cathy proves her love for him is greater than her affection for Edgar. Heathcliff's flight is similar in intent, if not in intensity, to Sequence B. In rating Sequence D positive we have three positives in a row, a powerful momentum against which the subsequence sequences move and clash.

Again Cathy convalesces at the Linton House, and Edgar wins Cathy's consent to marry. His sister Isabella is amused by the idea. The climax of Sequence E is on the church steps following the wedding:

62. (cont.) *She starts out, then stops. Her eyes seem to take in all the loutish yokels, one by one, with something frightened in her look.* EDGAR *takes her arm.*

EDGAR

Come, dear . . . Whatever are you staring at?

CATHY *comes to with a little shudder and clings to* EDGAR. CAMERA PRECEDING *them,* BEGINS TO MOVE UP ON CATHY.

CATHY

A cold wind went across my heart just then. A feeling of doom . . . (*smiling at him*) You touched me and it was gone.

They look at each other. He is anxious, but smiles.

EDGAR
(*looking around at the cold stones*)
It's just the dampness, darling—these old stones—

CATHY
(*with sudden ecstasy—clinging to him*)
Oh, Edgar, I love you! I do!

FADE OUT

As may be seen, Heathcliff is present *in absentia* via "the dampness" and Cathy's frightened look. It is as though she feels unfaithful to Heathcliff. It is Cathy's sequence, and she is at the apex:

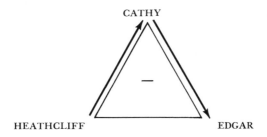

Triangle E is negative: Cathy chooses Edgar over Heathcliff.

Heathcliff returns in Sequence F, buys Wuthering Heights by paying Hindley's bad debts with the fortune he acquired in America. He impresses Isabella, who comes wooing him against her brother's wishes. Cathy warns Isabella that Heathcliff is using her in order to get close again to Cathy, but Isabella believes Cathy is jealous. "Yes, you love him! And you're mad with pain and jealousy at the thought of my marrying him!" Whereupon Cathy calls at Wuthering Heights:

100. ANOTHER ANGLE

Which includes the approaching figure of HEATHCLIFF.

> HEATHCLIFF
>
> Well, what brings you to Wuthering Heights, Cathy? Does Edgar know? I doubt he'd approve.

> CATHY
>
> Heathcliff, is it true?

> HEATHCLIFF
>
> Is what true?

> CATHY
>
> That you asked Isabella to marry you? (*She waits for his reply. As none comes:*) It is true, then. (*desperately*) Oh Heathcliff, you must not do this villainous thing. She hasn't harmed you.

> HEATHCLIFF
> (*stonily*)
>
> *You* have.

> CATHY
>
> Then punish me.

HEATHCLIFF
(*cruelly*)
I am going to. When I hold her in my arms . . . when I
kiss her . . . when I promise her life and happiness.

CATHY
(*horrified*)
You'll marry her—for that . . .

HEATHCLIFF
Yes . . . to teach you the ways of pain and to let you taste
the hell I am in!

Triangle F:

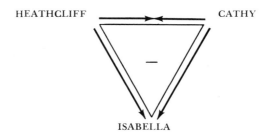

In the final sequence Cathy has lost her will to live and is dying of
lung inflammation. She sends Edgar to gather heather from the
"castle" on the moors. Heathcliff calls, and they have a final love-hate
session. The housekeeper Ellen comes to warn them that Edgar is
returning, but Heathcliff refuses to leave.

CATHY
(*wailing*)
It's true. It's true! I'm yours, Heathcliff . . . I've never been
anyone else's . . .

ELLEN
(*frantically*)
She doesn't know what she's saying . . . You can still get
out. Go, before we're done for!

CATHY
(*raising herself weakly*)
Heathcliff—take me to the window . . . Let me look at the

moors with you once more . . . Oh, my darling . . . once
more . . .

HEATHCLIFF

(carrying her from the bed)

Yes . . . yes!

CATHY

(faintly at the window)

How lovely the day looks . . . the sweet blue sky . . .
Heathcliff, can you see the Crag? Over there, where our
castle is—I'll wait for you till you come.

She droops and stiffens in his arms. HEATHCLIFF *stands holding her,
her night dress trailing and stirring faintly in the breeze. . . .*

As he stands, EDGAR LINTON, *followed by* DR. KENNETH *enters in b.g.*
EDGAR *stands staring at* HEATHCLIFF *holding the silent* CATHY *near
the window.*

The final triangle, G:

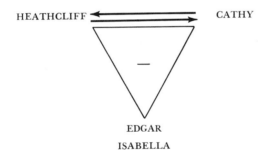

The last three triangles are negative; the tragedy is inevitable and
finished. There are a prologue and epilogue, a frame in which the
seven sequences fit. The structure is most exceptional. After the
initial sequence, placing the young lovers at a disadvantage, there
follow three positives demonstrating the unique power of their
neurotic love attachment. In traditional structuring the conflict rages
back and forth, a positive followed by a negative, and occasionally
there are two of a kind, back to back. Similar to evenly matched
prizefighters wherein the outcome is in doubt, the scoring fluctuates
from one opponent to the other. Suspense mounts. When it is a
lopsided fight there is no doubt as to the winner. Though there are

three negatives in a row at the end of *Wuthering Heights,* no one expects a twist, a happy ending, a positive rescue at the last minute. Dramatic impact is not only maintained but intensified.

In the final analysis, character motivation permits fresh and original structuring of conflict. The players—not the play's—the thing to catch whatever is to be caught.

CHAPTER SEVEN 🪶

The Obligatory Scene

1. THE NATURE OF THE CINEMATIC OBLIGATORY SCENE

The moment when expectation is fulfilled is *la scène à faire*—what William Archer, the English playwright and dramatic critic, called the "obligatory scene." "It is precisely this expectation," wrote the critic Francisque Sarcey, "mingled with uncertainty which is one of the charms of the theatre." There is a French expression: *Vous allez avoir de quoi faire*—You have your work cut out. *Scène à faire* is the scene to be made, almost inevitably toward the conclusion of the drama.

How does this nineteenth-century dramatic observation apply to twentieth-century cinema? Many contemporary films deliberately ignore or unwittingly discard the obligatory scene, with varied results. The question, regardless of fashion or style, centuries or modes, deals with tensions and anticipations in storytelling. Film audiences universally expect an acceleration of some sort, an accumulation of rising actions and reactions. The absence of an anticipated fulfillment can be a frustration comparable to the interruption by commercials during televised movies. To be frustrated in the viewing of any art is irritating, to say the least, and can be nihilistic. What appears to be neglected in much of contemporary cinema is an appreciation of the emotional need for anticipation.

More than audience psychology obliges the writer-director to go beyond excitement. He is obliged as a craftsman to fulfill the promises he planted in his opening scenes. If he is an artist, he is obliged to culminate the emotional experience he has been sharing with some sort of a significant catharsis—not necessarily through the "pity and fear" that Aristotle proposed.

"There are works of art that merely excite," wrote John Dewey in his *Art as Experience*, "in which activity is aroused without the composure of satisfaction, without fulfillment within the terms of the medium. Energy is left without organization. Dramas are then melodramatic; paintings of nudes are pornographic; the fiction that is read leaves us discontented with the world. . . ." The organization of energy—which for our purposes we might call "plot"—can be achieved, Dewey suggests, through symmetry and rhythm. "The connection of intensity and extensity and of both with tension is not a verbal matter," Dewey continues. "There is no rhythm save where there is alternation of compressions and releases."

The obligatory scene is precisely a rhythm factor. Contemporary cinema has so much more compression of action and plastic imagery of movement than traditional drama that there exist both minor and major obligatory scenes. A screenplay may have half a dozen minor concentrations of intensity that are the goals of those sequences toward which the idea is moving. The major obligatory scene would be the goal of the entire action, the greatest compression and the most intense anticipation. What has been ordinarily called the "obligatory scene" is the obvious confrontation between warring characters, the long-awaited clash between hero and villain, "the big scene." David confronts Goliath and throws his stone; Hamlet at last kills the King; Golden Boy turns to brass.

After an obligatory scene the mind of the viewer should behave differently. No character leaves a cinematic obligatory scene the same as when he entered, or else it isn't obligatory. It is expository or narrative or flatly dramatic.

As indicated, the cinematic obligatory scene differs from the dramatic *scène à faire*. Cinematic obligatory scene is the physical, photographable action that has maximum conflict intensifying and sometimes resolving that conflict.

2. DELIBERATE OBLIGATORY SCENES

Moments of maximum fulfillment are usually registered in the viscera during viewing. For an intellectual analysis we might facilitate identification by classifying obligatory scenes into the deliberate and the indirect types.

Orson Welles' masterpiece, *Citizen Kane,* is an excellent example of a psychological chase, a deliberate pursuit, a search for the secret of a complex man. Here is the plot's frame established in the opening scene when Charles Foster Kane dies:

DISSOLVE

THE WINDOW— (MINIATURE)

11. CAMERA MOVES IN *until the frame of the window fills the frame of the screen. Suddenly the light within goes out. This* STOPS *the action of the* CAMERA *and cuts the music which has been accompanying the sequence. In the glass panes of the window we see reflected the ripe, dreary landscape of* MR. KANE'*s estate behind and the dawn sky.*

DISSOLVE

INTERIOR: KANE'S BEDROOM—FAINT DAWN—1940

12. *A* VERY LONG SHOT *of* KANE'*s enormous bed, silhouetted against the enormous window.*

DISSOLVE

INTERIOR: KANE'S BEDROOM—FAINT DAWN—1940

13. *A* SNOW SCENE. *An incredible one. Big impossible flakes of snow, a too picturesque farmhouse and a snow man. The jingling of sleigh bells in the musical score now makes an ironic reference to Indian Temple bells—the music freezes—*

KANE'S OLD OLD VOICE

Rosebud!

THE CAMERA PULLS BACK, *showing the whole scene to be contained in one of those glass balls which are sold in novelty stores all over the world. A hand—*KANE'*s hand, which has been holding the ball, relaxes. The ball falls out of his hand and bounds down two carpeted steps leading to the bed, the* CAMERA FOLLOWING. *The ball falls off the last step onto the marble floor where it breaks, the fragments glittering in the first rays of the morning sun. This ray cuts an angular pattern across the floor, suddenly crossed with a thousand bars of light as the blinds are pulled across the window.*

14. THE FOOT OF KANE'S BED. *The* CAMERA *very* CLOSE. *Outlined against the shuttered window, we can see a form—the form of a nurse, as she pulls the sheet up over his head.* THE CAMERA FOLLOWS THIS ACTION *up the length of the bed and arrives at the face after the sheet has covered it.*

FADE OUT

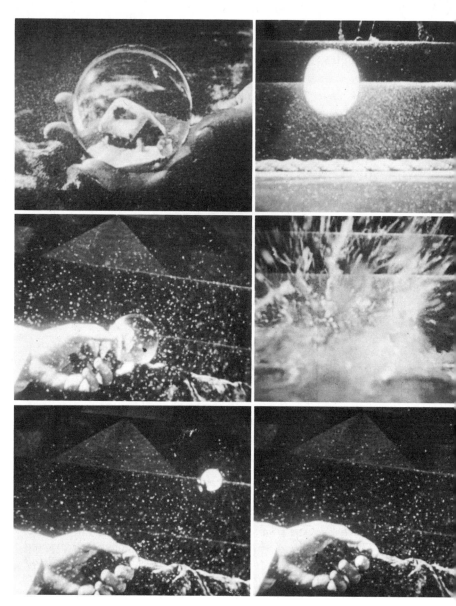

Citizen Kane. Courtesy of RKO.

The curiosity planted over "Rosebud" is propelled forward by screen playwrights Herman Mankiewicz and Orson Welles during the parody on "The March of Time" scene in the projection room. Editor Rawlston discusses "Rosebud" and assigns Reporter Thompson to the chase. Written as one continuous shot, 16, the scene was photographed and edited into over a dozen shots:

RAWLSTON
(*walks toward* THOMPSON)
I tell you, Thompson—a man's dying words—

SECOND MAN
What are they?

THOMPSON
(*to* SECOND MAN)
You don't read the papers.

Laughter.

RAWLSTON
When Mr. Charles Foster Kane died he said just one word—

THOMPSON
Rosebud!

FIRST MAN
Is that what he said? Just Rosebud?

SECOND MAN
Umhum—Rosebud—

Almost together.

FOURTH MAN
Tough guy, huh? (*derisively*) Dies calling for Rosebud!

Laughter.

RAWLSTON
(*riding over them*)
Yes, Rosebud!—Just that one word!—But who was she—

SECOND MAN
Or what was it?

Tittering.

RAWLSTON
Here's a man who might have been President. He's been loved and hated and talked about as much as any man in

our time—but when he comes to die, he's got something on his mind called "Rosebud." What does that mean?

THIRD MAN

A race horse he bet on once, probably—

FOURTH MAN

Yeah—that didn't come in—

RAWLSTON

All right— (*strides toward* THIRD *and* FOURTH MEN) *But what was the race?*

There is a short silence.

Thompson!

THOMPSON

Yes, Mr. Rawlston.

RAWLSTON

Hold the picture up a week—two weeks if you have to—

THOMPSON
(*feebly*)

Don't you think, right after his death, if we release it now— it might be better than—

RAWLSTON
(*decisively; cutting in on above speech*)

Find out about Rosebud!—Go after everybody that knew him—that manager of his— (*snaps fingers*) —Bernstein. —His second wife—she's still living—

THOMPSON

Susan Alexander Kane—

SECOND MAN

She's running a night club in Atlantic City—

RAWLSTON
(*crosses to* THOMPSON)

See 'em all. —All the people who worked for him—who loved him—who hated his guts— (*Pause.*) I don't mean go through the City Directory, of course.

The THIRD MAN *gives a hearty "yes-man" laugh. Others titter.*

THOMPSON
(*rising*)

I'll get to it right away, Mr. Rawlston.

RAWLSTON
(*pats his arm*)
Good! Rosebud dead or alive! It'll probably turn out to be
a very simple thing.

FADE OUT

(NOTE: *Now begins the story proper—the search by Thompson for the facts about Kane—his researches—his interviews with the people who knew Kane.*)

With expectation aroused, the psychological chase begins. What is the clue in "Rosebud" that will reveal the inner truth of a fabulously complex man? The chase is conducted through a juggling of time and place, avoiding the usual chronology of a character's life. This radical form, imitated in part twenty-two years later by Fellini in *8½*, adds to the jigsaw nature of the search. Welles, newly arrived from New York stages, is overly committed to dialogue, as we can see, but his natural genius for the theatrical, coupled with Gregg Toland's inventive perspective in his camera work, produces pure cinema and an exceptionally rare balance between auditory and visual impact. "I'll admit that I defied a good many conventions in filming *Citizen Kane*," Toland confesses.

Aside from Reporter Thompson's verbal questioning, which fails, there is only one visual clue to "Rosebud." There is a sled with which the six-year-old boy Kane plays at the time his mother and father sign him over to a stranger who, as young Kane's guardian, will take him east and raise him. "You won't be lonely, Charles," is Mother Kane's pathethic promise. All we see of the sled is in Shot 28:

EXTERIOR: MRS. KANE'S BOARDINGHOUSE—DAY—1870
28. KANE, *in the snow-covered field. He holds the sled in his hand. The Kane house, in the b.g., is a dilapidated, shabby, two-story frame building, with a wooden outhouse.* KANE *looks up as he sees the procession,* MRS. KANE *at its head, coming toward him.*

Thatcher is the guardian appointed by the bank that in turn will administer the Colorado Lode, worth millions. The sled appears once again:

28 (*Continued*)

THATCHER

We're going to have a lot of good times together, Charles
. . . Really we are.

KANE *stares at him.*

Come on, Charles. Let's shake hands.

KANE *continues to look at him.*

Now, now! I'm not as frightening as all that! Let's shake,
what do you say?

*He reaches out for Charles' hand. Without a word, Charles hits him
in the stomach with the sled.* THATCHER *stumbles back a few feet,
gasping.*

(*With a sickly grin.*) You almost hurt me, Charles. Sleds
aren't to hit people with. Sleds are to—sleigh on. When we
get to New York, Charles, we'll get you a sled that will—

He's near enough to try to put a hand on KANE's *shoulder. As he
does,* KANE *kicks him in the ankle.*

MRS. KANE

Charles!

He throws himself on her, his arms around her. Slowly MRS. KANE
puts her arms around him.

KANE
(*frightened*)

Mom! Mom!

There is a shot in the film, relating to sleds, that is not in the
script. On Christmas Day Thatcher gives young Charles a fancy sled
with curled runners, which Charles rejects bitterly. There is, similarly, a shot in the script that is not in the film. It occurs when Susan
Alexander, his second wife, leaves him, and Kane, now an aged,
lonely anachronism runs amok in Susan's childlike bedroom and
wrecks everything in that incongruous playroom. He retains "the
little glass ball with the snowstorm in it." The action, as written,
continues (Mrs. Tinsdall is the housekeeper, Raymond the butler) :

INTERIOR: CORRIDOR OUTSIDE SUSAN'S BEDROOM—XANADU—1932

114. KANE *comes out of the door.* MRS. TINSDALL *has been joined now
by a fairly sizable turnout of servants. They move back away from*
KANE, *staring at him.* RAYMOND *is in the doorway behind* KANE. KANE
still looks at the glass ball.

KANE
(without turning)
Close the door, Raymond.

RAYMOND
Yes, sir. *(Closes it)*

KANE
Lock it—and keep it locked.

RAYMOND *locks the door and comes to his side. There is a long pause
—servants staring in silence.* KANE *gives the glass ball a gentle shake
and starts another snowstorm.*

KANE
(Almost in a trance.)
Rosebud.

RAYMOND
What's that, sir?

In the film Kane places the glass ball in his pocket, and does not
speak. As we shall see in a moment, it would have been fallacious to
link "Rosebud" to the glass ball, even though snow was involved.
Needless to say, the glass ball is another clue. Throughout the film
our expectation is mounting; we demand to know "Rosebud."

The major obligatory scene coincides with the climax of the
picture. Thompson and a team of researchers and still photographers
from what might be *Life* magazine are finishing up at Xanadu,
Florida, the fabulous castle of Kane—intended as a dark version of
San Simeon, California, the princely estate of Hearst. A Girl Reporter asks:

GIRL
If you could have found out what that Rosebud meant,
I bet that would've explained everything.

THOMPSON
No, I don't. Not much anyway. Charles Foster Kane was a
man who got everything he wanted, and then lost it. Maybe
Rosebud was something he couldn't get or something he
lost, but it wouldn't have explained anything. I don't think
any word explains a man's life. No—I guess Rosebud is just
a piece in a jigsaw puzzle—a missing piece. *(he drops the
jigsaw pieces back into the box, looking at his watch)* We'd
better get along. We'll miss the train.

He picks up his overcoat—it has been resting on a little sled—the little sled young CHARLES FOSTER KANE *hit* THATCHER *with at the opening of the picture. Camera doesn't close in on this. It just registers the sled as the newspaper people, picking up their clothes and equipment, move out of the great hall.*

DISSOLVE OUT

DISSOLVE IN

INTERIOR: CELLAR—XANADU—NIGHT—1940

117. *A large furnace, with an open door, dominates the scene. Two laborers, with shovels, are shovelling things into the furnace.* RAYMOND *is about ten feet away.*

RAYMOND

Throw that junk in, too.

CAMERA TRAVELS *to the pile that he has indicated. It is mostly bits of broken packing cases, excelsior, etc. The sled is on top of the pile. As* CAMERA COMES CLOSE, *it shows the faded rosebud and, though the letters are faded, unmistakably the word "Rosebud" across it. The laborer drops his shovel, takes the sled in his hand and throws it into the furnace. The flames start to devour it.*

EXTERIOR: XANADU—NIGHT—1940

118. *No lights are to be seen. Smoke is coming from the chimney.*

CAMERA REVERSES *the path it took at the beginning of the picture, perhaps omitting some of the stages. It* MOVES *finally* THROUGH *the gates, which close behind it. As* CAMERA PAUSES *for a moment, the letter "K" is prominent in the moonlight.*

Just before we fade out, there comes again into the picture the pattern of barbed wire and cyclone fencing. On the fence is a sign which reads: "PRIVATE—NO TRESPASSING."

FADE OUT

THE END

When this film was first projected in 1941, there was considerable confusion as to "Rosebud." Currently, students, raised on Freudian insights and aware of adult delinquency, find "Rosebud" rather obvious. Nonetheless, it is today a classic example of a cinematic obligatory scene.

In *Tom Jones* the major obligatory scene and the climax of the plot do not coincide. The good Squire Allworthy returns home after a quarter of a year in London to find an infant baby between his sheets. The elderly woman servant, Mrs. Deborah Wilkens, assumes the foundling is illegitimate. "Faugh, how it stinks! It doth not smell like a Christian." In Fielding's novel she advises her master to leave it in a basket at the churchwarden's door: ". . . it is perhaps better for such Creatures to die in a State of Innocence, than to grow up and imitate their Mothers; for nothing better can be expected of them."

Mr. Allworthy, one of his fingers being pressured by the infant's hand, ruled otherwise, and "gave Mrs. Deborah positive orders to take the child to her own bed. . . ."

Thus ends Chapter III, with Allworthy off "to those pleasing slumbers which a heart that hungers after goodness, is apt to enjoy when thoroughly satisfied. . . ."

Though Henry Fielding does unleash curiosity and plot dynamics, screenplaywright John Osborne heightened both in his rendition of the scene that demands an eventual obligatory confrontation. Allworthy's sister Bridget enters, appears stricken, and demands the presence of Jenny Jones. "Find Jenny Jones." The script continues:

12. INTERIOR: ALLWORTHY'S STUDY—NIGHT

JENNY JONES, *a large, rosy, not too comely, but intelligent girl, stands before the* SQUIRE *and his* SISTER. *The* BABY *is gurgling away happily in a basket on* ALLWORTHY'S *desk.* ALLWORTHY *looks very stern indeed.*

ALLWORTHY
Will you still not reveal the father's name?

JENNY *shakes her head.*

Come, Jenny. The whole shame with all its dreadful consequences will fall entirely upon you.

BRIDGET *looks very distressed.*

BRIDGET
Brother, if the girl has been deceived by some wicked man, she is to be pitied.

But ALLWORTHY *is doing his magistrate's best at the moment.*

ALLWORTHY
The dreadful nature of this conduct is sufficiently apparent to every Christian. It is committed in defiance of the laws of our religion and of Him who founded it.

JENNY

Sir, I beg you not to persist in asking me to reveal the father of my baby. I promise you faithfully that one day you shall know. But I am under the most solemn ties of honour, and religion, to conceal his name now. You would not want that I should sacrifice either my honour or my religion.

The SQUIRE *sighs.*

The misfortunes of Tom, being considered a bastard, multiply as the plot unfolds. He is disinherited, cast off by Allworthy, rejected by Sophie Western, hounded by Blifil, and carted away after a duel to be hanged. In Newgate Jail two old friends, Mrs. Waters and Partridge, visit Tom, and say they will seek Mr. Allworthy's help. The following is the major obligatory scene, clearing Tom's legitimacy, a talky scene not in this form in the film:

202. INTERIOR: SITTING ROOM—SQUIRE WESTERN'S HOTEL—DAY

ALLWORTHY, BLIFIL, WESTERN, PARTRIDGE, MRS. WATERS (JENNY). *We are present at a general "post mortem."*

PARTRIDGE

Now, sir, I have told your honour the whole truth. I am not the father of Tom Jones.

ALLWORTHY
(*to* MRS. WATERS)

Then was this man not the father of your child? . . .

MRS. WATERS

You had a sister, sir.

ALLWORTHY

Oh no!

MRS. WATERS

As there is truth in heaven, sir, your sister was the mother of that child you found between your sheets. Thus, sir, you have at last discovered your true nephew.

PARTRIDGE *and* MRS. WATERS *look pleased.* SQUIRE WESTERN *not displeased.* BLIFUL *looks disappointed.* ALLWORTHY *looks dumbfounded.*

ALLWORTHY

And what of poor Tom? Where is he now?

DISSOLVE TO

203. INTERIOR: NEWGATE JAIL—FETTER ROOM—DAY

The obligatory scene having been concluded, two climaxes await their turns. First, Tom is about to be hanged and needs to be rescued by Squire Western on horseback. Second, Sophie and Tom are to be reconciled. Suspense is not present here any more than in the obligatory scene, but expectation of fulfillment is very much alive. The screenplay concludes:

> SOPHIE
>
> Let it then be your business to show me you deserve forgiveness.

> TOM
>
> I beg you to fix a period for the wedding.

> SOPHIE
>
> A twelve-month, perhaps.

> TOM
>
> Oh, my Sophie, you have named an eternity!

The obligatory scene in *Tom Jones,* as we have seen, evolved out of a narrative complication, the climaxes out of dramatic complications, but the effectiveness of the film is the direct consequences of cinematic invention, achieved through editing tempo and juxtaposition, camera composition and movement—all aided and abetted by superb performances of lusty parts.

In the patriotic films of Eisenstein, plot evolution of idea is considered secondary to the idea itself. Such are the limitations of posters compared to paintings. *Potemkin* in 1925 served as a recruiting poster on the walls of Western Europe, enticing enlistments in favor of the new people's republic between the Black Sea and the Baltic.

When Hitler threatened, the Kremlin permitted Eisenstein to extol the glory of the prince who defeated the invading Teutonic knights. Alexander Nevsky was a national hero under the czars, exhumed by the Communist Party for propaganda purposes. The release of *Alexander Nevsky* (1938) soon embarrassed the Kremlin when both Stalin and Hitler carved up Poland in a nonaggression pact.

The plot in *Nevsky* is the defeat of the invader. The expository theme is the special love Russians have for Russian soil. This is expounded in the opening sequence when Khubilai, the Mongol

Chieftain, meets Alexander. The compositions are statically interesting, illustrating the beauties of the land and the sea. The dialogue is as follows, translated too literally for literary value:

The Mongol Chieftain leaves. ALEXANDER *and his aide,* NIKITA, *watch the sedan chair depart with the Mongol soldiers.*

> NIKITA
>
> A hard people, strong. It will be difficult to beat them.
>
> ALEXANDER
>
> Is there any wish to?
>
> NIKITA
>
> It's about time to avenge our father's bones.
>
> ALEXANDER
>
> With the Mongols we can wait. There is a more dangerous enemy than the Tartar . . . nearer, more evil. You can't buy them off with tribute. The German! But destroy him, and you can then turn around and settle with the Tartar.
>
> NIKITA
>
> Well, if it's the German, then it's the German; you know better whom to start with, but for us it's all equally unbearable.
>
> ALEXANDER
>
> Without Novgorod you can't cut off the German. . . . From Novgorod we must take him. The last of free Russia is there—but the fish are getting away!

They hasten toward the peasant fishermen in the background.

The main obligatory scene is thus announced in Reel One: the inevitable battle with the German invaders. This begins in Reel Seven. The expository idea of patriotism is repeated in the following dialogue declarations of six Russian warriors, following the general retreat to the wagons in the rear:

> VASSILISSA
>
> Shall we take away the wagons?
>
> BUSLAI
>
> Hush! Die where you stand!
>
> IGNAT
>
> It's time, Yaroslavich.

ALEXANDER

For Russia! For Russia!

GAVRILO

For Russia!

MIKULA

Well, muzhik, let's strike at the German!

The cinematic obligatory scene is the battle on the ice, climaxing in the invaders sinking in their heavy armor as the ice breaks into chunks. The motions within these shots are so staged they have a theatrical quality. Prokofiev's lively music is so moving that an illusion of greater action and movement exists than what is actually being photographed. It is Eisenstein's design, according to his drawings and essay on *Nevsky*, to direct the eye over compositional lines from shot to shot—possible because the pictures are static.

What follows after the battle in Reel Eleven is an anticlimatical speech from Alexander, who hushes the victorious voices with these words:

All shouting, all shouting, but no thought of the important thing! People of Pskov and Novgorod! If you had lost the battle on the ice, Russia would not forgive either you nor me for lack of courage! So remember it, and tell your children and grandchildren . . . And if you forget, you'll be traitors to the Russian land. And now we'll administer justice!

In Reel Twelve Alexander has a final speech:

Go and tell all in foreign countries that Russia lives, let anyone come to us without fear as a guest. But if anyone comes to us with a sword, he will perish by the sword. On that stands and will stand the Russian land.

So ends the oratory and the opera of *Nevsky*, a pictorially interesting film with an obvious obligatory scene.

Curiously, an almost identical pattern is repeated in *Ivan the Terrible, Part One* (1944), with Ivan, like Alexander, devoted to Mother Russia. The Prologue, called "The Approaching Storm," announces the conflict (this translation by Herbert Marshall, Eisenstein's scholarly disciple, is superior to the later Ivor Montagu–Marshall collaboration) :

Clouds surge across the screen. . . .
Voices sing:

See the cruel treachery
of Boyar blood
'gainst the Emperor's power
to battle go.

The eight-year-old Ivan is warned by his dying mother, the Grand Princess Helena Glinsky: "I am dying . . . they've poisoned me. . . . Beware poison! . . . Beware the Boyars!"

In this Hall of Darkness sequence Ivan sees the handsome Telepnev-Obolensky, the princess' lover, dragged away before his terrified eyes. Then appears a Boyar of gigantic stature, Andrey Shuisky, who orders Telepnev-Obolensky murdered, and Telepnev throws himself at the feet of the boy with the cry, "Great Prince of Moscow, protect me!"

The sequence reaches its second climax:

Telepnev is caught and dragged away from the feet of Ivan. Telepnev desperately catches hold of the thin feet of the Crown Prince. From above, through the darkness, comes the harsh voice of Andrey Shuisky:

Take him away!

Telepnev is dragged to the stairs below. He is beaten and kicked. His silk shirt is torn open.

The torches move down. Telepnev is dragged into the cellar.

The tapers disappear above. The torches below. . . .

The boy Ivan trembles alone in the darkness.

FADE OUT

The question is planted: How is Ivan going to meet the Boyars when it becomes his turn?

In an extraordinary reversal of pattern, the major obligatory scene occurs as the climax of the Prologue—two sequences later—in the Ivan's Apartments sequence. The effect of fulfilling expectations so quickly is a preemption of the remaining tensions so that anticipation is reduced, as we shall see. In this initial and predominant clash "the richly clad Boyars" are quarreling among themselves whether tribute is to be paid to the Livonian merchants, favored by Boyar Shuisky who has been bribed by the Livonian ambassador, or to the Hanseatic League. In their midst the eight-year-old Ivan is being disrobed by an old woman attendant, following an elegant court session, and now "looks almost poverty-stricken."

The Boyars roar with laughter at the child, and Shuisky drops into a chair and flings his feet on the bed. "Ivan jumps forward, panting

with anger" and orders Shuisky to take his "feet off my mother's
bed . . . my mother, worried to death! By you dogs!"

> SHUISKY
>
> I'm a dog, eh? (*Rises from his chair like a wild beast*) **She
> was a bitch herself!** That He-dog Telepney and she were
> thick together; no one knows who sired you!

The gigantic figure of SHUISKY *towers over* IVAN, *brandishing his iron
staff.*

> Son of a bitch!

IVAN *covers his head with his arms to ward off the blow, then suddenly, unexpectedly even to himself, he screams out hysterically.*

> IVAN
>
> Arrest him!

Everyone, including IVAN, *is dumbfounded at its unexpectedness. The*
BOYARS *creep to the door.* SHUISKY *seems as if petrified.*

IVAN *searches with his eyes. On the threshold to his private chapel he
notices his* HUNTSMEN. *They also stand motionless.*

And now with a voice of decision, IVAN *commands.*

> Take him away!

And . . . the HUNTSMEN *take hold of the Chief Lord of the Realm—*
ANDREW SHUISKY. *They hustle him from the apartment.*

Ivan's reaction to his confrontation of Shuisky is most humanly
depicted, an exceptional insight into character motivations for a
Sergei Eisenstein script. Poster figures and symbols, coupled with
camera and set compositions, have been Eisenstein's chief means of
conveying character impact. But here the boy Ivan is now frightened
by his determination and startled by what has happened, and he
collapses.

The script continues:

> *He presses his face against the covers on his mother's bed and sobs
> as though his head lay on her breast. His skinny shoulders shake.
> Hurried footsteps are heard in the corridor. The door creaks.* IVAN
> *cowers, afraid to turn around. Through the door fearfully comes one
> of the* HUNTSMEN. *Cautiously he touches* IVAN *on the shoulder.* IVAN
> *turns. Shifting from foot to foot, the* HUNTSMAN *says guiltily.*

HUNTSMAN

We got a bit overzealous . . . strangled the Boyar . . .

CLOSE-UP *of* IVAN'S *face. At first at a loss. Then stern and concentrated. The "royal" look in his eyes. And in his glance—approval.*

IVAN

I'll rule myself . . . without the Boyars . . .

The HUNTSMAN *looks apprehensively at* IVAN.

I'll be a Czar! (*The eyes of* IVAN *gaze into the distance.*)

FADE OUT

In the subsequent sequences the pattern of the above anticipation and fulfillment is repeated with astounding pictorial power but with less dramatic impact. At seventeen the Grand Prince of Muscovy is crowned Czar of all Russia, and proceeds to dominate Staritsky Boyars, the Metropolitan and his clergy, and the foreign ambassadors. Though these conflicts are enacted with the firm countenance of Ivan, in juxtaposition to the hateful glances of the villains, little or no suspense exists because Ivan had already won the fight when he was eight years old. Eisenstein had shot his obligatory-scene bolt.

The first of these occurs upon the deathbed of the czar, taken ill on the return trip from Kazan. As Ivan lies dying, his face partially covered by a heavily jeweled book of the Gospel, and surrounded by seven black-cloaked priests holding seven candles—the question is whether the Boyars will kiss the Cross for Ivan's son Dmitry or for an idiotic fly-catcher Vladimir Staritsky. This undramatic choice of unequal alternatives is conveniently resolved. Ivan recovers. This is not an obligatory scene.

The next climax occurs when Anastasia, the czarina, is poisoned by Euphrosyne of the Staritsky Boyars, and other Boyars desert Moscow for foreign soil. Ivan ponders in a whisper:

> Am I right in what I am doing?
> Am I right?
> Is this not the chastisement of God?

Doubt is resolved by gazing into the dead features of his wife— "The face of Anastasia seems to shine with approval." The resolution is oratorical as he swears a great oath, his hand above Anastasia:

> In this summons from the people
> I shall read the will of the Almighty.

Into my hands I shall take the Lord's avenging
  sword.
The great task I shall accomplish:
a Sovereign almighty upon earth shall I become!

This similarly is no obligatory scene.

Nor at the conclusion of Part One is there a climax or an obligatory scene. Ships from England have sailed into the White Sea, the
Great Russian realm flourishes, the czar's men are in command, but
the rumor is that Ivan has abdicated, gone from Moscow, and living
in a monastary, the Alexandrov Liberty. And so he is, now thin and
haggard. The czar's men repeat their loyalty oath; the people of
Moscow stream in an Eisenstein-controlled line (reminiscent of the
lines of people on the breakfront in the Odessa harbor in *Potemkin*),
streaming in a pilgrimage from Moscow. "Return to thy kingdom!"
the people cry. "Dear father of ours." Yes, he will return.

Ivan the Terrible. Courtesy of Artkino.

Ivan the Terrible, Part Two (1946) is a continuation of this anti-climax. Though pictorially brilliant it lacks dramatic acceleration. There is no release of tension in a fulfillment of expectancy; there is no obligatory scene.

It would be criminal to Eisenstein's memory to conclude this script analysis without reference to his battles with the Stalin bureaucracy, which killed him by literally breaking his heart. For a man of Eisenstein's genius artistic integrity was indivisible. His scripts and production plans were repeatedly shelved by inferior mentalities. They were his scripts for a comedy *MMM* (Maxim Maximovich Maximov), his partly finished *Bezhin Meadow* (1935–37) inspired by a Turgenev tale, his script for *The Black Consul* with Paul Robeson, his biography of Moscow as seen through several generations of a family, his *Ferghana Canal* to be set in Uzbekistan (Samarkand), starting in the time of Tamberlane, and a script about Pushkin—all rejected.

In accepting the suggestion of *Ivan the Terrible* as a possible subject, this exceptionally astute man—one of the most cultured minds of his time—utilized the opportunity to revenge himself against his tormentors. By glorifying the tyrant in Part One, Eisenstein would be explaining Stalin, ironically, as "the new hero." In Part Two—subtitled "The Boyars' Plot"—he went further, and depicted the fratricidal murders of a paranoic Ivan, which Stalin resembled. Similarly, Ivan's private army, the Oprichniks, paralleled the GPU, the secret police of Stalin.

While filming the intrigues and murders of "The Boyars' Plot" (The Commissars' Plot), Eisenstein was begged repeatedly by anxious friends not to take the tremendous risk. "This is my Ivan the Terrible," he is reported to have replied. "Such will it be. When you have made your Ivan, you may do otherwise."

In a personally artistic way, the whole of *Ivan the Terrible, Part Two* was Sergei Eisenstein's obligatory idea. As a result, its creator was castigated and condemned by the Communist Party of the USSR; the picture was promptly banned, and lay buried for thirteen years.

The long-delayed encounter between the monomaniac Captain Ahab and the White Whale is indeed an obligatory scene, be it narrated in a novel, described offstage in a play, or photographed in a film. What renders this classic obligatory scene so meaningful is the contrapuntal and interchangeable idea of good and evil. Is the White

Whale symbolic of destructive nature, while Ahab is man bent on slaying the sea serpent? This is not so simple, Melville instructs us. Here is the first description of the demon in Ahab, excerpted from Chapter XXVIII:

His bone leg steadied in that hole; one arm elevated, and holding by a shroud; Captain Ahab stood erect, looking straight out beyond the ship's ever-pitching prow. There was an infinity of firmest fortitude, a determinate, unsurrenderable wilfulness, in the fixed and fearless, forward dedication of that glance. Not a word he spoke; nor did his officers say naught to him; though by all their minutest gestures and expressions, they plainly showed the uneasy, if not painful, consciousness of being under a troubled master-eye. And not only that, but moody stricken Ahab stood before them with a crucifixion in his face. . . .

The lust to kill Moby Dick is in turn evil, as depicted in the drunken climax of Chapter XXXVI when Ahab revels and rants:

Drink, ye harpooners! drink and swear, ye men that man the deathful whaleboat's bow—Death to Moby Dick! God hunt us all, if we do not hunt Moby Dick to his death!" The long, barbed steel goblets were lifted; and to cries and maledictions against the white whale, the spirits were simultaneously quaffed down with a hiss. Starbuck [chief mate] paled, and turned, and shivered.

Nor does Melville depict Moby Dick as wholly evil, but with majestic beauty:

A gentle joyousness—a mighty mildness of repose in swiftness, invested the gliding whale. Not the white bull of Jupiter swimming away with ravished Europa clinging to his graceful horns . . . not Jove, not that great majesty Supreme! did surpass the glorified White Whale as he so divinely swam.

This awesome power is visually described in the same chapter, CXXXIII, dealing with the first day of the chase:

Ahab could discover no sign in the sea. But suddenly as he peered down and down into its depths, he profoundly saw a white living spot no bigger than a white weasel, with wonderful celerity uprising, and magnifying as it rose, till it turned, and then there were plainly revealed two long crooked rows of white, glistening teeth, floating up from the undiscoverable bottom. It was Moby Dick's open mouth and scrolled jaw; his vast, shadowed bulk still half blending with the blue of the sea.

Before the obligatory scene enters its first stage we know that evil and good are interwoven, as Ahab literally becomes enmeshed with the harpooned whale, and goes down with him. Prior to that climax, which coincides with the obligatory scene, Captain Ahab and his whaling ship *Pequod* experience storms, lightning, loss of compass, the drowning of a man, the insanity of Pip, and the slaughter of ordinary whales. On the second day of the chase Ahab declares the inevitability of the encounter when Starbuck begs him to desist—"In Jesus' name no more of this, that's worse than devil's madness. Two days chased; twice stove to splinters; thy very leg once more snatched from under thee; thy evil shadow gone—all good angels mobbing thee with warnings:—what more wouldst thou have?—Shall we keep chasing this murderous fish till he swamps the last man? Shall we be dragged by him to the bottom of the sea? . . ."

Ahab answers:

. . . This whole act's immutably decreed. 'Twas rehearsed by thee and me a billion years before this ocean rolled. Fool! I am the Fates' lieutenant; I act under orders. Look thou, underling! that thou obeyest mine.— Stand round me, men. . . .

What distinguishes the obligatory scene in the novel *Moby Dick* is not only the commingling of good and evil, but the counterpoint between mysticism and realism that, in the end, raises the obligatory scene to a classic significance while endowing it with extraordinary reality. All the little essays and discourses, expository and descriptive, full of information and lore about the nature of the whale, the history of the science and art relating to whales, facts about the industry, footnotes, the tools of the trade—all labor indirectly on behalf of the mysticism by giving it a frame of realism. Unfortunately, these are the elements ignored in the two motion-picture versions: *The Sea Beast* (1925) with John Barrymore grimacing over the gunwales, and *Moby Dick* (1956) with the jaw of Gregory Peck hardly a match for the grin of the White Whale.

The most truly cinematic passage in the John Huston effort is the opening shots, those of Ishmael striding down a wooded hillside, a young man on his way to the sea and a whaling ship. All the artificiality of rubber whales and miniature ships in studio tanks, with water churned by gigantic rockers and airplane motors, is an artificiality that is rendered more offensive by our keen expectancy of witnessing one of the most classic obligatory scenes in all storytelling.

The significance of *Moby Dick* for cinema is not that rubber whales, miniatures, and studio tanks are artificial—they can be instruments making for mystical reality when properly applied—but that an obligatory scene should not be executed perfunctorily merely because an audience takes its coming for granted. The obligatory three-day scene in *Moby Dick* still awaits fulfillment in cinematic form.

The opposite, an overfulfillment, is the case in *The Seventh Seal,* an allegorical encounter with death wherein a series of anticipations create a total of no less than six obligatory scenes. This pessimistic drama of man's quest for answers about God and death has exquisite moments of carefully chiseled photography—the vision, to name one, of the Virgin Mother strolling with the Christ Child through the meadow like princess and son. The concern of Bergman is how each of us faces death. The suspense is not in the when, but the how. With so many obligatory scenes Bergman appears to transcend the necessity for any of them (in surplus there is excess), and demonstrates that an audience can become involved without the traditional suspense of the obligatory scene, but purely on the sheer force of intelligence, style, performance, and theme. All the horrors of witch-burning, flagellations (*Totentanz*), rape, thievery, and deceit appear as sensational illustrations of an idea that is already explicit.

Here are the six obligatory scenes (translated by Lars Malmstrom and David Kushner). The first:

The KNIGHT *returns to the beach and falls on his knees. With his eyes closed and brow furrowed, he says his morning prayers. His hands are clenched together and his lips form the words silently. His face is sad and bitter. He opens his eyes and stares directly into the morning sun which wallows up from the misty sea like some bloated, dying fish. The sky is gray and immobile, a dome of lead. A cloud hangs mute and dark over the western horizon. High up, barely visible, a sea gull floats on motionless wings. Its cry is weird and restless.*

The KNIGHT's *large gray horse lifts its head and whinnies.* ANTONIUS BLOCK *turns around.*

Behind him stands a man in black. His face is very pale and he keeps his hands hidden in the wide folds of his cloak.

KNIGHT

Who are you?

DEATH

I am Death.

KNIGHT

Have you come for me?

Black for you!

The Seventh Seal. Courtesy of Janus Films.

DEATH

I have been walking by your side for a long time.

KNIGHT

That I know.

DEATH

Are you prepared?

KNIGHT

My body is frightened, but I am not.

DEATH

Well, there is no shame in that.

The KNIGHT *has risen to his feet. He shivers.* DEATH *opens his cloak to place it around the* KNIGHT's *shoulders.*

KNIGHT

Wait a moment.

DEATH

That's what they all say. I grant no reprieves.

KNIGHT

You play chess, don't you?

A gleam of interest kindles in DEATH's *eyes.*

Knight Antonius Block makes a condition "that I may live as long as I hold out against you. If I win, you will release me."

Though the outcome is foreordained, curiosity centers upon the length of the reprieve. On this strung-out clothesline Bergman hangs his episodic sermons, propping their weight at regular intervals with poles. The second expected meeting occurs when the knight enters a confession booth—"The face of Death appears behind the grille for an instant, but the knight doesn't see him." The knight confesses his doubts over God—he is returning from a Crusade—"My life has been a futile pursuit, a wandering, a great deal of talk without meaning." He confides his tactic for beating the Devil at chess—"In the next move I'll shatter one of his flanks." Death replies: "I'll remember that."

DEATH *shows his face at the grille of the confession booth for a moment but disappears instantly.*

KNIGHT

You've tricked and cheated me! But we'll meet again, and I'll find a way.

DEATH

(*invisible*)

We'll meet at the inn, and there we'll continue playing.

The third pole props up the story line before the inn scene:

The KNIGHT *picks up his chess game and carries it toward the beach. It is quiet and deserted; the sea is still.*

DEATH

I've been waiting for you.

KNIGHT

Pardon me. I was detained for a few moments. Because I revealed my tactics to you, I'm in retreat. It's your move.

DEATH

Why do you look so satisfied?

> KNIGHT
> Don't worry about my laughter; save your king instead.

> DEATH
> You're rather arrogant.

> KNIGHT
> Our game amuses me.

> DEATH
> It's your move. Hurry up. I'm a little pressed for time.

> KNIGHT
> I understand that you've a lot to do, but you can't get out
> of our game. It takes time.

The defiance of Death is a positive alteration that serves to heighten anticipation. The fourth meeting serves to postpone a decision, and, hence, to add further expectancy. The scene comes during the preparation for burning Tyan, the young girl accused of consorting with the devil:

> *They take her down from the cart and lead her toward the ladder and the stake. The* KNIGHT *turns to the* MONK, *who remains seated in the cart.*

> KNIGHT
> What have you done with the child?

> DEATH *turns around and looks at him.*

> DEATH
> Don't you ever stop asking questions?

> KNIGHT
> No, I'll never stop.

Death appears next in the forest, but his encounter this time is with Skat, the lecherous actor, who has just feigned suicide to escape death at the hands of a cuckold smith, Plog. It is an amusing scene in which Bergman comments on actors' vanities: Skat is up a tree, which Death is sawing, and pleads—"my performance . . . my contract . . . Aren't there any special rules for actors?" The scene also reminds us that Death is more than a chessplayer. He can kill.

The sixth and final appearance of Death also occurs in the forest. It is curiously anticlimactical for an obligatory scene, since anticipation has run dry. Death takes the knight's queen. The knight does not move.

He pretends to be clumsy and knocks the chess pieces over with the hem of his coat. He looks up at DEATH.

> KNIGHT
> I've forgotten how the pieces stood.

> DEATH
> (*laughs contentedly*)
> But I have not forgotten. You can't get away that easily.

Death announces to Antonius Block that he is mated on the next move, and asks if the knight enjoyed his reprieve. Block admits he did:

> DEATH
> I'm happy to hear that. Now I'll be leaving you. When we meet again, you and your companions' time will be up.

> KNIGHT
> And you will divulge your secrets.

> DEATH
> I have no secrets.

> KNIGHT
> So you know nothing.

> DEATH
> I have nothing to tell.

The KNIGHT *wants to answer, but* DEATH *is already gone.*

The final image is a silhouette against a stormy sky of Death leading his troupe of dancers "toward the dark lands. . . ." The sight is witnessed by a symbolic Adam and Eve, the players Jof and wife Mia, who holds her son Mikael in her lap.

The Seventh Seal, we may note, suffers from a plethora of obligatory scenes, which are more like statements than dramatic resolutions.

3. INDIRECT OBLIGATORY SCENES

When an obligatory scene is so implied without "maximum expectation," but semisubmerged through design or disaster, it may possess the subtle values of indirectness. Unfortunately, in such examples there is more frequently an imbalance between an accelerating anticipation and an intensifying uncertainty of outcome. Subtlety, not unlike satire, more often fails than succeeds, even for specialized audiences, if cinematic impact is missing.

An excellent example of an indirect obligatory scene is in *The Magician* (1958, titled *The Face* in England). Written and directed by Ingmar Bergman two years after *The Seventh Seal*, this film is a crowded composite of mental quests and cinematic tricks. Into 102 minutes Bergman crams his perpetuating inquiry into truth, religion, illusion, women, and artists, all in an elaborately baroque style, yet kept so lively through camera and editing, composition and lighting and special effects that we are dazzled and confused—but curiously satisfied by the rarity of the experience.

Truth is the idea behind this comedy about a hypnotist, challenged by the Royal Counselor on Medicine who believes the magician is a fake. Indeed, Bergman tells us, we are not what we appear to be. The magician Vogler's young gentleman assistant turns out to be an attractive girl; Vogler's dark hair and beard are removed to disclose a clean-shaven blond. At times Vogler resembles Christ.

In a mid-nineteenth-century Sweden that has a touch of Kafka's *The Trial,* the police chief, Starbeck, reads from a newspaper: "Sensational marvels never shown before. Magic acts based on the philosophies of the Orient. Health-giving magnets. Spine-tingling thrills of the senses." Vogler does not defend himself; we are informed he is mute. Medical Examiner Vergérus demands answers of Vogler, "who sits with his head bowed and his hands resting on his knees."

VERGÉRUS

Why do you look so furious, Mr. Vogler?

VOGLER *looks at him.*

You have no reason to hate me. I only want to find out the truth. That should be your wish as well.

VOGLER *doesn't answer.*

Open your mouth.

VOGLER *obeys.*

Stick out your tongue.

VOGLER *obeys.* VERGÉRUS *leans over* VOGLER *and carefully squeezes his throat and windpipe.*

The Magician. Courtesy of Janus Films.

I regret to say, Mr. Vogler, that I find no reason for your muteness.

Vergérus later informs Manda, the boy who turns out to be Vogler's wife, that he cannot leave them in peace:

> VERGÉRUS
> Because you represent something which I most abhor.

MANDA *looks questioningly at him.*

The unexplainable.

> MANDA
> Then you can immediately stop your persecution, Mr. Vergérus, because our activities are a fraud from beginning to end.

> VERGÉRUS
>
> A fraud?

> MANDA
>
> Pretense, false promises, and double bottoms. Miserable, rotten lies throughout. We are the most ridiculous scoundrels you can find.

> VERGÉRUS
>
> Is your husband of the same opinion?

> MANDA
>
> He doesn't speak.

> VERGÉRUS
>
> Is that true?

> MANDA
>
> *Nothing is true!*

With Vergérus personifying truth and Vogler personifying tricks, an obligatory scene is anticipated. It comes, most indirectly, when Vogler appears to have been strangled and the Medical Examiner will perform an autopsy. Now Bergman uses cinematic tricks to argue in favor of mystical tricks, and truth—on any level or in any relationship—ceases to exist. We are tricked by camera and editing.

Vergérus is in the attic, where he has performed the autopsy, and is now writing his report. "When he is about to put the pen back into the inkwell, he stops. A human eye stares at him from the top of the inkwell. . . . Then the clock behind the mirror begins to strike quickly and repeatedly, but falls silent just as suddenly. . . . Another hand lays itself quietly over his left hand. Vergérus looks long and thoughtfully at this strange phenomenon. The hand which rests upon his own is cut off, amputated. . . . He strokes his hair and straightens his glasses, tries to focus his image in the mirror, but sees something else deep in the room behind him. It is a face, floating formlessly above the body of the dead man. A glaring face, lit from inside, with pale, tense features and a look of hatred. When he turns around, the vision disappears immediately. He runs over to the dead man and rips away the sheet, but everything is unchanged—dead and tangible. . . . Then his glasses are ripped off and thrown into the darkness. . . . The large clock behind the mirror has begun ticking slowly and unevenly. The door to the pendulum opens on a dark emptiness. . . . He peers into the mirror. Once again he sees the face floating behind him in the dim light. A hand stretches out suddenly toward his neck, but he steps back and gasps for air. At the same moment, a sharp report is heard, and the mirror shatters into whirling slivers. The face disappears immediately. Vergérus staggers backward toward the table, holds his breath and listens in the heavy silence. He hears someone breathing close to his ear, then light, quick steps across the floorboards. . . . A hand stretches out again from the darkness and touches his throat. . . . He runs toward the staircase, stumbles on the top step, rolls down the stairs, throws himself against the door, pounds and cries. Finally he sinks down and crouches at the threshold like an animal. . . . Again the hand approaches and touches his throat. . . ."

Manda rescues Vergérus by ordering Vogler to release him. Vogler is "dressed in the actor Spegel's rags."

What we observe is not an explicit obligatory scene, though we might relish the smug Vergérus getting his comeuppance while being mystified and frightened ourselves. So indirect is this obligatory scene that Bergman is obligated later to explain it with Vogler having regained his speech:

VERGÉRUS

It would interest me to know whom I've actually dissected.

VOGLER

A poor actor who wished for nothing better than to be dissected and scraped clean.

VERGÉRUS

And you lent him your face. Changed places on the floor in the hall. You were never dead. Not even unconscious, perhaps?

VOGLER
(*humble*)

It was a cheap trick.

The ironic climax comes later when Vogler departs to give a command performance at the Royal Palace in Stockholm. Truth and trickery are never to be resolved.

When there is a double plot whereby protagonists operate in overlapping and parallel contexts, obligatory scenes have the disadvantage of being shared with or eclipsed by the accompanying plot, and become, in effect, indirect. *Greed* (1925) is such an example. For powerful moments of maximum expectancy no film can surpass

Erich Von Stroheim's masterpiece, based on Frank Norris's *Mc-Teague*.

As an impoverished immigrant in New York, washing dishes and sleeping in cheap rooming houses, Von Stroheim dreamed of making a film of Norris' realistic novel. He slept with the book under his pillow and carried it from one lodging to another. In the following decade, after a series of successful sex films, his opportunity came, and so faithful was Von Stroheim that he filmed *McTeague* almost page by page. His final editing (from a rumored 150 reels) was 40-odd reels, or over ten hours on the screen. He attempted a further cut, but finally became adamant. The Goldwyn company, original producers, and Metro-Goldwyn-Mayer, releasers, cut *Greed* by three-quarters, June Mathis and assistants doing the horrendous and thankless butchery. Of the quarter that remains there are certain passages that indicate the uncompromising originality of the writing and directing. Von Stroheim bitterly remarked to this writer on the occasion of seeing M-G-M's *Greed* for the first time, and years after he had departed from Hollywood, "It is like seeing your child, your flesh and blood, its body opened and dismembered on the slab of the autopsy table."

The double story lines, in the novel and Von Stroheim's script, are: (1) the friendship and ensuing hatred between McTeague, the dentist, and his "pal" Marcus Schouler, assistant at a Dog and Cat Hospital; (2) the love and hatred between Mac and his wife, Trina.

The anticipation is launched for both plots in Chapter VII of the novel when Trina is told she has won $5,000 in a lottery, an enormous sum in 1899. Trina had been Marcus's girl, but is now engaged to Mac. Trina's Germanic mother, Mrs. Sieppe, asks, "Vhat efer will you do mit all dose money, eh, Trina?"

The novel continues:

"Huh!" exclaimed Marcus. "Get married on it for one thing." Thereat they all shouted with laughter. McTeague grinned, and looked about sheepishly. "Talk about luck," muttered Marcus, shaking his head at the dentist; then suddenly he added:
"Well, are we going to stay talking out here in the hall all night? Can't we all come into your 'Parlors,' Mac?"

The complete script, Von Stroheim's personal copy preserved by Mme Denise Vernac, offers the comparative passage (Trina is played by Zazu Pitts, Marcus by Jean Hersholt, McTeague by Gibson Gowland):

TITLE:

"Vhat efer vill you do mit all dose money, Trina?"

CLOSE-UP—MARCUS

Smiles cynically in direction where MAC *is, says:*

TITLE:

"Get married on it for one thing."

MEDIUM SHOT—ALL IN

They shout with laughter.

CLOSE-UP—MCTEAGUE

Grinning and looking about sheepishly.

CLOSE-UP—MARCUS

Shaking his head at the DENTIST, *says:*

TITLE:

"Talk about luck."

BACK TO CLOSE-UP—MCTEAGUE

Grins.

BACK TO CLOSE-UP—MARCUS
Says:

TITLE:

"Well are we going to stay talking out here in the hall all
night. Can't we all come into your parlors, Mac?"

*Says that with accompanying gestures pointing in direction of "par-
lors."*

This stroke of fortune alters all three main characters: Trina from
being a shyly passive maiden to a calculating, miserly bitch; Mac
from being a stupid, amiable giant to a sadistic brute; and Marcus
from "the life of the party" clown to an embittered, revengeful
monomaniac. The alterations are painfully progressive, done in dark
detail, each neurosis moving gradually toward psychotic actions. On
Trina's wedding night her exceptional fear of sex leads eventually to
her going to bed naked with her golden coins. That scene immediately precedes Mac's revenge, when he returns from a bum's life to
collect the gold.

In the novel the revenge scene occurs in Chapter XIX:

"You ain't going to make small of me this time. Give me that money."

"No."

"For the last time, will you give me that money?"

"No."

"You won't, huh?" You won't give me it? For the last time."

"No, no."

Usually the dentist was slow in his movements, but now the alcohol had awakened in him an ape-like agility. He kept his small dull eyes upon her, and all at once sent his fist into the middle of her face with the suddenness of a relaxed spring.

Beside herself with terror, Trina turned and fought him back; fought for her miserable life with the exasperation and strength of a harassed cat; and with such energy and such wild, unnatural force, that even Mc-Teague for the moment drew back from her. But her resistance was the one thing to drive him to the top of his fury. He came back at her again, his eyes drawn to two fine twinkling points, and his enormous fists, clenched till the knuckles whitened, raised in the air.

Then it became abominable.

In the schoolroom outside, behind the coal scuttle, the cat listened to the sounds of stamping and struggling and the muffled noise of blows, wildly terrified, his eyes bulging like brass knobs. At last the sounds stopped on a sudden; he heard nothing more. Then McTeague came out, closing the door. The cat followed him with distended eyes as he crossed the room and disappeared through the street door.

In the script the corresponding obligatory scene, which also happens to coincide with the climax of the Trina-Mac plot, begins with Trina scrubbing the floor in the schoolhouse. The cat is frightened and runs out; Mac swings the door open:

CLOSE-UP—MAC

With one sweeping glance he surveys the ground, then he concentrates on TRINA *and his eyes reduce to little pin heads.*

SHOT FROM HIS ANGLE—TRINA

She is kneeling, sitting back on her heels, she brings the back of her dripping hand in a frightened way to her mouth, she is paralyzed.

SHOT FROM HER ANGLE—MAC

His fists clenched, never looking away from her, slowly walking toward her with lowered head.

SHOT FROM PERAMBULATOR

Moving toward TRINA, *she wants to scream, but her voice has left her. With the greatest effort she rises, camera pans up with her and comes so close until face covers entire screen.*

SHOT FROM HER ANGLE BIG HEAD CLOSE-UP—MAC

Coming nearer.

BACK TO HEAD CLOSE-UP—TRINA

With indescribable fear TRINA *speaks:*

TITLE:

"Mac—listen—
Oh don't—I'll scream—
I'll do anything!"

BACK TO CLOSE-UP—MAC

Looks at her, speaks:

TITLE:

"I want that five thousand."

BACK TO CLOSE-UP—TRINA

Shakes her head, says: "I haven't got it—it isn't here"—*points out, says:* "Uncle Oelbermann's got it."

BACK TO MACK

He looks at her, says:

TITLE:

"That's a lie—
Oelbermann told me that you got it."

BACK TO CLOSE-UP—TRINA

Shakes her head, says "No! That's a lie—that's not true."

BACK TO CLOSE-UP—MAC

Says: "You had it long enough, now I want it—do ya hear?"

BACK TO TRINA

Speaks:

TITLE:

"Mac, I can't give you that money."

BACK TO MAC

Speaks: "Yes you will—every nickel of it."

BACK TO TRINA

Shakes head, says: "No, No." *Speaks:*

TITLE:

   "I won't give it to you."

BACK TO SCENE—MAC

Says: "Give me that money!"

BACK TO TRINA

Shakes head, says "No!"

BACK TO MAC

Speaks:

                                TITLE:

   "For the last time—
   will you give me that money?"

BACK TO TRINA

She says "No! No!"

MEDIUM SHOT

Both full in against double door, leading into cloak room. TRINA *has regained her wits and with unbelievable rapidity brushes past him, squeezes through the open door.*

MEDIUM CLOSE-UP

on other side of door, she just locks door from inside then looks around terrifically frightened for something to put in front of door, there is nothing there.

MEDIUM SHOT

on other side in school room, MAC *lays one hand on knob and with move bursts open door, locks and everything. As door opens, he grabs* TRINA *who tries to brush past him out into school room, but he twirls her around so that they disappear into dark cloak room in which shades on the windows are down. One can see him hit her once, she staggers back into darkness, he follows her with clenched fists, camera keeps on grinding at open door with dark room behind for at least twenty feet. Right after* MAC *and* TRINA *have twirled into it the black cat runs out frightened toward camera. Then* MAC *backs out, his face scratched, his cheek bleeding, he turns, looks about, steps one step in, looks toward right from cloak room, disappears again.*

MEDIUM SHOT—TRINA'S ROOM

Door is burst open, MAC *enters, he strikes a match, then sees globe, turns on light, looks around, sees trunk under bed, pulls it out.*

MEDIUM SHOT

from school room toward open door of cloak room, black cat sneaks in very slowly and carefully.

MEDIUM LONG SHOT

front of kindergarten, two policemen saunter in, one of them is the one that had seen MAC, *they stop right in front of gate, talk.*

MEDIUM SHOT

in school room toward double door, black cat jumps out again, MAC *comes out with canvas sack, he puts it into top of pants, buttons coat over it, then turns, closes door, starts to walk toward right of camera.*

MEDIUM SHOT

front of kindergarten, two policemen standing there, they say "Good night" to each other, one walks one way, the other the other way. At the same time MAC *enters from school house, opens gate, looks up and down the street.*

CLOSE-UP—MAC

Looks up toward the sky, then mumbles:

                                        TITLE:
    "I bet it'll rain to-morrow."

BACK TO SCENE

He walks toward camera

                                        IRIS DOWN

On window of cloak room, hold for a second.

                                        IRIS OUT COMPLETELY

The above, written by Von Stroheim and printed as he wrote it, is a perfect example of a cinematic obligatory scene.

Marcus confronts Mac in the Death Valley desert, after a parallel orchestration of conflict, such as a fight in the local saloon, a wrestling match in Schuetzen's Park, and Marcus' betrayal of Mac to the State Dental Examiner for practicing without a license. After leaving San Francisco Marcus became a cowboy in the Panamint Valley, and eventually learned, by a poster outside the Wells Fargo office, that Mac was wanted for murder and was believed hiding in the vicinity. Marcus tells the sheriff and posse, "I can identify um, and you fellers can't. And I knew—I knew—good *God!* I knew that girl—his wife—in Frisco. She's a cousin of mine, she is—she was—I thought once of— This thing's a personal matter of mine—an' that money he got away with, that five thousand, belongs to me by rights. . . ." Marcus leaves the posse to strike across the desert alone, and self-driven by his lust for gold and revenge he finally captures McTeague and the canvas sack of gold. Marcus is "singularly puzzled to know what next to do. He had got McTeague . . . his enemy. . . ." Water is more precious than gold; they are a hundred miles from the Panamint hills. "We're dead men," says Marcus, but the moment Mac takes a step toward his canvas sack, saying, "I guess, even if we are done for, I'll take—some of my truck along," Marcus comes to life.

The novel continues:

"Hold on," exclaimed Marcus, with rising aggressiveness. "Let's talk about that. I ain't so sure about who that—who that money belongs to."

"Well, I *am,* you see," growled the dentist.

The old enmity between the two men, their ancient hate, was flaming up again. . . .

"You soldiered me out of that money once, and played me for a sucker, an' it's *my* turn now. Don't you lay your finger on that sack."

They fight. McTeague kills Marcus with blows from Marcus' revolver. The novel concludes:

As McTeague rose to his feet, he felt a pull at his right wrist; something held it fast. Looking down, he saw that Marcus in that last struggle has found the strength to handcuff their wrists together. Marcus was dead now; McTeague was locked to the body. All about him, vast, interminable, stretched the measureless leagues of Death Valley.

McTeague remained stupidly looking around him, now at the distant horizon, now at the ground, now at the half-dead canary chittering feebly in its little gilt prison.

In Von Stroheim's script, the irony of their mutual lust for gold is brilliantly executed in cinematic terms, one of the supremely great scenes in cinema. Marcus and Mac have agreed "to go somewhere," so Max moves toward his dead mule. The script continues:

TITLE:
"—even if we're done for, I'll take some of my truck along."

BACK TO SCENE—MARCUS

Very aggressive, says: "Hold on."

TITLE:

"I ain't so sure about who that money belongs to."

BACK TO SCENE—MAC

Says: "Well, I am." *They look at each other with ancient hate,* MAC *speaks:*

TITLE:

"—an' don't try and load that gun either."

BACK TO SCENE

He fixes MARCUS *with his eyes.* MARCUS *speaks:* "Then don't lay your fingers on that sack."

BACK TO SCENE—MARCUS

Drags handcuffs from his pocket, holds revolver in his hand like a club, speaks:

TITLE:

"You soldiered me out of that money once, and played me for a sucker—it's my turn now."

BACK TO SCENE

Says: "Don't lay a finger on that sack."

MEDIUM SHOT—BOTH IN

MARCUS *bars* MCTEAGUE'*s way.*

BIG HEAD CLOSE-UP—MCTEAGUE

His eyes draw to fine twinkling points.

CLOSE-UP

His fists knotting themselves like wooden mallets.

BACK TO SCENE

He moves a step nearer to MARCUS, *then another, suddenly the men grapple, in another instant they are rolling and struggling on the white ground.* MAC *thrusts* MARCUS *backwards until he trips and falls over the body of the dead mule; the little bird cage breaks from the saddle and rolls out on the ground.*

CLOSE-UP—MARCUS' HAND

holding the revolver like a club, MCTEAGUE'*s hand takes it from him.*

BACK TO SCENE—MCTEAGUE

Strikes with it blindly, clouds of dust envelop the two fighting men.

CLOSE-UP—MCTEAGUE

Panting, he looks to where his enemy is on ground.

SHOT FROM HIS ANGLE—MARCUS

Still, suddenly he regains energy.

CLOSE-UP—MCTEAGUE'S RIGHT WRIST

Being caught by handcuff.

BACK TO MARCUS

On ground, becomes motionless.

MEDIUM SHOT—BOTH IN

MCTEAGUE *tries to rise, he feels a pull on his right wrist.*

CLOSE-UP—MCTEAGUE

Looking down.

CLOSE-UP FROM HIS ANGLE—HANDCUFF TO BODY ON GROUND

SHOT FROM HIS ANGLE—BODY DEAD

BACK TO CLOSE-UP—MCTEAGUE

He turns, looks at canvas bag on saddle of dead mule.

SHOT FROM HIS ANGLE—SPLIT OPEN CANVAS BAG

Twenty dollar gold pieces falling into sand.

BACK TO CLOSE-UP—MCTEAGUE

He looks once more at handcuff and at body.

MEDIUM SHOT—ALL IN

He sits cumbersomely down, looks stupidly around.

SHOT FROM HIS ANGLE—DESERT

BACK TO MCTEAGUE

He looks at bird cage.

SHOT FROM HIS ANGLE—BIRD CAGE

Bird flops.

BACK TO MCTEAGUE

Nodding gravely.

FADE OUT

Von Stroheim concludes with four lines of moralizing verse, an indulgence he learned from his mentor, D. W. Griffith. He added a bit of business with the bird, a Freudian touch that has been a minor leitmotif throughout the filming of the novel. Mac kisses the bird's beak and throws it into the air, but it falls dead on the sack of gold spotted with blood. In two successively more distant shots we leave Mac sitting like a speck in the middle of the desert.

When fresh characters are powerfully motivated, the obligatory scene, which would ordinarily loom ahead with glowing intensity, might become an embarrassment to an original playwright. Often, in such cases, it is started but never completely shown, or it occurs off the set invisible to an audience, or is simply ignored.

Two of Tennessee Williams' scripts illustrate the success and the failure of such solutions. His rare talent for atmospheric suggestiveness, both dramatic and poetic, gives dimensions to his characters beyond surface conflicts. We are expected to feel more than we see.

In *A Streetcar Named Desire* (1951) the fragile, tragic Blanche DuBois, obsessed by sex as her only means of maintaining her illusions of ladylike gentility, is placed in juxtaposition to a crude, hedonistic animal, Stanley Kowalski, married to Blanche's sister Stella. In Scene Two of the play this triangle intimates the coming of two obligatory scenes. Blanche and Stanley as opposites are magnetically drawn toward each other, while Stella, a simple wife, is unsuspectingly accommodating: first, we expect a sexual contact between the stalking lion and the elegant zebra, and, second, we trust the sleeping lioness will wake up and roar. Here, in Shot 29 of the script, our expectations are planted; Stanley has been complaining to Stella about Blanche's expensive wardrobe, and Stella has been defending her sister:

29. (*Continued*)

STELLA *snatches up her white hat and gloves and starts for the outside door.*

STELLA
You come out with me while Blanche is getting dressed.

A Streetcar Named Desire. Courtesy of Warner Brothers.

STANLEY

Since when do you give me orders?

STELLA

Are you going to stay here and insult her?

STANLEY

You bet your life I'm going to stay here.

STELLA *exits.* STANLEY *turns at the sound of the bathroom door open-ing off shot.*

30. FULL SHOT—BLANCHE

She comes out of the bathroom in a satin robe.

BLANCHE
(*airily—as she approaches him*)
Hello, Stanley. Here I am, all freshly bathed and scented and feeling like a brand new human being.

STANLEY
(*lighting a cigarette*)
That's good.

> BLANCHE

Excuse me while I slip on my pretty new dress.

> STANLEY

Go right ahead, Blanche.

But he makes no move to go. BLANCHE *waits for him to leave. He moves sullenly into the bedroom. She draws the drapes, then reacts as she sees the open, disordered trunk.*

> BLANCHE

I understand there's to be a little card party to which we ladies are cordially not invited.

> STANLEY

That's right!

> BLANCHE

I'm going to ask a favor of you in a moment.

> STANLEY

What could that be I wonder?

> BLANCHE

Some buttons in back! You may enter.

She opens the drapes and STANLEY *enters the kitchen.*

Their obligatory scene occurs later, as the climax of Scene Ten in the play, when Stella has gone to the hospital to have her baby, and Blanche and Stanley are alone. The oaf Mitch has withdrawn his proposal to marry her; she is desperate and defenseless. She has been drinking heavily and trying to reach a former patron when Stanley, in the script, emerges from the bathroom in "brilliant silk pajamas." Stanley advances rudely toward her, Blanche smashes a bottle on the table and threatens to "twist the broken end in your face!" The action continues in Shot 94 of the script; the smashing of the mirror —symbolical and cinematic—is added to the play:

94.

> STANLEY

I bet you would do that . . .

> BLANCHE

I would. I will if you . . .

> STANLEY

Oh! So you want some rough house . . . all right let's have some rough house . . .

They have advanced so that we are now able to see the action in a large mirror only.

Let's have some rough house . . . Tiger . . . Tiger . . .

(*He is feigning . . . suddenly he leaps in and seizes her arm—then he has her.*) Drop that bottle-top. Drop it!

He has managed to wrest the bottle top from her . . . and throws it . . . It smashes into the mirror and the glass shatters . . . And the tortured face of BLANCHE *which was big, with it.*

Tiger . . . We've had this date with each other from the beginning . . .

And on the broken glass we dissolve.

95. EUNICE [MAID] WINDOW—FROM THE OUTSIDE
White curtains of ragged lace. BLANCHE's *face peers out into the street. It seems haggard, drawn and almost as colourless as her hair. She is looking apprehensively.*

Blanche is removed to a mental institution. But Stella only reproaches herself as a sister; she does not suspect her husband as the final straw on the frail frame of Blanche. There is no obligatory scene between Stella and Stanley, who continues his poker games, impervious to the end. Whatever frustrations dangle in the final moments are swept aside in Blanche's tragic departure.

In the play *The Night of the Iguana* an alternative is posed to the Reverend Shannon by blowsy Maxine, a choice that makes us anticipate an obligatory scene. At the very beginning of Act I, a "panting, sweating and wild-eyed" Shannon arrives on the veranda of the Costa Verde Hotel, of which Mrs. Maxine Faulk is the proprietress. The busload of schoolteachers are waiting below on the road with Hank, their driver:

MAXINE
You're going to pieces, are you?

SHANNON
No! Gone! Gone! (*He rises and shouts down the hill again.*) Hank! Come up here! Come up here a minute! I wanna talk to you about this situation!—Incredible, fantastic . . . (*He drops back on the steps, his head falling into his hands.*)

MAXINE
They're not getting out of the bus. —Shannon . . . you're

not in a nervous condition to cope with this party, Shannon,
so let them go and you stay.

SHANNON

You know my situation: I lose this job, what's next? There's
nothing lower than Blake Tours, Maxine honey. . . .

So we are informed at the very beginning that Shannon has a
protector in Maxine and he can stay with her at the Costa Verde.
The only question thus poised is whether he will, not a very critical
question, since his failures as a guide and a sober citizen are rather
obvious. Nonetheless, he is offered a choice.

No such offer is made in the film script (1964), though Shannon
begs for assistance. Maxine gives him no alternative at the beginning.
Here is the similar scene on the veranda in Shot 131 (it is interesting
to note how many more shots Mr. Williams uses in adapting his work
for cameras twelve years after *Streetcar*) :

SHANNON

Maxine . . . you got to help me.

MAXINE

(*massages his neck*)

Baby . . . you're really gone.

SHANNON

(*looks at her piteously*)

I can't lose this party, Maxine. I'm on probation now. If
I lose this party, I'll be sacked for sure. I lose this job,
what's next? There's nothing lower than Blake Tours,
Maxine honey.

MAXINE

Okay. Okay. They can stay here . . . if it's all that important to you.

Maxine does not tell him to "let them go and you stay." With no
choice poised there is only a narrative interest in what will happen
next. No dramatic tension exists, nor does any accumulate. It is a
curiously unstructured motion picture.

In the concluding moments of the play the obligatory scene is most
indirect. Maxine simply announces to Shannon that she wishes he
would stay with her:

SHANNON

(*taking the rum-coco from her*)

You want a drinking companion?

> MAXINE
> No, I just want you to stay here, because I'm alone here now and I need somebody to help me manage the place.

HANNAH *strikes a match for a cigarette.*

> SHANNON
> *(looking toward her)*
> I want to remember that face. I won't see it again.

> MAXINE
> Let's go down to the beach.

> SHANNON
> I can make it down the hill, but not back up.

> MAXINE
> I'll get you back up the hill.

They have started off now, toward the path down through the rain forest.

> I've got five more years, maybe ten, to make this place attractive to the male clientele, the middle-aged ones at least. And you can take care of the women that are with them. That's what you can do, you know that, Shannon.

He chuckles happily. They are now on the path, MAXINE *half leading, half supporting him. Their voices fade. . . .*

In the concluding moments of the film script Maxine offers what appears to be a choice, but is not. She has a proposition for Hannah Jelkes, the spinster daughter of the poet Nonno, namely, that Shannon and Hannah operate the hotel and share the profits, fifty-fifty, with Maxine. She'll head north to El Paso, but there's "no deal unless Shannon stays on." This is a false choice, dramaturgically, since the offer is made to Hannah, not to Shannon, and Hannah promptly rejects it. Shannon doesn't vote, one way or another. "I'll drive you into town," he answers Hannah when she says "Goodbye" as her decision. There is no obligatory scene, nor is there a climax.

The script (and film) conclude rather lifelessly with Maxine in her room packing:

239. INTERIOR: MAXINE'S ROOM

She stands over the open suitcase, now nearly filled.

> SHANNON'S VOICE
> She's gone, Maxine.

MAXINE
(turns towards the door . . . after a pause)
You're not accepting my proposition?

240. EXTERIOR: DOOR

to her room.

SHANNON
She's not. I am. If you really need a man here.

241. INTERIOR: MAXINE'S ROOM

She rises slowly, goes to the door . . . opens it. She and SHANNON
stand for a moment regarding each other. Then:

MAXINE
It's not too hot yet, Shannon. Let's go down to the beach.
(She turns back into the room, starts peeling off clothes.)

SHANNON
I can make it down the hill, Maxine, but I don't know
about back up.

MAXINE
(laughs softly)
I'll get you back up the hill, baby . . . I'll get you back up.

FADE OUT

This structurally weak ending, faulted by the absence of an obligatory scene, has its basic weakness rooted in the ambiguity of the
characters. The Reverend T. Lawrence Shannon is not in focus as a
human being, and the imposition of a triangle at the end does not
sharpen him. Even if he were intended to be fuzzy, he is not a clearly
delineated fuzz.

In an entertainingly satirical film, Mike Nichols' *The Graduate,*
character credibility is challenged by the absence of a most obligatory
scene: the confrontation between Elaine (Katherine Ross) and
Mrs. Robinson (Anne Bancroft) when the conventional daughter
learns that the dropout boy she loves has been her mother's lover.
Unless we see Elaine's long-festering hatred of her spoiled mother,
how can we possibly comprehend her acceptance of Ben (Dustin
Hoffman) as her husband-to-be? Or is Oedipus guilt a middle-class
hangup to Nichols?

CHAPTER EIGHT ✗✗

Scene Climax

1. THE NEED FOR CLIMAXES

Our progression toward more specific considerations is not unlike a plane descending through clouds (*idea*) to behold the earth (*conflict*) where we recognize landscape and towns (*character* and *triangle*), and upon coming close we see streets (*sequences*), and then approaching the runway we clear the trees (*scenes*) and upon landing we can discern the leaves (*shots*). Such progression is actually a creative process, the way many writer-director creators work— even if they begin in reverse with a single shot in mind, and then take off and fly. What is important in all these elements is their relationships and interactions.

We have seen the inevitability of rhythm in the flow of conflict, its stresses and accelerations, or, as Dewey describes the process, "the alternation of compressions and releases." Without this alternation there would be monotony, no interactions.

Shouldn't sequence climaxes and obligatory scenes suffice? Though obligatory scenes may contain stress and acceleration, they are but one form of scene climax. More often, the effective scene climax is the one unforeseen or totally unexpected.

In other words, why need there be more alternation in cinema than in other forms of drama or exposition? A novel needn't have many complications to keep its plot rolling, and an average play has three acts on which curtains fall on moments of major intensity.

The answer lies, of course, in the nature of cinema's unique compression and intensification. Seeing a movie can be a highly concentrated experience. When the film is suspenseful and engrossing, a viewer's perception is accordingly intensified; he seems to see more and feel more than during moments of reading or hearing comparable stimuli in other languages.

This phenomenon of cinema is due, in large measure, to the number and degree of scene climaxes. Quite similar to jazz, the vitality of cinema springs from the constant variations of the stimuli. This means the plastic intensity of shots, as we shall see in Chapter Nine, and the minor but insistent importance of climax intensities in scenes.

2. MAKING THE SCENE

In adapting *The Night of the Iguana,* Tennessee Williams wrote an introductory sequence for the purpose of visualizing the inner conflict that torments the Reverend T. Lawrence Shannon. No such series of scenes were necessary within a theatre, wherein the intimacy of atmosphere, the fixed ratio of stage to audience, the major dependency on dialogue—all the characteristics of staged drama—served to portray Shannon's dilemma. In the theatre we are inclined to believe what we hear. In his shooting script, Williams aims to make us see as well as hear the torment.

Sequence A (in cinema, sequences are lettered; scenes are numbered) begins in a "green Virginia countryside" church with Shannon in the pulpit and ends in Mexico with Shannon a guide to a third-rate tour. He starts high, quoting Proverbs—"He that hath no rule over his own spirit is like a city that is broken down and without walls"—and ends low, his reputation ruined, his job threatened by Judith, who leads the touring schoolteachers—"Come on, girls. It's the end of the road for Dr. Shannon."

Five scenes structure this sequence:

The first, A1 (Sequence A, Scene 1), can be readily analyzed by applying the principle of the IAC (*idea, action, character*). The idea in A1 is Shannon's masochistic compulsion to destroy himself without provocation. The action that implements this idea is Shannon raving in his pulpit in a manner to demonstrate "appetites that I inherited," his defying the congregation to "sharpen your scalping knives," and his driving them out of the church. The character who dominates the scene is the monologist Shannon.

The scene climax of A1 is Shot 17, which follows Shannon's pursuit of his fleeing parishioners down the aisle, and he stands on the deserted steps of his church, the rain pouring down on him:

SHANNON

. . . You have turned your backs on the God of love and compassion and invented for yourselves this cruel senile delinquent who blames the world and brutally punishes all He created for His own faults . . .

CAMERA NOW STARTS TO PULL AWAY *and his lone figure grows smaller and smaller and his voice fainter and fainter as he continues shouting:*

Go . . . go home . . . close your doors . . . close your windows . . . close your hearts against the truth about God . . .

He is now a very small, white-clad figure, surrounded only by thunder and lightning as:

DISSOLVE TO:

Scene 2 of Sequence A is wholly expository, informing us that Shannon is a tourist guide for teachers from a "Baptist Female College in Blowing Rock, Texas." That is the idea in A2. It is implemented by a series of little actions describing the nature of the job—Shannon buys Enteroviaforma for a suffering "little wisp of a woman"; he is the sex target of Charlotte Goodall, "not quite nineteen"; and the object of close scrutiny by group leader Judith Fellows. Shannon still carries the ball at the climax, Shot 24:

24. INTERIOR: BUS

SHANNON *swings the door shut with the lever provided for that purpose, drops onto the seat adjacent to the door. He pulls a bandanna handkerchief from his pocket, mops his brow, as:*

JUDITH
(*from rear of bus*)
Are we downhearted?

She is answered by a resounding chorus of "noes" and, an instant later, the bus is loud with "Happy Days Are Here Again." SHANNON *shakes his head, dazedly, mutters to himself.*

SHANNON

Fantastic!

DISSOLVE TO:

Thus far we have had two narrative scenes without conflict; we have been informed, but we are hardly involved. A3 continues in this expository manner by introducing a potential drama: Shannon is warned to leave Charlotte alone. This is the idea of A3. The action is a cozy chat in the bus between Charlotte and Shannon, followed by Judith exchanging places with Charlotte to make her threatening speech. It is Judith's scene, since she has become an active antagonist, climaxing in Shot 45:

> JUDITH
> (*rises*)
> Just remember what I've said, Dr. Shannon. Don't make me take steps. (*turns, faces her friends*) Well, girls, what about another song?
>
> *She moves towards them, past camera.* SHANNON'*s face glistens with sweat as the words* "Three Little Fishes" *flood over him.*
>
> 46. EXTERIOR: THE RUTTED ROAD
>
> *The bus, going away from camera, rounds a bend to disappear.*
>
> DISSOLVE TO:

Shannon's only defense in A3 is verbal (expository information) ; with phony dignity he reminds Miss Fellowes that she is speaking to an ordained clergyman, and assures her that the room clerk in Tierra Caliente got "our keys mixed up. That's all." Through these first three scenes, Shannon's inner torment is still discussed verbally.

A4 is cinematic. A blown tire stops the bus, giving Shannon an opportunity to go for a swim in his shorts. He is followed by Charlotte "wearing the bikiniest of bikinis." Upon her request Shannon holds her hand in the water. We see them at last together. Judith tardily summons Charlotte to shore, and in intermingled anger and frustration slaps Charlotte's face. This is the action that climaxes A4 in Shot 22, and Shannon responds with guilt:

> SHANNON
> What did you think we were doing out there, Miss Fellowes? Spawning?
>
> JUDITH
> (*glares at him, sputters*)
> Beast . . . beast—beast . . . beast . . .

CAMERA MOVES IN *on* SHANNON *as her denunciation continues over him. He begins to tremble as panic seizes him.*

DISSOLVE TO:

Judith continues as the leading character of this subsequent scene, since her action dominates it; but it is Shannon's demonstration of his capacity for sensuality—swimming in the near nude, and hand-holding with a nineteen-year-old sexpot—that is the cinematic idea (capable of being photographed) behind the scenes, and clinched by Shannon's reaction of guilt. ·Here we ·may put a finger on a fundamental flaw in *The Night of the Iguana,* thanks to a contradiction exposed by the IAC. Why isn't Shannon the dominant character in A4? He would have been if his sensuality were more evident and defiant, and if his guilt were more cinematically treated and not merely an actor's reaction. Actually, the flaw in A4 provides the key to the faulty structure throughout, and explains why the plot fails to involve us deeply, why Shannon remains shadowy and verbal. Idea should be implemented by the character who dominates the action. How to make a weak character strong dramatically has been a challenge to creators through the ages. Goethe did it with Faust; Fellini does it with Guido in *8½.*

A5 is largely anticlimactical, continuing what occurred in A4. Shannon attempts a letter to Bishop Williamson, presumably a plea for reinstatement, but fails to dislodge Charlotte when she parks herself in his room at three in the morning. "Honey girl, do you know what you're doing?" There is no visual struggle over temptation, but a discussion of it. Passively and in masochistic fashion, Shannon unlocks the door to admit Judith when she demands admittance. The IAC is the same as in A4. Again Judith has the climactic and concluding speech at the end of the scene. It is unfortunate that Judith makes the final speech in every scene with Shannon—four out of the five in the sequence—at the expense of Shannon, weakening his structural characterization. The climax of A5 provides the climax of Sequence A:

104. SHANNON *unlocks the door, pulls it open.* JUDITH *almost falls into the room.*

105. THE BALCONY: OUTSIDE

CAMERA IS SHOOTING PAST *the crowd outside the door.* SHANNON *faces* JUDITH.

JUDITH
(*spitting it out*)

You're through, Shannon. I'll see to that. When I finish, there won't be any place for you to hide.

CHARLOTTE

Why can't you mind your own business? (*and she stalks out*)

SHANNON

It's all right, Miss Fellowes. Virtue is triumphant. *Yours,* of course.

JUDITH
(*grimly*)

Wait . . . just . . . you . . . wait! (*She turns, starts out.*) Come on, girls. It's the end of the road . . . for *Dr.* Shannon!

She strides through them, after CHARLOTTE. *They turn and struggle after her.* SHANNON *is left alone in the open doorway. He is very, very close to the breaking point. He moves forward to the balcony railing, raises his head to stare up at the heavens. A violent trembling wracks his frame.*

DISSOLVE TO:

What is evident from these scene climaxes is the importance of structuring, at the more intimate depths, the clarity of idea, the impact of action, and the predominance of character. At the scene level, if there be no control of the dynamic forces at work, all fails: intent and execution.

This need for climaxes, fulfilled in making scenes parts of an accelerating whole, can be observed in studying the strengths and weaknesses in *Doctor Zhivago* (1965), a film curiously lacking in structure. A thematic, lyrical notebook, hardly a novel, has served as the basis for a film that is narrative in its theme and lyrical in its cinema, but whose characters are not dramatically delineated. Our eye is intrigued, but our emotions are not engaged. The first five minutes are meaningless; we are not involved. A Soviet general (Alec Guinness) interrogates a female laborer (Rita Tushingham) at a hydroelectric dam; he is searching for the lost child of his half-brother, Yuri Zhivago (Omar Sharif). Is hers the face that launches *Zhivago* as a film?

The thematic core of the film, and of the novel, is a humanistic identity with all suffering persons—the eternal theme of the Greeks—whether they be Red or White soldiers. The peasants of a village are burned out because of suspicions that they sold horses to the Whites. The pink-cheeked youths of St. Michel's Military Academy are machine-gunned by the Reds, and we suffer their needless deaths. Zhivago suffers, in close-ups, the horrible spectacle of what man does to man. On the other hand, he is capable of deserting, for long stretches, his wife, Tonya (Geraldine Chaplin), and his child, and does so without qualms. What is Tonya's reaction? We never see. What makes the marriage so intolerable when it appears so amiable? If Lara (Julie Christie) is called "a slut" at seventeen by her mother's lover Komarovsky (Rod Steiger) who has seduced her, why don't we see her in sluttish ways? Why is she lovely and unsluttish in her affair with Zhivago?

The film lacks character focus; there is hardly a story. Zhivago's torment over his principles rises only on three isolated occasions: when he confronts Comrade Yelkin who has appropriated his foster-parent's home; when he confronts General Strelnikov (Tom Courtenay) who could execute him; and when he confronts Razin, the political commissar of the forest Partisans. The absence of scene climaxes and of an obligatory scene leaves a void, which is only partially filled by an extraordinary production.

At this stage it might be rewarding to do a scene analysis of a classic formula executed in a commercial pattern, the TV adaptation of *Kitty Foyle*. The nine sequences of the shooting script, done by Dalton Trumbo, were confined to three sequences by Whitfield Cook in the video version.

Sequence A, Scene I, establishes the frame, or "hook," that is designed to capture the viewer so that he won't reach for the switching dial. The idea: inside the white-collar girl. The action: secretarial activity. The character: Kitty. Here is Al:

FADE IN: VERY CLOSE SHOT—KITTY FOYLE

She is staring wistfully past the camera into space. Over shot we hear her thoughts.

KITTY'S VOICE

Sometimes I get mixed up thinking about Wyn. I don't always remember just what came before that. But it doesn't matter . . . Dearest, let me think and just see how it feels. My blessed. My boy . . .

CAMERA PULLS BACK, *to show* KITTY *sitting at desk in her smart little New York office. A* STENOGRAPHER *comes in briskly, points to some letters, asks a question which we don't hear.* KITTY *nods. Scribbles on pad.* STENOGRAPHER *goes out.* KITTY *answers phone. We don't hear her speak, but over shot, we hear her voice continuing:*

> Even a busy white collar girl can't keep from thinking of the things closest to her heart. There has always been so much that was good and wonderful with Wyn. No matter how much it hurts, I don't ever want to forget it, darling, not ever—My crazy boy—I always think of him as almost a baby, even if he was seven years older than me when we met. That happened right in our old backyard in Philadelphia . . . It's funny when you think of it . . .
>
> DISSOLVE TO:

The use of voice-off-shot (O.S.) is a carryover from radio writing into television, though it is employed effectively on occasion in cinema, such as the camera on Eliza's face in *Pygmalion* while Higgins talks. It permits narrative bridges between dramatic moments, shortens time, and on the whole explains rather than emotes meaning—even in *Hiroshima Mon Amour*. The viewer is told; he need not search for motivation.

Kitty's father, Pop, is the straight man, in vaudeville usage, who counterpoints Wyn, the wealthy lover. Here is the climax of A2:

> POP
>
> Je*h*osophat, Kitty! —Thinking he was the man to fix the roof! Don't you ever read your Ledger? Strafford, Wynnewood and Company, the oldest private bank in Philly. Darby Mill, that's the name of their country place; there's an old sawmill on the creek out there where they cut up the logs for Washington at Valley Forge. Honey, those folks are so pedigree they'd be ashamed to press their pants. And you thought Wyn was—

CAMERA HAS PULLED BACK SLOWLY *to include* KITTY *standing dreamily by the rose vine.*

> KITTY
>
> Well, don't get your Irish up.

> POP
>
> And you'll do that typin' job for him, see?

> KITTY

I will if I feel like it.

> POP

That's what I mean. You will if you feel like it.

> KITTY
> (*sharply*)

Would I be your daughter if I didn't have a will of my own!

> POP
> (*their nonsense talk*)

Be's you got bugs?

> KITTY

Sure I are.

> POP

Everybody do.

They both relax and grin at each other.

I'm sure glad you're only a quarter Irish. That's like the mixture in a good highball. Half and half is too strong.

CAMERA *moves up on* KITTY's *face.*

> KITTY'S VOICE
> (*off shot*)

I'm grateful for that twenty-five percent of Irish in me. It gives me a private alibi for all sorts of grief and comedy . . . And there was plenty of grief and comedy with Wyn . . .

> DISSOLVE TO:

The structure of these scenes is rather simplified, emphasis being placed on the existence of the triangle rather than on character complications. An oversimplification of the triangle emasculates any story. This is the basic tragedy in TV dramatic writing: the pressures of time, the limitations of space. Often one looks forward perversely to an exciting commercial. As an indication of the erroneous belief that cinematic elements are the sole province of the director and the scene designer, we should note the insistence on dialogue as the earthbound rails to carry the freight that should fly.

Here are Wyn and Kitty in their first intimate rapport in A3; Wyn confesses his ambition to launch a magazine, a Philadelphia version of *The New Yorker:*

WYN

This is the first thing that I've thought up myself. It's important to me.

KITTY

But what about your banking business?

WYN

(*laughing*)

My banking business? All I do down at the bank is what some higher-up tells me to do. I'm pretty small potatoes down there. You know, some day I'm going to do something nobody ever told me to do. (*looking at* KITTY) What's **more**, I'm going to do it now.

He puts his arm around KITTY *and kisses her. She looks adoringly into his eyes.*

(*tenderly*) Surprised?

KITTY *shakes her head.* WYN *kisses her again.*

KITTY

Oh, Wyn—

WYN

I had all this planned, but I got so darned interested **in** talking to you, I almost forgot it. Almost, not quite.

KITTY

(*softly, happily*)

It seems so—so natural.

WYN

I hope everything that happens to us will always seem natural— (*His cheek against her hair*)

KITTY

"Us"—Isn't it funny and—nice to be able to say "us"—

That is their narrative, a continuation of their relationship as editor and secretary, as lover and mistress. There is no progression in terms of character or plot. The scene climaxes are static; the IAC is not dynamic.

A note of disinterest is introduced as the climax of A4:

WYN

Today we're in business. We start opening our oyster. I

hope it doesn't give us ptomaine. (*he holds up crossed fingers*)

KITTY

Maybe we'll find a pearl in it.

WYN
(softly)

I've already found one.

DISSOLVE TO:

VERY CLOSE SHOT—WOMAN'S HANDS TYPING VERY RAPIDLY

KITTY'S VOICE
(off shot)

After that first oyster-opening kiss, he scarcely looked at me, we got so busy . . .

DISSOLVE TO:

Their affair continues with an all-night session in the Poconos. Kitty, being a bit realistic, sees no marriage looming. When the magazine fails she thinks of a job in New York, selling beauty products. For the first time a note of conflict is introduced that serves as the TV climax of A5, and Sequence A:

KITTY'S VOICE

Looking back on it, it seems sad as a fairy tale. They're pretty sad if you read them again after you're grown up . . . But I can never forget Pocono, and I never want to . . .

WYN *gets up slowly, as* KITTY'*s voice continues, pokes at the fire, turns slowly, holds out his arms to* KITTY. *She rises, goes to him. Easily, dreamily, they start dancing to the soft radio music.*

KITTY'S VOICE
(over preceding)

Wyn didn't know anything about the small makeshifts and anxieties of life, but it was his love that taught me everything. Maybe not so much his love of me, but the love I gave him . . . Oh, Wyn, it was *good*. Would there be any way to tell other people to believe in the goodness of it? No matter how its hurts? —Partly I thought you were a god and partly I was just taking care of you. But I knew I could never be ashamed or humiliated or unhappy again. I knew what life was for . . .

CAMERA HAS BEEN MOVING UP ON THEM *as they dance. It moves in* VERY CLOSE *on* KITTY's *ecstatic face against* WYN's *chest.*

FADE OUT

END OF ACT ONE

The above climaxes of scenes have not moved us along from one complication to another. There is so little character conflict that the sequence is basically narrative, not even dramatic. Not until the climax of Sequence B, when Kitty defies Wyn and his Philadelphia Main Line family, do we have tension. Mere actions, movements of cowboys and Indians with traveling shots galore, are no substitutes for involvement. Thus gunfire and "big scenes" can bore us in TV dramas. The highest rating for the sponsor means the lowest denominator for entertainment.

What sort of cinematic scene structuring is possible when the dramatic is well defined? In Sequence D of Olivier's *Hamlet,* the shortest and most tightly knit of the five sequences, the Danish Prince declares his will to act—he will fight Laertes to prove he loved Ophelia. This scene, D4, will be the climax of Sequence D.

How do we arrive there? By starting off in the opposite direction in true dramatic logic. Claudius sends Hamlet packing for England, using the murder of Polonius as the reason—"This deed must send thee hence with fiery quickness. . . ." Hamlet rather passively complies, and the scene reaches its climax with the camera on King Claudius, emphasizing him as a visual counterpoint to the central character. Here is that moment in D1:

272. MEDIUM CLOSE SHOT—HAMLET

HAMLET
. . . my mother. Come! . . . For England.

HAMLET *goes out of picture and* CAMERA TRACKS BACK *to include the* KING, *who, during his dialogue walks across to a window, and leans against the wall.*

KING
Follow him, tempt him with speed aboard,
Delay it not; I'll have him hence tonight; Away!
For everything is seal'd and done,
That else leans on the affair;
Pray you make haste.
And, England, if my love thou holdst at aught—

Thou mayst not coldly treat
Our sovereign order, which imports at full the present
    death of Hamlet.
Do it, England,
For like the fever in my blood he rages,
And thou must cure me.
Till I know 'tis done,
How'er my haps, my joys, were ne'er begun.

CAMERA TRACKS BACK *through the window away from the* KING *and* PANS *up the Castle Wall.*

FADE OUT

In D2 the madness of Ophelia is the IAC, and serves as the *modus operandi* for reaching the sequence climax. In the midst of her mad speech, lamenting over her father "in the cold ground," she cries out: "My brother shall know of it! . . . Come, my coach . . . Sweet ladies, good night." This speech is delivered with CAMERA PANNING with Ophelia. She now goes out of picture, and we hear her final "Good night."

In D3, Hamlet's presence is felt via his voice in a letter Horatio reads, brought by a pirate captain. In a Medium Long Shot (M.L.S.) the pirates and sailors are shown fighting; the action between the ships is in miniature. These shots are in flashbacks while we listen to Hamlet's voice narrate the encounter. With the past finished, the flashback ends, and Hamlet bids Horatio to come to him with "as much speed as thou would'st fly death." Though he is not seen, the IAC is all Hamlet.

The graveyard scene with Laertes and Hamlet fighting in the grave is the climax of D4 and of the sequence. It is the first face-to-face confrontation in the drama, and a foreshadowing preparation for the face-to-face confrontation with Claudius to end the play.

In these four scenes we have witnessed a rather simple "alternation of compressions and releases."

F. Scott Fitzgerald wrote a *Saturday Evening Post* story (1931), keenly bitter with the sentiment of disillusionment, which he turned into a screenplay, called *Cosmopolitan,* as a vehicle for Shirley Temple. In his Author's Note for the Second Draft Revised, August 13, 1940, he asked that no one read a pat moral "about the life of the Wall Street rich of a decade ago. It had better follow the example of

'Hamlet,' which has had a hundred morals read into it, all of them different—let it stand on its own bottom."

A comparison of the scene climaxes in *Babylon Revisited*, a brilliant short-story unit, with those of *Cosmopolitan*, a Hollywood composite, demonstrates what different bottoms do to scenic superstructure.

There are four scene climaxes to *Babylon Revisited:*

1. Charlie Wales, currently a successful businessman in Prague after a Parisian period, visits the Men's Bar at the Ritz, deserted during the Depression, a nostalgic revisit that no longer has allure. Charlie is in Paris with the hope of regaining custody of his small daughter Honoria, now living with his dead wife's sister, Marion Peters. Charlie has guilts about the death of his wife, Helen, during a drunken period. Rehabilitated, he must prove his new sobriety to Marion. The love between father and daughter gives the scene its poignancy:

. . . From behind the maid who opened the door darted a lovely little girl of nine who shrieked "Daddy!" and flew up, struggling like a fish, into his arms. She pulled his head around by one ear and set her cheek against his.

"My old pie," he said.

"Oh, daddy, daddy, daddy, daddy, dads, dads, dads!"

Marion's cold dislike tests Charlie's control; he is determined to regain his daughter. Though he tours the old haunts, he goes to bed early and sober.

2. The scene climax of the second part extends the positive hope. Having lunch with her father, Honoria asks suddenly, "Why don't I live with you?" Ghosts from the past threaten in the shape of Lorraine Quarrles, on whom Charlie once had a passing fancy, and a college friend, Duncan Schaeffer, but Charlie avoids giving his address. He's going straight. "Daddy, I want to come and live with you," Honoria begs. ". . . he had wanted it to come like this."

Since Marion blames her sister's death on Charlie, we suspect the old playmates will ruin Charlie's chance at the most inopportune moment. The scene ends on his happiness over Honoria's love for him.

3. Marion, being Honoria's legal guardian, must agree to Charlie's request, so he suffers her bitter diatribe, motivated also by jealousy over her sister's wealthy marriage to Charlie. By refusing to be provoked—Helen's death is "something you'll have to spare with your own conscience," Marion cries out—Charlie wins.

4. Marion agrees Honoria can accompany her father back to Prague, but wishes to retain legal guardianship "a while longer." Charlie shops for a governess. Lincoln Peters says at lunch that "the big party's over now." He knows that it's his wife who's still envious. The details are to be settled at six that evening, "before Marion's too tired."

Charlie receives a letter from Lorraine, reminding him of their past escapades, and asking for a date "about five in the sweatshop at the Ritz." The Ritz barman had not given away Charlie's address, as instructed, but had forwarded the *pneumatique*. Charlie is awed by his former romps with Lorraine, who now "seemed trite, blurred, worn away." At five he buys gifts for all the Peterses. Marion has accepted the inevitable, but she can't get Honoria ready before Saturday.

Unexpectedly, Lorraine and Duncan Schaeffer arrive "roaring with laughter." Now Charlie makes two fatal mistakes. He presents them to Marion and Lincoln, and waits for them to explain themselves. The drunken couple have come to invite Charlie out to dinner. Here Charlie makes his third error. "Tell me where you'll be and I'll phone you in half an hour." Lorraine responds unpleasantly, reminding him when he once hammered on her door at 4:00 A.M. and she "was enough of a good sport" to give him a drink. After they have departed, Charlie bursts out—"What an absolute outrage!" He can't even sip his solitary drink. "People I haven't seen in two years having the colossal nerve—"

But it is too late. Marion doesn't believe him; he has lost. His departure is touching. Honoria hugs him:

"Good night, sweetheart," he said vaguely, and then trying to make his voice more tender, trying to conciliate something, "Good night, dear children."

The three positive scene climaxes have been a preparatory counterpoint for this negative conclusion.

5. The final scene is anticlimatic recrimination. Memories of the past—"The men who locked their wives out in the snow, because the snow of twenty-nine wasn't real snow." On the phone Lincoln tells him shortly: "Marion's sick . . . we'll have to let it slide for six months." Charlie tells himself that "they couldn't make him pay forever. . . . Helen wouldn't have wanted him to be so alone."

More than any other factor, the character of Charlie, his former weakness and his present strength, is the key to the mounting tension in *Babylon Revisited*. We want him to win.

By shifting to Honoria, called Victoria in the shooting-script version, Fitzgerald abandons the core of the tension in favor of a little girl's search for her father. The shift is disastrous. Wanting her to win becomes a structural movement, not a character action in search of love. Fitzgerald must have sensed the danger inherent in his shift, for in his Author's Note he implores "whoever deals with this script . . . to remember that it is a dramatic piece—not a homey family story. Above all things, Victoria is a child—not Daddy's little helper who knows all the answers."

Here in brief are the five sequence climaxes of *Cosmopolitan,* of which only two, in part, parallel *Babylon Revisited.* It is a wholly different story.

Sequence A: Paris, October, 1929. Victoria Wales runs away from home, aiming to reach Hautemont, Switzerland. We know nothing of her motivation, except at the conclusion, in the train compartment, she thinks aloud: "Daddy and Mummy and I—" She is being followed by a sinister "YOUTH IN THE CLOSE-FITTING TOPCOAT."

Sequence B: New York City. Charles Wales is retiring from the stock market and taking Victoria and his wife (never seen) to Europe. Wall Street boom fever has infected everybody (also noted in Paris, Sequence A). Wales' partner, Schuyler, has insured Wales' life for a cool million, and is ordered by Wales to transfer $350,000 from Wales' personal account into Liberty Bonds. Old Van Greff, worth half a billion, admires Charles as a potential partner. Charles becomes absorbed in playing the market to rescue an old friend— "They're pounding Radio! Poor old Bill Bonniman!" He neglects his wife, stays cooped in the ship's brokerage office, and finally goes looking for her. The following is a genuine cinematic moment in the script:

84. A MONTAGE EFFECT—CHARLES WALES' FACE

very distraught, with other faces around him—all speaking to him.

VOICES

Not here, Mr. Wales.
Not there, Mr. Wales.
Not in her room.
Not in the bar, Mr. Wales.
Not in there, Mr. Wales.

Throughout this, the ship's dance orchestra is playing tunes of 1929 in a nervous rhythm.

85. A DARK SKY FILLED WITH SEAGULLS

The sudden sound of a wild shriek—which breaks down after a moment, into the cry of the gulls as they swoop in a great flock down toward the water. Through their cries we hear the ship's bell signalling for the engines to stop.

86. MEDIUM SHOT—STERN OF THE SHIP

Ship receding from the camera as the awful sounds gradually die out.

FADE OUT

At Le Havre, Marion, "the personification of outrage and hatred," blames Charlie for her sister's suicide, and he, in a strange response, asks her to take care of Victoria. Marion's husband is a Frenchman impressed by rich Americans.

Sequence C: Schuyler calls on Marion and Petrie to tell them Charles is a hopeless drunk and abdicates business matters to him— "We could probably arrange a guardianship." At the Ritz, in a luxurious suite, Charlie is under the care of a sinister Dr. Franciscus, and, inexplicably, of a decent American, Julia Burns, "a nurse, but not in white." Schuyler brings Victoria to the hotel to see Charles in his condition, a presumption that angers Wales. Later, while half drugged, he signs the guardianship papers.

Sequence D: Stocks crash. Schuyler gets control of Victoria's money, a trust from her father, by conning Petrie into signing. Julie pulls Wales through the vapors of alcohol. Victoria calls on her father, a meeting that parallels Scene 1 of the original:

175. SALON: BY THE WINDOW—CLOSE SHOT CHARLES WALES IN AN ARM-CHAIR

His expression is rigid, tense. He doesn't know whether once again the contours of VICTORIA's *face will remind him of his dead wife. He makes an impatient gesture, then steels himself as he hears:*

VICTORIA'S VOICE
(*over shot*)

Daddy!

WALES *turns and faces them with a slow, difficult smile.*

176. ANOTHER ANGLE

VICTORIA
(*running toward him*)
Oh Daddy, Daddy, Daddy, Daddy, Dads, Dads, Dads!

She jumps up into his arms, struggling like a fish and pulls his head around by one ear and sets his cheek against hers.

                    WALES
Why you little fella, you.

They have ices in Rumplemayer's Tea Shop. "An orchestra would be playing *Blue Heaven* or *Among My Souvenirs*." This scene parallels Scene 2 of *Babylon Revisited,* except for an added poignancy, since they are alone in the world, surrounded by a vulturous partner, a vindictive aunt, a quack doctor, and a stupid uncle—only Julie is their friend. The scene is enlarged:

                    WALES
            (*trying to draw her out about her life*)
And Aunt Marion and Uncle Pierre? Which do you like best?

                    VICTORIA
                 (*thinking*)
Oh, Uncle Pierre, I guess. (*Pause.*) She gets so excited. (*as if she had often thought of this*) Why don't I live with you? Because Mother's dead?

Pause.

                    WALES
But you're learning French. (*Pause.*) And it would have been hard for me to take care of you.

                    VICTORIA
But I don't need taking care of, anymore than you do.

Pause.

                    WALES
                 (*slowly*)
Darling, do you ever think of your mother?

                    VICTORIA
Yes, sometimes.

                    WALES
I don't want you to ever forget her. Have you got a picture of her?

                    VICTORIA
Aunt Marion has.

> WALES

She loved you very much.

> VICTORIA

I loved her too. (*Pause.*) Daddy, I want to come and live with you.

Sudden joy comes into WALES' *face, but he controls it.*

> WALES

Aren't you happy?

> VICTORIA

Yes, but I like you better than anybody—and you like me better than anybody, don't you—now that Mother's dead?

> WALES
> (*this is a little difficult*)

Of course. Of course, I do. But you won't always like me best, honey. You'll grow up and meet somebody your own age and go marry him, and forget you ever had a father.

> VICTORIA
> (*tranquilly*)

Yes, that's true.

He looks at her as she glances around the room. He has found her at last. It is apparent that he wants her with him now.

> DISSOLVE TO:

This moment was the scene climax of the original; in the shooting script the sequence continues. Wales learns Schuyler is a crook, and remarks ironically—since Schuyler reminds him of the million-dollar insurance—"I suppose my duty is to jump out the window." Wales wants to take Victoria with him to America, but Marion threatens him with imprisonment for kidnapping, should he try. Now Wales dares not leave Europe; he will lose Victoria. His best chance to regain his fortune and good name is old Van Greff in Switzerland.

Sequence E: Hautemont, Switzerland. Wales makes an appointment to dine with Van Greff. Victoria takes "the Funicular (mountain railway)," and thus we resume the time sequence of the story begun in the introductory scenes. She is being followed by "the YOUTH IN THE CLOSE-FITTING TOPCOAT in a back seat of the Funicular." Victoria dresses in "a white long formal organdy," and sits where she can observe her father dine with Van Greff—Wales is touched to see her so grown-up. While Wales sits at Van Greff's table, the secretary of the multimillionaire arrives, grief-stricken—"Mr. Van Greff left us very suddenly fifteen minutes ago." There goes Wales' chance to recoup his fortune; but not wishing "to let his troubles touch her tonight," he dances with Victoria. The tune, which he ordered, is "I'm Dancing with Tears in My Eyes"—an unfortunate, untypical Fitzgerald touch.

Here, at this moment, Fitzgerald has chosen to introduce the couple from the jazzy past, Lorraine and Duncan, now called Cornelia and Tom. Cornelia throws her arms around Wales—"You've owed me a dance for ten years." He politely refuses, and "dances off with Victoria, CAMERA REMAINING on Tom and Cornelia, who feel snubbed." There are no consequences—the opposite reaction of the original. Victoria discloses that Schuyler got Uncle Pierre to sign a paper he didn't want Aunt Marion to see, and now Wales has Schuyler and Pierre in his pocket for conspiracy. He so informs Marion by phone, and hence regains custody of Victoria, though he is penniless.

Their happy ending is to be postponed. The YOUTH is waiting with a gun in Wales' room, and aims to force him out the window— presumably under Schuyler's orders—a million-dollar corpse. "Suddenly one foot from the gunman's ear, the telephone shrills. Involuntarily he starts and takes his eyes off Wales for half a moment. In that split second, Wales strikes, knocking him against the corner of a wardrobe. The YOUTH is out. . . ." Victoria is on the phone to say she'd like to keep the dress "to show it to Miss Burns. But I don't want to be extravagant, now we're out of Wall Street." Charlie's cup overfloweth as "the orchestra has begun to play the tune he and Victoria danced to."

WALES

Ah, there's a lot to live for.

The CAMERA MOVES *to a* CLOSE SHOT *of him.*

297. CLOSE SHOT: VICTORIA—ASLEEP

By the single light still lit in her bedroom, we see that her expression is akin to his, as if in agreement with his sentiment. Sleep has overtaken her just before she managed to really get into bed. Still in her dressing gown, with one slipper off and one on, she lies across the bed with her new white dress clasped in her arms.

FADE OUT

Aside from the sentimentality, done so deliberately by an ill author that it appears an act of Hollywood desperation, *Cosmopolitan* is an interesting screenplay because of its excessive scene climaxes. The slight drama is overburdened with narrative ideas not necessary for the advancement of the conflict. It is as though Fitzgerald, who died shortly after completing this second draft, were issuing his final testament. Amazingly, there are nine ideas in the space of twenty-two shots on eleven pages. Without commenting on content, this fact alone explains the unfortunate farcical pace of the conclusion, and the frenetic state of the exhausted author.

The nine are: (1) Van Greff is dead (narratively presented) ; (2) Wales loves his daughter (dramatically projected) ; (3) his jazzy past is politely but firmly rejected (dramatic) ; (4) he learns Schuyler conspired to steal Victoria's money (narrative) ; (5) Wales tells Marion he's assuming custody of Victoria (narrative) ; (6) Wales faces death and captures killer (dramatic) ; (7) Victoria loves Miss Burns (narrative) ; (8) Wales is proud to have "put a lot into a child . . . [and] there's a lot to live for" (narrative) ; (9) Victoria agrees as she falls asleep. Three-quarters of these are narrative ideas, not dramatized, and none are cinematic.

An excess of scene climaxes can lessen the impact of plot and character. "It is quality rather than quantity that matters," said Seneca in his *Epistles,* all of twenty centuries ago.

An opposite extreme is an insufficiency of scene climaxes, so that conflict is not mounted on successively higher plateaus. Tension can hardly accelerate if the rhythmic flow of the plot lacks those bursts of compression and release that stimulate, each time, a greater expectancy. More than any other factor, a shortage of scene climaxes can keep a conflict from achieving its full potential. *Lord of the Flies* (R 1963) provides an intriguing example, since other elements— amateur actors and editing tempo and an imbalance of sound—also contributed to a lessening of impact in this otherwise unusual film. None of these three factors, however, were as detrimental as the shortage of scene climaxes.

Contrary to popular myth, there is a shooting script of *Lord of the Flies.* Improvisation of some acting on a natural location, the island of Vieques off the east coast of Puerto Rico, and an excessive shooting of 415,000 feet—more than four times the usual amount—contributed to the myth. "Peter Brook wrote a screenplay directly from the novel and it became virtually interchangeable with the book," wrote the film's producer, Lewis Allen. What this means is that the motion picture has a narrative scene structure and is excessively dependent on dialogue for making points that, at least, should be dramatized and, at best and ideally, should be cinematic. Dialogue, when it does not dilute the visual flow, can be cinematic.

In the William Golding novel (1955) the master idea has been described by John Peter in the *Kenyon Review:* "Evil is inherent in the human mind itself, whatever innocence may cloak it. . . . This is Golding's theme, and it takes on a frightful force by being presented in juvenile terms. . . ."

A group of British schoolboys, ages six to thirteen, are evacuated from London at the outbreak of atomic war; their plane is shot down, and 34 of them, without grownups, are the sole survivors on a desert isle. To depict their gradual transition from well-mannered students to painted savages—the triumph of instinct over intellect—necessitates the artichoke treatment, the pealing off of one leaf at a time. This means carefully constructed scene climaxes. In the novel Golding gives us these little revelations, a steady unveilment as we move closer and more quickly toward the heart of the matter. The three main characters are Ralph, the initial leader representing a civilized assembly (Parliament, Congress, the UN) ; Jack, who starts as head of the choir that sings ironically *Kyrie Eleison* and becomes the leader of the anarchistic hunters; and Piggy, the reasoning intellectual whose spectacles, ridiculed and then shattered, symbolize the decline of reason.

The structure of the first two chapters launches the inner conflicts. Jack, being more naturally aggressive, is the protagonist. He carries a knife and attempts to kill a piglet, caught in creepers, but is unaccustomed to violence, and hesitates—"The pause was only long enough for them to understand what an enormity the downward stroke would be." The piglet escapes. "They were left looking at each other and the place of terror. Jack's face was white under the freckles." After laughing ashamedly, Jack explains—"I was just waiting for a moment to decide where to stab him." The others understood, but Jack feels challenged: "He snatched his knife out of the sheath and slammed it into a tree trunk. Next time there would be no mercy. He looked round fiercely, daring them to contradict." This is the climax of Chapter One.

In the shooting script, which is exceptionally extensive—listing 795 shots in 134 pages—the writer-director, Peter Brook, does not indicate the dramatic and cinematic importance of the scene, the first to depict the master idea. Here is the equivalent passage in the screenplay:

118. MEDIUM SHOT—PIGLET TEARS LOOSE

119. MEDIUM SHOT—THE THREE LOOK AT ONE ANOTHER

JACK *brings his arm down. All three laugh ashamedly.*

120/121. MEDIUM SHOT—THEY WALK AWAY

> JACK
>
> I was choosing a place. I was just waiting for a moment to decide where to stab him.

> RALPH
>
> You should stick a pig. They always talk about sticking a pig.

JACK *walks ahead, so they cannot see his face.*

> JACK
>
> I was choosing a place. Next time. . . .

He snatches knife from sheath and slams it into tree trunk. Then he looks around at them defiantly.

The above four shots, more blueprint than screenplay, depend obviously on acting quality and editing rhythm for their emphasis. A perfunctory execution will not indicate the essentiality of the scene.

Though improvisation and editing will compose the scene, what is manifestly clear is the necessity for emphasizing, first on paper, the continuity of theme. When a writer-director takes his eye off that spherical target, he is in danger of striking out. Instead of concluding on Jack, as does Golding in the novel (Chapter One), Brook ends Sequence A with a secondary scene, the disappearance of the Little One with the Birthmark. Thus the central line wanders astray, and the basic idea goes out of focus:

175. MEDIUM SHOT—PIGGY

> PIGGY
>
> Where is he now? I tell you I don't see him.

176. MEDIUM SHOT—*The boys look at each other, fearful.*

> PIGGY
>
> Where is he now?

> RALPH
>
> Perhaps he went back to . . .

177/179. MEDIUM SHOT

The pall drifts into the dusk. The rumbling continues (fire).

FADE OUT

Another factor mitigating cinematic effectiveness is an imbalance of dialogue, a tendency to depend on spoken words to carry the meaning of the scene.

The above scene (Shots 175–179) concludes Chapter Two in the novel. Here, briefly noted, are the points of emphasis that Golding makes in that chapter:

1. Jack slammed his knife into a trunk and looked round challengingly. Novel: P. 43; script: Shot 121.

2. Jack becomes excited over the prospect of punishing anyone breaking the rules. Novel: P. 44; script: Shot 123.

3. A small boy imagines he has seen "a beastie, a snake-thing." Novel: P. 47; script: Shot 137.

4. Jack leads the crowd to make a fire; the conch is forgotten. Novel: P. 49; script: Shot 146.

5. Jack violently snatches the glasses off Piggy, who shrieks in terror. Novel: Pp. 52–3; script: Shots 152–154.

6. Jack ignores the conch, symbol of free speech, and fiercely orders Piggy, "You shut up!" Novel: Pp. 54–55; script: omitted.

7. Piggy—"daring, indignant"—protests being the only one ordered to be silent. Novel: P. 56; script: Shot 173, minus reaction.

8. Piggy explodes in a tirade against anarchy, and at first they pay attention to his violence. Novel: P. 58; script: combined in Shot 173, minus reaction.

9. The small boys scream, imagining creepers illuminated by flames are snakes. The six-year-old with the birthmark is missing. Novel: P. 60; script: Shots 175–179.

What weakens the transition of the above points from novel to script is the dependency on statement, mainly via dialogue. Golding gives us clues to reactions so that we picture in our mind the total scene. Here the direction of actors, the control of rhythmic editing need to supply on film what the flow of words provide in reading.

Subsequent scenes in both script and on film demonstrate a similar lack of an accelerating emphasis on the transition from innocence to evil. The physical events are well photographed. However, like noisy children, empathy should be seen and not heard.

The slack structure of *Lord of the Flies* raises legitimately the question of the relationship, if any, between scene climaxes and the form of the writing. That is, does the verbal shape of the script—the manner and style of the writing—have anything to do with the structural design of the film, such as a scene climax? Theoretically, the answer should be in the negative. No matter in what literary form the words are arranged, the impact in terms of characters-in-conflict needs to be visualized so that upon reading—with moderate imagination—ordered images should leap into the mind's eye.

Nevertheless, there has been a literary temptation to compose scripts to be read, not seen. Like closet drama, closet cinema is the product of verbal-minded writers. An early example, interesting to note in juxtaposition to *Lord of the Flies,* is *Things to Come* (1936) by H. G. Wells. In 1935 the Cresset Press (London) published in book form what its author described as "A Film Story," based on his history of the future, *The Shape of Things to Come.* In his note to the reader, Wells, an impatient propagandist for the betterment of mankind, confesses he tried two screen treatments before deciding to "discard the elaborate detailed technical scenario altogether. . . ." It is his belief that "a competent director" can "produce directly from the descriptive treatment here given. . . ." The belief was personal and disingenuous, since he was advised by three highly competent film creators, Alexander Korda, Lajos Biro, and Cameron Menzies.

For our interest, the question is whether the following scene climax, basic to the idea that children's play is naturally violent, can be visualized without shots indicated but implied. How filmic is this film story? The setting is a children's party at Christmas. The adults, Passworthy and Cabal—heavy-handed names—disagree over the threat of war: "this little upset across the water. . . ." Their children, Horrie and Timothy—forerunners of Jack and Piggy—enact their disagreement. The counterpoint between the grown-ups and the boys is clear:

Passworthy: "Hullo Cabal! Christmas again!" (Sings.) "While shepherds watched their flocks by night, All seated on the ground. . . ."
Cabal nods at the paper. Passworthy takes it up and throws it down with disdain.
Passworthy: "What's the matter with you fellows? Oh, this little upset across the water doesn't mean war. Threatened men live long. Threatened wars don't occur. Another speech by *him.* Nothing in it, I tell you. Just to buck people up over the air estimates. Don't meet war

half-way. Look at the cheerful side of things. *You're* all right. Business improving, jolly wife, pretty house."

Cabal: "All's right with the world, eh? All's right with the world. Passworthy, you ought to be called Pippa Passworthy. . . ."

Passworthy: "You've been smoking too much, Cabal. You—you aren't eupeptic . . ." (Walks round and sings.) "No-el! No-el! No-el! . . ."

In Cabal's living-room. Christmas tree with freshly lit candles burning and presents being taken off and distributed. A children's party in progress. Each child is busy in its own way. Horrie Passworthy is donning a child's soldier's "panoply." Timothy is laying out a toy railway system. He is completely absorbed in his work, neither hearing nor seeing anything, working with the intensity of the born builder. A smaller girl and a very small boy enter the picture. They have been attracted by the work and the worker. They stare admiringly. In another corner of the room Horrie, now in full uniform, beats his drum.

Horrie: "Fall in! Fall in!" Three boys fall in behind him. "Quick march!" They march off to the drum taps.

Timothy finishing his layout. He surveys it with a last glance before starting the engine. Horrie enters the picture with his followers. The camera shows only the marching feet of Horrie's followers. Railway system spread out. Horrie's foot kicks aside some part of the system.

Timothy (nervously) : "Don't!"

The marching feet pass by. Timothy has but one thought, to save his gadgets. He succeeds. He lays out his railway again. To a little boy: "You work the signals." The little boy sits down happily. To the little girl: "You—you look on." The little girl sits down and plays her part; she admires. Timothy starts his train. The train moves. Timothy is earnestly observing it. The two children are delighted. Drum going. Horrie and his followers return and halt. Horrie stops and thinks.

Horrie: "Make an accident!"

Timothy looks up for a second: "No." Busy with railway.

Horrie: "Make an earthquake!"

Timothy: "No."

Horrie: "Let's have a war."

Timothy: "No."

Horrie goes off reluctantly.

The toy railway. Train going. One of the carriages collapses. It turns over. It has been hit by a wooden pellet. We see four guns being worked by Horrie and his friends. They are delighted. Timothy realises that the whole layout is being bombarded to pieces. He tries to protect the railway with his hands. Protesting desperately: "Don't—stop!" His hand is hit by a projectile. The little girl protests with Timothy.

Horrie directs the firing of the guns. More projectiles hit Timothy.

Timothy jumps to his feet and goes to attack Horrie. Horrie rises quickly, Timothy hits him. Horrie disengages himself from Timothy, kicks over the engine and disarranges the rails. Timothy claws hold of him, and they begin a tussle which ends on the ground.

The conflict between adults is confined to dialogue; the children fight. The size of an image is described directly—"The camera shows only the marching feet of Horrie's followers." And indirectly—"The toy railway. Train going." Editing, the crosscutting from one image to another, is indicated—from "only the marching feet" to "Railway system spread out" and back to "Horrie's foot kicks aside some part of the system." Three shots.

Many contemporary novels, written with an eye on a possible firm sale or written by an author naturally cinematic, may be called film stories in the Wellsian sense. However, *Things to Come* is neither a novel nor a shooting script. It is reasonable to suppose that a competent director could dictate a shooting script to a secretary while holding the Cresset Press book in his hand.

In the case of Henry Miller's book *Scenario: A Film Without Sound,* a director could devise a progression of shots that might be photographed with ingenuity and considerable audacity for private viewing. They would be primarily an exercise in imagery. The following poetical passage lacks dramatic structure but is uniquely visual. It has the quality of a dream, the symbols are personal. It could be pure cinema:

Mandra and Alraune are lying on a beautiful couch beneath a canopy studded with stars. They are lying naked, face to face, breathing into each other's mouth. The sun beats through the open window in long oblique shafts of powdered gold. There is the music of the lutes, soft, distant, incessant as the rain.

IX

The same scene except that the room is suspended in an enormous bowl flooded with an intense blue light. The bed sways gently to and fro as if it were a hammock. At the top of the bowl a few dead gold-fish are floating face up. A hand reaches into the bowl and removes the dead fish one by one. Mandra, who has been asleep, slowly opens her eyes and, seeing the enormous hand above her, the fingers closing around the dead gold-fish, she opens her mouth and screams—but there is only a faint echo of her voice. Alraune lies beside her, on her back, her legs slightly parted. The purple flower with the fleshy roots is planted between her legs. From the long bell-shaped corolla protrudes a pistil bursting with seed. Mandra bends over the body of Alraune and examines the flower attentively. She gazes and gazes until her eyes seem ready to pop out of her head.

The body of Alraune gradually changes color, the limbs stiffen, the half-opened mouth settles into a rigid grimace. As the color of her body changes, from flesh-pink to the dull black of a meteor, the heavily charged pistil bursts and the seed spills over the bed.

The scene alternates now from bed to garden, back and forth incessantly. We see the maid walking down the gravel path toward the pool in the center of the garden. She carries the dead gold-fish in a basket trimmed with palmetto leaves. She gets down on her knees and, lifting a plug from the bottom of the pool, she lets the water drain away. At the bottom of the pool is a jewel box. She opens the box, which is lined with satin, and deposits the gold-fish therein. Then she walks to a corner of the garden and, digging a hole, she buries the casket, making the sign of the cross when she is through. As she walks back towards the house, the gravel crunching beneath her feet, she moves her lips as if in prayer. The face is that of an idiot. She is cross-eyed, her hair unkempt, the tears streaming down her face, her lips moving mechanically. As she mounts the steps leading to the door her dress suddenly bursts open in back, exposing her bottom. She stands a moment on the steps, perplexed, makes the sign of the cross again and turns the door knob. As she does so two white doves fly out of her rectum.

Closet cinema, for commercial and censorship reasons, is a rarity, yet the possibilities for personal statements, comic effects, and sensual experiments are unlimited. Poetic cinema remains insufficiently explored, with very few examples on paper or film for study.

The script of *Que Viva Mexico* by S. M. Eisenstein (Vision Press, Ltd., London, 1951) is a literary treatment of poetic and tragic material. Although Eisenstein is a directorial genius and Wells and Miller are verbalists, the book script of *Que Viva Mexico* lacks the visual impact of either *Things to Come* or *Scenario*. It is heavy with intellectual comment and information. Obviously, Eisenstein wrote his films when he edited them. Here is the conclusion of the Prologue, a funeral in a cemetery, with very few shots implied:

In this ceremony, idols of the heathen temples, masks of the gods, phantoms of the past, take part.

In the corresponding grouping of the stone images, the masks, the bas-reliefs and the living people, the immobile act of the funeral is displayed.

The people bear resemblance to the stone images, for those images represent the faces of their ancestors.

The people seem turned to stone over the grave of the deceased in the same poses, the same expressions of face, as those portrayed on the ancient stone carvings.

A variety of groups that seem turned to stone, and of monuments of antiquity—the component parts of the symbolic funerals—appear in a shifting procession on the screen.

And only the quaint rhythm of the drums of the Yucatan music, and the high-pitched maya song, accompany this immobile procession.

Thus ends the prologue—overture to the cinematographic symphony, the meaning of which shall be revealed in the contents of the four following stories and of the Finale at the end of these.

First Novel: Sandunga

Tropical Tehuantepec.
The Isthmus between Pacific and Atlantic oceans.
Near the borders of Guatemala.
Time is unknown in Tehuantepec.
Time runs slowly under the dreamy weaving of palms and costumes, and customs do not change for years and years.

Concepción, an Indian girl from Tehuantepec, dreams of her forthcoming marriage to Abundio, her *novio* (future husband). Now there are images in a dream of reverie, but the sentences are more concerned with the meaning of the general image than with its visual aspect, or fragmentation into parts in true cinematic style. Here is a passage that is purely literary:

Under the caress of the waves of her hair she lets herself float into dream-land. A wreath of flowers crowns her brow. While listening to the song of her friends she closes her eyes, and in her imagination gold takes the place of flowers.

A necklace of golden coins, adorned with rough pearls strung on threads of golden chains, is glimmering on her breast.

A golden necklace—this is the object of all her dreams; this is the dream of all the Tehuanas—the Tehuantepec girls.

From tender childhood a girl begins to work, saving painstakingly every nickel, every penny, in order that at the age of sixteen or eighteen she may have the golden necklace.

The necklace—that is a fortune, it is an estate. The necklace is the future dowry.

And the bigger, the more expensive it is, the happier future, marital life.

That is why the dreams of Concepción are so passionate; that is why the visions floating before her mind's eye are so colourful.

Handsome youths alternate with the necklace dreams.

Youthful beauty blossoms on the screen. . . .

The dreamy song of the girls wafts over the dreamy voluptuous tropics. . . .

Oh, . . . we have let ourselves drift so deeply into dreams, that we have not even noticed how the girls got to work, when they went over to the market place, exhibited their wares: oranges, bananas, pineapples, flowers, pots, fish, and other merchandise for sale. The Tehuantepec market-place is an interesting sight. If you will look in this corner you may think yourself in India.

It would be difficult to imagine a scene based on the above sentences. Structural conflict is not the problem here.

Fellini is the first director since D. W. Griffith to evoke cinematic ideas on a Shakespearean scale. Like Balzac and Churchill, he continues to create on galley proofs and page proofs long after his penned sheets have gone to the printer. His final drafts on celluloid have the benefit of his preliminary evaluations on paper.

In the later Fellini, each frame and every shot is so vibrant with life that there is a sense of personal involvement, similar to the experiencing of a masterpiece in any art. *8½* is a subjective *La Dolce Vita,* a Dante's *Inferno* turned inside out into a modern Bunyan-esque *Pilgrim's Progress,* a sophisticated Christian in search of himself. Director Guido (Marcello Mastroianni) has made eight films, but cannot complete the script, and launch the production of a banal spectacular, dealing with the escape, from this world to an unknown planet, of survivors after a nuclear war. Guido has a creative block, which he attempts to resolve by remembrances of boyhood escapades and parents, by reveries fantasying an ideal Muse-like dream girl, by a fling with a simple-minded mistress, comic and uncomplicated, and by Walter Mittyish daydreams of sexual power.

Through juxtaposition of scene climaxes, Fellini indicates a direct connection between the psychological impotence of Guido as a cynical Italian male—revealed by his obsession with sex and his inability to have a sustained relationship with wife or mistress—and Guido's artistic impotence. This basic idea in *8½* provides a clarity of dramatic line in what appears to be, at first viewing, an excessively complicated film. The complications may overwhelm a viewer should he overlook Fellini's fundamental quest, namely: Is Guido getting to know himself? In the course of his psychological odyssey Guido encounters hypocrisy, pretension, ambition, money, age, artistic problems—all the complications of society that a modern-day Italian Christian could encounter on the road to his unsought-for salvation. In *La Dolce Vita* there is no quest. It is a clinical film

8½. Courtesy of Embassy Pictures.

without empathy, except in the aging-father scene, played first in the nightclub and then in the prostitute's apartment following the heart attack. In *8½* the quest is indirect and highly entertaining. Is Guido getting to know himself? Scene climaxes provide the clues.

The structure of *8½* is more at the scene level than in terms of sequences. This is because the fragmentation of the master image, the division of actions into shots, is done more in accordance with isolated events than via any chronology or plot evolution. Past and present fuse, as in *Marienbad*. The conscious and the subconscious blend. Time and place aren't essential. The child is father of the man, and the man is his own nurse of his childhood.

For our purposes at this point, a shot-by-shot continuity script is not necessary. The first scene climax occurs in Guido's bedroom when a doctor and nurse arrive, awakening him from a nightmare. He had been caught in a traffic jam in a tunnel, surrounded by dead-like faces in stalled cars. He escapes into the sky (not by rocket) and floats above the sea, but is jerked to earth by a rope attached to his foot. He cannot take off for another planet to escape his claustrophobia. We are all earthbound. Guido raises his hand for help, and sinks back on his bed in despair. Nightmare and reality are fused. With this first scene climax, Fellini has established his basic idea of psychic impotence.

The scene structure in *8½* is more designed than generally recognized. Two main streams surge through the film: the narrative line concerning the frustrations over the pending film production and a parallel line composed of flashback dreams and psychic fantasies, meant to explore childhood motivations or adult escapes. Each fantasy or flashback is triggered, directly or indirectly, by a character who makes Guido become introspective, and these total eleven scenes. Following the introductory nightmare, here is the chronological order of those scenes:

1. The scriptwriter Carini (also called Daumier) tells Guido that his film project lacks a point of view—a cruel attack—whereupon Guido, now standing in line at the spa for his drink of mineral water, envisages his ideal dream girl (Claudia Cardinale) emerging from the woods to serve him his glass. The implication is that all Guido needs, he believes, is the inspiration of a beautiful woman who serves him.

2. Guido tries the present-day escape into sex for sex's sake by importing his mistress Carla (Sandra Milo). He plays a game, paint-

ing her face to pretend she is a streetwalker, and then directs Carla to enter the room as though she were calling on a stranger and so reveal her body beneath the wrapped-around bedsheet. It is an adolescent game, a continuation of the voyeurism he indulged in as a boy on the beach when he paid La Saraghina, the monstrously fat prostitute, to dance obscenely. After coitus with Carla and while asleep, Guido dreams of his mother, who enters the room. With her, Guido visits the family tomb and talks to his father. The past weighs heavily on him, but he is summoned into the present by the arrival of his producer Pace (Guido Alberti) at the cemetery, demanding action.

3. At the spa's nightclub a magician acquaintance recites three words, "Asa, Nisi, Masa," and Guido, via a flashback, recalls his childhood when he was lovingly bathed and put into bed near the bed of his young female relations.

4. Conocchia, the elderly producer's assistant, quarrels with his friend Guido over the ambiguous character of the production, whereupon Guido retires to his room alone. There he imagines Claudia appearing to turn down the bed and bring his slippers. His ideal kisses his hand, gets under the covers, and promises to stay with him.

5. An encounter with a Roman Catholic cardinal, visiting the spa, triggers a flashback to La Saraghina and the beach where she dances, and where the priests catch the boy Guido and punish him.

6. At the baths he talks with Mezzabotta, an elderly man with a young girl friend, and imagines in fantasy that the cardinal summons him, Guido, for a conference amid the steam and mud—the least meaningful scene of the eleven.

7. Guido is seated with his wife, Luisa (Anouk Aimée), and her friend Rossella (reminiscent of Greta Garbo) when Carla arrives to sit in taunting solitude at one of the outdoor tables. Luisa recognizes her and is furious; Rossella is sarcastic. Whereupon Guido imagines in fantasy that Luisa behaves as a gracious friend and compliments Carla on her outlandish clothes and voice, and dances with her. Their comradeship expands, in Guido's rich fantasy, into a fabulous harem scene wherein all the women he has ever known are now his slaves, a Negress, a Scandinavian airlines hostess, assorted actresses, and others. Guido orders his first experience, Jacqueline Bonbon, an aging vaudeville performer, upstairs into retirement—the rules of the house. He cracks his whip; they all respond. They carry him about; they administer his bath; especially Luisa and Claudia. He rules; he is the lion-tamer.

8. In the theatre where film-rushes are being screened, Carini again provokes Guido by deriding the proposed film, and Guido imagines his annoyer executed by hanging.

9. Claudia materializes as an actress, dressed in black, calling at the theatre with her press agent. They flee in reality, and during their drive to a lovely Renaissance courtyard Guido imagines Claudia, now dressed in white, serving him dinner and wine on the spot where the car had been.

10. The climax of Guido's harassment is reached at a press conference, called to announce the commencement of the production. Production Manager Bruno whispers he has slipped a gun into Guido's pocket—in Guido's imagination—so he could escape the inane questions and derisions of the reporters. So Guido fancies himself crawling under the table to commit suicide, and imagines his mother on the beach crying to him, "Guido, you naughty boy, where are you running?"

11. Finally, the disaster is acknowledged as Guido sits in a car with Carini while the launching frame for the rocket is being dismantled. Now comes the final fantasy: The magician arrives to announce that everyone is ready. Guido raises the electric megaphone to direct a Noah's Ark finale. In his imagination he stops fighting his creative block. Instead, he accepts all who have been part of his life, past and present. He takes his wife, Luisa, by the hand, and together they join hands in a huge circle and dance along the rim of a circus ring, the band playing. Everyone is there—himself as a boy, his parents, La Saraghina, Carla, the muse Claudia, the actors and crews of technicians, the producer and screenwriter. Guido is reconciled with himself. He will go on, because life goes on here on earth—a simple affirmation is keeping with the vitality that characterizes the entire film.

Fellini's point of finish is conclusive for this film, and at the same time could be the point of attack for his ninth film, which apparently was his aim.

Although meant as a feminine companion piece to *8½*, *Juliet of the Spirits* (1965) fails in the very area in which *8½* triumphs. Fellini could identify more with the introspections of the masculine Guido than he could deal with the psychic searchings of his Juliet, played by his spouse, Giulietta Masina. It is a wise director who knows how to cast his wife. As a self-pun, and revealing of his unconscious derogatory attitude, Fellini chose an aging, paunchy version of Mastroianni to play Giorgio (Mario Pisu), the philandering husband of Juliet.

For all the varieties of cinematic techniques employed in *Juliet*—and it is a brilliant tour de force of movements and color—there is a sameness, an emotional flatness, due to the lack of character progression. Juliet is passive. She is more acted upon than responsive. Her pregnant sister takes her to the offices of a private detective (Giorgio is having an affair with a young model) ; her friend Valentina takes her to a hermaphrodite fakir Bhisma (Waleska Gert) ; her neighbor Susy (Sandra Milo) offers an Oriental lover who resembles the Hindu deity Krishna and the use of Susy's circular bed with mirror on the ceiling; the Spaniard Don Raffaele (Felice Fulchignoni) offers nonalcoholic stimulation, and the family lawyer offers to trespass into the private property should Juliet but nod. However, she accepts none of these would-be teachers and rescuers, not even the evidence supplied by the detective. The characteristics of her personality make the film a mood piece.

Juliet performs one conscious act. She calls at the apartment of her husband's mistress only to fail when the girl friend won't return. There is no obligatory scene. When Juliet finally denies her mother's power to frighten her, the ugly duckling offspring, she commits an act of psychic will and, in addition, is released from the vise of her Catholic upbringing.

None of this is dramatized. Instead Fellini gives us astounding sights in extraordinary color and costumes to the point where he appears trapped in his own compulsive inventions. In the end, Juliet, resigned to an unfaithful husband and her own lack of adventure, emerges from her house (complete with TV, maids, all the bourgeois comforts) to walk among the trees, the symbol of life with roots in the ground and foliage in the sky. It is an easy ending and an uneasy solution.

Juliet's submission, like her unprotesting acceptance, is evident throughout the film by the absence of scene climaxes. In *8½* there are scene climaxes because Guido is first of all a character, and then he has his psychic-creative blockage. Juliet never rises to any dramatic challenge, as Masina did as Gelsomina in *La Strada* and in *Cabiria*. Her passivity can not produce scene climaxes. Fellini unwittingly explains his failure when he described his ambition to a *Life* reporter: "But for *Juliet*, I gamble. I wanted this film to be a dream, and for the first time in my filming, colors might be even more important than faces. . . ."

One face is worth a thousand pigments.

CHAPTER NINE ✳❦

Orchestration of Shots

1. THE MYSTIQUE OF THE PLASTIC

Shots are the skin, hair, and clothes of cinema. Like people emerging from an exit door, they approach us. They flow toward our eyes in a relentless stream of fluctuating lights and shapes. We are bound to watch whatever is presented, and the shots, like views during a dream, may disregard all the temporal and spatial factors that ordinarily describe the familiar.

How applicable to cinema is the observation on poetry and dreams by Ella Freeman Sharpe in her lectures at the London Institute of Psychoanalysis (*Dream Analysis,* 1937) : "The laws of poetic diction, evolved by the critics from great poetry and the laws of dream formation as discovered by Freud, spring from the same unconscious sources and have many mechanisms in common."

Shots possess a mystique of their own. It is the allure of moving imagery, the plastic essence that molds, forms, fashions, and stylizes the reality or the fantasy. It may take three or four shots of a person, seen from different angles, to convey a certain emotion; or three or four shots of a fragment of an action in order to project a special flavor to the dramatic idea. Like a painter, Fellini will achieve a subtle effect with the strokes of half-a-dozen shots, such as his opening passage in *Juliet.*

The expensive manikin in a shop window, elegantly attired, wig of genuine hair, face realistically painted, body artfully poised, cannot sustain attention. Nor can shots be considered apart from their inner sources of life and vitality. On conscious and unconscious levels we anticipate more than surface stimuli.

A cinematic creator thinks as naturally in terms of images as a composer has a feeling for musical sounds, or as a painter intuitively thinks of design and light. He sees in his mind's eye his characters and their setting, their movements and reactions. A writer is a director of actors, a set designer, production designer, and editor of images first before he is a screen playwright. In a way, his omnipotence is the basis for all that follows during actual filming. One part of him needs to protect his script from the writer's verbiage, the other part from an excess of the director's shots.

Conversely, the film has been a source of new vitality for the novel, as seen in the sharper visualization of description and narration at surface levels, and the increased manipulation of time and space might be better understood with examples taken, ironically, from novels. Plasticity, after all, is the surface image. Here is a precinematic example from E. M. Forster's *Howards End* (1910); the author, without a camera eye, is our at-the-elbow guide while we stand at a London window:

She broke off and listened to the sounds of a London morning. Their house was in Wickham Place, and fairly quiet, for a lofty promontory of buildings separated it from the main thoroughfare. One had the sense of a backwater, or rather of an estuary, whose waters flowed in from the invisible sea, and ebbed into a profound silence while the waves without were still beating. Though the promontory consisted of flats—expensive, with cavernous entrance halls, full of concierges and palms—it fulfilled its purpose, and gained for the older houses opposite a certain measure of peace.

Now compare this with early Hemingway, *Cat in the Rain*. It is fifteen years later, and again we are at the window; but the author as The Man from Cooks has disappeared. We are our own guide:

The American wife stood at the window looking out. Outside right under their window a cat was crouched under one of the dripping green tables. The cat was trying to make herself so compact that she could not be dripped on.

"I'm going down to get that kitty," the American wife said.

"I'll do it," her husband offered from the bed.

"No, I'll get it. The poor kitty out trying to keep dry under a table."

The husband went on reading, lying propped up with the two pillows at the foot of the bed.

"Don't get wet," he said.

This is pure cinema. The first sentence is a full shot, establishing the woman at the window. The second sentence gives us the wife's vision in a medium shot, followed by a close-up of the cat. Characterization comes through action, or lack of action in the husband's case. Dialogue becomes a means of characterization, bearing the least amount of exposition or narrative. The eye tells almost all; the ear is descriptive.

Carried to extremes, the author, by removing himself as guide, has been content to call on central casting, wardrobe, the prop department, and the makeup man to do his work. Françoise Sagan, in *Aimez-vous Brahms?* for example, says merely that her heroine Paule "puts her coat on; she dressed very well." Alberto Moravia's female characters appear wooden but animated, cinematic puppets, who unwittingly reveal Moravia's attitude toward women as well as his debt to movies.

Dos Passos pioneered in the technique of writing novels directly through the camera eye. In his 1930 novel, *The 42nd Parallel,* he offers 56 illuminating short subjects, 19 "newsreels," and 27 "camera eyes" in addition to his feature picture. These insertions, which Dos Passos calls "newsreels" and "camera eyes," are factual or informational paragraphs of different typesetting on news events so that their juxtaposition in the course of the novel's narrative might give a contemporary and realistic dimension. In his 1925 novel, *Manhattan Transfer,* he presents three crosscuts on the very first page. "Three gulls wheel above the broken boxes . . . ," he says in the first paragraph. "The nurse, holding the basket at arm's length as if it were a bedpan, opened the door . . . ," begins the second paragraph. Then the third: "On the ferry there was an old man playing the violin. . . ."

The freedom from time and place as a strict narrative dictum permits a greater freedom in utilizing the stream of consciousness. William Faulkner, under the initial influence of James Joyce, was enthralled by its potentials, as he demonstrated in *The Sound and the Fury* (1929). Here, through three separate streams of consciousness, he followed the Compsons over a three-day period. Jason Compson could not forget the past; Quentin tried to forget the present, and Benjy had no sense of time.

Joyce, that fountainhead of original waters, was the legitimate father of the cinematic novel. It is possible to trace how the parturition came about. He read, at twenty, a novel that Remy de Gourmont reviewed as an "anticipation of the cinema"—Edouard Dujardin's *Les Lauriers Sont Coupés,* wherein, for the first time, the reader is constantly inside the mind of the main character. There was no immediate influence, however, nor was there any immediate reaction arising from Joyce's frequent attendance at the Trieste cinemas, the Edison and the Americano.

During those years in Trieste he was working on *Stephen Hero*, and its writing was not going well. He thought of Stephen as "growing from an embryo," told in direct narrative with episodes chronological and explicit—a purely naturalistic novel. In 1906, having cast the manuscript of *Stephen Hero* into the fire (not all its pages and possibly done by Mrs. Joyce in a wifely rage), Joyce began afresh, this time as *A Portrait of the Artist as a Young Man*.

While at work on this new version, Joyce significantly interrupted his writing for several months in order to establish and manage the first movie hall in Dublin, which he appropriately called "The Volta"—but the light failed to disclose a profit, and he returned to Trieste and his novel.

The technique Joyce uses in *Portrait* is highly cinematic, with the use of flashback and crosscut, the editing of time and space with the intensity and compression of the camera, minus the literary padding of *Stephen Hero*. For example, the first chapter is in four parts: Stephen as an infant; Stephen, years later, at school (playground, classroom, dormitory, infirmary); Stephen at home for Christmas; and Stephen again at school (playground, refectory, rector's study, and playground again).

The difference between *Portrait* and *Stephen* has been described by Theodore Spencer as the difference between things seen under a "spotlight" that were previously in "daylight." Here is a passage, selected at random from this jewel box, which foreshadows Faulkner, Dos Passos, Hemingway, Camus, and a host of later-day saints:

He stood still in the middle of the roadway, his heart clamouring against his bosom in a tumult. A young woman dressed in a long pink gown laid her hand on his arm to detain him and gazed into his face. She said gaily:

"—Good night, Willie dear!"

Her room was warm and lightsome. A huge doll sat with her legs apart in the copious easychair beside the bed.

His masterpiece, *Ulysses* (1922), Harry Levin observed, "has more in common with the cinema than with other fiction." Strick's *Ulysses* is extraordinarily faithful in narrative and exciting cinematically.

Contemporary cinematic writing has a tradition in the novel, as we have seen, dating back actually to Flaubert in *Bouvard et Pécuchet* and *Madame Bovary*. In *Madame Bovary* (1857) there is a classic cinematic instant when Flaubert, through the juxtaposition of dialogue, cleverly utilizes double time and double place—simultaneous action in the crosscut. The precision is of a lens, the rhythm that of a master editor.

The scene at the Agricultural Fair acquires cinematic significance for us when Rodolphe, Madame Bovary's would-be lover, escorts her to the Council Chamber on the first floor of the Town Hall, an empty place where they sit on stools, surveying through a window the speakers' platform and the crowd below. The rhythm here is slow, ornate, and ponderous, because the Prefect's deputy, Monsieur Lieuvain, makes eulogistic praises to the Government and "for Trade and for Industry, for Agriculture and for the Arts."

Here follows the Alan Russell translation:

> "I ought to get a bit farther back," said Rodolphe.
>
> "Why?" said Emma.
>
> But at that moment the official's voice rose to a remarkable pitch as he declaimed:
>
> "Those days are past, gentlemen, when civil discord stained our public places with blood, when landowner, merchant, and working-man alike, as they courted peaceful slumbers, would tremble lest they be awakened by the clang of the tocsin; when the most subversive slogans were aimed in all audacity at the very foundations—"
>
> "They might see me from down there," Rodolphe explained, "and then I'd have to spend a fortnight apologizing. And with my bad reputation . . ."
>
> "What a thing to say about yourself!"
>
> "No, no, it's abominable, I assure you."
>
> "However, gentlemen," the speaker proceeded, "if, driving those sombre pictures from my mind, I turn my gaze now to the present state of our fair land, what do I see? Everywhere, trade and the arts flourish. Everywhere new paths of communication, new arteries within the body politic, are opening up new contacts. Our great manufacturing centres thrive once more. Religion finds new strength and smiles in every heart. Our ports are full. Confidence returns. At last France breathes again!"
>
> "Though I dare say I deserve it by ordinary standards," Rodolphe added.

The rhythm reaches its climax when Flaubert enacts Emma's and Rodolphe's byplay against the more animated oratory of Lieuvain's successor on the platform, Monsieur Derozerays, who touched on history and farming. Rodolphe in turn "led on gradually from magnetism to affinities and while the Chairman alluded to Cincinnatus at his plough, to Diocletian among his cabbages, to the Chinese emperors ushering in the new year with the sowing of seed, the young man was explaining to the young woman that the cause of these irresistible attractions lay in some previous existence."

In Emma's case, "the previous existence" lies in her fatal commitment to romanticism as though it were a neurotic compulsion. The reason Jean Renoir's 1934 film adaptation and Vincent Minnelli's 1949 version (MGM) failed was that this idea was diluted or ignored. *Madame Bovary* is no ordinary tale of adultery; it is a masterpiece reflecting a woman's innermost romantic needs, presented without masculine prejudice.

Here follow the accelerated crosscuts. Rodolphe is continuing:

"We, now, why did we meet? What turn of fate decreed it? Was it not that, like two rivers gradually converging across the intervening distance, our own natures propelled us towards one another?"

He took her hand, and she did not withdraw it.

"General Prize!" cried the Chairman.

"Just now, for instance, when I came to call on you . . ."

"Monsieur Bizet of Quincampoix."

". . . how could I know that I should escort you here?"

"Seventy francs!"

"And I've stayed with you, because I couldn't tear myself away, though I've tried a hundred times."

"Manure!"

"And so I'd stay tonight and tomorrow and every day for all the rest of my life."

"To Monsieur Caron of Argueil, a Gold Medal!"

"For I have never been so utterly charmed with anyone before."

"To Monsieur Bain of Givry St Martain."

"And so I shall cherish the memory of you."

"For a merino ram . . ."

"But you'll forget me. I shall have passed like a shadow . . ."

"To Monsieur Belot of Notre-Dame . . ."

"No, say I shan't! Tell me I shall count for something in your thoughts, in your life?"

"Pigs: Prize divided! Monsieur Lehérissé and Monsieur Cullembourg, sixty francs each!"

Rodolphe squeezed her hand. He felt it warm and vibrant in his, like a captive turtle-dove trying to take wing. Whether she was trying to withdraw it, or responding to his pressure, her fingers made a movement.

"Oh, thank you, you do not repulse me!" he said. "How sweet you are! You know that I am yours! Only let me look at you, let me gaze upon you!"

A breeze from the window ruffled the cloth on the table, and down in the square the peasant women's big bonnets lifted up, fluttering like white butterflies' wings.

"Oil-cake," the Chairman continued. He began to go faster: "Flemish fertilizer—Flax—Drainage—Long Leases—Domestic Service."

Rodolphe had stopped speaking. They looked at one another, and their dry lips quivered in a supreme desire. Gently, effortlessly, their fingers interwined.

It is astonishing to realize that the rhythms of Flaubert's cross-cutting were conceived seven decades before Eisenstein's *Potemkin,* which revolutionized the creation of cinema. In this accelerating passage each line of dialogue crackles like a fresh shot flashed on the screen.

Awareness of shots is based on a trained capacity for visual perception, and therein lies the secret behind the mystique of the plastic. A novelist as supreme as Flaubert creates images in the mind's eye. A screen playwright of whatever talent he may possess has the advantage of creating his images more specifically in terms of a visual language—also the risk!

2.   LEARNING THE GRAMMAR THROUGH SHOTS

The ancient association of the word "grammar" with verbal languages should not handicap our awareness of its potential in a visual language. No other word—lexicon, syntax, vocabulary, or anatomy—properly describes the means and the manner of composition.

Grammar is what renders a language useful; without it there is gibberish. In an art form grammar is the study of what is to be preferred and what avoided. Unfortunately, cinema lacks an active grammar. Witness the hours of illiterate and meaningless imagery that flow from screen and tube, depending on other languages—dialogue, vaudeville, drama, journalism—for its content, and with only an occasional moment of lucid and literate cinematic expression. It may be argued that the study of grammar is not essential for a twenty-one day Cooks Tour through Italy; similarly, it is possible to spend a lifetime sitting before a TV lamp and not know what images could mean.

Emerson coined the phrase "creative reading" to indicate that there should be more in the mind's eye than what is read. So should there be creative viewing.

Nearly half a century ago Percy Lubbock in *The Craft of Fiction* complained of the handicaps in writing and reading the modern novel. "What is to be understood by a 'dramatic' narrative, a 'pictorial' narrative, a 'scenic' or a 'generalized' story?" Lubbock asks pertinently. "We must use such words, as soon as we begin to examine the structure of a novel; and yet they are words which have no technical acceptation in regard to a novel, and one cannot be sure how they will be taken."

Lubbock has an intriguing, speculative answer, one that could be applied as well to cinema. "The want of a received nomenclature is a real hindrance," he observes, "and I have often wished that the modern novel had been invented a hundred years sooner, so that it might have fallen into the hands of the critical schoolmen of the seventeenth century. As the production of an age of romance, or of the eve of such an age, it missed the advantage of the dry light of academic judgement, and I think it still has reason to regret the loss. The critic has, at any rate; his language, even now, is unsettled and unformed."

Similarly, the cinema critic is handicapped by the lack of an aesthetic terminology at most levels, and a common cinematic vocabulary at the reporting level. "His language" indeed "is unsettled and unformed." At least, the modern novel is today safely specimenized under the microscopes of "academic judgement."

Serious viewers learn to look for shot examples in terms of content that is shaped by cinematic grammar and also of grammar that affects content. For an analysis of a film or TV program to have any *sui generis* value, its passages of plot or character or sociology contain grammar that gives that passage its unique meaning—time, place, cognitive recognition, all our responses to emotions and ideas—and in the terminology of frame, shot, scene, sequence, and the varied movements in subject, camera, and editing.

Other approaches tend to talk about cinema as though it were somewhat of a cross between the novel and the theatre with a bit of painting thrown in—or an illustrated sociological essay.

Since a revolutionary alteration in viewing habits has begun, perceptional sensitivity is all the more interlocked with an ability to analyze shots. Content analysis, grammar, visual perception are all simultaneous and inseparable, beginning with the first shot flashed on screen or glass.

Could a lack of shot-consciousness be the reason why the grammar of cinema hasn't developed?

Historically, the tyranny of the fixed frame has long dominated creative and critical expression. The most immediate of the dictators has been the proscenium box, and the most ancient has been the dictatorship of the painter's frame. In cinema, space need not be restricted or confined any more than time is strictly a matter of consecutive seconds. This interplay and reliance are true in the art of the novel. Alfred Kazin has taken the novelist Lawrence Durrell to task: "When Mr. Durrell so sharply separates space from time he is attempting something which in the representation of actual human experience is impossible, since we do not think of space apart from time."

Men through the ages think generally of time in terms of past, present, and future. Men see objects or space, similarly, as movement and lights that activate those objects or that space—a painting has life because it has captured a fraction of time, frozen a moment in luminosity. Nor can feelings and thoughts exist in cinema without the rhythms of movement and light. Objects by themselves, animate or inanimate, have no cinematic vitality otherwise; a still photograph has a true but limited reality. Vitality springs more likely from rhythmic alterations.

These are the grammatical rudiments that give cinema its unique character, its special excitement, its particular pleasures and pains— all the strange possibilities, sights and sensations unlike any other language in the history of man.

Through cinematic grammar different meanings can be placed on ideas, emotions, and objects. Herein lies the key to shots and grammar. "What you see is what he [screen playwright] makes the camera see," observed T. S. Eliot in commenting on the film version of *Murder in the Cathedral*.

3.   ORCHESTRATION: CHOICES

A feeling for the multiplicity of shots, potentially available, is essential for understanding the nature of orchestration. Choice, or selection, may be partially intuitive, as with Griffith, Truffaut, or Kubrick; or, more deliberately designed, as with Eisenstein, Bergman, or Kurosawa.

The philosophy behind orchestration is cogently described by David Lean, who began his cinematic life as an editor: "Actually, I begin editing my films as I work with the writer on the script, getting a series of balances—light and dark, slow and fast, boredom and shock."

Orchestration exploits the plastic potential. How? By its distribution of harmony and dissonance in a proper balance of the whole, this structural manipulation always aims to maintain the prominent parts. The aim is for effective combinations, the mixing of contrasts, differences, and varieties. Pacing, or rhythmic alterations, exist primarily in the shots, though there are also patterns at the scene and the sequence levels.

Movement needs to be organized for the recording of reality or fantasy to become art. Cinema is movement organized, and this is accomplished through orchestration. It is an aesthetic not far from the philosophy of Pablo Casals who proclaims with bow and voice: Freedom with order. To persist as a truly independent art, cinema relies on the sensory elements of the visual that are organized. In sharp contrast, most of television is pictorial radio, dependent on objectives other than those that are *sui generis,* and is visually disorganized.

For unity of expression a dominant movement is preferred, such as a character walking, the camera traveling, or your eye jumping from one place to another setting. There are many areas within a frame that can have independent movement, but they need to be coordinated—even for dissonance and shock. Movement, as we shall see shortly, is in terms of character or nature, quality or ratio, velocity or tempo, and perspective or point of view. The thrush on the bough is maddening to the ear, since he never, in his descending sevenths, finishes off a lovely passage with an alteration.

We are concerned here with orchestration as a kinetic pattern, which is eloquently described by Monroe C. Beardsley in his *Aesthetics: Problems in the Philosophy of Criticism:* "Kinetic pattern is the pattern of variation in its propulsion, or intensity of movement. . . . Music, as a process in time, has varying regional qualities that can be described, metaphorically, by terms borrowed from physical motions: the music is rushing, hesitating, pausing, picking up speed, becoming calm, driving ahead, overcoming resistance, building up inertia, insisting, going pell-mell, dragging, exploding, withdrawing, creeping, fading." So goes cinema.

CHAPTER TEN ✖️ॐ

The Faces of Time

1. THE CONTINUOUS PRESENT

Cinema is unique among the arts in its projection of time primarily as the continuous present, the immediate moment being both of utmost importance and the accumulation of all that has gone before. The popular novel, now overly influenced by cinema, approaches this preoccupation with the second-by-second unfolding of events. The basic ongoing rhythm is the dominant characteristic, with variations in velocity and time tenses as secondary interruptions. Cinematic devices that uniquely affect pace and place, such as alterations in motion-speed (subjects in slow or fast motion, frame panning or traveling in slow or fast speeds, and editing), serve to relieve the rhythms of time continuing.

The constant challenge to the creator is how to capture, hold, and project the continuous present he sees as movements inherent in life. On this basic point, William Faulkner, the most talented American novelist to have written expressly for the screen, remarked in 1958 (echoing Conrad, 1897): "The aim of every artist is to arrest motion, which is life, by artificial means and hold it fixed so that a hundred years later, when a stranger looks at it, it moves again since it is life."

The writer-director, being primarily concerned with action of all sorts, asks: Does a character cross the room toward the door or is he already walking down the road? Do we follow him side by side or do we sit back and observe his movements? When he leaves the room, do we see him going down the stairs? Is another character involved simultaneously in another place, but at the same time? If so, do we shift back and forth between the two? There is a past experience in every person's life that might be utilized in a turning back of the clock to a previous scene; or, the moment, being precious, might be prolonged with a stretching out of time.

Actually, what the creator is selecting, during this questioning, is the proper means to convey most effectively the motion he envisages. What might be the preference of one writer-director could be rejected by another, or what might be suitable for one situation won't work in another. The choices made reflect the visual intelligence of the creator—his basic talent, his plastic sensitivity, his artistry. His choices create his style. Personal talent, in either sender or receiver of visual stimuli, is not to be taken for granted, as Emerson reminds us—"Hundreds of people can talk for one who can see."

Most of our waking hours are spent in the present tense. The predominant clock in our mind ticks away at the rate of sixty seconds to the minute. This primary movement, though varied by rhythms and velocity, may be called the continuous face of time.

The basic tenses in life and grammar—present, past, future—are useful means for recognizing the faces of time in cinema, but not in any proportion resembling their use in a verbal language. Past tense is dominant in the novel. The performing arts evoke the present tense. The faces or tenses are not to be considered a rigid decalogue or didactic means. Like parts of speech, they are tools that demonstrate the infinite variety of combinations uniquely possible. In association with subjective material, they could be three thousand or three million, limited only by imagination.

2. THE CONTINUOUS FACE WITHIN THE FRAME

The most frequent form of perception in cinema is the movement of persons and objects within the frame of the picture. From babyhood we are accustomed to seeing people and animals move about while we remain stationary. In crib and classroom this has been our basic pattern. The theatre reinforces this fixed equation. We observe actors move about within a box, one side of which has been removed. The arena style, or theatre-in-the-round, continues the rigidity of the equation, but with a different background.

In first noting continuous time within the frame as a separate and distinct movement (later we may observe it in conjunction with other movements) , we see the action as the total shot, like a scene in the theatre. In *Citizen Kane,* an open gold mine of excellent examples, there is a singing-lesson scene between an exasperated maestro and the inept Susan. The shot has an extreme depth of field, similar to a stage setting, in which Susan and the maestro are in the foreground by the piano, with Kane in the far background at the door. It is Kane's slow movement forward that intensifies the drama; we await his reaction to the maestro's inability to teach the talentless Susan. By the time Kane arrives in the foreground we know that the lessons will continue. Although this example is more dramatic than cinematic in that the action is recorded by camera, suspense is heightened by the steady, self-assured approach of Kane, a case of an actor dominating the scene.

Consider the moment when Caesar meets Cleopatra in Bernard Shaw's script (1944) , based on his stage play, produced by Gabriel Pascal (1946) . It is straight theatre. An actor speaks; a prop of silk moves; and a girl's voice is heard, though she is hidden:

12. MEDIUM SHOT—THE SPHINX SHOOTING PAST CAESAR (IN PROFILE)

CAESAR *is looking up at the Sphinx and the scene between the paws is hidden from him.*

CAESAR
(*earnestly*)

Sphinx, Sphinx: My way hither was the way of destiny; for I am he whose genius you are the symbol: part brute, part woman, and part god—nothing of man in me at all. Have I read your riddle, Sphinx?

A bunch of silk moves and raises itself up, peeping cautiously out like a bird to discover who is down below.

A GIRL'S VOICE
(*apparently from the Sphinx*)

Old gentleman.

In the following, which is a medium shot of Caesar alone, the action is solely a dialogue exchange, an example of Shavian wit, a piece of theatrical inheritance, though photographed by a camera:

12A. MEDIUM SHOT—CAESAR

He starts violently, and clutches his sword.

CAESAR

Immortal gods!

THE VOICE

Old gentleman, don't run away.

CAESAR
(*repeating to himself, stupefied*)
"Old gentleman, do not run away"! This, to Julius Caesar?

THE VOICE
(*urgently*)

Old gentleman.

CAESAR

Sphinx, you presume on your centuries. I am younger than
you though your voice is but a girl's voice as yet.

A straight action within the frame is another form of continuous
motion. Here is an amusing moment in American literature, the
scene in *The Adventures of Tom Sawyer* when Tom is being
punished for playing hookey. He is made to whitewash a fence, but
ingeniously pretends it is a privilege, and gets his friends to do the
job for him and pay as well. The moment in the John Van A.
Weaver script (1937), produced by David O. Selznick, is when Joe,
the first victim is induced to paint:

JOE

I'm goin' in a-swimmin', *I* am. But accourse you'd druther
work.

TOM
(*looking at* JOE *with feigned surprise*)
What do you call work?

JOE
(*genuinely surprised*)

Why, ain't *that* work?

TOM
(*resuming whitewashing—carelessly*)
Well, all I know is it suits Tom Sawyer!

JOE *stops nibbling his apple; thinking this over,* TOM *swipes his
brush daintily back and forth, steps back to note the effect, adds
a touch here and there—*JOE *getting more and more interested.*

JOE
Say—let *me* whitewash a little.

The camera is changed to another angle, the action continues within the frame:

38. ANOTHER ANGLE—TOM AND JOE

TOM
Think I'd let a dude whitewash? Where's that hat?

JOE
Aw, I only wear it when my Ma makes me. . . . Go on, let me whitewash.

TOM *considers the proposition, then finally speaks.*

TOM
(*reluctantly*)
No—no—if it was the inside, I wouldn't mind and Aunt Polly wouldn't, but she's awful partickler about the outside.

JOE
Aw, come on now—I'd let *you* if you was me.

TOM
I'd like to, honest Injun, but—no, I couldn't trust you.

JOE
Aw, shucks, I'd be careful! (*fishing into a pocket and hauling out a colored card of pasteboard*) Say—I'll give you a bible ticket I just found.

TOM
(*with scornful laugh*)
Bible ticket! Huh!

JOE *is not discouraged by this refusal. He offers his slightly eaten apple.*

An eccentric alteration, such as a makeup transformation in *Dr. Jekyll and Mr. Hyde* (1932), can be continuous motion. Here from *Lost Horizon* (1937), screenplay by Robert Riskin, directed by Frank Capra, is the face changing from eternal youth of Shanghri-La to a biological age. In James Hilton's novel the transformation is done indirectly in the imagination of the reader, unfolded through conversation in a London club over cigars and brandy. A beautiful Chinese lady, Lo-Tsen, accompanies the Englishman Conway out of a magical, mysterious land 1,100 miles west of the China border of Tatsien-Fu. Conway's journal ceases at this point in the narrative, and his memory lapses. In the epilogue of the novel, one of the clubmen, a novelist named Rutherford, recounts his visit to a hospital in Shanghai, years later, where a doctor recalls the case of the Englishman who had lost his memory but had been brought to the hospital by a Chinese woman. The novel on the final page gives us the opportunity to imagine the hidden mystery of Shanghri-La. Rutherford asks if the Chinese woman was young:

> Rutherford flicked his cigar as if the narration had excited him quite as much as he hoped it had me. Continuing, he said: "The little fellow looked at me solemnly for a moment, and then answered in that funny clipped English that the educated Chinese have—'Oh, no, she was most old—most old of any one I have ever seen.' "

On the screen we see the transformation of Lo-Tsen (Maria) in a series of shots of varying sizes, all predominately continuous motion.

In the first instance Conway is walking behind a companion who is carrying the girl on his back during their painful trek high in the unmapped mountain passes:

412. CLOSE-UP—CONWAY

staring at the girl's face as it hangs over GEORGE's *back. Suddenly his eyes widen.*

Conway's reaction arouses our curiosity, which is increased when we behold, in a subsequent close-up, what is happening to Maria:

413. CLOSE-UP—MARIA

A distorted view of her. Youth and beauty seem to be vanishing.

Though editing is a factor in the juxtaposition of one motion flowing into another, these adjacent images are dominated by one major element—the aging of Maria into her physiological years following her departure from Shanghri-La. Now the climax of the action, the continuous face, as continuous motion within the frame:

417. MEDIUM SHOT OF THE THREE

The only illumination comes from the moon. We cannot get a clear view of her face. But what we see seems to us to be small, withered, and aged. The men stare at her intently. After a few moments, the silence is broken by MARIA's *voice—which is a feeble whisper.*

MARIA
(scarcely audible)
George—please—hold my hand.

GEORGE *takes her hand in his.*

Forgive me, George—I lied to you. (*Pause.*) Everything they
told you is true—I should never have left—

Makeup transformation, even done via tricks such as single-frame
motion with the makeup man making alterations in gradual stages, is
confined to a subject, the actor. Actors generally make character
delineation without benefit of costume or makeup changes.

A classic example of an actor creating continuous motion is the arrival of Anna Christie in a waterfront saloon after we had been
informed by her tugboat-captain father, Chris, that Anna was a good
little girl, living on a farm in Minnesota with cousins. Anna (Greta
Garbo) enters, looking like a prostitute, and slumps down at a table.
Her first words:

ANNA
Gimme a whiskey—ginger ale on the side, and don't be
stingy, baby.

LARRY
Well, shall I serve it in a pail?

ANNA
Well, that suits me down to the ground.

All this, in a medium shot, runs seven seconds, but within that
short span Garbo gives us the character of Anna Christie.

For an actress revealing a fundamental alteration in character,
Sarah in *The End of the Affair* (1954) goes through a psychic trans-
formation. Though married to Henry, Sarah is in love with Maurice
Bendrix. She is a woman without faith in God. During an air raid in
London she believes her lover is killed, and conducts a dialogue with
herself. The following scene, written by Lenore Coffee from Graham
Greene's novel, is predominantly continuous motion (acting and
dialogue) :

129. INTERIOR: BENDRIX' SITTING-ROOM

as SARAH *comes in stunned and shocked by the belief that* BENDRIX
is dead. Suddenly, overcome with despair, she drops down on her

knees in a corner of the room. A shaft of light from the kitchen falls on her.

> SARAH'S VOICE

I knelt down on the floor. I must have been mad to do such a thing. I never even had to do it as a child; I wasn't brought up to believe in prayer. I hadn't any idea what to say—only that Maurice was dead and I knew that I had to cry out for help to someone.

The following dialogue is between SARAH *as she tries to pray and the whispered voice of her driving conscience.*

> SARAH
> *(slowly and painfully)*

Dear God—make me believe. I can't believe. *Make* me.

> HER WHISPERED VOICE

WHY "DEAR"? HOW CAN ANYTHING YOU DON'T BELIEVE IN BE "DEAR"?

> SARAH

I will believe. Only let Maurice be alive and I will believe.

> HER WHISPERED VOICE

THAT ISN'T ENOUGH. IT DOESN'T HURT TO BELIEVE.

> SARAH

Very well. I love him and I'll do anything—if you will let him be alive.

> HER WHISPERED VOICE

THAT STILL ISN'T ENOUGH. YOU KNOW IT ISN'T. AND WHAT DO YOU MEAN BY "ANYTHING"?

> SARAH

I'll never quarrel with him again or make him unhappy.

> HER WHISPERED VOICE

YOU KNOW THAT'S IMPOSSIBLE. THE VERY NATURE OF YOUR LIVES TOGETHER MAKES IT IMPOSSIBLE.

> SARAH

I'll be sweet, and kind, and patient to Henry—

> HER WHISPERED VOICE

YOU ALREADY ARE. AND IT DOESN'T COST YOU ANYTHING. YOU LIKE TO BE KIND.

As SARAH *fights with her conscience she digs her nails into the palms of her hands and the perspiration begins to stand out on her face*

*and forehead. It is a real battle of the soul. She takes a deep
shuddering breath and says, the words spaced out slowly—*

SARAH

I'll—give—Maurice—up—forever— (*Then in a rush of words*)
If you'll only let him be alive!

HER WHISPERED VOICE

FOREVER?

SARAH

(*with panic in her voice*)
People can love each other without being together, can't
they?

HER WHISPERED VOICE

CAN YOU?

SARAH

People love God all their lives without seeing Him, don't
they?

HER WHISPERED VOICE

PEOPLE WHO BELIEVE IN HIM.

SARAH

I *do* believe! I *will* believe! Make me. I can't do anything of
myself. Make him be alive—and I will believe. I *promise!*

HER WHISPERED VOICE

ARE YOU SURE YOU WANT TO PROMISE? REMEMBER YOU SAW
HIM LYING DEAD UNDER THAT DOOR. YOU SAW HIS DEAD HAND.
YOU TOUCHED IT.

SARAH

If there is a God, can't He heal the sick and raise the dead?
(*her nails digging deeper into her palms*) All I can feel
now is pain—and I accept pain. Give me nothing else and
I will bear it. (*opens her hands and we see the bloody
marks*) Oh God, they say You are merciful. But how can
there be a merciful God and this despair? Show me that
You are! *Prove* it to me! And I'll believe! If you are really
God, You can do anything!

As SARAH's *voice dies away there is the* SOUND *of the* "ALL CLEAR."
And it is still sounding when SARAH *hears* BENDRIX' *voice calling—*
"Sarah—Sarah"—*She crouches against the wall and turns a terrified
face to* BENDRIX *as he walks into the open door.*

Within-the-frame acting and action with dialogue are examples of continuous time, both being a theatrical inheritance. The purest cinematic invention is found in frame movement and editing. Though several motions may be present, the dominant movement is the one that characterizes the shot, and so we naturally describe a shot by its most effective face.

3.   CONTINUOUS TIME AND FRAME MOTION

The escape from the tyranny of the fixed frame was instigated by newsreel cameramen from France and England who photographed, during the late nineties, touring scenes in Venice and the Caucasus as panoramic shots from a fixed point of view (tripod). Later, in America, Niagara Falls was recorded in a pan shot, also a snowstorm in Madison Square. Panning is as natural as a baby in a highchair watching his mother move from stove to table. We pan every minute with our eyes; we pan with our eyes and heads.

The human eye is an extraordinary camera, superior to any invented or manufactured. We can observe a general scene one instant, and the next we can be focusing on an object under our noses. From horizon to fingernail with one blink. In cinema this is done through traveling forward or backward, the camera on trucks or a crane. If the camera remains on a tripod, the zoom lens sends us flying toward the outfielder catching the ball, or pulls us back from the quarterback to observe the passer throwing to an intended receiver.

Frame motion—right, left, up or down, in or out, or accompanying in parallels or diagonals—has a natural, physiological base in the capability of the human eye (though the eagle is superior in range and focus). Movement is also related to heartbeats and a psychological need for fulfillment—to be noted in terms of dramatic and pictorial tensions. The screen or tube itself is timeless as a blank page is wordless. Let an image appear, though projected via electricity, and there is motion, which is time.

A horse on the move evokes both an immediate and a timeless image. Take the charge of the English knights in the battle of Agincourt in *Henry V* (1944). Here starts the first pan shot, with Henry mounting his horse (note angle of view is included in the pan) :

143. CLOSE SHOT—HENRY

Shooting up. HENRY *turns off camera right from Westmoreland, who was presumably standing off camera right, to include all the people present and says:*

HENRY

You know your places! God be with you all!

He steps off the cart CAMERA PANNING *with him right, straight on to his horse which has been drawn up for him along the end of the ramp from the cart, his left foot in the left stirrup, horse facing left background. He mounts. Camera pans with him as his horse steps away from camera left, then wheels round right, camera following him as he draws his horse up to the standard bearer also on horseback, who is waiting in position for him facing camera right so that they are now in mid long shot surrounded by a joyous crowd all rushing to their appointed places.*

CUT TO:

Panning with Henry as he mounts his horse from the cart gives a sense of identification, which continues as his horse steps away. We (the camera) move with Henry. Movement in a parallel direction provides a continuing identity via frame motion that has psychological power. We become Henry.

In delightful contrast the head of the French forces, the Dauphin, is lowered onto his horse by a crane in subject motion. It is intended to be a comical sight:

144. SCENE 54: FRENCH—MID CLOSE SHOT

Shooting up on to the DAUPHIN *being lowered by crane on to his horse. The* DAUPHIN's *horse is facing slightly left. When he has arrived in his saddle, he releases the ropes from his arms with the help of the three or four grooms surrounding him and the man at the pulley in the background.*

When this business is completed, he turns his horse towards the camera and rides, wheeling camera right, away to the background camera right.

The Dauphin joins his nobles and standard bearer in a static composition, whereas Henry starts forward, leading a charge from a walk to a trot to full gallop, camera traveling in a parallel direction, the knights climaxing their charge by lowering their lances. Incidentally, this famous charge is not in the shooting script. Sir

Laurence Olivier had the artistic insight to see that an extensive traveling-shot charge evolved most naturally out of shot #143, the pan on the mounting and stepping off.

Too frequently we see frame motion executed without an apparent design that aims at character delineation or plot progression, but merely as travel, crane, or a zoom for a compositional change that neither adds nor subtracts anything. This is directing without traffic. More likely to be significant is the frame motion that is used to accompany subject motion so that continuous time is given a double impetus that stylizes the action, as just noted when Henry mounts his horse.

Another effective use of the pan shot in *Henry V* relates to the archers and their arrows. First of all, suspense is created and accelerated by a series of shots showing the bowmen preparing their weapons, including crosscuts between the line of archers and the French knights charging on horse. We anticipate the release of the arrows with growing intensity, so that when that moment comes we fly with the arrows. This is achieved visually via a pan shot, followed by a trick shot, but there is no doubt—for anyone who has seen the images —that there exists an exhilarating psychological release:

CUT TO:

183. Scene 82   (Sketch No. 85) : english—mid long shot

Shooting camera right from a back view, the bowmen *release their arrows.* camera pans *quickly right as they take the air.*

CUT TO:

184. Scene   (Sketch No. 86) : trick shot

Arrows flying through the air.

CUT TO:

Obviously, sketches of images were drawn prior to the writing of the shooting script, a useful practice employed extensively by Eisenstein. The grand climax of the Battle of Agincourt is depicted in panning and traveling shots:

214. Scene 113 (Sketch No. 116) : tracking and panning

from the cannon muzzle to disclose gunners falling about deafened by the noise. We describe an 180 degrees arc and discover two or three tents with boys, wounded men and priests. People are moving

*in the direction of camera left. Finally at the end of the pan is dis-
covered a tent from which singing is heard.* CAMERA TRACKS *into the
interior of the tent from which pages are looking out.*

At the end of the scene camera moves forward and PANS *up close to
the cross on the altar.*

DISSOLVE TO:

215. SCENE 117   (SKETCH NO. 117): CLOSE SHOT

The English standard against the sky advancing left to right,
CAMERA TRACKS *left to right with it.. CAMERA then PANS down to reveal a melee showing the English advancing and the French retreating in disorder,* HENRY *and the* STANDARD BEARER *keeping in the
centre of the picture. Now* CAMERA PANS *up to the standard still
moving right. (In this shot* HENRY *and the* STANDARD BEARER *will
have to describe an angular movement away from the camera and
back towards it again.)*

DISSOLVE TO:

216. SCENE 118 & 120   (SKETCH NO. 118): CLOSE SHOT

The French standard traveling right, CAMERA PANNING *with it as the
standard moves away from the camera. Still in direction right, we
discover the French party, including* DAUPHIN, MOUNTJOY, STANDARD
BEARER, BOURBON, ORLEANS, *and three or four others, riding up to the
top of the hill.*

Though action on a large scale, battles and mob scenes, provides
readier opportunities for frame motion, a simple pan or dolly might
prove correspondingly effective within a room, such as a packed
prison cell or a crowded steerage on a boat.

Orson Welles in *Citizen Kane* introduces us to the eccentricities
and mysteries of Kane in the dim opening shots by having the
camera travel downward, close to a wire fence, from a "No Trespassing" sign. The sensory impact is unmistakable. We had just seen
previously the dark castle of Kane on a foreboding horizon, so that
the down movement gives us a sense of being locked out; we are
outsiders. Similarly, a bumpy dolly right shot, shooting through the
wire fence at an aged and robe-wrapped Kane being pushed in a
wheelchair, approximates cleverly a newsreel quality; we feel we are
peeking in at a famous and elusive recluse.

This sense of zeroing in on a character is also accomplished by a
travel-in and tilt-down combination over a model roof of El Rancho,

then a trick dissolve through the glass skylight, and we are in a full-sized, third-rate nightclub. The frame movement continues, now on a crane, as we swoop down upon Susan Alexander, Kane's second and tragic wife, drunkenly weeping at a table in the deserted Atlantic City club. Already, she is characterized. How visually unprepared and sensorily dull it would be if we met Susan Alexander in an ordinary cut—the reporter, Thompson, of "Time on the March" is ordered to bring back Kane "dead or alive," and the next shot would show him interviewing Susan.

Frame movement can be no assurance by itself of adding artistry to content. Often and blatantly this is the intent as seen in television dramas. Here from *Crime in the Streets* (1956) by Reginald Rose we have a perfect example of movement minus empathy; it is merely action for action's sake:

FADE IN:

1. EXTERIOR: WAREHOUSE STREET—LONG SHOT—LOW ANGLE—NIGHT
The street is empty save for a truck parked by a single gas pump. At the far end of the street is a closed wooden gate. Looming above is a huge gas storage tank. There is absolute silence. As the CAMERA DOLLIES *slowly down the street we hear the scuffling of feet accompanying it. A small figure climbs over the fence followed by another. The* CAMERA STARTS FORWARD AGAIN *as does the sound of the scuffling feet.*

2. CLOSER ANGLE: SHOOTING UP AT FENCE—THE HORNET GANG
The last of the gang jumps down from the fence. These are the Hornets: BLOCKBUSTER, FIGHTER, GLASSES, BENNY, LOU, BABY, LENNY, PHIL, HERKY, REDTOP, CHUCK. *Their leader,* FRANKIE DANE, *stands slightly in front of them, weaponless. Most of the others have sticks, baseball bats, belts, rocks, etc.* FRANKIE *calmly smokes a cigarette. He and the rest of the gang look* OFFSCENE.

3. REVERSE ANGLE: LONG SHOT—THE DUKE GANG

They are advancing slowly. In the distance there are about ten of them of varying sizes, some carrying weapons. . . .

11. OVERHEAD SHOT—SHOOTING DOWN ON STREET FROM HIGH ANGLE

The SCREEN *is empty. From opposite sides the two gangs approach. When they are about a yard apart their two leaders stop. There is complete silence. This is the pause which lasts until one or the other leader strikes first.*

This alleged pause is also the moment for a message from the sponsor. No gangs with gang psychology (emotions keyed, strong through numbers, bravado enhanced, lusting for blows and blood) will pause in "complete silence" merely because the script so orders them. The typical shock opening is the sort of "hook" designed to keep hands off the channel-switcher knob.

A frame motion can be slight in extent of movement and be quite significant. Consider in *Lord of the Flies* the short pan up the pole to the severed head of the pig, offered as a tribal sacrifice to "The Beastie." The brief movement gives us a jolt. Also, in *Flies* there are some excellent low-angle traveling right shots through the jungle when Ralph, the leader, is being pursued by the tribe bent on killing him. Suddenly there is a panning right to alter perspective, and the frame motion ceases. We see in close-up a pair of white shoes and white stockings—civilization!—then panning up—the bare knees, the white baggy shorts with a double buckle of a British naval officer. It is an effective combination of traveling, climaxed by panning.

Another example of a frame motion that is slight in degree but effective in quality is a moment in the beginning of *Caesar and Cleopatra* when Caesar confronts the Sphinx, which in turn personifies the Nile kitten. This is done through a pan-down shot:

Sᴘʜɪɴx ᴀɴᴅ Cᴀᴍᴘ

10. ᴛʜᴇ sᴘʜɪɴx ɪᴛsᴇʟғ

A most beautiful, impressive angle of the face.

ᴄᴀᴇsᴀʀ
(over)
And here at last is their sentinel—an image of the constant
and immortal part of my life, silent, full of thoughts, alone
in the silver desert.

The camera pans down from the head of the Sphinx and reveals a strange and unexpected sight. A mass of colour between its great paw defines itself as a heap of red poppies on which a girl lies motionless, her silken vest heaving gently and regularly with the breathing of a dreamless sleeper, and her braided hair glittering in a shaft of moonlight like a bird's wing.

How gently and poetically we are eased into an awareness of Cleopatra through a brief frame motion.

Introductory scenes frequently start with a variety of traveling shots, in which compositional size is maintained or subject moves and size alters, executed by both experienced and novice directors. It must be concluded, in the face of such empirical evidence, that frame motion tends to involve the viewer promptly, that it can evoke identification more readily, and can be provocative to the eye. Take Sidney Lumet's *Long Day's Journey into Night* (1962) when we are first introduced to the father and the mother. Assume we know nothing of James Tyrone, a talented but self-defeating actor, a maudlin Irishman; or of Mary Cavan Tyrone, a sweet and lonely lady turned inside out by her family, and now a dope addict. How do we learn these facts visually—or at least intimations that all is not a surface image?

From a high angle and long shot the frame moves with the mother and father as they walk and talk after breakfast. They move toward the porch swing. It is their summer home on an August day. The action follows to the letter the stage directions. The camera makes the difference: from a high angle at a distance of about 12 feet the camera, on a crane, moves in and down. This master movement is the foundation on which tension is built.

Close-up shots on faces and hands orchestrate the basic cinematic movement; we begin to sense that Mary is far from normal, something is askew. We float in on them to study their faces.

This curious relationship between frame motion and the close-up can be observed also in the introductory scenes of *Great Expectations,* both the 1934 and the 1947 versions. First, the Dickens original of 1861: it is the beginning of Chapter I when Pip is in the churchyard, a very young boy, an orphan, looking at the tombstones of his family:

. . . My first most vivid and broad impression of the identity of things, seems to me to have been gained on a memorable raw afternoon toward evening. At such a time I found out for certain, that this bleak place overgrown with nettles was the churchyard; and that Philip Pirrip, late of this parish, and also Georgiana wife of the above, were dead and buried; and that Alexander, Bartholomew, Abraham, Tobias, and Roger, infant children of the aforesaid were also dead and buried; and that the dark flat wilderness beyond the churchyard, intersected with dykes and mounds and gates, with scattered cattle feeding on it, was the marshes; and that the low leaden line beyond was the river; and that the distant savage lair from which the wind was rushing, was the sea; and that the small bundle of shivers growing afraid of it all and beginning to cry, was Pip.

"Hold your noise!" cried a terrible voice, as a man started up from among the graves at the side of the church porch. "Keep still, you little devil, or I'll cut your throat!"

Dickens moves quickly from exposition to narrative to dramatic—the line of dialogue cutting in like a sudden close-up.

The Gladys Unger screenplay of 1934 breathes a full cinematic vitality into the scene. The fifth shot begins with a close-up of a tombstone, the camera pulls back to disclose Pip seated, reading the inscription:

5. (*Continued*)

PIP'S VOICE
(*off*)
Sacred to the mem-ory of Phil-lip–Pir-rip—late of this Par-ish.

PIP
(*in scene*)
Also Georg-iana—wife of the above.

6. CLOSE-UP—AT THE STONE

PIP *turns to f.g.—hand up to chin—thinking—he turns—speaks to tombstone—camera pans slightly.* MUSIC.

PIP
I didn't mean to be late, Sarah— (OFF SCENE) but Mrs. Joe wouldn't let me out—

7. CLOSE-UP—PIP

LOOKING DOWN—TALKING

PIP
She was on the rampage—you don't know what a rampage is, do you? She likes to go-whack! What's that to laugh about . . .

8. CLOSE-UP—TOMBSTONES

Camera pans from one marked SARAH *to another—*ALEXANDER. *Camera pans to one marked* TOBIAS—*pans to one marked* ABRAHAM—*pans to another marked* ROGER. MUSIC.

PIP
She's your sister, too? She'd uv brung you up by 'and too if sh'd 'ad the chawnce—Lend us your ball, Tobias—Abraham and I want to play—Don't be a cry baby, Roger.

9. CLOSE-UP—PIP

Seated—talking—he looks off—startled as he hears—MUSIC

> PIP
> I'll play with you next even if you are an infant!

> MAGWITCH
> (*off scene*)

Hold your noise!

10. CLOSE-UP—MAGWITCH

looking to f.g.—starts towards camera.

11. MEDIUM SHOT—INTERIOR GRAVEYARD

MAGWITCH *going towards* PIP *takes hold of him suddenly as he tries to run.* MAGWITCH MUTTERING.

12. CLOSE-UP—OF THE TWO

MAGWITCH *grasping* PIP—*turns him.*

> MAGWITCH
> Keep your mouth shut, you little devil . . .

What has happened via frame motion? We have dollied back from the tombstone, followed by a close-up of the stone with camera panning from Pip's face to the stone, then a close-up of Pip alone, followed by a camera pan over five tombstones: three out of four shots involve frame motion—then Magwitch explodes. The movement keeps us fluid, so that the close-up of Magwitch, in Shot 10, startles our eye. We are jarred by the abrupt cessation of frame motion and the exceptional content.

The interplay between dramatic material—action, actors, setting, dialogue, makeup, costumes—and cinematic form is tremendous. In frame motion the sensuality of movements—shapes changing forms, light changing texture—affects and is in turn affected by the ideas and emotions at work, perhaps more so than in other faces of time. The eye can be stimulated, with such variety of light and movement alterations in frame motion (continuous time) that the physiological potential makes a happy wedding with the more subtle and less obvious psychological stimuli. In all art, seldom can there be such a joining of realism and romanticism.

When thirteen years after the American production David Lean adapted, as both writer and director, *Great Expectations* for J.

Arthur Rank, this interplay became brilliant and vastly rewarding. Note, in this parallel introductory passage, how much more frame motion Lean introduces:

4. VERY LONG SHOT OVER RIVER ESTUARY (WIND—FOOTSTEPS)

On PIP *running right, camera trucking and panning. Movement stops as* PIP *toward foreground, glancing nervously at gallows pole at right as he exits right foreground.*

DISSOLVE TO:

CLOSE SHOT (SUNSET) (WIND—BRANCHES)

PIP *as he appears above broken wall at left. Camera moves right and down with him as he climbs over wall to churchyard, glancing nervously about. He walks toward background, and stops at gravestone.*

5. CLOSE MEDIUM (WIND—BRANCHES)

On PIP *as he tears weed from grave and puts flowers on it.*

6. CLOSE SIDE ANGLE—PIP (WIND—BRANCHES)

As he lifts head. He faces camera looking up left.

7. MEDIUM LONG UPWARD (WIND—BRANCHES)

On tree as it sways toward camera moved by wind.

8. CLOSE-UP—PIP (WIND—BRANCHES)

As he reacts to off shot noises.

9. MEDIUM LONG (WIND—BRANCHES)

On heavy tree stump and bare stretching branches as they sway and creak in the wind.

10. LONG MEDIUM (WIND—BRANCHES)

PIP *as he rises from grave and runs left, camera panning, bringing in* CONVICT *in chains whom* PIP *bumps into suddenly.* CONVICT *grabs* PIP *by throat in close shot.*

PIP

Oh! . . . Oh . . .

11. CLOSE-UP—PIP

as he screams, shooting past CONVICT*'s hands at left as they cover* PIP*'s mouth smothering scream.*

12. CLOSE-UP—CONVICT

WIND.

Keep still, you little devil, or I'll cut your throat.

Now what has happened via frame motion? Lean is what the French call *sérieux;* he is more professional. He felt the same need for traveling and panning; he utilizes the interplay with more rhythmic control. The first two units of frame motion run a total on the screen of slightly over three-quarters of a minute—a very long time. During that period we join Pip in his running fright; we acquire physical and psychic empathy. Then follow five shorter shots of subject motion, totaling only twenty-two seconds—less than half the length of the fluid flow. During this pause, however, our identity is intensified because of the rather simple sentiment involved—an orphan lad alone in the graveyard while the wind howls in the branches. Now Lean is at us again (Shot 10), and for eleven seconds we are fleeing with Pip as he rises from the grave and runs, camera panning—eleven seconds can be a long run—into the arms of a monstrous man. Then comes two quick close-ups: Pip as he screams, which is barely over a second in duration, and a close-up on the convict when he speaks.

For sheer excitement and keen identity Lean's rhythmic uses of frame motion in the opening of *Great Expectations* are superb.

When the point of view of the camera becomes subjective in frame motion, identification is enhanced. Another dimension, like a fourth to the three of traditional depth, heighth, and breadth, is added, and it is an addition in both physical and psychic reality. When the camera is placed inside a moving object, like a gondola in Venice in 1894, or on a motorcar racing around Picadilly Circus in 1900, or in an airplane crash-landing on TV—our perspective is that of a participant, and so our perception is altered.

Consider the excruciatingly painful moment in the classic *Odd Man Out,* which Carol Reed directed and produced for J. Arthur Rank in 1947. The screenplay, by F. L. Green and R. C. Sherriff, contains that car-getaway moment when four out of six shots are subjective frame motion. Johnny McQueen (James Mason) is the leader of an Irish Rebel unit, and raids the treasury of a local mill so that they might have cash for their operations. As amateur thieves, stealing for a noble cause, they have our sympathy. Sad to see, they are inept Robin Hoods who fail to haul a wounded comrade into the getaway car. Such touches of realistic humanity give the film its tragic tone. Here is that cruel and ironic moment when the Rebels with the stolen money are fleeing in the car, an open touring style of World War I vintage, and Johnny McQueen, wounded and bleeding, is being dragged along outside, held precariously by his confederates, Nolan and Murphy. Pat is in the driver's seat, and not a very good driver. Repeatedly, subjective points of view enhance our perception and deepen our involvement:

103. SHOOTING DOWN—NARROW STREET (MOTOR—ALARM)

Camera pans as car races toward corner—swerves around corner.

104. CLOSE-UP—IN MOVING CAR

MURPHY *and* NOLAN *hanging on desperately to* JOHNNY *as car swerves.*

MOTOR—ALARM.

NOLAN

Steady. Steady.

105. LARGE CLOSE-UP—JOHNNY (MOTOR—ALARM)

Gropes for hand hold on top of car. Loses hold and starts to fall backward out of car.

NOLAN
(off shot)

Look out.

106. CLOSE-UP PAN SHOT—FROM MOVING CAR

Camera tilts down and pans as JOHNNY *falls from car and onto pavement.* MOTOR—MUSIC—ALARM. JOHNNY *rolls over at street corner. Camera car races down street.*

MURPHY

Hold him. Hold him.

107. CLOSE-UP—NOLAND

Looks up—speaks urgently—looks back and outside of car.

MUSIC—MOTOR—ALARM

NOLAN

Stop, Pat. Stop. Johnny.

108. TRAVELING SHOT—DOWN STREET FROM REAR OF CAMERA CAR

JOHNNY *lying near corner of side street in b.g.* MUSIC—MOTOR—ALARM.

MURPHY
(*off shot*)

Stop. He's dropped off.

Failure at the moment of victory and the fallibility of men are timeless tragic themes, capable in themselves of only evoking intellectual understanding. Shot 104 introduces perspective. We are inside the moving car and see not only Murphy and Nolan desperately holding on to Johnny, and we see Johnny's upturned face as he's being dragged outside the car. Terrible as the moment is, our eye is concurrently startled by seeing the background move as we move—the pavement, the street, the passing buildings—identity is extented into an exciting reality. The rescue of Johnny becomes more urgent each split second. The subsequent close-up of Johnny, losing hold and starting to fall backward, is the most painfully felt in the film.

When Johnny finally falls, the camera, still shooting from the moving car, pans with him as he hits the road and rolls over, and holds him within the frame while he diminishes in size on the pavement. Then a change of angle. Our point of view is from the rear of the car as we speed away, "Johnny lying near corner of side street." We are left limp.

As a concluding note, it is fascinating to observe that Japanese directors are more inclined to pan and dolly from right to left, whereas Western directors generally go from left to right. Could the reading habits of centuries influence visual preferences as well as condition perception?

4. CONTINUOUS TIME EDITED

The continuing problem in cinema, as in all modern languages, is the relations between order and disorder. The search for structural symmetry is countermanded by the urge toward random groupings. The former positives in values have become the negatives of a newer generation. More than old-fashioned impulse versus discipline are in conflict when the total environment appears to be unanchored. Witness the amount of confusion, juxtaposed to passages of clarity, during scenes and sequences in the works of director-writers such as Antonioni, Buñuel, Fellini, Godard, Kubrick, Lumet, Renais, Richardson, Truffaut, and others.

Through its ability to edit relationships of time, light, and materials, cinema is equipped to focus the external chaos of man while he retains his individual form. In contemporary cinema this theme runs through the Western world like a Mississippi through drought-stricken lands: man half searching in a world half seen. Witness *Ashes and Diamonds* (1958, Poland), *L'Avventura* (Italy), *Ballad of a Soldier* (R 1959, USSR), *The Bridge on the River Kwai* (Britain), *East of Eden* (1955, USA), *My Life to Live* (R 1962, France) —to name a few at random.

This possibility of editing relationships is interlocked with structural and destructional factors, unlike any expression in other arts. These cuts (edits) create patterns of order or disorder. Cinema may walk, it may jump, trot back and forth on two legs, leap backward, and it may crawl on its knees. These five types we shall examine.

In continuous-time editing, the action alters in size and light, but the pulsebeat is familiar. It is slightly reminiscent of stage movements—up front, sideways, to the rear, and so on—dependent on entrances and exits, but on the whole a representational time. The flow is normal; the temporal structure is familiar. Inventiveness lies in the rhythmic length of shots, sizes of shots, and lighting values.

Pip's first meeting with Miss Havisham is a unified moment in *Great Expectations*. The poor boy is to meet the grand lady. Pip is "very uncomfortable" and "half afraid." Dickens describes the eccentric Miss Havisham and her dress in visual narration:

. . . I saw that everything within my view which ought to be white, had been white long ago, and had lost its lustre, and was faded and yellow. I saw that the bride within the bridal dress had withered like the dress, and like the flowers, and had no brightness left but the brightness of her sunken eyes. I saw that the dress had been put upon the rounded figure of a young woman, and that the figure upon which it now hung loose, had shrunk to skin and bone. Once, I had been taken to see some ghastly waxwork at the Fair. . . . I should have cried out, if I could.
"Who is it?" said the lady at the table.
"Pip, ma'am."
"Pip?"
"Mr. Pumblechook's boy, ma'am. Come—to play."
"Come nearer; let me look at you. Come close."
It was when I stood before her, avoiding her eyes, that I took note of the surrounding objects in detail, and saw that her watch had stopped at twenty minutes to nine, and that a clock in the room had stopped at twenty minutes to nine.
"Look at me," said Miss Havisham. "You are not afraid of a woman who has never seen the sun since you were born?"

The Gladys Unger script of 1934 maintains the time order and attempts to enliven the scene with compositional alterations, mainly close-ups. In this pre-World War II version Miss Havisham weeps in self-pity:

23. CLOSE-UP—INTERIOR ROOM

MISS HAVISHAM *dressed in bridal dress and veil—looking at her reflection in the mirror—crying—she turns.* MUSIC. MISS HAVISHAM CRYING SOFTLY.

24. INTERIOR ROOM

MISS HAVISHAM *turning from the mirror—goes slowly across—room festooned with cobwebs.* MUSIC.

25. CLOSE-UP—NEAR DOOR

PIP *clutching his coat—watching off—fearfully.* MUSIC.

26. CLOSE SHOT—MISS HAVISHAM

Standing near chair—sobbing softly. MUSIC.

27. CLOSE-UP—CLOCK

hands pointing to twenty minutes to nine—clock covered with cobwebs. MUSIC.

28. CLOSE SHOT—INTERIOR ROOM

MISS HAVISHAM *moves across.* MUSIC.

29. CLOSE-UP—INTERIOR ROOM

PIP *looking off—frightened—clutching his jacket.* MUSIC.

30. INTERIOR ROOM

MISS HAVISHAM *moving slowly across to the mirror.* MUSIC.

31. CLOSE-UP—AT THE MIRROR

MISS HAVISHAM *looking at her reflection—turns, suddenly.* MUSIC.

32. CLOSE-UP—INTERIOR ROOM

PIP *startled—looks off.* MUSIC.

33. MEDIUM SHOT—AT FIREPLACE

MISS HAVISHAM *moving up—takes candles—goes across—walking with cane—camera pans following her to* PIP—*she questions him.*

MISS HAVISHAM

Who are you?

PIP

I'm—I'm Pip, mum—

MISS HAVISHAM

What are you doing in this room?

MUSIC.

34. CLOSE-UP—PIP

Clutching his hat—speaks, terrified.

PIP

You—you sent for me.

MUSIC.

35. CLOSE-UP—MISS HAVISHAM

Looking off—speaks.

MISS HAVISHAM

So you are the boy who's come here to play.

36. CLOSE-UP—PIP

Looking off—nods—starts forward slowly.

MISS HAVISHAM
(*off scene*)

Come nearer.

37. CLOSE SHOT—INTERIOR ROOM

PIP *moving closer to* MISS HAVISHAM.

MISS HAVISHAM

You're not afraid of a woman who has never seen the sun
since . . .

Using tears and music are stylistic appeals of a type once popular.
In the following David Lean treatment continuous time is orches-
trated through compositional movements (Estella is Miss Havisham's
young ward, Pip's age) :

24. CRANE SHOT—ON STAIRCASE

On ESTELLA *and* PIP *as they move up stairs—he follows her—he looks
around in wonderment—camera cranes over to landing as they come*

*forward to door—turns—goes to b.g.—*PIP *moves slowly to door—he knocks as he exits.* MUSIC. FOOTSTEPS. KNOCK.

ESTELLA

This door, boy.

PIP

After you, Miss.

ESTELLA

Don't be silly, I'm not going in.

MISS HAVISHAM
(*off shot*)

Come in.

25. CLOSE-UP—EXTERIOR DOOR

PIP *opens door slowly—*PIP *steps inside doorway, opening door wide, revealing* MISS HAVISHAM *seated in chair in room b.g.—*MUSIC STOPS— *she wearing bridal costume of many years past—room shows devastation of the time.*

MISS HAVISHAM

Who is it?

PIP

Pip, Ma'am.

MISS HAVISHAM

Pip?

26. CLOSE SHOT—PIP

Looking off hesitantly—speaks.

PIP

Mr. Pumblechook's boy—come to play.

27. CLOSE SHOT—IN ROOM

PIP *in f.g. looking at* MISS HAVISHAM*—camera dollies up and angles around as* PIP *crosses hesitantly to* MISS HAVISHAM*—she questions him —she puts hand over her heart.*

MISS HAVISHAM

Come nearer. Let me look at you. Come close. Look at me. You aren't afraid of a woman who has never seen the sun since before you were born?

PIP

No.

Though Shot 24 is frame motion (crane shot) and in Shot 27 the camera travels up and angles around, the major movement dominating the scene, via the editing, is continuous time. Variables make for artistic freedom. How vastly more variable cinema has become in those short thirteen years.

On the other hand, continuous time may be dominated by frame motion, as we have seen in *Henry V*. Or dominated by subject motion as in *Lost Horizon* or *The End of the Affair*. Rather, it is the predominant quality that characterizes any given passage, and this in turn is usually determined by the style the director gives to the movements.

For example, Fred Zinneman in *From Here to Eternity* solves the problem of suspense in the knife fight between the sadist Fatso and Prew by having them battle in "the shadows." In actual shooting, he went further and had the fight off camera. Our suspense is based on continuous time, second by second. Fatso is almost twice the size of Prew; we fear he will win. When, in the actual shooting, Fatso emerges alone from the shadows we are crushed but hardly surprised. Here is that classic knife fight in script form (Prew had been waiting for Fatso outside the New Congress Club to revenge the death of Angelo Maggio) :

PREW

You killed him.

FATSO

Did I? If I did, he asked for it.

PREW

The Army'll catch up to you sooner or later, Fatso. But before they do, I want a piece of you myself.

There is the snick of a blade snapping open as FATSO *pulls a knife. He moves toward* PREW, *who steps swiftly to one side.*

I kinda thought you'd try that.

There is the same sound as PREW *pulls a knife from his pocket, snaps it open, holds it out flat in his hand, showing it to* FATSO.

This here's the one you pulled on Maggio.

FATSO *darts at* PREW, *knife raised.* PREW *moves back, but* FATSO *is on him and they both roll to one side along the building. The movement throws them deep into the shadows.*

From Here to Eternity. Courtesy of Columbia Pictures.

298. ANOTHER ANGLE—SHOOTING INTO THE SHADOWS

The two figures feint and dart. There is the occasional silver flash of the knives as light hits them. The men go deeper into the shadows, are all but lost to view. There is a startled, pained cry. Then one of the figures falls to his knees and starts to crawl toward camera.

299. CLOSE SHOT—SHOOTING NEAR GROUND

as the figure comes directly to camera, REVEALING *the anguished face of* FATSO. *It slowly turns, is upside-down in the frame.*

300. MEDIUM SHOT

FATSO *is on his back, his stomach gushing blood, his eyes already glazing.* PREW *staggers into the light now. His left side has two vicious cuts; he is bleeding badly. He stares down at* FATSO, *who manages a small, reproving voice.*

> FATSO
> You've killed me. Why'd you want to kill me?

PREW *backs away from* FATSO, *turns, staggers down the alley away from camera.*

> DISSOLVE TO:

Fatso's dying words are omitted. Time, second-by-second, tells the action.

The lynching scene in *The Ox-Bow Incident* (1942) provides an illuminating variable on continuous time. The gruesome action occurs off camera, particularly the clumsy lynching of Martin who has won our affections. Donald Martin (Dana Andrews), a newly arrived rancher is suspected of killing a popular rancher and of stealing his cattle; also suspected are Martin's aged helper and his Mexican cowhand (Anthony Quinn). The three suspects are mounted on horses with hands tied behind and ropes around their necks. It is the climactic moment in the film. The lynching posse is about to taste blood; the innocent three (a modern Calvary) are to be murdered. Each second becomes increasingly critical. Director William Wellman and Lamar Trotti, the screen playwright, wisely move the actual hanging out of camera range. Our eyes focus on the faces of a variety of characters: Gerald, the bullied son of the sadist Major Tetley who orders him to stand behind Martin's horse and whip it upon the signal from Deputy Mapes; the other two executioners are Ma Grier (Jane Darwell), the town boardinghouse keeper, and

Farnley, bent on the revenge of a friend, believed to be shot by the three suspects. Against this array are the feeble voices of Davies, the storekeeper, who pleads for a fair trial, and the singing of Sparks, the Negro preacher-handyman.

We see the three victims on the horses (206) . At the climax we see only the rear of the horses in the shot (209) :

205. CLOSE SHOT—GERALD

as like a sleepwalker he crosses behind the horses, takes his stand.

206. WIDER ANGLE

as the men move back out of the way of the horses.

207. CLOSE SHOT—MAPES

He has a pistol in his hand ready to give the signal.

208. CLOSE-UP—DAVIES

DAVIES

No—no!

The SOUND *of* MAPES' *pistol drowns out his cry.*

209. MEDIUM SHOT—MA, FARNLEY AND GERALD

with just the rear of the horses in the SHOT *as* MA *and* FARNLEY *cut their horses sharply. Their horses leap forward.* GERALD *doesn't move and his horse merely walks out of scene. As he stands motionless,* TETLEY *steps up behind him and strikes him with the butt of his pistol.* GERALD's *knees slump and he falls to the ground unconscious.*

TETLEY
(indicating MARTIN *off scene)*

Finish him.

FARNLEY *raises his gun and fires. As he does so,* GIL *and* DAVIES *step over to* GERALD *and lift him.*

210. ANOTHER ANGLE—SHOOTING AWAY FROM THE LYNCHING

The men are all starting toward their horses, silent, speechless. It is now getting bright. TETLEY *moves past them and goes to his Palomino.*

211. CLOSE SHOT—TETLEY

his face set, as he mounts his horse, turns and, without looking back, rides off.

212. GROUP SHOT—MEN GETTING ON THEIR HORSES

Some glance back, then quickly away. DAVIES *and* GIL *come in among them, carrying the still unconscious* GERALD. GIL *looks back—then quickly shifts his eyes. Off scene comes* SPARKS' *voice softly singing* "In Dat Great Gittin'-up, Mawnin'."

FADE OUT

Grim climaxes, when sustained through continous time, have a cumulative power.

In his feature films Alfred Hitchcock has an unerring instinct for the values of time beheld in a normal rhythm, which can have the affect of emphasizing the character conflict or plot complication. Here from *Dial "M" for Murder* (1954) our villain Tony is trapped:

380. INTERIOR: HALLWAY—SEMI LONG SHOT—DAY

TONY *is opening the hall door once more. He comes down to the* CAMERA *until his* HAND FILLS THE SCREEN. *It goes to the stair carpet and takes out the concealed key.*

381. CLOSE-UP—TONY

Looks down at it with an expression of relief and satisfaction.

382. CLOSE-UP

The key in TONY's *hand. It moves over to the door—is inserted in the lock and as the door opens we see the figure of* HUBBARD *in the room beyond being slowly revealed as the door opening widens.*

383. INTERIOR: WENDICE LIVING ROOM—SEMI CLOSE-UP—DAY

TONY *enters the room and closes the door. He switches on the light. He turns and sees:*

384. SEMI LONG SHOT

MARGO *and* MARK *staring at him. She is in the f.g.*

385. CLOSE-UP

TONY *reacts and then turns and sees:*

386. SEMI LONG SHOT

HUBBARD *standing by the desk.*

387. MEDIUM SHOT

TONY *springs into action and quickly turns and opens the door. A detective bars the way.* TONY *closes the door and remains turned away for a fraction of a second. Then he turns and the* CAMERA PANS HIM *to the drinks. He recovers his customary nonchalance as he pours himself a straight Scotch. . . .*

This screenplay by Frederick Knott, author of the original play, is designed to give the sense of a trap closing from all sides. Hitchcock not only works closely with his writers but designs each shot in detailed sketches.

One of the most common usages of continuous time is the interplay between characters, or the establishment of a personality. We have both types in *The Private Life of Henry VIII* (1933), directed by Alexander Korda with story and dialogue by Lajos Biro and Arthur Wimperis. This script was published in 1934 with an introduction by Ernest Betts: "This is the first complete script of a British film to be published in book form . . . and—if it is not too wild a claim—introduces a new form of literature."

The script is rather conservative; it includes a bit more acting instructions, but presents continuous time in traditional style (Charles Laughton plays Henry; Binnie Barnes is Katherine Howard) :

SCENE 115: MEDIUM SHOT

HENRY *on his dais with* CROMWELL *and* NORFOLK. HENRY *scowling, but eating voraciously. There is a pile of dishes before him.* CROMWELL *and* NORFOLK *silent.* HENRY *pushes away his empty plate with a gesture of disgust.*

He punches a chicken in the breast.

> HENRY
> Pah! What with the cooking and the company I can touch nothing!

Still grasping a bone, he turns to his house-steward, who waits behind his chair:

> (*punching a chicken in the breast*) Call this a capon? Look at that! All sauce and no substance— (*he tears off a leg*) — like one of Cromwell's speeches—and just as difficult to swallow. (*he tears it limb from limb*) Too many cooks, that's the trouble. Above stairs as well as below. (*he throws a leg over his shoulder*) Marry again—breed more sons! coarse brutes! (*he plunges his fingers inside the bird*)

There's no delicacy nowadays. No consideration for others. Refinement's a thing of the past! (*he throws the carcase over his shoulder; off*) Manners are *dead!* Have the cooks whipped from the kitchen! (*he swings round on* CROM-WELL) And *you,* Master Cromwell, you may tell my loyal Guild of Barbers to mind their own business and leave me to mine! Marry, *marry, MARRY!* Am I the King or a breeding bull?

SCENE 116: FULL SHOT

Everybody in the room silent, including CROMWELL *and* NORFOLK. *Everybody stops eating.*

SCENE 117: MEDIUM SHOT

Back to HENRY, CROMWELL, *and* NORFOLK. *Silence. The house-steward puts a new dish before* HENRY *with great caution.* HENRY *sulkily begins to eat, throwing bones over his shoulders to the great peril of pages and servitors. Suddenly he bursts out in a blaze of temper.*

HENRY

God's truth! Are you all dumb? I have known funerals merrier!

One of the GENTLEMEN USHERS *comes forward.*

Have we no singers at the Court?

SCENE 119: MEDIUM SHOT

HENRY *and his guests. Into the picture comes* KATHERINE *with a guitar. She bows to the King and sits down near the dais, as if, so to speak, at his feet.*

HENRY

What will you sing?

KATHERINE

Whatever pleases you—if I know the song.

HENRY

Do you know, "What shall I do for love?"

KATHERINE

Yes, indeed.

HENRY

Good music, do you think?

KATHERINE

Yes, and lovely words.

HENRY

Did you know that both were mine?

KATHERINE

How should I not? It is my favourite song.

HENRY

Then let us hear it, child.

SCENE 120: CLOSE SHOT

KATHERINE *singing*.

KATHERINE
(*sings*)
"Alas! What shall I do for love?
For love, alack! for love what shall I do?
Since none are kind I do not find unto!
Alack!"

HENRY

Very good, my child.

SCENE 121: MEDIUM SHOT

KATHERINE *at once retires, although* HENRY *makes a gesture as if he would like to speak to her.* CULPEPER *behind* HENRY, *at once delighted with* KATHERINE *and jealous of her.*

SCENE 122: CLOSE SHOT

HENRY *turns to* CULPEPER.

HENRY

What's her name, Thomas?

CULPEPER

Katherine Howard, Your Majesty.

HENRY

Ah, I remember—

He turns back to his guests.

So with the uses of power and persistence (continuous time) Henry gets his fifth wife.

Finally, the climax of a scene, sequence, or finale may have a narrative continuity that is executed in successive shots, or would be enhanced with the cumulative power of continuous time. Such an example can be seen in *The Heiress* with its powerful ending, when Catherine wilfully rejects Morris who has come to take her away from spinsterhood. The ironic tragedy of this conclusion—a plain but proud girl and an ambitious but weak man, each with faults—is compounded in mounting impact, shot by shot:

H-14. EXTERIOR: SLOPER HOUSE— (LATER THAT NIGHT)

The house is dark and the parlor curtains are drawn. The only light to be seen is that which comes from the street lamp. A carriage drives up to the house, and we hear the SOUND *of the horse's hoofs and wheels of the carriage as it approaches and stops in front of the Sloper house. There is some luggage piled on top near the driver. When the carriage stops,* MORRIS *gets out, runs up the steps and rings the front door bell.*

H-15. INTERIOR: FRONT PARLOR

The SOUND *of hoofs and the carriage stopping outside is heard.* CATHERINE *is still; she is not surprised; she has expected it. We hear the sound of the door bell as it rings.* MARIA *comes by the front parlor door on her way to answer the bell.* CATHERINE *calls to her.*

> CATHERINE
>
> I will attend to that. It's for me.

> MARIA
> *(stops)*
>
> Yes, Miss.

We hear the SOUND *of the bell as it rings again.* CATHERINE *takes a last stitch and breaks off the thread.* MARIA, *puzzled, watches* CATHERINE *a moment. Then we hear the* SOUND *as* MORRIS *uses the knocker.*

> MARIA
>
> Miss Catherine . . . ?

> CATHERINE
>
> Bolt it, Maria.

> MARIA
>
> Bolt it . . . ?

> CATHERINE
>
> *Bolt the door, Maria!*

> MARIA
> *(weakly)*
>
> Yes, Miss.

MARIA *exits.*

H-16. INTERIOR: FRONT HALL

MARIA *comes from the door of the front parlor to the front door and slides the bolt.*

H-17. EXTERIOR: SLOPER HOUSE—AT FRONT DOOR

MORRIS *hears the bolt slide. He registers his astonishment. We hear the* SOUND *as he uses the knocker again.*

H-18. INTERIOR: FRONT PARLOR

MARIA *has come in from the hall and is standing near the front parlor door.*

CATHERINE

Good night, Maria.

MARIA

Good night, Miss.

MARIA *exits to the back of the house.* CATHERINE *rises. We hear the* SOUND *of the knocker as* MORRIS *uses it again, this time with impatience.* CATHERINE *extinguishes the lamp at her embroidery frame, and walks into the hall.*

H-19. INTERIOR: FRONT HALL

There is a lamp on a side table just inside and very close to the front door. As CATHERINE *picks it up, we go outside and see—*

H-20. EXTERIOR: SLOPER HOUSE—AT FRONT DOOR

MORRIS *is looking at the faint light that comes through the fan over the door. We hear the* SOUND *as he knocks on the door with his fist— loud and a little frantically. He calls:*

MORRIS
(calling)

Catherine!

H-21. INTERIOR: FRONT HALL AND STAIRWAY

Inside, CATHERINE *is standing looking at the door and holding the lamp. She again hears* MORRIS *call.*

MORRIS' VOICE
(calling)

Catherine!

She turns away from the door and starts for the stairs. Again we hear the SOUND *as* MORRIS *knocks and calls.*

MORRIS' VOICE
(calling)

Catherine!

The Heiress. Courtesy of Paramount Pictures.

CATHERINE *continues up the stairs to the* SOUND *of* MORRIS' *knocking furiously and frantically on the door and calling her. She disappears up the steps, the light of the lamp going with her, until the hall is in darkness, and we hear the* SOUND *of* MORRIS' *voice, calling.*

FADE OUT

END OF SEQUENCE "H"

THE END

Continuous time has an insidious capacity to outlast its welcome. Since the clock is ticking along normally, the stroke of midnight is not always heard, and what was once an entertaining guest has become a garrulous bore. Redundant and anticlimactical shots occur more frequently in this most natural of the faces of time. In subsequent types of editing we shall see why this fault is less likely to happen.

In *The Heiress,* for example, the playwrights had an extra shot, ending the film, in a month-earlier version of their shooting script (May 10, 1948) :

CATHERINE *continues up the stairs to the* SOUND *of* MORRIS *knocking furiously and frantically on the door and calling her. She disappears up the steps and as she does, the hall is in darkness.*

H-18. EXTERIOR: WASHINGTON SQUARE AND SLOPER HOUSE— (NIGHT)

The fan light is now dark. The whole house is dark, but we can see a small figure standing at the Sloper door. A light comes on in CATHER-INE's *third-floor room. And the figure seen by the light of the street lamp turns from the door and walks down the steps to a waiting cab.*

FADE OUT

THE END

Obviously the frame motion and subject motion of Catherine with her lamp disappearing up the stairs, leaving the hall in darkness, have different dramatic and cinematic values than a light coming on (via continuous time) in a third-floor room and Morris descending the steps under the streetlamp.

"One of the worst plagues of society is this thoughtless, inexhaustible verbosity," observed the pre-cinema English novelist Mrs. Humphry Ward. The contemporary decline in conversation appears to have been replaced—in magazines, galleries, theatres, and living rooms—by a visual verbosity.

CHAPTER ELEVEN ✻

The Faces of Time Edited

1. ACCELERATED TIME

In the continuous present, which can provide such magical fluidity, the most frequent variation, or rhythmic interruption, is the use of acceleration, the editing that elliptically omits segments by jumping ahead. In the jargon of the technicians this device is appropriately termed a "jump-cut."

Accelerated time is the motion that contrives to compress less than sixty seconds to the minute, so that action and place leap forward beyond normal expectation. Accelerated time is taken at the cut between the last frame of one shot and the first frame of the next. On a sudden your heartbeat may accelerate, perception quicken, and you are propelled into the future at a faster-than-normal speed. You are living at the rate of forty-five or thirty seconds to the minute. When images are progressing in continuous time at the normal pace of 1, 2, 3, 4, an expectant structure, suddenly 5 is omitted and we are looking at 6. The banal or obvious might have been edited out.

Another kind of accelerated time may be a series of structured leaps, as when a deer that has been nibbling its way forward suddenly bounds off, covering territory at great speed. The structure then might be 1, 3, 6, 9 (with variations). This would be a whole sequence edited by jump-cuts.

Also, a third kind is the accelerated cut that moves us ahead in time and place from one sequence to the next, usually done with a dissolve. In other words, time may leap ahead within the same scene, or from scene to scene, or between sequences.

The uses of accelerated time give most evidence of maturity in this art form. The rate of creator and audience sophistication might be charted by the increased usage of this type of cut since World War II. Psychologically astute receivers of stimuli perceive relationships that would have been lost a generation earlier. The visual-minded seek structural relationships in fresher forms than the dramaturgy of Shakespeare or the mosaics of Mozart. Accelerated time satisfies a nervous need for the unexpected. The tempo has been rising through the years. The leap ahead is no longer from 4 to 6, or from 4 to 8. In the search for an unanticipated association—psychological, physiological, or whatever—rapid editing can be freshly inventive, as seen in the works of many *nouvelle vague* directors. Godard's *Breathless* has Jean Seberg and Jean-Paul Belmondo hopping and posing on a bed in all sorts of accelerated times. Indeed, breaking step or rhythm or a pattern can become in itself a stimulant, as seen in the humorous Mack Sennett leaps in *The Graduate.*

Accelerated time is achieved in other ways than through jump-cuts, such as rapid movements of the camera (traveling shots) in approaching or withdrawing from objects and persons at velocities in excess of normal speed or perception. The camera permits us to run, leap, skip, jump, and dive. Also, acceleration is possible by manipulating subject motion (done by mechanical alteration of shutter speeds within the camera), and so gives the illusion that a person or object is moving at greater velocity. Editing is the most common form of all three types.

Gestalt psychology with its emphasis on relationships of organized structures has been an indirect, atmospheric encouragement. We prefer certain film creators for their kind of stimulation through their uses of the cut for accelerated action. Truffaut's *Shoot the Piano Player* and Fellini's *8½* are special favorites. Insights into French or Italian cultural attitudes are possible at the instant of the cut for accelerated time in those films. Certainly, we may glimpse the individual attitudes of the writer-director, his taste, judgment, humor, or anger—more so in this movement, so unique to cinema.

Conversely, instability of structure may be quickly revealed when a creator is just jumping for exercise. Today, disjointed organization ruins more potentially good films than mediocre acting. Unstructured images may be charming to a point. Louis Malle's *A Very Private Affair* (1962) is an example of cinematic tricks, as is Édouard Molinaro's *Man Hunt* (1964). The latter, however, uses acceleration for very good ends; the fast cutting giving a feeling of the hectic, constant motion in the life the man is leading, with continuous time used in the more ordinary, normal sequences. *The Loved One* is a series of lively cartoons, linked through acceleration that, in this case, is no substitute for structure. Acceleration should not only be motivated; it should have a goal. Otherwise, we travel for traveling's sake, which can get tiresome.

Crosses and exits on the stage kept a character in constant view until he disappeared. In early cinema the logical extension was to shoot him as he emerged from the exit and walked down the hall, and down the stairs, and into the street. In contemporary cinema the character may complete his action without crossing the set, and the next shot is of the character entering a taxi or walking in Tokyo.

Many accelerated uses are conceived in editing rooms, largely because the screen playwright hadn't written them at the point where he might have. In *Tom Jones* there is a scene at an inn when Tom and Mrs. Waters eat and drink in an escalating rhythm. With each cut they leap forward in consumption of varied foods and toward the consummation of their affections. The scene as written

Tom Jones. Courtesy of United Artists.

has this idea behind it, and without which the editor and his scissors could not have operated:

120. INTERIOR: THE INN AT UPTON—DINING ROOM—NIGHT

TOM *eats tremendous 18th-century-type meal while* MRS. WATERS *watches him, obviously entranced by him. As his appetite is slowly satisfied, so she gets to work on him, and his eyes and attention slowly shift from his food to her.*

CAPTION 1:
Heroes, notwithstanding the high ideas they may entertain of themselves have more of mortal than divine about them. However elevated their minds may be, their bodies at least are subject to the vilest offices of human nature. Among these, the act of eating.

CAPTION 2 (*as* MRS. WATERS *makes headway*) :
And devious other acts.

Note in the film how the idea was used more cinematically by employing jump-cuts instead of captions.

The more traditional narrative acceleration may be observed in *Abe Lincoln in Illinois* (1940) in a scene, written by Robert E. Sherwood, in which Ann Rutledge and Abe are together for the last time. Sherwood warns us in the appendix to his play version, "This whole affair has been so clouded by the mauve mists of romantic legend that it is impossible to say for sure whether Abe ever proposed marriage to Ann and, if so, whether he was ever accepted." Nonetheless, Sherwood in the screenplay applies accelerated time to cover a sensitive moment and to enhance the tragedy. These shots were not represented in the play; the dissolve merely indicates a short curtain. Shots 184 and 185 occur under the same roof:

184. CLOSE MEDIUM SHOT—THE TWO

A moment's silence save for the off-scene ticking of a clock.

ANN
(*softly*)
Tell me we're going to be happy.

ABE
(*passionately*)
We *will* be happy, Ann! I know I'm not much, Ann, for a girl like you to care about. I've got less than nothing to offer

you. But for whatever I am—whatever I can be—my life belongs to you—and it always will, till the day I die.

ANN

I—I love you . . . Oh, I do love you . . . I knew you'd come back to me . . . Don't ever go away from me again . . . We *will* be happy.

We see that she is clutching MCNIEL'S *locket. But* ABE *doesn't see it. His head is bent over her other hand, which he holds in a fierce, desperate grip.*

DISSOLVE

INTERIOR: RUTLEDGE LIVING ROOM—NIGHT

185. ABE *comes out of the bedroom, walks in silent agony to the door. The* RUTLEDGES *look at him and know that* ANN *is dead.*

Since Abe was not present at her death, Sherwood keeps to the literal truth by not depicting the actual demise.

The following shot, Number 186, leaps ahead to another scene:

EXTERIOR: NEW SALEM STREET—NIGHT

186. *Presumably some distance down the street from the* RUTLEDGE *home. Torch lights, men, excitement.* JACK ARMSTRONG *and his boys are prominent among them—also* BOWLING GREEN, JOSHUA SPEED, *and* MENTOR GRAHAM.

GREEN

Abe carried New Salem by 205 votes to 3!

Wild cheers.

The association in this accelerated time, presumably, is the motivation Ann's death gave to Abe. We make that imaginative leap by the juxtaposition of Abe "in silent agony" and Abe victorious at the polls. This might be one of the "mauve mists" of which Sherwood complained—that behind a great and lonely man lies a love unrealized.

What distinguishes the jump-cut within the bedroom scene in *Breathless* from any narrative jump from one sequence to another? Only the cut's relativity to an idea or an emotion that dominates that passage, as in poetry, the novel, or drama.

Since 1901 (English pioneer directors), narrative jumps have provided cinema with a unique power that thrilled audiences accustomed to such leaps at the leisurely pace of the theatre, where a curtain would end an act and a notation in the program would inform the theatergoer that it was "six months later." In silent films the leaps were announced by titles of captions. Sometimes these were bits of verse composed by the director, as in the case of D.W. Griffith who fancied himself a poet and published verses in *Collier's*. His disciple, Erich von Stroheim, did the same in *Greed*.

From the script of *Greed*, here is its first narrative leap, the time when McTeague leaves the mining camp at his mother's instigation to seek his fortune as an apprentice to the itinerant dentist:

CLOSE-UP—MOTHER

through two layers of veil, tear dimmed eyes. She stuffs her handkerchief, bit by bit into her mouth, then pulls on edge of handkerchief so hard she tears it.

REVERSE SHOT

From behind her back with road stretched out in front of her at the end of which the wagon of the DENTIST *just then is silhouetted against the sky.*

SLOW IRIS DOWN

on wagon, hold for second and as wagon disappears

IRIS OUT COMPLETELY

FADE IN TITLE

Ah! curst ambition! to thy lures we owe,
All the great ills that mortals bear below.

FADE OUT

IRIS UP—ON MCTEAGUE'S FACE

He is apparently watching something with quite some interest, hold there for second.

PAN

to right until face of some patient leaning back with napkin around neck comes to be in iris, while hands of unseen person are working on tooth in mouth of patient

IRIS OPENS

completely while camera on perambulator moves simultaneously back until scene in

MEDIUM SHOT

shows quite some crowd of village folks standing around chair with patient in it, while our friend the TRAVELING DENTIST *is working on him.* MCTEAGUE *stands very close to him.* DENTIST *turns, holds out hand to instrument from small table next to him. This scene is taken at Colfax.*

SLOW IRIS DOWN

on MCTEAGUE's *face watching, hold for second*

IRIS OUT COMPLETELY

It is amusing to note the silent film technique of titles rejuvenated by John Osborne, the screen playwright of *Tom Jones,* and that the uses of the iris (controlling the size of the image by focusing on a portion of it) has been adapted by the French new wavers (Malle, Godard, Truffaut) .

The novel, of course, preceded cinema in the concept of accelerated time, as Elizabethan drama preceded the novel, but in cinema the acceleration is instantaneous to the eye.

In *Anna Karénina* the climactic suicide occurs at the end of Chapter XXXI, Part VII. Tolstoy's narrative instinct is to flee far from the gruesome tragedy in the subsequent chapter to the activity of a secondary character, Sergei Ivanovitch:

She tried to fling herself below the wheels of the first carriage as it reached her; but the red bag which she tried to drop out of her hand delayed her, and she was too late; she missed the moment. She had to wait for the next carriage. . . . And exactly at the moment when the space between the wheels came opposite her, she dropped the red bag, and drawing her head back into her shoulders, fell on her hands under the carriage, and lightly, as though she would rise again at once, dropped on to her knees. And at the same instant she was terror-stricken at what she was doing. "Where am I? What am I doing? What for?" She tried to get up, to drop backwards; but something huge and merciless struck her on the head and rolled her on her back. "Lord, forgive me all!" she said, feeling it impossible to struggle. A peasant muttering something was working at the iron above her. And the light by which she had read the book filled with troubles, falsehoods, sorrow, and evil, flared up more brightly than ever before, lighted up for her all that had been in darkness, flickered, began to grow dim, and was quenched forever.

In that stunning passage, sensitively translated by Constance Garnett, Tolstoy depicts an action on narrative, psychological, and philosophical levels. The counterpoint follows immediately in Chapter I, Part VIII:

Almost two months had passed. The hot summer was half over, but Sergei Ivanovitch was only just preparing to leave Moscow.

Not until Chapter IV does this minor character—he had just finished six years of writing "Sketch of a Survey of the Principles and Forms of Government in Europe and Russia"—see Vronsky, Anna Karénina's lover. Not until Chapter V does Sergei Ivanovitch talk to him, and we hear Vronsky's expressions of guilt.

In the Garbo film the juxtaposition is immediate with a brief pause for an old-fashioned lap dissolve. Here is the editor's record, a continuity script. Accelerated time occurs between shots 65 and 66:

59. CLOSE SHOT—TRAIN WHEELS

going out right more rapidly—

60. CLOSE-UP—ANNA

looking down f.g.

61. CLOSE SHOT—TRAIN WHEELS

pulling out to right more rapidly.

62. CLOSE-UP—ANNA

looking down f.g.

63. CLOSE SHOT—TRAIN WHEELS

going out right rapidly—

64. CLOSE-UP—ANNA

looking f.g., then jumps off f.g.

65. LONG SHOT—TRAIN

pulling out toward b.g. (Sound of whistle.)

LAP DISSOLVE

66. MEDIUM CLOSE SHOT—INTERIOR: VRONSKY'S APARTMENT

VRONSKY *and* YASHVIN *seated at table drinking—talking—*

YASHVIN

Vronsky, can't you forget? You're a young mar yet, your life's before you. Can't you forget?

67. CLOSE-UP—VRONSKY

looking up f.g. and speaks—

> VRONSKY
>
> I'll tell you what I can't forget; that the last time we were together and she turned to me with pleading eyes, she wanted sympathy . . . a kind word. I didn't give it to her. I didn't speak, I just turned away.

This blueprint, taken as specifications after the film was photographed and edited, replaces Sergei Ivanovitch by Yashvin, another secondary character. There is an undeniable directness in the emotional association achieved by going from Anna's suicide to Vronsky. This is the power possible in the jump-cut.

Progressing from one stage to a successive one within the idea of a scene is a familiar form of accelerated time. In *Pygmalion* Higgins (Leslie Howard) is teaching Eliza (Wendy Hiller) to speak the King's English in queenly style. In the following passage there are four leaps illustrating Eliza's progress: she goes from "the rain in Spain" drill to an exhausted slumber, then to the exercise with marbles, followed by a recorded playback of a previous exercise, and then into a live drill with her professor. Though two of these five segments contain shots running in parallel time, the predominant characteristic of the scene is accelerated time (MIX TO is an editing term) :

CLOSE-UP—HIGGINS

> HIGGINS
>
> The rain in Spain.

CLOSE-UP—ELIZA

> ELIZA
>
> The rain in Spain.

CLOSE-UP—HIGGINS

> HIGGINS
>
> Stays mainly in the plains.

CLOSE-UP—ELIZA

> ELIZA
>
> Stays mainly in the plains.

CLOSE-UP—HIGGINS

> HIGGINS
> The rain in Spain stays mainly in the plains.

MIX TO

CLOSE-UP—ELIZA ASLEEP

MIX TO

CLOSE TWO SHOT—ELIZA AND HIGGINS

> HIGGINS
> Now, Eliza, you see these three marbles. . . . I want you to put them into your mouth. . . . Yes.

CLOSE SHOT—ELIZA AND HIGGINS'S HAND

popping marbles into mouth.

> HIGGINS
> *(off)*
> One . . . two . . . three.

CLOSE TWO SHOT—HIGGINS AND ELIZA

> HIGGINS
> Now don't be alarmed . . . it's just an exercise. . . . Now then, repeat slowly after me. The shallow depression in the west of these islands is likely to move slowly in a westerly direction.

> ELIZA
> "The shallow depression in the west of these islands is likely to move in . . ." (*Breaks off suddenly, spits out marbles into hand.*) . . . Lumme, I swallowed one.

> HIGGINS
> Don't worry, we have plenty more.

MIX TO

CLOSE-UP—RECORD REVOLVING ON TURNTABLE

MIX TO

CLOSE-UP—SPEAKER

> (ELIZA *off, in refined voice*)
> The shallow depression in the west of these islands is likely to move slowly in an easterly direction.

MIX TO

CLOSE-UP—SPEAKER

MIX TO

CLOSE-UP—HIGGINS

> HIGGINS
> Hampshire, Hereford, Hertford.

CLOSE-UP—ELIZA

> ELIZA
> Hampshire, Hereford . . . Coo lumme it jumps.

CLOSE-UP—HIGGINS

> HIGGINS
> And so it will, Eliza . . . every time you say "H" correctly.
> Now try again . . . In Hampshire, Hereford and Hertford,
> Hurricanes Hardly ever Happen.

CLOSE-UP—ELIZA

> ELIZA
> H'in Hampshire, Hereford and Hertford, Hurricanes
> Hardly ever 'appen.

The Jack L. Warner production of this scene, while more elaborate and expensive, was based on the same accelerated principle. Time is elemental whether it be noted on a child's wristwatch or a Tiffany jeweled setting.

Often the development of an idea within a scene combines accelerated time with other movements. In *Citizen Kane* there is a thrilling use of swish, or rapid, panning combined with jump-cuts. When two or even more movements are involved and interrelated, the problem is to discover which one dominates or carries a larger portion of the idea. This may pose a challenge. Orson Welles chooses to combine frame movement with accelerated time to depict the deterioration of a marriage. The result is an elliptical thrust, condensing years into a minute. It is a series of breakfasts sittings, beginning with Kane and his first wife seated close together after an all-night party, he in white tie, she in daring décolletage. He will cancel his morning appointments to remain with her (the marriage does produce a son). Then the table is lengthened, and by swish pans from one end to the other—an accelerated edit interjected during the panning—we see husband and wife literally farther apart. They are dressed more soberly; Kane has a breakfast jacket, a pipe, a moustache. They lady of the house is in her dressing gown and inquires politely into her husband's newspaper attacks on the entrenched interests; they quarrel. The dialogue becomes a link in the acceleration as each retort flows into another; then there is silence at the breakfast table while wife reads the opposition paper. Kane is in his business suit.

In this scene we have (1) frame motion in the use of a swish pan, (2) subject motion in terms of slight movements of the actors, (3) accelerated time in that the cutting jumps us ahead in years, and (4) parallel time since we cut via the swish pan from Kane to wife within the same time reference. These four movements are interrelated and work in harmony. No separate one could create the final impact, and together they total more than their sum.

Since neither subject nor frame movement could produce this extraordinary compression of time in this style, this particular example is one of accelerated time, an effective means for conveying the dissolution of a marriage.

The swish pans at the conclusion of John Huston's *Reflections in a Golden Eye* (1967) fail to evoke horror or depict the end of that marriage, since the technique is self-consciously tricky.

Films for television have adopted this device: the combined swish pans and jump-cuts in *The Man from U.N.C.L.E.*, for example, take us from Moscow to New York with the blur of a moving image.

The leap forward to a future possibility or daydream is another usage. The opening scene in *Hiroshima Mon Amour* contains a shot, symbolic in intent, that projects the lovers into the future should there be another war. Their intertwined arms and legs, nude and fleshly real, become ghostly and dead. Here is the text by novelist Marguerite Duras in her *Scenario:*

As the film opens, two pairs of bare shoulders appear, little by little. All we see are these shoulders—cut off from the body at the height of the head and hips—in an embrace, and as if drenched with ashes, rain, dew, or sweat, whichever is preferred. The main thing is that we get the feeling that this dew, this perspiration, has been deposited by the atomic "mushroom" as it moves away and evaporates.

The two shots in the film, the now and the after in juxtaposition, are violent and conflicting, exacting as Duras demands in her poetical text.

Mother McTeague in *Greed* visualizes her dream for her son. She is with the traveling dentist and stares "into space with wide eyes" and her look becomes concentrated on the dental chair at the rear of the dentist's wagon (prior to her son's departure) :

SHOT FROM HER ANGLE—OF DENTAL CHAIR

First empty, no one around. Suddenly into dental chair dissolves figure of a patient, one of the miners perhaps, with DENTIST *working on him so that his face could be seen from* MOTHER'S *angle. Some miners on left as well as on right looking on. Figure of* DENTIST *slowly dissolves into figure of her son* MCTEAGUE *in a similar suit as* DENTIST *wears.*

QUICK LAP INTO

MEDIUM SHOT—PATIENT IN CHAIR AND MCTEAGUE

as dentist, seems to have finished his work, removes napkin from PATIENT'S *neck,* PATIENT *rises, asks price.* MCTEAGUE *as dentist answers with gesture of two fingers indicating $2.00.* PATIENT *extracts two silver dollars, and one by one lays them into* MCTEAGUE'S *palm.* MC- TEAGUE *bows comically as he should in* MOTHER MCTEAGUE'S *imagination, one hand on abdomen and the other on back. Unusually graceful.* PATIENT *starts to leave.*

DISSOLVE OUT

DISSOLVE INTO *empty dental chair with no one around as it is in reality.*

MEDIUM CLOSE-UP—MOTHER AND DENTIST

both in [*the shot*], MOTHER *with faint trace of smile.* DENTIST *seems to understand her thoughts, at once follows up idea accompanied by gestures.*

IRIS DOWN ON DENTIST TALKING

In *The Knack* writer-director Richard Lester uses a plotless pushing of an iron bedframe through London streets, including a passage on the Thames, as a series of jump-cuts, each acceleration depending on inventive novelty for its humor. The total impact of so many jumps forward is to create curiously a sense of the continuous present with variations. A similar instance is a tandem bicycle ride through Manhattan's streets and parks in *A Thousand Clowns* (1965).

2.   PARALLEL TIME

Cinema enables the viewer to be in two or more places concurrently and also at two or more different times simultaneously. This type of editing is called the crosscut. Two clocks are running in separate settings, and the viewer may see them both. Parallel time may also be normal time, but a particular kind of normal, a variation of continuous time, like the breakfast scene in *Citizen Kane*.

For a more classic example, wherein chronological time is ignored, there is D. W. Griffith's *Intolerance* (1916). The master of the cross-cut has us in four different countries and in four different centuries with only a blink of an eyelid. Time is thematically related through the depiction of historical dramas in which man is intolerant to man—modern time with its crime, poverty, and capital punishment; the Babylonian time when invasion by armies and betrayal within were examples of hatred; medieval time when Roman Catholics persecuted Huguenots on St. Bartholemew's Eve; and biblical times when Jesus of Nazareth was not tolerated by the Pharisees.

On a simpler scale we had the moment prior to Anna Karénina's suicide, an example when crosscutting within a scene is not parallel time, but parallel place. We recall seeing in close shots the "train wheels going out right more rapidly" from the perspective of Anna. We also see Anna's face in a close-up from the angle of the train. We are omnipotent. We are the wheels and we are Anna.

In the following example from *High Sierra* (1941) the killing of Roy Earle (Humphrey Bogart) by a marksman in the sheriff's posse is rendered cruelly real by a subjective shot—our outlaw hero seen through the telescopic sight of the rifle—placed in parallel juxtaposition between a shot of Roy alive and Roy dead. The dog Pard was attached to Roy and the girl friend Marie, and had followed Roy on his flight high into the Sierra Mountains:

290. CLOSE SHOT—ROY

scowling. PARD *runs into scene, jumps to lick* ROY's *face in a frenzy of delight.* ROY *puts his hands on the dog to feel if he is real. Then he pushes him aside, gets to his feet, shouts:*

ROY

Marie!

291. CLOSE SHOT—TIM, THE MARKSMAN

as he puts his eye to the telescope sight of his rifle.

292. LONG SHOT—ROY

through the telescope sight. The cross lines in the sight are on his middle. OVER SCENE *the crash of the rifle. The recoil of the rifle throws* ROY *out of view.*

293. CLOSE-UP—ROY'S HAND

PARD *comes into the picture, sniffs the fingers.*

DISSOLVE TO

It would be difficult to imagine another way of conceiving that scene. The perfect choice if the possible faces of time, in this instance, is parallel time, the being at both places.

A series of three separate but linked parallel structures may be observed in a passage from *Beat the Devil* (1954), another Humphrey Bogart-John Huston adventure. Here, in the screenplay by Truman Capote, is the moment when the elegant car escapes from its occupants who are pushing it, eludes an onrushing bus, and dives into the sea:

174. MEDIUM SHOT—EXTERIOR: CAR—COAST ROAD

the DRIVER *pushing the car—the* CAMERA PANS *to show* DANNREUTHER *and* PETERSEN *pushing it from behind—suddenly the car runs away from them.*

175. LONG SHOT—THE CAR

it runs away from them down the declining road.

176. MEDIUM SHOT—PETERSEN, DANNREUTHER AND DRIVER

they are all running after the car.

177. LONG SHOT—THE CAR

going away from camera around the bend and down the road, right to left.

178. MEDIUM SHOT—PETERSEN, DANNREUTHER AND DRIVER

all running down the road.

179. MEDIUM LONG SHOT—THE CAR

going away from camera, right to left.

180. MEDIUM SHOT—THE BUS

it comes towards camera, left to right.

181. MEDIUM SHOT—THE CAR

it comes towards camera right to left—camera PANS LEFT *with it as it passes the bus and crashes through the wall.*

182. LONG SHOT—THE CAR

it falls down into the sea from the cliff.

183. MEDIUM SHOT—THE BUS

the passengers jump out and come to the wall and look over.

184. LONG SHOT—THE SEA

showing the bubbles where the car has sunk.

185. MEDIUM SHOT—DRIVER, PETERSEN AND DANNREUTHER

they are all looking down over a part of road wall. Then the DRIVER *turns to them.*

DRIVER
My car. My car . . . my beautiful car.

The first of the parallel structures can be noted in shots 174–178, the stalled car and the three pushers in juxtaposition. Then follows the impending collision of bus and car in shots 179–181. As the climax of this delightful scene, we behold four parallel actions: the car dives off the cliff; the bus passengers rush to see the demise; the sea swallows the car; and the three fated pushers are desolate.

A three-way parallel structure climaxes *The Bridge on the River Kwai*. The irony that renders the scene painful must be viewed from the omnipotence of being everywhere at once. In a Japanese prisoner-of-war camp for British soldiers, the English commander Nicholson (Alec Guinness) discovers that the bridge he has so proudly built as a matter of personal and national pride is about to be exploded by a commando unit. Tracing the demolition wire, he heads downriver for the plunger to stop the destruction. En route he is hit by a mortar shell fired by the commando leader Warden (Jack Hawkins); this occurs in Shot 67 of the continuity script based on the final reel. To add another time bomb to the tension, the target of the blowing is the oncoming train, which Warden is determined to destroy. Thus we have Nicholson heading for the plunger, though mortally wounded; we have the train pounding toward the bridge; and we have Warden in his commando camp:

68. EXTERIOR: RIGHT BANK OF RIVER—DAY

MEDIUM SHOT—*Plunger Box below rock.* SOUND OF TRAIN'S APPROACH *(off shot).*

69. EXTERIOR: RIGHT BANK OF RIVER—DAY

MEDIUM SHOT—NICHOLSON

stumbles forward—staggers.

CUT TO:

70. EXTERIOR: NICHOLSON'S BRIDGE—DAY

The train moves forward on to the bridge. SOUND OF TRAIN AND WHISTLE.

71. EXTERIOR: RIGHT BANK OF RIVER—DAY

CLOSE SHOT—NICHOLSON

he falls. SOUND OF TRAIN WHISTLE.

72. EXTERIOR: RIGHT BANK OF RIVER—DAY

MEDIUM CLOSE SHOT—THE PLUNGER BOX

NICHOLSON's *body falls forward on to it and pushes down the handle.* SOUND OF TRAIN *(off shot)*.

CUT TO:

73. EXTERIOR: BRIDGE AND RIVER—DAY

LONG SHOT—*The bridge blows up.* SOUND OF EXPLOSION.

CUT TO:

74. EXTERIOR: COMMANDO CAMP ABOVE BRIDGE—DAY

WARDEN *in f.g. with* SIAMESE GIRLS *behind him*—SOUND OF EXPLOSION *(off shot)* —*looks out towards the bridge.* WARDEN *starts to rise.*

CUT TO:

75. EXTERIOR: NICHOLSON'S BRIDGE—DAY

The train and carriages falling into the river.

Our omnipotent point of view enables us to witness all sides of the ironic tragedy. In a concluding shot, Number 81, Clipton, a junior officer under Nicholson, cries out one word—"Madness!"

The tempo in parallel time is essential to its effectiveness. Glancing at the figures above, we note the following rhythmic tensions: having been wounded in Number 67, Nicholson is still short of his objective—thus comes a two-second glimpse of the plunger box in a medium shot. Back we go to Nicholson, who stumbles and staggers onward for four seconds. The train, full of sound and whistle, is moving onto the bridge in a one-and-a-half-second shot. Again back to Nicholson for three seconds as he falls. From a different angle and for only one second we see his inert body collapse upon the plunger box, pushing down the handle. The bridge blows up for three and a half seconds. At the sound of the explosion Warden starts to rise to his feet—two and a half seconds. Finally, for five and a half seconds the train and cars fall with the bridge into the river Kwai.

The quick shot of the train pounding forward (one and a half seconds) climaxes previous longer shots of the train. Similarly, Nicholson's dead body setting off the explosion (one second) climaxes previous shots of longer duration. Pressure is most intense when it is briefest, provided there has been preparation. Indeed, parallel structure requires not only a rhythmic interrelationship but also implies an intensification of tempo. A writer-director like David Lean provides exceptional examples of these principles at work.

Occasionally, parallel time is not in contactual juxtaposition but is adjacent in structure. *Splendor in the Grass* (1961, screenplay by William Inge, directed by Elia Kazan) offers an interesting illustration. Mrs. Loomis has a heart-to-heart talk with her daughter Deanie, admonishing her not to "let things go too far" with boyfriend Bud. Deanie promises she won't, but once alone she has "tears in her eyes. It's as though she longed for the act of fulfillment."

Ten shots later, Ace Stamper, wealthy and bullish, has a heart-to-heart talk with his son Bud, admonishing him not to quit school and marry Deanie—"You pull a crazy stunt like that and I'll cut ya out of everything." Father advises son to "get a little steam outa his system . . . with one of the *other* kind" of girl. But to Bud "no other girl looks good to me, but Deanie. I can't even notice anyone but her. . . ." The parental parallel is obvious: Morality of a sort is at work in both homes.

Parallel time can be uniquely impressive as descriptive cinema, especially during moments when gigantic actions submerge plot and character. The earthquake sequence in *San Francisco* (1936) illustrates this type. Mary (Jeanette MacDonald) and Burley (Jack Holt) are about to leave the music hall where Mary has been entertaining the customers when the first quake begins. Mary stops to ask, "What was that?"

Shot 95 (Reel 10) is a close shot of a large glass chandelier shaking with plaster dropping from the ceiling. There is a rumble. The shot is exceptionally short—one and one-sixth seconds.

Shot 96 is a close shot of glasses of beer on a table shaking. It is only two-thirds of a second.

Shot 97 is a medium shot, shooting down on the people at a table.

They are reacting to the rumble. The length is the same as Shot 95—one and one-sixth seconds.

We are experiencing the earthquake within one setting. With Shot 121 begins a series of earthquake shots in a montage:

> Walls of building fall—lamp posts falling and crashing to street—dust and smoke fills screen. Then shots of people rushing through streets. Large brick wall falls. Large tower building crumpling and falling, CU reaction of woman. Bricks falling over people on ground. Dust fills screen. People rushing out of buildings. More brick walls falling. People fall to ground—bricks fall over them. Dust fills screen. More bricks falling over people as they run through streets. Water main bursts—water sprays fill screen. Many lying on ground. Little girl looks up o.s.—reacts—then wall of building falls—dust and bricks cover man on the ground. Dust fills screen. Then shot of woman looking up o.s. Corner wall of building crumples—falls—piano is hurled out of window—crashes to pieces on ground. People rushing past camera. Others running through dusty street. Large statue on building as it rocks. CS of horse rearing—statue in f.g. starts to fall—man below with horse and buggy—man looks up o.s.—reacts—statue falls forward toward camera. Man jumps out of buggy—dust and bricks falling. Statue falls on vegetable wagon. Flashes showing wheel of wagon spinning off—head of statue rolling on the ground.

These shots were created out of footage shot by cameramen in special sets, and are credited to the editor John Hoffman, not to the screen playwright Anita Loos. Nonetheless, descriptive uses of parallel time are within the realm of imaginative writers as well as directors.

The mysterious, psychological flow that characterizes the style of *Marienbad* creates a dreamlike unreality. Actually, time loses its dimensions when one tense so interwinds with another that there is no clock. The clue to this timelessness of the clock is established in a parallel-time scene near the beginning of the film.

The elegant guests in their evening clothes have gathered in a reception hall of their spa. They sit or stand in separate poses, chairs scattered about—no theatre rows. On a small stage are an actor and actress in the evening dress of the previous century, and whose postures and gestures are wooden and baroque—even the stage is lighted by eight oil lamps as footlights, and the curtain is a crudely painted setting of a classical landscape. By crosscutting between the stilted actors acknowledging the applause of the audience and the

Last Year at Marienbad. Courtesy of Astor Pictures.

equally stilted audience applauding, Resnais presents his provocative theme (assisted by scenarist Alain Robbe-Grillet) : there is no difference between playacting and life-acting, between illusion and reality, between the performers and the viewers.

The script employs detailed camera instructions with the aim of involving the reader in a fuller visualization:

> Having reached the first row of the spectators, the camera continues its movement, passing in review, from almost directly in front now, the faces aligned, frozen with attention, and brightly illuminated by the light from the stage. But the camera speed has gradually decreased and the image finally comes to rest on a few motionless heads.
>
> Then the shot cuts abruptly to the stage itself, brilliantly lit and occupying the entire screen.
>
> The stage represents a garden. . . . .

The timelessness of the real and the unreal makes *Marienbad* extraordinary.

3.   PAST TIME

Another type of interruption, altering the flow of continuous time, is the cut to a previous place and time, called a flashback. This is a momentary reverse, like a swirling eddy before the river resumes its dominant direction downstream. Accelerated time, as we have seen, acts to send the river on a sudden into white water. Parallel time acts like a division into companion channels.

The interruption to the past may be characterized often in terms of sentiment. Memory, being one of the most powerful determinants of present conduct, hovers constantly in our conscious and subconscious backgrounds. There is in everyone a latent love of time remembered, of places in the past.

Past and parallel times are the only two types of variations on continuous time that are achieved solely through editing, and in a way parallel is a two-or-more-faced version of continuous. Accelerated time, as observed, may be created not only through editing but also by decelerating the rate of the film speed of the camera and by exaggerating the frame movement in pans, tracks, and zooms. However, once the past has been evoked through the flashback, time becomes once again continuous. The unfolding of movements— through action, acting, editing, or frame motions—is time present even though the setting might be in a previous period. This realization reiterates the basic nature of cinema, its predominant occupation with the ongoing moments. The flashback to a previous continuous time might be concluded, ironically, with an accelerated time leap back to the present.

The nostalgic D. W. Griffith preferred to exploit the sentimental values possible in the flashback. Remembrance of previous actions could be established by having a fade-out on a character, say Elsie Stoneman (Lillian Gish) in *The Birth of a Nation* (1915), and a fade-in on Elsie and the Little Colonel in a tender embrace, a vignette by itself; then back to Elsie recovering from her reverie. The flashback pattern had precedence in the novel, the form that inspired Griffith to adapt the technique to cinema, and in the epics of Homer.

The classic value of the flashback is its information coming to us privately, unknown to some of the key characters. It serves the role of the Greek chorus or oracle, and, as Aristotle points out, stimulates our curiosity—we know something about the villain or the hero that others haven't yet realized, and we watch to see when they will awaken. We feel subtly superior.

Mildred Pierce (1944) as a novel has a natural opening without shock, but the film begins melodramatically with three shots that are a flash-ahead, rendering the main story a flashback. The technique becomes a frame in which the story fits. *The Lavender Hill Mob* (1951) provides a perfect illustration of a narrative use of past time, including a surprise ending when we discover Holland (Alec Guinness) is handcuffed to a police officer when they both rise from the table where Holland has been drinking and recounting his adventure.

The Loneliness of the Long Distance Runner is structured repeatedly on the flashback. Whenever the young thief (Tom Courtenay) in the reformatory runs crosscountry for sport—alone through the woods and fields—his mind flashes back to previous episodes: the sordid family life with an unfaithful, unfeeling mother, a father dying after a hard life of labor, the barrenness of existence compelling the boy to defy the deadly patterns by stealing a car, spending an overcast weekend at the shore with a girl, and stealing a cashbox. The flashbacks provide the means for presenting the main narrative, which, in turn, becomes an explanation for his incarceration—a parallel structure—crime and punishment on an obvious level, and boredom and running on a philosophical plane. The running of the

The Loneliness of the Long Distance Runner. Courtesy of Woodfall.

Borstal boy becomes an expression of freedom sought and felt in his body, a joyous and hopeful expression. Thus when the pompous chief warden (Michael Redgrave) robs our runner of this free flavor by insisting that the Borstal boy win in competition against a private school team of wealthy young gentlemen, he balks, deliberately and subconsciously, upon nearing the finish line. The series of flashbacks at this finale serve a thematic aim. They summarize the social system, the barren life, the artificial values. It is a Tony Richardson attack on the Establishment, the director assisted by novelist and screen playwright Alan Sillitoe.

John Brooks' *In Cold Blood* also relies on flashbacks for its structural continuity and hence for its suspense.

Narrative and thematic flashbacks characterize *The Pawnbroker* (R 1965), ranging from split seconds to entire scenes. A German-Jewish refugee from a Nazi concentration camp, Sol Nazerman (Rod Steiger), operates a pawnshop in Harlem. He sees the hell of his present life in previous terms, so sensitized internally is he to self-torment and self-pity while externally he wears a turtle shell of indifference. Seeing a jammed subway car of New Yorkers, tired, silent, dispirited, his mind flashes back to a shot of a railroad car packed with victims heading for the concentration camp. The sight of a half-naked prostitute offering herself to him in his pawnshop evokes a flashback to his witnessing of his wife stripped naked and forced into a brothel for Nazi officers. Unfortunately, these interruptions are frequently heavy-handed and arbitrary; their editorial flavor overburdens the narrative.

Time remembered, as a series of nostalgic and self-recriminative recollections of an old man's past, gives the flashback a thematic significance in *Wild Strawberries* (1957). On the day Professor Emeritus Isak Borg (Victor Sjöström) is to be made a Jubilee Doctor at Lund University, he has dreams, remembrances, and nightmares. Within this one-day frame Ingmar Bergman as writer-director employs the flashback as counterpoint to contrast the rigid, self-centered state-of-mind of Isak Borg today. The first of the series has a Scrooge-like premonition of Time Future and is, in effect, a flash-ahead. The seventy-six-year-old professor dreams of a funeral. The hearse is wrecked, the coffin partly smashed:

> . . . When I leaned forward, the dead hand clutched my arm and pulled me down toward the casket with enormous force. I struggled helplessly against it as the corpse slowly rose from the coffin. It was a man dressed in a frock coat.
>
> To my horror, I saw that the corpse was myself. I tried to free my arm, but he held it in a powerful grip. All this time he stared at me without emotion and seemed to be smiling scornfully.
>
> In this moment of senseless horror, I awakened and sat up in my bed. . . .

Borg's sour nature is revealed in his relations with his house-keeper, his son and daughter-in-law, and his ninety-six-year-old cynical mother. That he seeks affection and sentiment is portrayed in his visit to the wild-strawberry patch he knew near the family summer home. After a series of contrasting episodes during the long day, including flashbacks to his family when he was a boy, to his wife when she was unfaithful, and in a flash-ahead to a catechismal examination into his incompetence as a doctor, the script and film conclude with a flashback to Isak's father and mother:

> . . . I looked for a long time at the pair on the other side of the water. I tried to shout to them but not a word came from my mouth. Then my father raised his head and caught sight of me. He lifted his hand and waved, laughing. My mother looked up from her book. She also laughed and nodded. . . .
>
> I dreamed that I stood by the water and shouted toward the bay,

but the warm summer breeze carried away my cries and they did not reach their destination. Yet I wasn't sorry about that; I felt, on the contrary, rather lighthearted.

There is a feeling of catharsis and resignation in this ending with the old professor lying "lighthearted" in his bed.

The thematic uses of past time in *Hiroshima Mon Amour,* the references to Nevers and the German lover, have been noted. Turning the clock back repeatedly to demonstrate that time is timeless as humanity is brotherhood, Resnais in his subsequent *Marienbad* dissolves completely the familiar landscape of time. The hypnotic appeal—the timelessness of human relations—lies in its schizophrenia. Sophisticated, sensitive persons are likely to live on more than one time level, their awareness split or fragmented, often disassociated. Primitives prefer the present as romantics seek the future and cynics recall the past. By fusing the three, Resnais demonstrates that one is not more essential than the other two, nor can one exist without the others. Curiously, he achieves this blurring of the clock in the beginning of the film by utilizing past time.

At first the girl X is dressed in black during continuous time. During previous times, via flashbacks, she wears white. For a while we can keep track through costumes, an adventurous experience.

The camera travels in trucks and pans to depict a static existence within a massive mausoleum; organ music summons memories of departed encounters. Life is baroque and stationary. The first half hour has the stylized grace of an aristocratic chess game, and gradually the illogic of the schizophrenia takes over, and we are confused observers. We lose conscious track of shifts. The girl X becomes the sum of her past, present, and future.

Resnais is pioneering—not unlike Joyce and Picasso—in his particular style by utilizing the face of time most taken for granted: past time.

4. DECELERATED TIME

The final and least common of the cinematic rhythms, which interrupt continuous time, slows the clock to 70, 80, 90 seconds to the minute, and may be called decelerated time. The moment is stretched. Holding back the clock is opposite to jumping it forward in a cut for accelerated action. Since this technique disturbs our normal rhythm, it can be aesthetically revolutionary, like having our heartbeat retarded while our eye is being enlivened.

The means of prolonging the experience of a certain moment is usually done by altering the normal shutter speed of the camera so that the characters move in slow motion. Dream scenes and sports events are popular examples of velocity reduced by mechanical means within the camera or the video playback. Decelerated time may be created also by exaggerating the pace of frame movement below normal, so that with slow pans, trucks, or zooms we may follow a character in his ambulations with greater emphasis. This is an unnatural retardation of frame motion (cinematic) for the dramatic requirement of that moment.

Fragmenting a moment into many parts, by repeating a portion of a previous shot, is to achieve decelerated time through editing. The Sioux, and other tribes, have a Bunny Dance, performed by jogging two steps forward, followed by one back—a decelerated action.

Pare Lorentz's *The River* (1937) has such a moment depicting the descent of a tall fir tree crashing into a river. Nature lovers would wish to hold back time and the tree, and for a few precious seconds Lorentz grants our romantic urge. The fall is interrupted and repeated through editing. Finally, the crash of the giant tree into the water is doubly painful.

A superb example in contemporary cinema is the climax in the French version, directed by Robert Enrico, of *An Occurrence at Owl Creek Bridge* (1962), based on the Civil War short story by Ambrose Bierce. The Bierce tale begins:

A man stood upon a railroad bridge in northern Alabama, looking down into the swift water twenty feet below. The man's hands were behind his back, the wrists bound with a cord. . . .

The man, Peyton Farquhar (Roget Jacquet), is about to be hanged by Union soldiers. Is it that we would wish him a last-minute reprieve? What is flashing through his tormented mind? As written and directed by Enrico we see the rope break and Farquhar submerged under the waters of Owl Creek. He frees himself miraculously from his bonds, eludes drowning, eludes the bullets of the soldiers and their cannon, and survives the swirling waters of the creek. Gasping for breath, exhausted almost beyond endurance, he escapes through the woods toward his home and his wife, Abby Farquhar (Anne Cornally). The moment he beholds her emerge from the plantation house in her hoop skirt and dotted crinoline dress with lace trimmings, long tresses over her right shoulder, locket around her neck—that moment becomes decelerated.

Occurrence at Owl Creek Bridge. Courtesy of Contemporary Films.

Four times he repeats his emergence from the woods (the shot is repeated) and his crossing the lawn. In an accompanying mood of deceleration within the frame, Abby gracefully descends the garden stone steps and moves toward her husband in a slight but distinct slow motion (velocity). The camera travels with her in a combined pan and truck to underscore her tearful grace in juxtaposition (parallel time) to the shots of Farquhar rushing—repeatedly rushing —toward her. The moment they come together within one shot and she places her outstretched hands on his bruised neck, decelerated time ceases. He drops out of her arms, leaving her alone, hands empty. . . . Peyton Farquhar, tied at ankles, knees, and wrists, is swinging stiffly at the end of a rope.

The shock achieved by writer-director Enrico is unique in cinema, and opens psychic possibilities not heretofore seen.

Fragmenting subject movement into disjointed bits or snatches of shots—a Griffith-Eisenstein technique—may extend time by actual count while extracting every drop of emotional or intellectual meaning. The prolongation of the experience, however, may give an opposite impression, an aesthetic effect of contracting time. That is, the time it takes for an irate sailor, washing dishes in *Potemkin,* to smash the plate with its lettering, "Give us this day our daily bread," is a matter of two seconds in normal subject movement. By editing this action into nine shots, Eisenstein prolongs the actual motion, but the total impact so stimulates the eye that the doubled lapsed time of four seconds seems less than two. *Ten Days That Shook the World* (1928) has another such moment when the raised bridge holds the dead horse. By deceleration the moment appears enlarged, not an unusual psychic phenomenon.

Repetition of an action can have the effect not only of extending time but also of prolonging an idea. This is done in *The Knack* when the young leading man (Michael Crawford) discovers his bathroom is jammed full with beautiful young ladies clothed only in towels. He flees across the hall and down a flight of stairs three times. Though this action is accelerated through camera shutter speed, the total impact of the repeat editing is a prolongation. Time is momentarily arrested while the fantastic idea is relished.

François Truffaut in his script of Ray Bradbury's *Fahrenheit 451* (1966) indicates a scene is to be shot in slow motion, so that the cruelty and insanity of book-burning by firemen of the State will be more fully felt. A fire engine, with siren going, arrives at a "middle-income housing development" on a raid for books (all books are subversive). The Captain sits majestically on the fire engine, children gathering around in natural curiosity, while Montag leads the raiding party of firemen. Books were discovered in a chandelier and inside a TV set. Now comes the time for burning and the script indicates how this should be done:

(Filmed in slow motion). The firemen open the sack and throw the books in a pile. One book escapes from the pile and bounces to the side, lies open, its pages exposed. A child squats down to gaze curiously at it.

A look at him from the silent CAPTAIN, *still seated in the front of the fire engine.*

THE CAPTAIN's *look is noticed by the child's father who very quickly kicks the book away from the boy. A second kick sends it into the pile.*

Another look from the father to THE CAPTAIN.

THE CAPTAIN *almost smiles.*

At this moment, we see MONTAG *and his men leaving the building. Two men surround* MONTAG *and busy themselves with him, passing him a helmet protector for his head and eventually asbestos overalls not unlike those worn by deep sea divers. Finally,* MONTAG *is given the flame-thrower . . . it is a much smaller, more casual weapon than its World War II prototype.*

MONTAG, *armed with the flame-thrower, goes to the books.*

CLOSE-UP *on him. We easily recognize him under his helmet.* CLOSE-UP *on end of flame-thrower.*

TRAVEL FORWARD *toward the pile of books.* TRAVELLING *stops.* GROUP-ING—*the pile of books and* MONTAG.

Again CLOSE-UP *view of* MONTAG *who lowers his eyes to the apparatus.*

CLOSE-UP *of the cocked flame-thrower out of which streams a very strong flame.*

GROUP VIEW—MONTAG *adjusts the flame and directs it onto the books. We stay for a moment on this view in order to watch* MONTAG *burning the books, going around the pile, etc., until all are thoroughly on fire.* MONTAG *stops the flame-thrower, then goes back to the two men who help take off his helmet. He then goes to the fire engine to stand at attention beside* THE CAPTAIN.

MONTAG *salutes with style. Around them, the firemen set about arranging equipment. The books are all but consumed. The flames are lower. The books crumbling in ashes.*

The scene, done in normal tempo, would not have this impact of deliberate, methodical burning. Truffaut and his assistant writers, Jay Presson Allen and Jean Louis Richard, have fitted the proper form to such improper subject matter.

So much slow-motion velocity has appeared in films (as well as fast, reverse, frozen or stop motion) that directors and editors have monopolized its uses. Nor is it often possible to credit the writer with the original inspiration. In the case of known literary sources, such as Lafcadio Hearn's *Kwaidan* (Ghost Stories), which sixty years later became a film (1964), it was the director Kobayashi who created several stunning decelerated times. One was when the child emperor Antoko was drowned in the arms of his nurse when she leaped—in slow motion—into the sea to avoid capture by the victorious enemy. Nor was it Lafcadio Hearn who wrote of that moment in the third episode of the film, *Chawan No Naka* (Inside a Teacup), when time is arrested in a stop motion at the instant the bedeviled Kamnio believes he kills two ghostly assassins—the frame holds like a still picture. Also, when Kamnio proceeds to attack in decelerated time, legs moving in slow motion, the three ghostly emissaries from their lord whose face Kamnio had swallowed in a teacup. But the ultimate in decelerated time is the fashionable freeze ending, so effective in Truffaut's *The 400 Blows* (1958).

In *Fahrenheit 451* we do have decelerated time notes in the script. Fresh experiments should begin with the writer-director, with whom all beginnings commence.

Arthur Penn concluded *Bonnie and Clyde,* caught in a police ambush, with them writhing slowly to death in decelerated shots, an excruciating purge.

CHAPTER TWELVE ✖️

The Auditory Image

1. SIGHT AND SOUND UNEQUATED

Modern architecture may appear to be enhanced by the cacophony of city streets, while painting and sculpture continue to require no auditory supplement. The novel is best read in silence. Poetry carries its own rhythmic sound. Music, of course, is sound, and the dance cannot be performed apart from some beat or rhythm. Drama is obviously sight and sound, and so is cinema—but with auditory differences. The problems arising from relating sound to image—dialogue, music, sound effects—are questions of proportion. In the Ninth Art proportion is a unique challenge.

People talk, often too frequently and excessively. The silent film was not an organic art form—though many extraordinary works survive—because it was unnatural, either as a talkless performance of actors or a title-dependent narrative. The auditory image does extend cinematic effectiveness. When misused, or lacking in coordination, it can ruin cinema. The utterance of words is normal, though not always wise. Characters do converse—"But any attempt to convey thought and feeling exclusively, or even primarily, by speech," Professor Erwin Panofsky observed in 1934, "leaves us with a feeling of embarrassment, boredom, or both."

The eye in civilized man has become the thief of all other senses. We have come to depend almost exclusively on sight for our daily intercourse; *Gestalt* psychologists assert that 80 to 90 percent of all we learn comes through our eyes. Where once in jungle life we could catch sounds from far distances and our olfactory capability was keen, today hearing and smelling have become secondary senses. Today the optic nerve is the shortcut to the brain, figuratively and literally (only one-quarter inch).

When we are visually engaged in the movements and light alterations that delineate characters, places, plots, and expository events, we become irritated, embarrassed, or bored by assaults upon our ears aimed at giving us the thought of the moment or the emotion we should be feeling. Even the newsreels on television (the liveliest daily feature because of the editing and hand-held cameras) would be enhanced if speech were radically reduced; or, in documentaries, confined merely to statements of fact: who, what, when, and where.

Why should this imbalance between sight and sound persist through the decades, when it has become increasingly evident that no sound—words, music, or noise—can equate consistently with a picture on a fifty-fifty basis? Even in so deliberately visual a film as *Lady in the Lake* (1946) there are passages of dialogue replete with redundance. Here is the dialogue between two policemen who have discovered the drunk in Marlowe's wrecked car while the private eye is hiding behind a nearby tree, recording it all:

1ST POLICEMAN

Anybody in there?

2ND POLICEMAN

No, he was alone. Looks like everybody's celebrating tonight except us.

1ST POLICEMAN

He won't do any more celebrating for about six months.

2ND POLICEMAN

Why? Is he hurt?

1ST POLICEMAN

Naw. Just passed out. Here's his wallet. Phillip Marlowe—private dick.

2ND POLICEMAN

A plum pudding—all cooked up nice for us. Come on, let's get him out of here. He's gonna feel great in the morning. Oh, just a second until I get this license number. Call Headquarters and tell them to send out a tow car and that we're bringing in a Mr. Marlowe.

1ST POLICEMAN
Car 71 calling Headquarters. Car 71 calling Headquarters.
Come in, please.

The gentlemen occupants of Car 71 have given us an example of
radio-drama dialogue, explicit and surplus.

At the conclusion of *Lord of the Flies* there is an exchange, in the
script, between a rescuing officer and the painted young savages. As a
moral buttress to the implied theme, the Naval Officer asks if the
boys were playing some sort of war game, and they appear to assent.
In the final edited version there is no dialogue at the end. The point
is made visually.

Imbalance persists when there is confusion over the various roles
of dialogue and the proportion required at a given moment. Actually, there are three general types of dialogue: those that are to be
read, or heard, or seen. These might be called narrative, dramatic,
and cinematic dialogue.

All dialogue carries freight, a burden of information, thought, or
emotion. Some freight rolls ponderously on rails; others roar on four-
lane thruways, and some freight flies.

2.   NARRATIVE DIALOGUE

When dialogue is the sole source of evoking in the mind's eye an
image of what is happening; then it carries heavy burdens. The
reader of a novel doesn't seem to mind. Herman Wouk's *The Caine
Mutiny* (1951) offers, in its crucial scene, an interesting basis of
comparison. Here is the moment when Executive Officer Maryk
stages his paper mutiny by taking command from Captain Queeg,
who is physically and psychically incapable of commanding. Stilwell
is the helmsman during the typhoon, Willie is the OOD in the wheel-
house:

"Hold it, Stilwell," said Maryk.

"Mr. Maryk, fleet course is 180." The captain's voice was faint, almost
whispering. He was looking glassily ahead.

"Captain, we've lost contact with the formation—the radars are blacked
out—"

"Well, then, we'll find them—I'm not disobeying orders on account of
some bad weather—"

The helmsman said, "Steady on ooo—"

Maryk said, "Sir, how do we know what the orders are now? The guide's antennas may be down—ours may be—call up Sunshine and tell him we're in trouble—"

Butting and lunging, the *Caine* was a riding ship again. Willie felt the normal vibration of the engines, the rhythm of seaworthiness in the pitching, coming up from the deck into the bones of his feet. Outside the pilothouse there was only the whitish darkness of the spray and the dismal whine of the wind, going up and down in shivery glissandos.

"We're not in trouble," said Queeg. "Come left to 180."

"Steady as you go!" Maryk said at the same instant. The helmsman looked around from one officer to the other, his eyes popping in panic. "Do as I say!" shouted the executive officer. He turned on the OOD. "Willie, note the time." He strode to the captain's side and saluted. "Captain, I'm sorry, sir, you're a sick man. I am temporarily relieving you of command of this ship, under Article 184 of *Navy Regulations*."

"I don't know what you're talking about," said Queeg. "Left to 180, helmsman."

Only the seventh paragraph, containing expository description, might be compared to camera work. It appears to be a talkative bridgehouse for being in the midst of a terrible typhoon. This is from the final draft of the 1953 script (by Michael Blankford, Stanley Kramer Production 1954):

251.

MARYK

Excuse me, Captain (*to* STILLWELL) Hold her at hard right!

252. MEDIUM LONG SHOT—THE CAINE (MINIATURE)

as it rolls up a little on the surface of the water, slowly starts moving against the wind.

253. MEDIUM SHOT—BRIDGEHOUSE

MARYK

(*to* WILLIE)

We'll do much better heading into the wind. She'll come around.

QUEEG, *clutching the telegraph stand, blinks and shakes his head as though he has just awakened.*

QUEEG

Who gave those orders? Fleet course is left to one-eight-zero!

MARYK

Captain, we're in trouble . . .

> QUEEG
>
> Mr. Maryk, if you question my decisions once more, I'll order you off the bridge. Come left . . .

MARYK *hesitates a second, then speaks with complete firmness.*

> MARYK
> (*to* HELMSMAN)
>
> Stilwell, steady as you go. (*to* WILLIE) *Willie, note the time.* (*to* QUEEG; *saluting*) Captain, I'm sorry, but you're a sick man. I'm relieving you as captain of this ship, under Article 184, Navy Regulations.

> QUEEG
>
> I don't know what you're talking about. Left to one-eight-zero, helmsman!

The miniature of *The Caine* replaces the paragraph of expository description, and the dialogue remains similarly explicit as in the novel. This is embarrassing since such vocalizing occurs during a 100-mile-an-hour typhoon with the ship almost on her side—death is howling around the bridge; the moment is agonized with terror. We accept such dialogue in the novel, since the image needs to be evoked in our mind. When we hear it while viewing the action of very specific images, the imbalance irritates as we sense something unreal and unnatural.

A fundamental test of imbalance can be made by closing one's eyes or by listening to TV in an adjoining room. Soon we discover the amount of freight being hauled on the sound track.

At the conclusion of the film there is a scene that goes beyond its progenitor in the novel as a concession to the United States Navy, without whose cooperation this film could not have been made. There is a victory dinner to celebrate Maryk's acquittal, but the defense lawyer Greenwald uses the occasion to extol Queeg, whom he had demolished in court. "Queeg deserved better at my hands. I owed him a favor, don't you see? He stopped Hermann Goering from washing his fat behind with my mother." The novelist-intellectual Keefer should have been on trial instead of Queeg because he ran out on his fellow officers in court by not saying "straight out that he always insisted Queeg was a dangerous paranoiac." This anti-intellectual argument was made at a time when Senator Joseph R. McCarthy was holding his court in Washington. These thoughts in the script are conveyed, as in the novel, primarily by speech. The additional argument, not in the novel, is the principle of indivisible command—

my commander, right or wrong. This concession twists the story into reverse; the picture faults itself with "a happy ending." Here is Greenwald admonishing the *Caine* officers for not appreciating Queeg, for not "figuring him out a paranoid":

301.

> GREENWALD
> (*continued*)
> about him and figuring him out a paranoid—do you think the whole issue would have come up in the typhoon? . . . I'm asking you—do you think it would have been necessary to take over for him?

WILLIE *and the other* OFFICERS *look at* MARYK *tensely, awaiting his answer.*

> MARYK
> (*slowly, to* GREENWALD)
> It probably wouldn't have been necessary.

> WILLIE
> (*impressed*)
> Then we're really guilty . . .

> GREENWALD
> Ah—you're learning, Willie! You're learning! You're learning that command is—indivisible. . . . You don't work with a Captain because you like the way he parts his hair! You work with him because he's got the job!— (*pounding on the table*) —or you're no good!

He straightens up and looks at the startled and uncomfortable faces of the men around him, then he smiles sourly, and pours himself a drink.

> Don't look so worried . . . You're all safe. The case is over. (*bitterly*) It was like shooting fish in a barrel . . . (*then, with contempt*) Now—we come to the man who should have stood trial—the Caine's favorite author—the Shakespeare whose testimony nearly sunk us . . . [Keefer]

The freight has sunk the scene.

Trials are tribulations because speech commands so prominent a role among the means of depicting thought. In *The Devil and Daniel Webster* by Stephen Vincent Benét, the short-story form helps preserve a neat balance. Defense lawyer Webster requests a trial for his farmer-client after The Stranger (The Devil) asserts that his name is older in this country than Webster's. The door of the barn opens ". . . and twelve men entered, one by one. If Jabez Stone [client] had been sick with terror before, he was blind with terror now. For there was Walter Butler, the loyalist, who spread fire and horror through the Mohawk Valley in the times of the Revolution; and there was Simon Girty, the renegade, who saw white men burned at the stake and whooped with the Indians to see them burn. His eyes were green, like a catamount's, and the stains on his hunting shirt did not come from the blood of the deer. . . ." Others filing in are King Philip, cruel Governor Dale, Morton of Merry Mount, Teach the bloody pirate, and Reverend John Smeet. The Devil asks Daniel Webster mockingly, "Are you satisfied with the jury, Mr. Webster?"

"Quite satisfied, though I miss General Arnold from the company."

"Benedict Arnold is engaged upon other business."

Benét's narration and dialogue keep a pleasing proportion. In the film version, called *All That Money Can Buy* (1941), the Devil, now called Scratch, introduces each member of the jury as he appears; but since there is an element of visual suspense and surprise in wondering which scoundrel will materialize next, a balance does exist. It is clever, also, to move their entrances from barn door to cellar door in the floor (hell). The adaptation is by the author, screenplay by Dan Totheroh:

> *Then* SCRATCH *goes to a door in a dark corner of the floor that opens into a cellar. He throws the door back and a black hole yawns at his feet. A ruffian in pioneer dress,* CAPTAIN KIDD, *appears, others follow.*
>
> SCRATCH
>
> You must pardon the leathery toughness of one or two . . . Captain Kidd—he killed a man for gold; Simon Girty—the renegade—he burned men for gold; Governor Dale—he broke men on the wheel; Asa, the Black Monk—he choked them to death; Floyd Ireson and Stede Bonnet, the fiendish butchers; Walter Butler—the King of the Massacre; Big and Little Harp—robbers and murderers; Teach, the Cutthroat; Morton, the vicious lawyer . . . and . . . General Benedict Arnold—you remember him, no doubt. Dastard, liar, traitor, knave—*Americans* all . . .
>
> *They now go toward the stalls that in a crude way resemble a jury box.*

Listening to Scratch (Walter Huston) introduce such a jury would force anyone testing the sight-and-sound ratio to open his eyes. When the opposite is the case, when speech supplies the image, why have a picture?

The use of a voice off-shot automatically makes speech supplementary—provided the image, in its own terms, remains primary. Here is a favorable example from the climax of *A Tale of Two Cities* In Dickens' novel (1859) there are many cinematic passages—the film is equally cinematic—such as the vivid opening scene of the coach drive to Dover, one of the finest in Dickens, and vivid pictures of Paris, modeled on Carlyle's *The French Revolution*. Sydney Carton, reckless and in disrepute, smuggles Charles Darnay out of the Bastille, since he resembles him, and takes his place on the scaffold. Dickens concludes with a description of Carton's face and his inner thought:

. . . peacefullest man's face ever beheld there. Many added he looked sublime and prophetic. . . . If he had given any utterance to his [thoughts], and they were prophetic, they would have been these: ". . . It is a far, far better thing that I do, than I have ever done; it is a far, far better rest that I go to, than I have ever known."

In the David O. Selznick production (1935), screenplay by W. P. Lipscomb and S. N. Behrman, this thought of Carton's is heard off the shot. The last six shots of the film contain only two examples of dialogue, as noted in the continuity script:

REEL 13

SHOT 36. MEDIUM CLOSE SHOT—ROW OF DRUMS

as roll is given—

37. CLOSE SHOT—KNIFE OF GUILLOTINE

Knife is released—drops off shot—crowd below at b.g. all cheer— (Crowd noise).

38. CLOSE SHOT—CARTON

*looking off shot—*GUARD *enters at right—*CARTON *exits with him.*

OFFICIAL
(*off shot*)

Twenty-three.

39. MEDIUM LONG SHOT—CARTON AND GUARDS

at bottom of stairs. They come forward up steps. CARTON *looks up off shot.*

40. MEDIUM SHOT—MAN TURNING WINDLASS OF GUILLOTINE

Blade raises off shot. CARTON *enters right—crosses to guillotine.*

41. MEDIUM CLOSE-UP—CARTON NEAR GUILLOTINE

CAMERA TRUCKS *back.* CAMERA PANS *up—past guillotine—shooting out over city.* PANS *up, holds on setting sun and clouds.*

CARTON
(off shot)

It's a far, far better thing I do than I have ever done. It's a far, far better rest I go to than I have ever known.

To make certain the thought of Christian charity and redemption is fully appreciated throughout the English-speaking world, Mr. Selznick superimposes a title over the setting sun and clouds:

"I AM THE RESURRECTION AND THE LIFE:
HE THAT BELIEVETH IN ME, THOUGH HE
WERE DEAD, YET SHALL HE LIVE."

Titles and voices off-shots are forms of narrative dialogue that pose special problems of balance, since the intensity of the image should determine the amount of speech or caption. One of the better balances is the opening of *How Green Was My Valley* (1941), screenplay by Philip Dunne, directed by John Ford. Only the pictorial beauty and rhythm of these opening shots keep the image abreast of the voice:

2. FULL SHOT—VALLEY

The ugly coal Valley. Smoke, blackness, poverty. The SHOT DIMS *slowly down as the Valley as it was appears, fresh and green.*

VOICE

So I can close my eyes on the Valley as it is today—and it is gone—and I see it as it was when I was a boy. Green it was, and possessed of the plen of the earth. In all Wales, there was none so beautiful, for the colliery had only begun to poke its skinny black fingers through the green.

3. MINIATURE SHOT—COLLIERY

with only a small slag heap.

VOICE

The black slag—the waste of the coalpits—made only a small pile then—

4. EXTERIOR: THE CHAPEL—LONG SHOT

Dominating the street.

VOICE

—and our little Chapel was master of the Valley from where it stood at the head of the street.

5. LONG SHOT—FROM HILLTOP

Far down the hill a man and boy appear, slowly climbing the hill. They are GWILYM MORGAN *and his ten-year-old son, the same* HUW *who is the narrator of our picture.*

VOICE

Everything I ever learnt as a small boy came from my father, and I never found anything he ever told me to be wrong or worthless.

6. CLOSE PANNING SHOT—MORGAN AND HUW

They wear the clothes of the period around 1890. They are of a family of coal miners and should be attired accordingly. MORGAN *is smiling down at* HUW *as the boy struggles to keep up with his father's great strides. His lips move as he speaks to his son, who looks up at him with wide eyes.*

VOICE

He used to tell me of my Valley and its people—the brave men of Wales who never bowed to Roman or Danish or Saxon conquerors until so many had died that the women could not bear enough children to fill the ranks. The men of the Valley, long since gathered to their Fathers—

Though the Voice (Roddy McDowell) evokes images, quite similar to the words of Richard Llewellyn, the author of the novel—and they could be sustained in part by themselves—their aural combination with the visual results in another dimension. The whole can be greater than part sight, part sound.

Voice is most embarrassing when action stops. Such cessations of fluidity when plot and characters are humming along—abrupt and unnatural stopping points—irritate because they frustrate our impulse to witness what is coming next. Such is the example of *Double*

Indemnity (1944), screenplay by Billy Wilder and Raymond Chandler of the James M. Cain novel. An insurance salesman, Walter Neff (Fred MacMurray), meets a lecherous wife Phyllis (Barbara Stanwyck). In conjunction they plan a double crime of murder and fraud. In the end, Walter Neff, mortally wounded, bleeding profusely, staggers late at night back to his insurance office where he dictates his confession to his superior Keyes (Edward G. Robinson). This dictation introduces a flashback. The action is rolling with Phyllis and Neff proceeding to formalize intimately their partnership in his apartment (she came calling) :

1. INTERIOR: NEFF'S LIVING ROOM

CLOSE-UP—NEFF AND PHYLLIS

seated on a couch. He pulls her closer.

NEFF
Stop thinking about it, will you.

CAMERA TRUCKS BACK. SYNCHRONIZATION STARTS

NEFF'S VOICE
So we just sat there and she started crying softly, like the rain on the window, and we didn't say anything. Maybe she had stopped thinking about it, but I hadn't.

DISSOLVE INTO

2. INTERIOR: NEFF'S OFFICE

MEDIUM LONG SHOT—NEFF

seated at desk talking into dictaphone. CAMERA TRUCKS UP *to him.*

NEFF
(into dictaphone)
I couldn't. Because it was all tied up with something I had been thinking about for years, since long before I ever ran into Phyllis Dietrichson. Because you know how it is, Keyes. In this business you can't sleep for trying to figure out all the tricks they could pull on you. You're like the guy behind the roulette wheel, watching the customers to make sure they don't crook the house. And then one night you get to thinking how you could crook the house yourself, and do it smart, because you've got that wheel right under your hands. You know every notch in it by heart. And you figure

all you need is a plant out front, a shill to put down the bet. And suddenly the doorbell rings and the whole setup is right there in the room with you. Look, Keyes, I'm not try- ing to white-wash myself. I fought it, only I—I guess I didn't fight it hard enough. The stakes were fifty thousand dollars,

CAMERA TRUCKS BACK *slowly.*

but they were the life of a man, too—a man who'd never done me any dirt, except he was married to a woman he didn't care anything about. . . .

DISSOLVE INTO

3. INTERIOR: NEFF'S LIVING ROOM

LONG SHOT—PHYLLIS

seated on couch, putting on lipstick—NEFF *stretched out on couch, smoking.* CAMERA TRUCKS UP *slowly and* PANS *as she rises, crosses, gets coat, puts it on.*

NEFF'S VOICE

. . . and I did.

PHYLLIS

Will you phone me? Walter!

What happens to our eyes while we watch Fred MacMurray glibly, with painful grimaces, dictate? The greatest actor could hardly command our full attention while our imagination is back at the couch.

A respectful disregard of the original source, novel or play, can prove beneficial. Graham Greene's novel *The End of the Affair* is a first-person narrative, and opens in a rather meandering fashion:

A story has no beginning or end; arbitrarily one chooses that moment of experience from which to look back or from which to look ahead. I say "one chooses" with the inaccurate pride of a professional writer who— when he has been seriously noted at all—has been praised for his techni- cal ability; but do I in fact of my own will choose that black wet January night on the Common in 1946, the sight of Henry Miles slanting across the wide river of rain, or did these images choose me? . . .

Lenore Coffee's screenplay (1954) starts differently, and with a fresh action not in the novel:

FADE IN:

1. EXTERIOR: A SQUARE IN LONDON—A DARK RAINY NIGHT

DURING *the following narration the* CAMERA MOVES *in a* PANNING SHOT, *taking in the Square, the houses surrounding it, the pub*—MOVING IN DIRECTION *of* BENDRIX' *house.*

BENDRIX' VOICE

A story has no beginning or end. One merely chooses that moment of experience from which to look back—or from which to look ahead. And yet, do I choose that black wet night on the Square—or did this image choose me? Still, it is convenient to begin just there—after the war had ended and the lights were beginning to come on again.

By this time the CAMERA *has paused outside of the house in which* BENDRIX' *rooms are located. This is an old-fashioned house, converted into flats or rooms. As the* CAMERA TILTS UPWARD *to take in the lighted windows of* BENDRIX' *sitting-room, we see his silhouette as he looks out into the wet night.*

In this low-voltage opening the camera meanders, the voice ambles on, and we are somewhat intrigued, for this is the opening when we have our greatest expectations. The balance between visual and auditory images is unsuitable, since this literal transcription from novel to film renders Bendrix' voice superfluous. No previous shots have prepared us or prejudiced us.

Titles replace images, an easy but tricky solution. Having to read words introduces another language that necessitates adjustments. These could be a pleasant interruption when done very sparingly and for relief, comic or otherwise. When constant, as with every other shot in subtitling foreign-language films, a subtle irritation exists. Even under the most favorable circumstance (which is rare) we are under a double strain of receiving stimuli in two languages, verbal and visual. The eyes must drop from reading a human face, expressing a feeling or thought, toward the bottom of the frame and shift gears to read words. The process forces a slight detachment. Our involvement is handicapped.

The compulsion to be elliptical in subtitling captions exposes the dangers inherent in relating the verbal with the visual. Titles are anticinematic, though at best they strive for the brevity of cinematic dialogue. At worst, subtitles mock it.

In Teinosuke Kinugasa's *Gate of Hell* (1953), a period film set in the middle of the twelfth century during the Heiji Rebellion, there is a climactic scene done in classic severity between husband and

wife. The tableau, in color, imitates a Japanese print. The acting of
Lady Kesa (Machiko Kyo) is restrained in style and substance as she
pours sake for her husband. It is her farewell scene, since she plans to
substitute herself on the couch of her husband, about to be murdered
in his sleep by Moritō, the hero who quelled the rebellion and who
demands that Lady Kesa leave her husband for him. So in rolling,
honorific verbs, such as a medieval wife would employ in addressing
her lord and master, Lady Kesa offers the cup of sake amid great
ceremony.

The English subtitle read: "Have one." Tokyo audiences erupted
in laughter.

To conclude narrative dialogue an appropriate example comes
incongruously from a Western, a type that is generally the most
cinematic. In *Quantrill's Raiders* (1958) the first four shots contain
four titles and the next two very heavily freighted dialogue, all of
which is a harrowing lesson to behold:

FADE IN:

1. STOCK SHOT OF BAND OF RAIDERS—NIGHT

They pound down on a back-country road. NARRATION OVER—OR
SUPERIMPOSED FOREWORD:

> "In the dark days of the Civil War guerrilla raiders led by
> WILLIAM CLARK QUANTRILL terrorized the Kansas-Missouri
> border. . . ."

DISSOLVE THRU TO

2. ANOTHER STOCK SHOT OF RAIDERS—NIGHT

*They bear down on a farmyard, scatter the stock, set fire to the out-
buildings.* FOREWORD CONTINUES:

> "Quantrill fought for the South—with a savagery that
> shocked even his own allies . . ."

DISSOLVE THRU TO

3. CLOSER STOCK SHOT—THE BURNING BUILDINGS—NIGHT

(If possible with the figure of RAIDERS *silhouetted in f.g.)* FOREWORD
CONCLUDES:

> "His fury reached its peak when he attacked the friendly
> little town of Lawrence, Kansas. This is the story of that
> raid. . . ."

DISSOLVE TO

4. EXTERIOR: TENT ENCAMPMENT—DAY—FULL SHOT

(POSSIBLE STOCK—IF NOT, USE INSERT)

The tents are in a meadow, soldiers in Confederate uniform guarding them. Horses are picketed in b.g. OVER SCENE A TITLE FADES IN:
   "Field Headquarters of General Sterling Price, C.S.A."

5. INTERIOR: GENERAL'S TENT—DAY—MEDIUM SHOT

GENERAL PRICE, *a middle-aged gentlemanly officer, stands before a large map which is fastened to the canvas wall of the tent. Near him is a table on which reports are spread out.*

Facing him, back to CAMERA, *is* CAPTAIN ALAN WESTCOTT—*known as* WES—*a lean, muscular man whose features, we see when* CAMERA INCLUDES HIM, *are attractive and keen. He listens alertly as the* GENERAL *talks, occasionally referring to the map.*

> GENERAL PRICE
>
> I tell you in confidence, Captain Westcott, the overall situation of the South is grave. The Chiefs of Staff have decided that a diversionary thrust will take some of the pressure off General Lee. Therefore my brigade is to make an advance here. (*Indicates*) A sweep through Missouri and into Kansas will threaten the Union Army's supply lines to the West. However, to make the maneuver successful, we must destroy the Union's biggest arsenal west of the Mississippi, at Lawrence, Kansas. (*Again indicates*)

> WES
>
> I see, sir.

> GENERAL PRICE
> (*with a slight smile*)
>
> We can't count on our enemies being asleep. They may get wind of our advance in time to move the arsenal to Fort Scott. We must prevent that by destroying the ammunition while it's still at Lawrence. Since we have no troops in the area, we must rely on Quantrill and his raiders to do the job. You are to deliver the orders to him personally.

6. ANGLE FEATURING WES

He is none too happy at this.

> WES
>
> Quantrill has a pretty bad reputation, General. Suppose he doesn't stick to orders—goes ahead and plunders the town?

> GENERAL PRICE
>
> It's up to you to see that he doesn't. The town is not to be sacked and this is no license to murder civilians.
>
> WES
> (*dubiously*)
>
> Yes, sir. As I see it, the best method is to make a surprise attack on the arsenal, then get out of town at once before the garrison can go into action.
>
> GENERAL PRICE
>
> Exactly. You must get information for Quantrill as to the number of troops, location of artillery, if any, picket-posts, and so on.
>
> WES
>
> I understand, sir.
>
> GENERAL PRICE
>
> We have provided you with an identity—and papers. You'll be known as "Michael Davis," an ex-Union artillery officer. In Lawrence make contact with an agent of ours, Fred Thomas. He runs the gunshop there. He will put you in touch with the guerrillas. Here is the coded dispatch for Quantrill. Keep it in a safe place.
>
> *He hands* WES *a small folded paper. As* WES *takes it.* . . .
>
> DISSOLVE TO

Though the novel with its structural freedom in the use of time and place may be closer to cinema than to drama, narrative dialogue is not per se suitable for direct transposition to screen or tube. We are indeed most frequently left "with a feeling of embarrassment" when words by themselves are meant to convey motivations. At best, dialogue by itself can only flavor motivation. In *The Sandpiper* (1965) when Richard Burton, playing an Episcopalian minister happily married with two children, cries out to Elizabeth Taylor, "Laura, I want you"—we squirm, but not in empathy.

3. DRAMATIC DIALOGUE

In the theatre, first we hear and then we see. This is the nature of drama, its almost total dependence on spoken words for meaning. The primacy of the ear, eager to catch every syllable, is entrenched by the eye becoming accustomed to the size, depth, and angle of the stage image. The ratio between audience and actors never varies. The purchase of an admission ticket determines if your entire evening is to be spent viewing long shots, should you sit in the balcony, and at a high angle. The rear of the orchestra is a long shot at medium angle. Front rows orchestra are medium shots at low angles. Only in Elizabethan theatre when wealthy patrons sat on the stage was a close-shot possible. As in life, your purse may decide your perspective.

In cinema the camera is your constant usher, regardless of where you sit. Whether you lie outstretched on a home sofa or remain upright before a public screen, the camera-usher transports you up and down aisles without paying more money or moving leg muscles. As recounted, the flexible ratio between the action and the audience, which alters the size and shape of the proscenium, is frame motion.

The role of dramatic dialogue is loaded with responsibilities: the development of plot, the unfolding of character, the exchange of conflict, and so on. Only the mime theatre is free of the tyrannical rule of dialogue. Attractive dialogue on stage can be seductive, and many film producers have been led astray; some have taped Broadway performances, including the full length of laughs, and handed such tapes to screen playwrights. As an axiom, it might be proposed that the closer a screenplay is to the original drama, the more likely its failure.

Under rare circumstances dramatic dialogue, either through novelty or sheer force of rhetoric, can sustain a visual as well as an auditory interest. Here in *Ruggles of Red Gap* (1935) is such a moment when an English butler (Charles Laughton) recites Lincoln's Gettysburg Address in a frontier saloon to a group of fast-sobering American drinkers:

EGBERT
Why—say, Sam, what did Lincoln say at Gettysburg?

SAM
Who? Oh—why— (*he turns and shouts off toward her*) Hey, Curly, what did Lincoln say at Gettysburg?

C-8. CLOSE SHOT—CURLY

A typical bar fly, CURLY *pauses with glass half raised and looks at* SAM *dully but thoughtfully.*

CURLY

Search me. Ask Ike. He reads the papers.

C-9. LONGER SHOT

SAM *yells at* IKE, *a cowboy.*

SAM

What did Lincoln say at Gettysburg? (*as* IKE *scratches his head*) Hurry up before I come over and bust you one.

IKE *turns to* ED, *another cowboy who, with legs crossed, is seated at a table, sound asleep.*

IKE

Psst! Hey, Ed. What did Lincoln say at Gettysburg?

ED
(*sleepily*)

I wasn't there. (*he goes back to sleep*)

C-10. SHOT AT TABLE

EGBERT
(*to* SAM)

What kind of a saloon is this, where nobody knows the answer to a simple little question like that?

SAM *is really incensed. He's always been pretty proud of his bar flies but this is too much.*

SAM

I'm ashamed of em, Sourdough. (*turns angrily on the crowd*) Fine bunch of Americans you are. (*Overcome by disgust, he starts for them.*) Go on. Get out! And don't come back until you know what Lincoln—

RUGGLES
(*touches* SAM'*s sleeve*)

Pardon me, sir, but I think I can tell you what Lincoln said.

SAM
(*stares at him*)

You?

C-11. LONGER SHOT

RUGGLES *rises and begins to speak. The room becomes hushed except for his voice. One by one the occupants of the room drift over and stand in open-mouthed amazement.*

RUGGLES

Fourscore and seven years ago our fathers brought forth on
this continent a new nation, conceived in liberty, and dedicated to the proposition that all men are created equal. . . .

It is a moment, though anticipated, that is gratifying to eye and
ear. Generally, dramatic dialogue when accompanied by moving
images is a bore, no matter who recites the lines or how distinguished
is their author. Oscar Wilde's *The Importance of Being Earnest*
(1953) as a film was directed by Anthony Asquith; at the finale of
the last act, Jack discovers from the army lists of the past forty years
that General Moncrieff's Christian name was Ernest. Lady Bracknell
has been telling Jack that as eldest son he was naturally christened
after his father. Jack concludes his discovery by saying, "I always told
you, Gwendolen, my name was Ernest, didn't I? Well, it is Ernest
after all. I mean it naturally is Ernest."

The play continues:

LADY BRACKNELL

Yes, I remember that the General was called Ernest. I knew
I had some particular reason for disliking the name.

GWENDOLEN

Ernest! My own Ernest! I felt from the first that you could
have no other name!

JACK

Gwendolen, it is a terrible thing for a man to find out suddenly that all his life he has been speaking nothing but the
truth. Can you forgive me?

GWENDOLEN

I can. For I feel that you are sure to change.

JACK

My own one!

The dialogue is identical in the film. Here it continues in the
continuity version of Reel 10:

SCENE 32. MEDIUM CLOSE SHOT—MISS PRISM AND DR. CHASUBLE

DR. CHASUBLE
(*to* MISS PRISM)

Laetitia, at last.

CUT TO:

33. MEDIUM CLOSE SHOT—JACK AND GWENDOLEN

> JACK
> (*to* GWENDOLEN)

Gwendolen, at last.

> LADY BRACKNELL
> (*off to* JACK)

My nephew.

CUT TO:

34. MEDIUM SHOT—LADY BRACKNELL

> LADY BRACKNELL
> (*to* JACK *off*)

You seem to be displaying signs of triviality.

CUT TO:

35. MEDIUM CLOSE SHOT—GWENDOLEN AND JACK

> JACK
> (*to* LADY BRACKNELL *off*)

On the contrary, Aunt Augusta, I have now realized for the first time in my life . . .
the vital importance of being earnest.

CUT TO:

36. MEDIUM CLOSE SHOT—JACK AND GWENDOLEN

CAMERA TRACKS BACK *to show* MISS PRISM *and* DR. CHASUBLE, ALGY *and* CECILY *and* LADY BRACKNELL *in background. Stage curtain falls.*

The film ends, as does the play, on the directional word: *tableau.*
Nor does action per se assure speech of vitality in conjunction with the vividness of camera work. Consider one speech in a melodramatic thriller, *The Cat and the Canary* (1939) . The Cat is pursuing the canary (Paulette Goddard) when a confederate, Hendricks, interrupts the chase. Joyce is searching for help from Wally (Bob Hope) :

C-45. THE LAPPING OF THE BAYOU WATERS

She turns to retrace her steps when she sees a flashlight behind her.

JOYCE
(*calling*)

Wally?

The flashlight goes out. Nervously she proceeds on.

C-46. CLOSE SHOT—THE CAT

The CAT *is stealthily coming around a bend.*

C-47. THE ALCOVE IN FOREGROUND—LONG SHOT

HENDRICKS *remains concealed as the* CAT *now enters scene and advances* TOWARD CAMERA. *When the* CAT *comes abreast of* HENDRICKS *the latter seizes him.*

HENDRICKS
(*in a cold whisper*)

No, you don't! One killing's enough. Ringing gongs and scaring women is one thing. Murder is something else. I'm washed up. Give me that necklace. That's all I want out of this.

The CAT, *lost in* HENDRICKS' *powerful grip, reaches in his pocket and draws out the necklace. As* HENDRICKS *reaches for it the* CAT *with his other hand pulls out a wicked-looking blade.* HENDRICKS *crumples to the ground with a deathly groan. The* CAT *looks down the passageway, removes the necklace from* HENDRICKS' *limp grip and continues his pursuit.*

Talkative accomplices inevitably meet bad ends. Hendricks is neither comedy nor camp.

Parallel structure leads to speeches that are often set as opposites. *Splendor in the Grass* offers such an example in terms of dramatic dialogue. Mrs. Loomis is admonishing her daughter Deanie:

MRS. LOOMIS

Now see here, Deanie, you watch yourself with that boy. Don't let things go too far. Boys don't respect a girl they can go all the way with. Boys want a nice girl for a wife. Don't let things go too far. You know what I mean.

Ace Stamper has a bit of parallel advice for his son Bud:

ACE
(*confidentially*)

I tell you what you need now, son. You need another kind

of girl. BUD *looks at him closely*. When I was a boy, there were always two kinds of girls. We boys never mentioned them in the same breath. But once in a while a boy'd sneak off with one of the *other* kind and . . . get a little steam outa his system.

These speeches on a stage sound appropriate and to the point; they also read well. They diminish in value when our eyes are on Dean (Nathalie Wood) in the bathtub and her mother—in the notation of the director, Eli Kazan, to himself—"treats her back like she was grooming a horse." Ace and Bud do nothing but talk and listen, so we are forced to concentrate on spoken speech.

In this age of speed and fragmentation, dramatic dialogue needs to hit its targets with dispatch, even when heard in the theatre. When transcribed for the screen as dramatic dialogue the obligation is doubled. To conclude on this point, here is the dialogue in *Pygmalion* first as a play (1913), demonstrating the timelessness of Shaw's lines; the scene is the Embassy Ball when Nepommuck, a former pupil of Higgins and a phonetics expert, is suspicious of poor Eliza. There is suspense:

HOSTESS

Ah, here you are at last, Nepommuck. Have you found out all about the Doolittle lady?

NEPOMMUCK

I have found out all about her. She is a fraud.

HOSTESS

A fraud! Oh no.

NEPOMMUCK

Yes, yes. She cannot deceive me. Her name cannot be Doolittle.

HIGGINS

Why?

NEPOMMUCK

Because Doolittle is an English name. And she is not English.

HOSTESS

Oh, nonsense! She speaks English perfectly.

NEPOMMUCK

Too perfectly. Can you show me any English woman who

speaks English as it should be spoken? Only foreigners who have been taught to speak it speak it well.

HOSTESS

Certainly she terrified me by the way she said "How d'ye do." I had a schoolmistress who talked like that; and I was mortally afraid of her. But if she is not English what is she?

NEPOMMUCK

Hungarian.

ALL THE REST

Hungarian!

NEPOMMUCK

Hungarian. And of royal blood. I am Hungarian. My blood is royal.

HIGGINS

Did you speak to her in Hungarian?

NEPOMMUCK

I did. She was very clever. She said "Please speak to me in English: I do not understand French." French! She pretended not to know the difference between Hungarian and French. Impossible: she knows both.

HIGGINS

And the blood royal? How did you find that out?

NEPOMMUCK

Instinct, maestro, instinct. Only the Magyar races can produce that air of the divine right, those resolute eyes. She is a princess.

In comparing this passage to the filmed version of 1938 there are obvious surface changes: Nepommuck is called Kharpaty; the role of the hostess is expanded to include Perfide and Ysabel; the schoolmistress speech of the Hostess is dropped; the words "Film Star" and "high cheek-bones" are added. Wendy Hiller replaces Mrs. Patrick Campbell.

Though shots are designated, indicating the visualization of the characters, all thought is carried primarily by spoken words. Here is an exception to Panofsky's observation, rendered so by the sheer brilliance of the lines. Bernard Shaw is credited for the screenplay. It is the Ambassadress Ball, and Higgins is confiding in Pickering (an addition): "If he [Kharpaty] gives the game away to the Ambassadress . . . there'll be a deuce of a row. . . . I wouldn't miss it for worlds. . . ."

MEDIUM SHOT—KHARPATY

watching dancers. ELIZA *and* PRINCE *seen amongst dancers.* PERFIDE *enters shot, and swings* KHARPATY *round.*

PERFIDE
(dragging him away from doorway)

Come on, Aristid . . . you've got to . . .

CAMERA PANS *with them, and* YSABEL *enters shot from left. Guests wander in and out of shot.*

   . . . tell us.

They both drag him over left.

YSABEL

Yes, tell us all you know about this Miss Doolittle.

KHARPATY

This is my secret . . . but I'll tell her Excellency . . .

HOSTESS *and* GUEST *enter from left,* CAMERA *stops, holding the group in* MEDIUM SHOT.

   . . . she has the right to know.

HOSTESS

Well, who is she?

KHARPATY

She is a . . .

CLOSE TWO SHOT—HOSTESS AND YSABEL

YSABEL

Film Star.

CLOSE TWO SHOT—KHARPATY AND PERFIDE

HIGGINS *enters shot, stands between them.*

KHARPATY

Oh no . . . no . . . She is a fraud.

HOSTESS
(off)

A fraud? Oh, no.

KHARPATY

Yes . . . yes . . . She cannot deceive me, her name cannot be Doolittle.

HIGGINS *pushes* PERFIDE *out of shot right.*

HIGGINS

Why?

KHARPATY

Because Doolittle is an English name, and she is not English.

HIGGINS

Oh!

CLOSE TWO SHOT—HOSTESS AND YSABEL

HOSTESS

But she speaks English perfectly.

CLOSE TWO SHOT—HIGGINS AND KHARPATY

KHARPATY

Too perfectly. Can you show me any English woman who speaks English as it should be spoken. There is no such thing. The English do not know how to speak their own language. Only foreigners who have been taught to speak it, speak it well.

HIGGINS

Yes, there's something in that.

CLOSE SHOT—HOSTESS AND YSABEL

HOSTESS

But if she's not English, what is she?

MEDIUM SHOT—KHARPATY, HIGGINS, HOSTESS, PERFIDE, AND YSABEL

KHARPATY

Hungarian!

GROUP

Hungarian?

KHARPATY

Yes, Hungarian . . . and of royal blood. I am Hungarian . . . my blood is royal.

HIGGINS

Did you speak to her in Hungarian?

KHARPATY

I did. She was very clever. She said, "Please speak to me in English, I do not understand French."

CLOSE TWO SHOT—HIGGINS AND KHARPATY

French! She pretended not to know the difference between Hungarian and French. Nonsense, she knows both.

HIGGINS

And the blood royal? How did you find that out?

KHARPATY

Instinct, Maestro . . . Instinct. Only the Hungarian, the Magyar Race, can produce that air of divine right, those high cheek-bones, those resolute eyes. She is a princess.

And so is Shaw's dialogue.

More likely than otherwise, dramatic dialogue is the pauper not the prince in a script. In *Those Magnificent Men in Their Flying Machines* (1965) someone rushes toward whoever happens to survive a plane crash and asks, no less than seven times, that impoverished question: "Are you all right?"

4   CINEMATIC DIALOGUE

Differing from the dialogue that is aimed to be read or heard, cinematic dialogue is meant to be seen. It is as though we were accomplished lip-readers, and in the course of responding to the facial expressions of a character we come to understand what he is thinking or feeling, because we already sense the scene visually and sort of vaguely hear what is being said. While looking, we are aware of, but not made conscious of, or interrupted by, spoken speech. Like dutiful and charming children, cinematic dialogue should be seen and not heard.

The effort to avoid stilted or unnatural speech has been the goal of writer-directors since the days of the talkies. One of the latest experiments has been *Nobody Waved Goodbye* (1964), written and directed by Don Owen of Canada, a poet. Microphones were hidden on the chests of the actors, a television technique used by Edward Murrow in visiting the homes of famous personages of the fifties. Two cameras were employed to shoot simultaneously from different angles. Photography took four weeks with a basic three-man crew. The actors improvised their dialogue.

Quoting *Variety:* "According to Owen, the amount of improvisation which went on during production would make an average Actors Studio workout look like a Bolshoi production of *Swan Lake*. Little if any dialog was given the actors. Instead, Owen provided them with the situation, scene by scene, and let them take it from there."

A natural approach and technical felicity allow the dialogue in *Nobody Waved Goodbye* to be refreshingly cinematic. It is not, nonetheless, consistently credible. Chronicling the disintegration of a high-school dropout, the film depicts rather poignantly several months in the life of a boy in revolt. He won't study; he cuts classes; he is flunking three courses; he refuses to understand why his father won't permit him to drive without a license. Yet he is portrayed as an intelligent boy. His background is apparently wholesome and his parents seem to have common sense. His girl has better sense than he although she is not intellectually superior. When asked to state his own values, the boy, Peter Kastner, becomes inarticulate or silent. He has no values. He is effective in commenting on the authority of parents, the state, and a society orientated to a moneyed success. Such passages are amusing in their honesty, but inasmuch as he is not mentally unbalanced his character, as portrayed, lacks motivation.

In the final judgment, dialogue, no matter how momentarily free of cliché or poignant with frustration, can not be divorced from character or plot.

A more traditional form of cinematic dialogue can be seen in *The Big Sleep* (1946), directed by Howard Hawks from a screenplay by William Faulkner and Leigh Brackett, based on the novel by Raymond Chandler. Marlowe (Humphrey Bogart) is keeping a rendezvous with Mars, the heavy, and makes a point of arriving first at Geiger's house on Laverne Terrace:

182. EXTERIOR: LAVERNE TERRACE—NIGHT FOG

MARLOWE *drives up in a car and stops at curb. He and* VIVIAN *[Lauren Bacall] get out of car and go toward house,* CAMERA PANS WITH THEM.

183. EXTERIOR: GEIGER'S PLACE

As MARLOWE *makes his way like a stalking cat through the garden,*

toward the front door. Nothing stirs. There is no sound but the rain.
MARLOWE *crosses the exposed bridge at a crouching run. Nothing happens. He pauses in the shadows by the front door, then tries the knob. Silently the door swings open. He waits, then darts swiftly inside.*

184. EXTERIOR: LAVERNE TERRACE

The dark convertible, still shrouded in the heavy shadows of the trees, parks quietly behind MARLOWE's *car across the road.*

185. INTERIOR: GEIGER'S HOUSE—LIVING ROOM

MARLOWE *stands beside the door, which he had closed, listening. He is only a shadow among shadows. The house is utterly still.* MARLOWE, *still cautious, crosses into the rear part of the house, then returns.*

> MARLOWE
> *(laughing softly)*
> Okay, Eddie. I get it—on the way out. (*He draws the heavy curtains quickly across the windows, turns on the lights and sheds his hat and coat. . . .*)

Marlowe, "laughing softly" to himself as he figures out the setup for his impending showdown with Mars, speaks nine words after a long passage of silence. Even these words are not essential, since we see him relax, but they provide an adjunct explanation: Marlowe is to be gunned down when he leaves Geiger's house after his session with Eddie Mars.

Now follows the showdown scene. At first glance it appears talkative; Marlowe is keeping up a barrage of words. Actually, they carry no explanatory freight. They are another gun in his other hand. He is using words like bullets to panic Mars into rushing from the house. This is dialogue of low content and high voltage, of sounds, barks, snarls—the Bogart dialogue when he confronts the killer and turns the tables. For his purpose he might as well be snapping out the Lord's Prayer in staccato:

187.

> MARLOWE
> *(firing a shot at the Chinese statue)*
> What do you think's going to happen now, Eddie? Now what are your boys going to think? What'll they do to the first one out that door? Who's it going to be, Eddie—you or me?

MARS

Now, look, Marlowe—

MARLOWE

You look at this. What's the matter, haven't you ever seen
a gun before? What do you want me to do—count three like
they do in the movies? That's what Canino said to little
Jonesy—

MARS

Now don't go crazy.

MARLOWE

—and Jonesy took it better than you're taking it. (*Shoots*
MARS *in the hand*) That's one, Eddie.

MARS

Don't, Marlowe, don't.

MARLOWE
(*shoots wild*)

That's two—

MARS *breaks and runs out the front door, yelling.*

*He is cut down by machine gun fire. There is a silence as the door
slowly swings open again and* MARS' *body falls back through the
door.* VIVIAN *gets up from the floor and comes through the curtains
to watch* MARLOWE *and he goes first to the window to peek through
the curtains and then to the door. He stays hidden behind the door
jamb while he reaches out with his foot and kicks the door shut.
Then he goes to the desk and dials the telephone.*

Cinematic dialogue, it may be observed, is more involved in the
action of the scene, the performance of the actors, and the mood and
rhythm of the movements. It is a secondary not a primary factor.
This involvement is at the level of another contributor, like lighting
or setting. It helps propel the film on its tracks, similar to an extra
pair of wheels on a giant locomotive, but it is not the steam or the
diesel oil or the electric juice.

This characteristic might be observed in the adaptation of Niccoló
Machiavelli's *Mandragola* by Alberto Lattuada in his film *La
Mandragola* (1966). In this medieval masterpiece of the Italian
comic theatre, an elderly husband wishes an heir from his young wife
and contrives diabolically to achieve her compliance by forcing her
to take for one night a lover supposedly ugly. That night is never

seen on stage. Lattuada photographs it. Machiavelli did describe it in a speech by Callimaco, the lover, who beneath his disguise is handsome (Nicia is the husband, Lucrezia his wife). This is from Scene 4 of Act Five:

I had some misgivings about being there until around three in the morning; for, although it gave me great pleasure, it didn't seem quite right. But then, when I was finally able to tell her who I was and how much I loved her and how easily, because of the simple-mindedness of her husband, we could find happiness together without the slightest scandal, promising her that whenever God should will to take him away I would make her my wife; and when, on top of these good reasons, she had tasted the difference between my embrace and that of Messer Nicia, and between the kisses of the young lover and those of an old husband—after sighing a little, she said: "Since your cunning, my husband's stupidity, my mother's foolishness, and the wickedness of my confessor have led me to do what I would never have done of myself, I'm ready to believe it was heaven's will that it should all happen in this way, and I don't have it in me to reject what heaven wants me to accept. Therefore, I receive you as lord, master, guide. . . ."

The approximately parallel passage in shots from Scene 60 of the script contains more than cinematic dialogue:

They [NICIA et al] *go out and shut the door followed by the glance of* CALLIMACO, *who still feigns timidity. But once alone, he is seized with delight and throwing himself forward, he says in his normal voice:*

CALLIMACO
I am called . . . (*but at once recalling that he must play the boor and changing his tone*) I am called **A**.

LUCREZIA *at last turns around to look at him and jumps back with a cry of horror.*

Ooohhhh! (*then she extinguishes the candle with one breath, plunging the room in darkness and retiring herself as much as she can to the edge of the bed*) Do not speak, I do not wish to know who you are.

La Mandragola. Courtesy of Arco Films.

CALLIMACO *meanwhile is trying to slip into the bed beside* LUCREZIA.

CALLIMACO

I just wanted . . . that we two should get to know each other.

LUCREZIA

For me you are a medicine.

CALLIMACO

Yes.

He begins to stretch out his hands. But she pushes him straightaway out of bed, making him roll on the floor.

LUCREZIA

Nothing more than a medicine!

LUCREZIA, *aroused and infuriated, almost to the point of a hysterical breakdown, pulls the bedclothes up to her bosom while calling in desperation upon heaven.*

Whatever was the reason to send me a monster!

CALLIMACO *meanwhile slowly rises again from the floor and, in the uncertain light of night, his disguised face seems fearful and comically monstrous.*

LUCREZIA

Whatever they may have told you, know that you are a medicine that I should not wish to take.

He is now on his feet in all his height before the bed; he takes a corner of the sheets.

CALLIMACO

There are some medicines that seem bitter . . . and instead—

Pulls sheets away and throws himself upon LUCREZIA, *and kisses her wildly with gestures made confused by agitation.*

LUCREZIA

Oh no, no, no!

She resists him, denies him her mouth, and sobs beneath the man.

And as LUCREZIA *struggles in her own defense so* CALLIMACO *with a stronger push falls headlong from the bed with her. . . .*

The dialogue obviously is more seen than heard. Machiavelli would have approved.

Cinematic dialogue is best when not essential. It may even verge on the obvious, the mundane, the ordinary—but shouldn't seem so— or, it may be nonsensical information, not meant to be retained or recalled. A passage from *Les Liaisons Dangereuses* (R 1959) illustrates this point. From the novel of Choderlos de Laclos, the adaptation is credited to Roger Vadim and Roger Vailland with the collaboration of Claude Brule, and dialogue by Roger Vailland. At a social gathering in a salon the camera travels, in this passage, continuously so that we overhear bits of conversations from three sets of guests. The total effect of their voices, blending together as we move along, is not unlike organ music, reminiscent of *Marienbad:*

We are now in the presence of a 35-year-old man with a pale face and cold, somewhat cruel eyes.

THE MAN

She came here from the province. She wore very simple little dresses . . . She always seemed to walk about in riding-boots and with a riding-whip in her hand. She went out freely with the boys. At the end of the first year each of them swore he had made her. But since no one could prove it . . . they stopped boasting from fear of being ridiculous.

A WOMAN

Basically she was as discreet as she is now?

THE MAN

Who will ever know? He perhaps.

The camera continues to move into the salon.

A YOUNG WOMAN

But where did she meet him?

A 40-YEAR-OLD WOMAN

At the Sciences Politiques. He married her the year he took the big exam.

The guest who has just answered is MME. VOLANGES. *Her very charming face has hardened and one feels that she is always ready to be aggressive.*

THE YOUNG WOMAN

And what does he do in the Foreign Office?

MME. VOLANGES

He's waiting to leave. On his father's side: Moselle rolling-mills, or on his mother's side: United Shippers Bank.

We are now behind the sofa where two men are chatting. We see only the bald head and thin neck of the first; only the black lacquered hair of the second man's head.

BALD HEAD
(German accent)
My dear friend, I don't understand why we were invited to this nice, so very Parisian party.

BLACK HEAD
(no accent)
She wants to get a mission for her husband in the O.M.A.P.A.

BALD HEAD
I thought that this young man was busier winning the hearts of women than in winning U.N. commissions.

BLACK HEAD
She has ambition for two.

The CAMERA *now frames, in* CLOSE-UP, *a girl's face.*

Such conversation can be heard in salons anywhere and, as background, soon fades when out of earshot. The problem is more complex when cinematic dialogue carries ideas and feelings.

In a concluding scene from *Fahrenheit 451* the dialogue is freighted with a powerful idea of revolt and subversion, personified in the character of Montag (national hero) who has turned from burning books to a desire to perpetuate them. He seeks the underground in a scene of momentous power, visually and aurally:

FORESTER
I am the Forester; are you looking for someone?

MONTAG
But . . . *(indicates TV)* I am Montag!

The FORESTER *is silent, as if awaiting proof.* MONTAG *draws packet of papers from beneath his shirt and presents them slowly, like credentials.*

FORESTER
(glances at papers, visibly relaxes)
Ah! *(he replaces rifle on rack on wall)* We didn't expect you quite so soon. My name is Marcus. *(they shake hands)* Marcus Aurelius. I am also Plato's *Republic*, in case you

should ever wish to read me. (*indicates* OLD MAN) And this is Faust.

> OLD MAN
> (*cheerfully*)
> You've come a bit late for *my* Faust, I'm afraid, but with any sort of luck, my grandson . . . (*takes* BOY'S *wrist*) will know it before I go.

> FORESTER-MARCUS
> (*to* OLD MAN)
> You've worked too hard today—I'm giving you a sedative.

> OLD MAN
> Not yet.

OLD MAN *and* BOY *softly commence recitation of* Faust, *which continues to end of scene.*

The informational burden embodied in the dialogue could hardly be presented in any other form, but two factors mitigate against the spoken words becoming narrative dialogue: the use of props that can be photographed (rifle, TV set, packet of papers), and the sheer novelty of the idea (the perpetuation of books from generation to generation through memorization and the uniqueness of persons in the underground being known by the titles they have memorized). Montag has brought with him a book he has saved from burning: *Tales of Edgar Allan Poe*. Marcus-Plato invites Montag to gaze through a telescope; the scene continues:

> . . . *through* MONTAG'S *eyes we get fleeting glimpses of a cottage, of a man working along railroad tracks, etc., as* MARCUS *calls out:* "Discourse on Reason! Canterbury Tales! The Red and the Black!" *etc.*

> MONTAG
> (*trying to hold telescope on a certain point*)
> Isn't that place near the—

> MARCUS
> (*cheerfully but firmly, he spins telescope away*)
> Never mind. Look here—! (*Grandiosely, using a stick, he taps at random on an enormous topographical map covering one entire wall. His voice rises in excitement as he locates on the map the various names he calls out. He moves rapidly to cover the distances across the face of the great map*) Here is The Prince! The Odyssey! Plutarch! Over there is Proust!

As MARCUS *speaks,* CLARE *appears in doorway behind them. Though she sees* MONTAG, *she does not interrupt* MARCUS, *until he glimpses her, and turns, pointing his stick at her with a culminating flourish.*

Kafka!

CLARE

(softly)

"Someone must have been telling lies about Joseph K., for . . . (*hesitates briefly, then smiles and with quick authority, continues*) . . . for without having done anything wrong he was arrested one fine morning . . ." (*she smiles at* MONTAG, *moves toward him*) I think you'll like me . . .

MARCUS *grins merrily, resumes chant of names and titles . . . pointing them out as he calls them. And his voice is joined by that of* OLD MAN *and* BOY. *Slowly, looking directly into* MONTAG's *face,* CLARE *too begins to recite, carrying on the story of poor Joseph K. The voices augment and rise.*

As if in a dream MONTAG *opens the book he brought with him and begins to read:*

MONTAG

"I am going to recount a story whose essence is full of horror. I would suppress it gladly, if it weren't a . . . (*frowns, falters over the word*) . . . a chronicle of feelings, more than facts . . ." (*he lowers the book, raises his head, and in concentration, recites the phrase*)

In the beginning there was the word. Now it is the image and the word.

5. MUSIC ON A SOUND TRACK

Frequently music is not on a sound track when tied to the moving image. Sound and sight are inclined to contradict rather than complement, since they are separate stimuli. The observations pertaining to dialogue apply as principles to music; the plethora of spoken words is often matched by plenty of musical accompaniment.

A silent sound track, even for a few minutes, is viewed by an excessive number of producers as a wasted opportunity. Even the documentary for television is seldom free of a musical burden. The problem is the blending of visual and aural images so that no imbalance will intrude and interfere with the flow of emotions or ideas. The best musical score is not the one that is unheard, but rather the tonal rhythms of which you are consciously aware without loss or dilution of the primary stimuli, which are visual. We see before we hear; a movie theatre is not a concert hall. The sad exception is in television, where the picture pattern is generally less engrossing than the audio information, especially so between the commercials.

In cinema the more likely box-office rule is the opposite of an excellent editing axiom—when in doubt, out—but rather when in doubt, add music. Tragic Spencer Tracy in *The Old Man and the Sea* (1957) is not permitted the solitude of his rugged soul, à la Hemingway, as he sits day after day in his little boat on a greenish Caribbean sea under a punishing sun. A hundred-piece orchestra, playing the noisy concoctions of Dmitri Tiomkin, must accompany him to be certain the audience is not lonely.

Music meant to underscore an emotional moment may indeed defeat its aim by signaling to the viewer what to expect or what he should be feeling. The generations being raised on TV drama have long ago learned these signals. The badman enters the saloon where the hero is minding his business at the bar, and music starts. "Pay attention," says the music, "there is going to be a fight." Or the hero pauses at the door, long enough for the music to begin, and crosses toward the girl in the rocking chair. "Watch now, they will kiss," says the music. No perceptive member of an audience likes to be told, "You are about to feel sad . . . now comes comedy."

The effective uses of music appear to be those that avoid an imbalance of excess caused by more music than image. It is a happy marriage when the music is an integral part of the drama or the idea, and is cinematically projected.

Thematic music, meant to coincide with a visual mood, can be subtle and sophisticated, and still have problems of balance. The objection to the unrelated symphony in *The Old Man and the Sea* is that it is *non sequitur*. Such is the function of most action music. An exciting exception is Dmitri Tiomkin's thematic music in *High Noon* (1951), wherein a haunting melody becomes a refrain like a conscience returning in different keys and tempos at crucial moments. Alfred Newman performs a similar service with his theme song in *Love Is a Many-Splendored Thing* (1955) (an unfortunate verbal arrangement), though his score in *The Greatest Story Ever Told* has a self-conscious religiosity. Moras Hadjidakas' lilting jingle in *Never on Sunday* (1959) accomplishes the same purpose, as did

André Previn's score for *Irma la Douce*. Elmer Bernstein has effective march music in *The Great Escape* (1963). Alex North captures with lute, harps, flutes, and recorders a Renaissance flavor in *The Agony and the Ecstasy* (1965), not so effective as his background music in *A Streetcar Named Desire*. However, these are really set pieces. They can be appreciated by the blind; shots add nothing to them, and vice versa; whereas the absence of music in *Othello* is truly noticeable.

East of Eden has music that provides a thematic underscoring that contributes uniquely, though the rhythms of composer Leonard Rosenman have echoes of the opera *Wozzeck* by Alban Berg. When the estranged son (James Dean) opens the door of the brothel, operated by his mother (Jo Van Fleet) there is a blast of low tavern music that informs our ears in no unmistakable terms of the true nature of the boardinghouse.

Nino Rota's scores for *La Dolce Vita* and *8½* are more effectively integrated than his intrusive bars in *Juliet of the Spirits*. Maurice Jarre's rhythmic contributions in *The Longest Day* (1962) and *Lawrence of Arabia* (1962) have a unity and significance that contribute in ways not felt in *Doctor Zhivago*. Or, the deliberate sophistication of Henry Mancini's polished and ironic scores in *Breakfast at Tiffany's* (1961), *The Pink Panther* (1964), or *A Shot in the Dark* (1964) give an impression of having been composed for record sales.

John Addison, on the other hand, makes a musical distinction in his score of *Tom Jones,* which, in its mischievous romp, is a perfect blend. John Barry's wit in his crisp score for *The Knack* is satirical in its own terms, and also appropriately fresh for the images it accompanies. His *Thunderbird* (1965) score is offensively apropos. But Bacharach's music in *What's New, Pussycat?* (1965) has a wild theme song that gives bright meaning to a film devoid of thought or purpose. Similarly, Ron Goodwin makes a distinct addition to the fairy-tale romanticism of *Those Magnificent Men in Their Flying Machines* by composing music in the manner of a pre-World War I carnival, rollicking and sparkling and full of pace. Nobody crashes fatally or drowns while banjos twang, brasses blare, and trombones slide.

Such examples of cinematic projection are music designed as much as light-and-shadow compositions. The musical coincides with the visual idea.

When music is an integral part of the drama the problem is less complicated. David O. Selznick's *Intermezzo* (1939) is the story of a violinist, Holger (Leslie Howard), who falls in love with a young piano teacher of his child, and deserts his family for her, Anita (Ingrid Bergman). Without the music in the following passage there could be no drama, and the music, fortunately, is balanced by editing on a rhythm of continuous present (they play together for the first time):

96. CLOSE SHOT—ANITA

She looks up at HOLGER, *profound admiration in her expression.*

97. CLOSE SHOT—HOLGER

He is lost in his music.

98. CLOSE TWO SHOT—ANITA AND HOLGER

She plays with fervor. An expression of satisfaction on her face. She is accompanying HOLGER'*s music beautifully.*

99. CLOSE-UP—CHARLES

Watching them reflectively.

100. CLOSE-UP—THOMAS

Listening. He turns to GRETA, *beside him—and smiles complacently.*

101. MEDIUM LONG SHOT—HOLGER AND ANITA

The two playing beautifully together.

102. CLOSE-UPS—ANITA AND HOLGER—PLAYING

103. MEDIUM SHOT—MARGIT AND ANN MARIE

Listening intently to the music.

104. CLOSE SHOT—ANITA AND HOLGER

The two finishing.

105. CLOSE-UP—HOLGER

HOLGER
(*looks down at* ANITA *approvingly*)

Bravo!

106. CLOSE-UP—ANITA

She is shy and pleased, but embarrassed.

ANITA

Thank you.

How different is the use of music in this flirting than the inci-
dental music of Katherine Howard singing "Alas! What shall I do for
love?" in *The Private Life of Henry VIII* when Katherine entertains
while Henry ravishes his food. Katherine's solo song is hardly secondary; the violin and piano are primary.

Music as foreground, the major factor of the scene, may be noted
in *The Red Shoes* (1948). Here is music that dominates—"Lac de
Cygnes," of Tchaikovsky, and Delibes' "Coppélia." Not only does
this music provide opportunities for dancing; it also serves as mood
for plot and transitions between scenes:

404. INTERIOR: NIGHT—STAGE—MONTE CARLO

"Lac de Cygnes." VICKY *dancing.*

405. INTERIOR: NIGHT—LERMONTOV'S BOX—MONTE CARLO

RATOV *enters.*

> LERMONTOV
> Look at her dancing!

> LIVY
> With pleasure. (*He applauds*) *Bravo!*

> LERMONTOV
> A debutante at a charity matinée.

RATOV *and* LIVY *exchange a look. Both know* LERMONTOV's *jealousies
and how they can upset the company.*

> RATOV
> Boris, Dimitri has Paris on the telephone. It's about your
> business trip tomorrow.

> LERMONTOV
> (*rising*)
> I'll come. Livy, when you take over, send Craster to me.
> *He goes.*

The music of Tchaikovsky changes to the music of Delibes.

DISSOLVE TO:

406. INTERIOR: NIGHT—ORCHESTRA PIT—MONTE CARLO

LIVY *conducting the orchestra.*

407. INTERIOR: NIGHT—STAGE—MONTE CARLO

"Coppélia." COPPELIUS, *played by* LJUBOV, *winds up the doll, played by* VICKY. *Angles should emphasize the comedy of the scene.*

DISSOLVE TO:

408. INTERIOR: NIGHT—LERMONTOV'S OFFICE—MONTE CARLO

The music of Coppélia *continues.*

CLOSE *on a pile of rough sheets of a music score. The title is written on the top sheet in big capital letters in ink:* "LA BELLE MEUNIÈRE."

A musical film differs from a film accompanied by a musical underscoring during certain scenes. The appeal of *The Red Shoes* lies in its colorful song and dance. Similarly, *My Fair Lady* is a musical comedy, a form that depends in a major measure on music for its structural rhythm as a whole. The writer-director of a musical film, knowing this intrinsic feature, constructs his story on the basis of key musical numbers. This is a specialty.

Perhaps here the writer-director has a clue to why background music so frequently fails in its mission, and more often contradicts the mood or intent of the scene. Consider the complexity of musical rhythms and qualities in juxtaposition to the visual elements and visual rhythms at work. The composer is concerned with the direct or indirect beat in his composition, its pitch in melody, its type of harmony, the tonal timbre, the inner dynamics. All these are likely to be incompatible to the complex rhythms and tempos in subject motion, frame motion, and various editing movements. No wonder an uneasiness often develops during a scene in which the eye is engaged but through the ear come discordant disturbances. Sergei Prokofiev's studied score for *Alexander Nevsky* is a rare example of music working together with cinema for thematic effectiveness. So is the unobtrusive music of Georges Delarue and Giovanni Fusco in *Hiroshima Mon Amour.*

On such occasions there is a matching. Whenever Tom Courtney takes off across country in *The Loneliness of the Long Distance Runner,* camera traveling with him through rolling English scenery, the music runs with him.

It is easier for the creator when a set piece of music becomes the theme (morale) of the film, such as the whistling of "Colonel Bogey" in *The Bridge on the River Kwai.* Nicholson and his men are marching and whistling as they arrive at the Japanese prison camp. It is the first time we hear "Colonel Bogey," and we do so from the point of view of British prisoners in the camp hospital; then we march with the men for four shots, then two shots from the Japanese Saito's hut, and conclude back at the hospital, all moments of movement and evocative feeling.

Here are continuity shots 38–46 of Reel One measured for time:

SHOT 38. EXTERIOR: CEMETERY—LONG SHOT—THROUGH TREES TO GRAVES. 36⅓ seconds.

TRACK BACK *with* NICHOLSON *and* MEN *marching and whistling.* TRACK THROUGH CAMP HOSPITAL *past backs of* ASIAN PRISONERS *watching.*

VOICE
(over)

Pick 'em up, men.

39. MEDIUM CLOSE SHOT. 4 seconds.

onto backs of NICHOLSON, HUGHES *and* REEVES *leading men*—TRACK AFTER *them.*

40. CLOSE SHOT—REEVES AND HUGHES. 4 seconds.

with MEN *behind them*—TRACK BACK *with them.*

VOICE
(over)

It won't be long now.

41. CLOSE SHOT—GROGAN AND BAKER. 5 seconds.

with MEN *behind them all whistling*—TRACK BACK *with them—they move out.*

42. MEDIUM LONG SHOT—NICHOLSON. 12 seconds.

leading men—TRACK R–L *with them*—NICHOLSON *stops in f.g.—turns back to camera.* HUGHES *stops and faces him.*

VOICE
(over)

Right, smarten up there now.

43. EXTERIOR: SAITO'S HUT— MEDIUM CLOSE SHOT—PUNKAH WALLAH. 4 seconds.

pulling rope.

VOICE
(over)

A company—mark time!

44. LONG SHOT. 9⅔ seconds.

down from SAITO's *hut to* MEN *as they move* R–L—*whistling*— A COM-
PANY *move into position, mark time.*

45. INTERIOR: CAMP HOSPITAL—MEDIUM LONG SHOT. 3½ seconds.

over backs of PATIENTS *to* SOLDIERS *in b.g.—passing* R–L.

VOICE
(over)

B Comp . . .

46. INTERIOR: HOSPITAL CLOSE SHOT—SEARS AND WEAVER. 3⅔ seconds.

VOICE
(over)

. . . any . . . mark time!

SHEARS *shakes head (deeply moved).*

The long shots and medium long shot are relatively longer in
duration, while the close shots are briefer. The rhythms of marching
men and whistling men simplify the coordination between sight and
sound. It is a wise screen playwright who knows tunes to write by.

Ordinarily, background music is especially composed by the foot
and frame per second and for support to a scene. A typical example is
the scene immediately following the suicide of Anna Karénina. Her
lover Vronsky is disconsolate, sitting at a table with his friend
Yashvin. They drink and talk, Vronsky admonishing himself for not
giving Anna sympathy—"a kind word"—when they were last together. Yashvin asks, "Would it have mattered if you had?" At this
point, music of a sentimental character is introduced to be heard
under the dialogue. It is listed as *"Original" by Stothart:*

69. CLOSE-UP—VRONSKY. 10½ seconds.

looks f.g. and speaks to YASHVIN *off shot.*

VRONSKY

No, perhaps not. But I shouldn't have this awful sense, this
awful guilt, which I know will never leave me . . . Never.

70. CLOSE-UP—YASHVIN. 3 seconds.

YASHVIN

It was fated. She was doomed.

71. CLOSE-UP—VRONSKY. 19⅓ seconds.

looks f.g. and speaks, then faces right.

VRONSKY

I didn't turn to her . . . I remember I felt suddenly I must ask her forgiveness and then immediately I . . . I hardened my heart. For this I shall never forgive myself. . . . This I . . . I shall never forget.

72. CLOSE-UP—YASHVIN. 2½ seconds.

smiles.

YASHVIN

She's forgotten. And she's forgiven.

It is doubtful whether this sort of musical accompaniment added anything to the dialogue. The rhythm during Vronsky's close-ups is visually three to one, and they are held six times longer than the duration of Yashvin's close-up. There is no discernible beat.

At the climax of *An Occurrence at Owl Creek Bridge* when decelerated time produces a moment of touching pathos, the musical underpinning is brilliantly effective, written expressly by Henri Lanoe. The beat is slowly measured to the graceful flow of Abby Farquhar moving to meet her husband. It is a beat that seems to decelerate our own heart pace, and saddens us, all in a unique blend of our senses. Similarly, the song *Le Tourbillion* and thematic music *Brouillard* by Georges Delerue enhance the melancholy in *Jules et Jim*.

Variations on a musical theme can help interpret a scene by altering the rhythm or the number of notes in the same phrase, that is, by playing the music in waltz time, foxtrot, or in triplets, and so on. Such are the shifting interpretations in *Mondo Cane* (R 1963). In that potpourri of box-office attractions a few themes are being constantly adapted to each sensational scene. In Pare Lorentz's *The River* there is an upbeating of the song *There'll Be a Hot Time in the Old Town Tonight*. First it is played straight; and then as the frenzy of denuding the virginal American forests increases, the song is raised in pitch and tempo as we see shots of trees falling, logs racing down sluices, splashing into rivers.

A possibility worth exploring is the use of organized sounds instead of melodic patterns for background buttresses. A new aesthetic for film music might evolve that could avoid the communication theories. Nonmelodic sounds so arranged to blend with image movements and verbal expressions could add a fresh aural dimension. Electronic music, unfortunately, is too frenetic, attracting attention out of proportion, but hopefully it might be controlled.

6. SOUNDS EFFECTIVE

The term "sound effects" is a carryover from radio, and is intended to describe the use of natural noises, such as doors slamming, horses' hooves, dogs barking, bells ringing, etc.

The screen playwright is responsible for all he hears as he visualizes. Here, too, the principles useful in applying dialogue and music to the moving image are apropos. Sound effects are more likely to be above than under normal patterns in terms of decibel intensity and duration. Patterns are to be modified and broken, of course, as well as observed and applied. Progress in art proceeds apparently at the rate of effective rule breakage.

Exaggerated sound in the climax of *A Tale of Two Cities* adds to that gruesome moment: the crowd noises, the roll of drums announcing another drop of the guillotine blade, the cheers, and the squeaking of the windlass as the huge blade is raised. Since sound can't be divorced from its intensity, some sort of a scale is needed. In music there are many gradations of tonal power with their abbreviations:

fff	fortissimo assai	As loud as possible
ff	fortissimo	Very loud
f	forte	Loud
mf	mezzoforte	Moderately loud
mp	mezzopiano	Moderately soft
p	piano	Soft
pp	pianissimo	Very soft
ppp	pianissimo assai	As soft as possible
fp ⎫ pf ⎭	forte piano or piano forte	A quick transition from loud to soft, or soft to loud
sfz	sforzando	A sudden increase of tone, applied to single notes
rfz ⎫ rf ⎭	rinforzando	A sudden increase of tone, applied to musical phrases
cresc	crescendo	A gradual increase of tone
dim decresc	diminuendo ⎫ decrescendo ⎭	A gradual decrease of tone

An indication of such dynamics at work in sound effects could contribute to the power of the script.

There is a pathetic moment in *Odd Man Out* when Johnny,

wounded in the holdup and bruised from his fall after the getaway car made a sharp turn, arrives in a junkyard. Here in hostile Belfast, the night coming on, Johnny is on his own awaiting a potential rescuer or a betrayer. The character Shell is such; music and rain are mixed with other noises to underscore the confused uncertainty:

63. LOW CAMERA IN JUNKYARD

JOHNNY *slumped in tub near camera*—SHELL *runs on to plaster-of-Paris angel at side—looks at* JOHNNY. MUSIC—RAIN—AD LIB NOISES.

64. CLOSE SHOT IN JUNKYARD

JOHNNY *sitting in tub—leans back unconscious.* MUSIC—RAIN.

65. CLOSE UP—SHELL

Looking off bug-eyed—starts to exit at side. MUSIC—RAIN.

66. EXTERIOR: STREET IN JUNKYARD

SHELL *runs forward down alley in junkyard*—CAMERA *pans as he looks about anxiously—starts down street.* MUSIC—RAIN—FOOTSTEPS.

. . . DISSOLVES INTO

The *mezzopiano,* moderately soft, use of music and rain intermingled gives the scene a dimension not possible otherwise. Sir Carol Reed uses *fortissimo assai,* as loud as possible, during the flight from the scene of the holdup. The noise of the racing motor and the alarm bells in the rear add maddening tension, and to these two sound effects music is added when Johnny falls from the car onto the pavement. The high volume makes the moment excruciatingly painful.

The rumbles and screams in *crescendo* and *fortissimo assai* in *San Francisco* render that montage sequence more realistic, plus the shouting of names, the roar of brick walls collapsing. Prior to the first rumble there was a gay tune in the music hall—"All right, Professor, give us a little music here." The piano is tinkling out "Smokey Mokes" by Holzmann when the earth faults. The contrast makes the horror more unexpected.

Another example of excess volume being momentarily effective is the climax of *The Bridge on the River Kwai.* Nicholson is in a panic, trying to reach the plunger to prevent the destruction of his bridge. The train is approaching, making a racket on the rails. The train and the bridge are the targets. The roar of the engine increases; the whistle blows in *crescendo* and *fortissimo.* It is an unbearably noisy moment. In the confusion over Nicholson's fall upon the plunger box, there can be no doubt as to what happens. *"SOUND OF EXPLOSION"* accompanies the blowing up of the bridge, train, rails, and timber.

Sound effects as counterpoint are a dramaturgical asset as well as an auditory tool. Having written the quiet scene when Abe last sees Ann Rutledge, Robert E. Sherwood moves us immediately to the opposite end of the decibel range. It provides a release for our pent-up grief. Here again is that change of pace (also accelerated time), Abe having left the Rutledge home without speaking:

186. EXTERIOR: NEW SALEM STREET—NIGHT

Presumably some distance down the street from the RUTLEDGE *home. Torch lights, men, excitement.* JACK ARMSTRONG *and his boys are prominent among them—also* BOWLING GREEN, JOSHUA SPEED, *and* MENTO GRAHAM.

GREEN
Abe carried New Salem by 205 votes to 3!

Wild cheers.

Orson Welles in both *Citizen Kane* and *The Magnificent Ambersons* (1942) employs sound for counterpoint, and utilizes echoes of sounds to add tonal quality. The possibilities of an enhanced realism is there for the creator to use, and once employed the effect is not forgotten. The emergence of Peyton Farquhar from Owl Creek is believable as he lies exhausted on the bank because we hear his heavy breathing.

Silence as a manipulated element can be employed creatively, which may make it doubly golden. In the first story, *Kurogami* (Black Hair), of *Kwaidan,* the samurai husband is performing on horseback at a court tournament. Because he is unhappily separated from his wife, living alone at their country house, he cannot keep her from his thoughts. So while testing his skill with bow and arrow at full gallop, the camera is in a close-up of the horse's hooves pounding on the track, the sound loud and furious. Without warning the hooves are silent. The samurai is recalling his wife at her spinning wheel, and so blots out the present, sight and sound.

The thundering score of Dmitri Shostakovitch in the Soviet *Hamlet,* on the other hand, seems composed apart from the images. In a film so actively visual with Hamlet's first entrance on horse, the

Queen rushing on horse to the duel, armies marching in a Kremlin coup d'état, the thunder and musical shouts are in opposition to Grigori Kozintsev's pageantry. Shakespeare is lost in the shuffle. Neither music nor cinema is of a piece, whereas in Olivier's *Hamlet* the pounding of the Prince's heart when he first meets the ghost is startlingly effective, as are the clashes and rasps of steel in the dueling scene.

CHAPTER THIRTEEN ✻

Refinements

1. LIGHT

Little noted and less appreciated than the powers of motion, light is nonetheless a unique quality in cinema. Without it, the image can not be recorded.

More than technical luminosity is involved. Light is a major ingredient that gives texture to both feelings and ideas. It combines naturally with motion to affect frame, shot, and scene structures. The response is in optical, physiological, and psychological-intellectual reactions. In its most elemental form cinema is light in movement.

Since the writer-director is the first to see the image in his mind's eye, long before the cameraman gets the script, the shades of light in the scene are his responsibility unless he abdicates it. Marguerite Duras in her scenario of *Hiroshima Mon Amour* describes the opening shots of the lovers: "The shoulders are of different colors, one dark, one light. . . . The difference between the hands is also very marked. The woman's hand lies on the darker shoulder. . . ."

Throughout the *Hiroshima* scenario there is a reference to light whenever it is appropriate. During one of the flashbacks to Nevers, Miss Duras describes: *"At Hiroshima. The light is already different. . . . At Nevers. A German crosses a square at dusk. . . . At Hiroshima. She is lying on the bed, pleasantly tired. Darker now. . . .* [later] *In the room, the light has faded even more."*

Gregg Toland, who photographed *Citizen Kane*, wrote that "the photography should fit the story." He saw his job as providing "a proper photographic vehicle for the plot. Fitting *Wuthering*

Heights, Grapes of Wrath (1940), and *Long Voyage Home* (1940) to an identical photographic pattern would be unfair to director, writer, actors, and audience." This exceptional acknowledgment was written in 1941.

Cinematographers, beginning with Griffith's G. W. Bitzer, have varied their key of lighting in visual efforts to enhance emotional moods. The three general keys are low, medium, and high. Low-key lighting in black and white indicates a somber time; the heavy shadows carry a gloomy, depressing, and dismal feeling. Medium key in monochrome is ordinary reality. High-key effects, created with definitions that sparkle in a general brilliance, suggest gaiety and lightness. Melodrama is underscored when contrasts are harsh, caused by sharp highlights in juxtaposition to soft shadows.

Much of the satirical tone in *The Graduate* is due to a hilarity enhanced by the high-key lighting of cameraman Robert Surtees.

As the maturity of cinema continues, the writer-director rediscovers that all elements are at his command: light and movements as well as characters and plots. *Last Year in Marienbad* opens satiated eyes to fresh possibilities offered by light. For example, time is labeled by the dark or light dress; a golden lamé indicates an intermediate stage. The lovers dance in shadow-and-light patterns.

What a saving in artistic frustration and financial commitments when the creator solves the challenge first on paper, which is indeed cheaper than celluloid or electronic tape.

2. COLOR'S THE THING

Though the compulsion toward colored cinema (films and TV) has monetary motivations, the artistic result is to be compared to reality and to imagination, the two contradictions that render modern man a candidate for schizophrenia.

Cinema in color presents a special challenge to the writer-director, since viewing habits are traditionally conditioned either by an indifference to color or by a color-blind ignorance of emotional possibilities.

Color is really an extension of light, a refinement, so that a creator in cinema—whether he acknowledges it or not—is part painter as well as a writer. If his eye is the eye of a poet, he will see shades of meaning in the subtle gradations of color. No two shades mean the same, any more than two words of dialogue or two notes of music.

The mood of war and of impending danger as signified by faint reds growing more reddish with each shot is an example of a creative use of color in *Becky Sharp* (1935). In the William Makepeace Thackeray novel *Vanity Fair* a ball is given on the eve of the Battle of Waterloo (conclusion of Chapter XXIX). This moment in the screenplay by Francis Edwards Faragoh is enlarged to permit what its director Reuben Mamoulian calls "controlling color for dramatic effect." Here is the beginning of that scene, based more on the play by Langdon Mitchell than on the novel:

88. INTERIOR: BALLROOM—BRUSSELS—NIGHT

MEDIUM SHOT ON DANCE FLOOR

The dance is on, but only for a flash. For now there is a sudden piercing sound, like a thunderclap. . . . The dancers slow down, there is amazement on their faces.

VOICES AD LIB
What was that? . . . Did you hear it? . . . Shh, listen to it!

Another cannon-shot, louder than the first.

88A. INTERIOR: ANTEROOM—BALL—BRUSSELS—NIGHT

CLOSE-UP—WELLINGTON

near the area of the cardtables. His face is set, he is listening.

89. INTERIOR: BALLROOM—BRUSSELS—NIGHT

CLOSE SHOT—*A* COUPLE

as they stop.

FIRST WOMAN DANCER
There! Did you hear it now?

FIRST MAN DANCER
(*a civilian*)
Yes. . . . like cannon . . .

90. INTERIOR: BALLROOM—BRUSSELS—NIGHT

CLOSE SHOT—ANOTHER COUPLE

standing still, but in a dancing position. They are listening intently.

Though the screenwriter failed to indicate color in his shots, for whatever reason, the director employed the dramatic acceleration as a basis for a color escalation. Olivier in *Richard III* (1955) used black shadows on the stone floors. This is using color as narrative.

Color as merely pictorial is seen in *Henry V,* where many scenes and costumes are copies from the Duc de Berry's *Book of Hours.*

Color as description can be seen in *Blood and Sand* (1941). For his second color film Mr. Mamoulian developed "a color-plan which would coordinate the emotional aspects of action and dialogue with the physical production and with the fact of color. . . . color-treatment of each sequence must be keyed to the dominant mood of the production. . . ." He sought models among painters—"What does it matter if our picture moves and speaks; it is still fundamentally a picture." Murillo in such paintings as "Young Spanish Beggar" served as a model for the abject poverty of the boyhood period: "bronze-browns and blacks dominated."

The bullring scenes: "we followed the style of Goya with his dramatic and vivid colorings."

For the luxurious home of the patrician seductress Donna Sol (Rita Hayworth) the model was Velázquez, "the great master of light and shadow who so flashingly depicted the richness of court life."

Similarly, for the scenes in Juan's dressing room prior to a bull-fight—"We tried to capture something of the luxury of color and strong suggestions of bustling movement that such painters as Titian and Veronese put on their canvases."

Sorolla was used for street and market scenes.

For the scenes in the chapel the color-mood came from El Greco, the prime religious painter of Spain. Here is a short chapel scene when Juan Gallardo (Tyrone Power) prays:

303. INTERIOR: A LARGE WHITE-WASHED HALL—FULL SHOT

The hall is quite bare of furniture; it's occupied at the moment by a couple of other matadors who are to take part in the afternoon performance, together with their cuadrilla and friends. JUAN *makes his way through the hallway and into a doorway at one end.*

304. INTERIOR: CHAPEL—FULL SHOT

A small, dark and narrow room, at one end of which lights are burning. The back of the altar contains a wood carving with Christ on the Cross. On a table four tapers are burning and several bunches of dusty, moth-eaten flowers stand in common pottery vases. The chapel, too, is full of people. The aficionados of humble class have assembled so as to see great men close at hand. They stand, bare-

headed, in the darkness at the rear of the chapel. JUAN *goes up to the altar, elegant and graceful, his cape loose over his shoulder. He bends his knees before the altar.*

305. CLOSE SHOT—JUAN—AT ALTAR

He mutters a short prayer, crosses himself and rises, walking backward toward the door, while the spectators in the chapel nudge each other and watch him.

DISSOLVE TO:

Using this screenplay by Jo Swerling, based on the novel by Blasco-Ibáñez, Mamoulian added his color concepts: "In the chapel scenes, we again heightened the mood by spraying the altar-ornaments, the crucifix, and so on, a green like the patina of old bronze." The greenish light aided "the emotional feeling of the sequence."

Reading color as though it were a separate guide to be integrated into the full script and production, Mamoulian describes the introduction of Juan in a fourth-class carriage en route to his fame as a bullfighter. His *cuadrillo* of three companions discuss their progress; Juan's voice is heard off-shot. Mamoulian continues, ". . . we cut to a full-screen shot of a newspaper, which he is pretending to read. The paper comes down, and we have a big head close-up of the young matador, reclining in his seat, his head resting against the folds of his brilliant red *muleta*. In monochrome, we could hold that close-up for almost any footage—one hundred, three hundred, a thousand feet if need be. In color, the emotional impact of that red background is so strong that the shot could only be held for a few seconds. Yet it was necessary: it gave Juan's first appearance the necessary impetus which helped him build and carry his vivid characterization throughout all the ensuing reels."

Involving color in plot conflict is another usage. Mamoulian speaks of the dinner scene when Donna Sol, seen in a white evening gown, ensnares Juan Gallardo: "Later, as she sings to him, playing the guitar, a close-up of her fingers highlights the scarlet paint on her nimbly-flying finger-tips. In another scene, where she and Tyrone Power play their most passionate love scene we see her in a close-up, after which the camera dollies back to reveal the flaming orange bodice she wears, as her scarlet-tipped fingers entwine themselves in Power's black hair. (The combination of red and black has always been symbolic of danger—passion—and evil menace). This costume, incidentally, forms an effectively dramatic contrast with the simple black dress worn by Linda Darnell [Juan's wife] when she enters the scene later."

Color as idea is most evident in fantasy. *The Red Shoes* uses ballet scenes to give the feel in color of motion and the realization (idea) of what ballet means, at least to Michael Powell. Mr. Powell and Emeric Pressburger wrote and directed *Stairway to Heaven* (1946) with color differentiating between reality and fantasy. Squadron Leader Peter Carter is doomed within his burning bomber, returning to England, and he has no parachute:

20. INSIDE THE LANCASTER

PETER *is sitting on the edge of the open hatch, his legs dangling into space.*

PETER
(*quietly*)

"The pine-tree drops its dead;
　They are quiet, as under the sea.
　Overhead, overhead
　Rushes life in a race,
　As the clouds, the clouds chase; and we go,
　And we drop like the fruits of the tree,
　Even we,
　Even so."

He says the poem very solemnly and seriously, as if it were a Grace. He looks back at the dead radio operator.

See you in a minute, Bob—you know what they wear by now. Propellors or wings. . . .

He takes the jump.

21. THE LANCASTER

The aircraft flying through the fog. PETER *falls from the hatch and instantly vanishes. The aircraft flies on. In a few seconds there is only the yellow fog.*

22. THE FOG— (TRANSITION SCENE)

Something very strange is happening. Until now our film has been in colour. The fog, greyish, yellowish, dun-colour, swirls about; what colour it has seems to be draining away, until shades of black and white are all that remain.

The Sequence that follows and all other sequences in the Other World are in black and white.

The reverse technique is applied when the office in Upstairs World discovers that Peter hasn't arrived. The Chief Recorder in heaven is a lady with extraordinary eyes:

34. CHIEF RECORDER'S OFFICE— (TRANSITION SCENE)

CHIEF RECORDER

. The question is, what has happened to Squadron Leader Peter Carter since 04.10 British Double Summer Time?

She pauses. Her eyes become concentrated on one particular man, on one particular spot at one particular time on the morning of May the Fifth 1945: the colours of Life start to pour back into the black and white image: we see what seems to be the colour of her eyes, bluish green, white: then we see through her eyes, steadily looking backward, that the colours are the colours of a long Atlantic roller, curling in on an immensely long, lonely sandy beach.

35. THE BEACH

The effect of this sequence is that Earth should be made to look like Heaven. It must be shot very early in the morning to do that.

A foggy, greenish dawn is breaking over an illimitable sandy beach, upon which surf-rollers are lazily pounding, as the tide goes out over the miles of yellow sand.

Some object is being carried in on one of these rollers, a dark object which is hurled beyond the tide in a flurry of surf and spray and left behind by the retreating wave.

36. THE BEACH

A nearer view reveals it to be the body of PETER CARTER, undamaged, the face we last saw covered in blood and oil now washed clean, his clothes a mixture of flying-suit and uniform, his expression extraordinarily impersonal as he lies there on his back: just the body of a young pilot, baled-out over the sea and washed-up drowned on the English coast. . . .

Color in the scripts of the thirties and forties has this decorative usage for the enhancement of plot and character. In *Red Desert* color becomes a separate and major element, of which we are aware as color apart from other determining factors (motion, plot, characters, editing, dialogue, and so on) . Antonioni is a writer-director obsessed with what cinema can create uniquely.

Life witnessed through the color prism of a neurotically unsmiling woman is the idea behind *Red Desert*. Explorations into the color perception of a disturbed psyche is more than the subjective emotion of a character for Antonioni. It is a new form of the art—Impressionistic, to use a painting term—possible for Antonioni because of his primary emphasis on the image in all his films. "My aim," he declares, "is to achieve the suppression of outward physical action with the narration of the film and, where possible, eliminate dialogue." Color, then, is to be used as a further concentration on mountain peaks in the progression of events, and with an avoidance of valleys and preparatory slopes. Proceeding from the top of one sequence climax to another, Antonioni reduces scene structure to a minimum—the opposite of traditional plotting.

"That which in ordinary life is unconscious must be made conscious," Antonioni says of his theory of color. The problem is "the habit of looking at colors as they are, of looking at reality as it is." Whereas the color in *Red Desert* "makes us see the world with other eyes, allows us to change our way of thinking. When I first saw *8½* I realized the limits of black-and-white films. For instance, the scene shot in the grave of the father, the interior of the hotel, the memories of childhood, all should have been in color. It has a meaning and function in modern life that it never had in the past. Black-and-white films will soon be shown only in museums. If I could, I would remake almost all mine in color."

How does Antonioni's color differ? In *Red Desert* he continues his study of the spiritually sterile professionals. Giuliana (Monica Vitti) is a mother of a young boy and married to a chemical engineer, Ugo, who works in the industrial district of Ravenna. Ugo's friend Corrado (Richard Harris) is recruiting skilled workers for a South American plant. Ugo leaves on business for a few days, the boy becomes ill with imaginary paralysis. Giuliana's inability to adapt to reality increases. She visits Corrado in his hotel, but she seeks a further encounter with a Turkish sailor on board a ship, only to turn away. In the final scene she appears somewhat adjusted as she walks with her son and tries to avoid, as the birds do, the yellow smoke from Ugo's factory.

The industrial ugliness is displayed in factory dumps, black and gray and foggy, strewn with refuse, as disordered as a field after a battle. Industrial beauty is in the arrangement of pipes, tubes, retorts, tanks of chemicals in red, yellow, black. Giuliana sees these colors as she walks about; her apartment is cold, functional, and gray. The black giant prow of an oil tanker gradually blocks out the view at a window. She is in a land of nightmare and grief. The most modern space-age antennae tower in rows beside a little green house. Ponds are stagnant, poisoned by purple and yellow chemicals. She is a prisoner of her environment, a theme emphasized by having the background slightly blurred, out of focus, and then through a pan or a subject motion Giuliana arrives very close in the foreground, as though demonstrating cause and effect. The color is at once static and beautiful, but so is she in her sickness.

Giuliana is neurotically disturbed to the point of a suicide attempt in a car accident (we are told) ; her illness is portrayed in a shameless expression of herself. While walking, the world she sees—a fruit vendor, the fruit, the street—is gray, which is the monotonous, non-discriminative color of indecision. The walls of her house are the same color as the factory walls. Her color is blue, which distracts her lover Corrado while he talks in a conference and happens to notice a panel painted blue.

Modern painters, Impressionists from Mondrian onward, are the ghosts behind Antonioni's compositions. A marsh is painted gray to indicate the feelings of Giuliana and Corrado as they gaze at it. The inside of a shack on a wharf is painted red wherein a rather lifeless orgy is verbally conducted. When Giuliana leaves that place she forgets her handbag left behind (symbology) , and they stand on the wharf discussing its rescue—her husband, her lover, and two friends. In a thickening misty fog she blots them out, one by one, as her neurosis isolates her by erasing them from her conscious mind.

This subjective utilization of color can be observed in excerpts from the screenplay by Antonioni and Tonino Guerra. When Giuliana bursts into Corrado's hotel room she complains of feeling ill, being cold, and not knowing where to go:

> . . . *The room is in disorder: suitcases and clothing scattered everywhere give a feeling of temporariness.* GIULIANA *removes her overcoat and begins to pick up a jacket, a tie, some handkerchiefs, a shirt, some colored envelopes, and place them on the bureau or on chairs, not following a logical order but according to her own system: all the green objects together, all the red together, all the yellow, etc. She goes about doing this like an automaton. Presently she stops. She is completely bewildered.* CORRADO *goes to her to calm her.*

Seeing the world illogically in terms exclusively of color is a unique means of characterization. She is preoccupied with color. Later, they are both seated on the bed:

. . . GIULIANA is paying no attention to him. She is observing a wall with great attention.

CORRADO

What are you looking at?

GIULIANA

There *(indicating the wall)*

She lies back on the bed. Her glance moves to the ceiling on which appears a multicolored stain. Then she covers herself with a blanket in order not to see. CORRADO observes her form on the bed. The temptation to touch her is enormous. After a moment, seeing that GIULIANA does not move, he extends his hand. GIULIANA starts violently. She uncovers her face and looks fixedly at CORRADO with her fists holding tightly the hem of the blanket.

Sometimes I have the desire to attack someone.

Her illness and what she sees are inseparable. In the next moment she begs for help:

. . . with an anguish which must be unbearable to judge from her movements, which she makes with her entire body, with her very voice, broken and panting. She is beside herself. CORRADO grasps her arms.

CORRADO

I'm here, Giuliana, calm yourself . . . tell me from what you wish me to protect you.

GIULIANA speaks in bursts, trying at first to control her voice and then abandoning herself to her need to shout louder and louder:

GIULIANA

From the streets, from the factories, from the colors, from the sky, from people!

And as if she wished to prevent her eyes from seeing, she throws her arms around CORRADO's neck and squeezes him as tightly as she can, bursting into desperate tears. CORRADO in turn embraces her and begins to caress her tenderly, as if to calm her. At first it is with a softness in distinct contrast with the impulse to stretch her body out on the bed and throw himself upon it. But then his gestures, at first tentative, acquire a precise objective. The caresses become bit by bit more explicit. GIULIANA is not even capable of realizing what is happening. Thus, when CORRADO intensifies his embrace, she suc-

cumbs inertly. CORRADO *begins to kiss her and the kiss becomes gradually more intense, violent.* GIULIANA's *whole body shakes violently. Her earlier bewilderment is submerged by a new, sensual confusion: a sort of frenzy, an unconscious lewdness mixed with the impulse to resist and with newly discovered pleasure. In a last glimmer of conscience,* GIULIANA *leaps from the bed and cowers seminude on an armchair.* CORRADO *goes to her and resumes kissing her, softly.* GIULIANA *abandons herself completely.*

Some time later, GIULIANA *and* CORRADO *are in the bed, completely naked, motionless, immersed in an unreal pink light. The entire room is pink: the objects, the furniture, the clothing.*

The scene ends, all is bathed in pink: lamp, bottle, books, fruit, papers, chest of drawers, chairs. The sheets are white. There is blue, Giuliana's color, in the silky curtain drawn across the window.

Taking Mamoulian's color plan and Antonioni's color in the script as indicators, the contemporary creator needs to be a color-conscious chronicler. The Czech feature *The Cat* (1963), for example, includes faces and hands as part of the color vision—green face for envy, red for anger, and so on.

In his perpetual dissatisfaction as he presses for perfection, Antonioni seeks to control every stage of the color process, including laboratory printing. As though he were working on a color reproduction of such modernists as de Kooning or Rothko, he strives for the exact color harmony, the precise dissonance. His sense of contrast and perfection recalls such a portrait as Hans Holbein's the Younger *Sir Thomas More,* with its finely defined features set against a green draped background, a black hat above, the tan-brown fur collar below, and the scarlet sleeves with their dark shadows. Such contrasting colors delineate more clearly the high flesh tones on the face. Holbein got what he wanted. "To give Antonioni what he wants," the Roman Technicolor technicians confess, "we would have to invent new film, new lenses, new chemical coloring components, everything."

Everything makes the difference between repetition and exploration.

Like Antonioni's initial color production, Fellini's first film in color also seeks to explore a troubled woman's psychic world in *Juliet of the Spirits.* To a lesser intent, Resnais's *Muriel* (1963) attempts the same in a discursive plot that is not, however, blacked out by color. Where Resnais lets the hues of his camera's palette enrich characterizations, Antonioni and Fellini employ color primarily as a character's subjective stance.

Juliet is a combination of red and white. For her, red means the devil and fire, and she wears red for her tentative, housewifely excursions toward the erotic. However, white is more her natural color, and when she concludes her explorations and rejects her vagabond visions and accepts her role as wife of a philanderer Juliet sallies forth in white against the soft browns and greens of the pine trees.

Throughout the film Fellini uses color as idea. The puritanical and childish past is depicted in pale and sweet tones that remind the viewer of ice-cream flavors. The black, funereal gowns and hoods of the nun-figures are color symbols of repression and death. The hectic and erotic present is shown in riotous reds, fierce purples, glamorous greens, and hot flesh tints.

There is, however, a general tone of absurdity cast over the whole production, seen in the erotic imagery so excessive that at times it is unintentionally grotesque. The excess is most evident in the sets, decorations, and costumes of the art director, Piero Cherardi, and his accomplice, the director of photography, Gianni di Venanzo. The music of Nino Rota is similarly exotic to the point where it is frequently absurd and repulsively distasteful, carbon copies of his previous music in *La Dolce Vita* and *8½*. It is as though Fellini had lost control of his film, or had abdicated to Cherardi.

A moment of exceptional unity, for both design and execution, is the use of color in the opening. It is a moment never equaled in the film. Following an initial head-on truck-in over the greenery, as though floating toward the ideal white house in fairyland, Fellini introduces Juliet in joyously hectic preparations for dinner. Her husband is expected; it is their wedding anniversary. The elaborate table is set for two. In eleven swift shots with pans right and left, coupled with trucks right and left, as we accompany Juliet's movements—the love-theme music lively—Fellini creates a mood. At first Juliet's face is not seen, she is the anonymous little woman behind the busy executive. She instructs her maids; she prepares her hair; she lights tall red candles. Shadows play sensuously as images race back and forth on a horizontal plane. The moment is highly fragmented, each second relished. In Shot 8 the dining-room lights go dark. In Shot 9 the darkened room is suddenly lighted as husband arrives. He enters in Shot 10, surprised. He had forgotten the date—was it her birthday?—and brought six guests. In Shot 11 Juliet's reaction is fleetingly poignant, as in *Nights of Cabiria* or Gelsomina in *La Strada*. The theme in all its radiant color has been introduced. Never again do we behold it so clearly.

The imbalance in Juliet is caused by Fellini directing a serious clown who is not a clearly delineated character caught in the comic irony of life. We are soberly dazzled, but not thrillingly satisfied. It is a *film d'auteur* with Fellini improvising his attitudes in the tradition of the writer-director of the *commedia dell'arte*. Though Michelangelo Antonioni lacks humor, and so his men and women go pessimistically through the alien world searching without a capacity to love, Federico Fellini enjoys the world and its foibles. His characters suffer with smiles; Antonioni's can't smile, they are so absorbed in their pain. In the end we suspect Antonioni, though far less entertaining, is more truthful.

Modestly Alfred Hitchcock admits that "I am doing well if I get 60 per cent of my original conception onto the screen. . . . This is a business that is full of compromises." Yet he persists in exploration, aiming for a new style of color photography in *Torn Curtain* (1966). Instead of direct lighting, the standard brilliance of what Hitchcock calls "Hollywood gloss," he uses soft light that has been reflected and diffused. There is more shadow, backgrounds become fuzzy, the camera at times deliberately out of focus, the impact impressionistic. Such color in an East German setting creates a different realism, though the characters are unreal and the story unrealistic.

Richard Lester in *A Funny Thing Happened on the Way to the Forum* aims to create with color a different comedy. Based in part on the comedies of Plautus, the film is a mélange of mixed identities, double entendres, and outrageous jokes, off color to the eye and ear. A courtesan at one point screams at a eunuch, "Don't you lower your voice to me!" To create the bad taste of the *nouveau riche* in Roma in the first century after Christ, the interior settings are dominated by what Lester calls "awful purple." The bedrooms of the courtesans are washed in torrid colors, variations of reds and pinks and purples. Color in itself can be funny, though the frenetic editing emasculated the humor. The techniques of TV commercials don't travel very far.

Color can be mystical. In Kobayashi's *Kwaidan* (Ghost Stories) there are four separate episodes; *Yuki Onna* (Snow Woman) was omitted in the English version. The most spectacular and inventive use of color was in the medieval sea battle, *Dan-No-Ura*, in the

Earless Hōichi segment. The sky is canvas and painted in fierce slashes, both during the battle sequence and behind the temple, which had been built to commemorate the 1185 battle. Choppy waves are reddish for anger and to indicate bloodshed. When the nurse, holding in her arms the child emperor Antoko, leaps from the royal warship to drown together under the colored waters, the moment has a curious fairy-tale credibility. This impressionistic flavor fits the narrative. When Hōichi, the young neophyte priest and mute musician, has his body painted with sacred prayers to protect him from the evil ghost warrior, we see, in the startling clarity of the color contrasts, his nude ears, overlooked and vulnerable. Color speaks, in this case, for the narrative. Again there is a plausible reality about the horror that follows.

Color demands style. What would that pioneer color film, *The Red Shoes,* be in black-and-white, or what would be the pageantry of *Henry V* if done in monochrome? *Doctor Zhivago* is more richly endowed in its colorful settings, interior and exterior, than in its characterizations, which lack motivation in depth. The bluish white of snowy expanses, for example, give an awesome dimension to the Siberian steppes, photographed in Finland at 40 degrees below zero by Fred A. Young who had captured the shimmering desert heat in *Lawrence of Arabia*. The golden wheat field in brilliant noonday summer, where the pink-cheeked youths of St. Michael's Military Academy are machine-gunned to death, is a cruel color.

An extraordinary infusion of motivation and color might be studied in Sir Laurence Olivier's projection of *Othello*. That any husband, so profoundly in love, could strangle his wife to death through suspicion, jealousy, and circumstantial evidence has been one of the most difficult dramatic motivations to accept. Making Othello a Moor has helped by adding mystery to his nature, the implication being that love and hate then flow in fury. But to see Othello as a black Moor with pink palms, reddish inner mouth, thick, chocolate lips, black kinky hair, and whose walk is a jungle shuffle with arms loose, whose speech is indolently sensuous and includes a chuckling humor—is to believe Othello a human animal capable of murdering the one he loves. The Christian cross around his neck is but an ornament he discards the moment the sleeping wolves are aroused. Accusations of trickery and witchcraft on the part of Desdemona's father now sound fitting, coming from a parent who has been fooled. Othello's colorful costumes add to his exotic appearance. The electrifying vibrancy in Olivier's voice has an extra dimension while we watch his black face reflect an inner fire. That agony in his voice as he holds the dead Desdemona in his arms, and is about to kill himself, is the terrible tonal despair of a colored man who has been victimized by his racial gullibility.

Color has rescued Othello from a black-and-white stereotype. Similarly, the presence of color in the epic *Chushingura* (*42 Ronin*, directed by Hiroshi Inagaki, 1963), is as natural an element, decorative and unobtrusive, as the absence of color in *Who's Afraid of Virginia Woolf?* adds to the black-gray-white realism of that lower-depths drama. The reverse in either case (*Chushingura* in black and white, *Who's Afraid* in color) would have created an unhappy imbalance of visual and dramatic values.

Color in Antonioni's *Blow-up* is more decorative than interpretative, adding little to the significance of Antonini's depiction of illusion and reality; whereas the uses of color for mood in *A Man and a Woman* (1966) raises that ordinary love story to the exquisite heights of an intimate experience. The director Claude Lelouch photographs a lovemaking scene in sensuous oranges, but when the widow Anne (Anouk Aimee) is reminded of her husband Pierre (Barouh) as her partner not only does the soft focus disappear but the flashback to her life with Pierre is in vivid, sharp color contrasts. When the lover Jean-Louis (Trintignant) remembers his dead wife Valerie (Legrange) the flashbacks are in brownish sepia. After their lovemaking scene the film remains in sepia to the end, as though their world had gone flat, but the final embrace is happy.

3. CONCLUSION

What should be manifest by now is the extraordinary opportunity to portray ideas and emotions in ways never experienced by creator or audience. And with these rare means go an equally enormous responsibility. The innate artist, self-propelled toward humanistic goals in a world of contradictions and confusions, feels this constant challenge. He is the bearer of the word, now in the form of the moving image.

In the tradition of the arts he is the new seed carrier, double-fisted, sowing a fascination that could stimulate either cruelty or energize affection. No other historical period has had the magnitude of this dual responsibility and in a language that has become so universal for the literate and the uneducated around the world.

Great cinema creates great audiences. "Public taste until a few years ago," says Michelangelo Antonioni, "was tied to certain routines for storytelling, to certain narrative orthodoxies. A film had to be superficial, to follow a mechanical rhythm of narration which held the attention of the audience. Then people began to understand that the rhythm could be broken, that films could be written differently, that more realistic stories could be told, based on individual feelings or relationships between individuals."

The creation of great audiences is accelerated by the personal identity the rising generations have with cinema, but the appeal of art is ageless. When one of Antonioni's films met with boos and jeers, a little old lady rose to shout at the Cannes crowd: "If you want a movie you can understand, go see Cops and Robbers!"

Television is creating a larger audience by making the moving image more accessible, a part of daily stimuli, and since familiarity with mediocrity breeds boredom—and hopefully contempt—TV creates a need for great cinema. Hollywood has retooled itself into becoming the television capital of the world. Perversely, this is the first step toward being one of the great cinema centers, the equal eventually in experimentation with ideas and an easeful familiarity with honest feelings—a Hollywood that is in aspiration the cinema equivalent of the best of Rome, Paris, Tokyo, London, and Stockholm.

More than any art, cinema manipulates physical objects and utilizes machinery. Nothing can be too technical or too detailed for the attention of the writer-director, nor will it be if he sees what he is looking at. He knows intuitively that cinema can never afford to be formless; since it is a manipulated art, it depends on structure. So limitless is his freedom of choice in selecting effects that chaos can result if the writer-director lacks a sense of order in his handling of ideas and feelings, or if his mastery of his craft materials is inadequate, or if his sense of cinema aesthetics is inept.

When the word-orientated creators write scripts and direct them, their films have a certain recognizable emphasis on narrative sequence, including a heavy reliance on dialogue or narration, and a curious lack of cinematic vitality. No verbal description can adequately describe the visual, but to bridge this gap a screen playwright is obliged to indicate on paper—to the utmost of his visual capacity—how a shot should look cinematically as well as dramatically.

Sergei Eisenstein, while writing and directing *Ivan the Terrible II* in 1945, says:

The most important thing is to have the vision. The next is to grasp and hold it. In this there is no difference whether you are writing a film-script, pondering the plan of the production as a whole, or thinking out a solution for some particular detail.

You must see and feel what you are thinking about. You must see and grasp it. You must hold and fix it in your memory and senses. And you must do it at once.

The immediacy of the image, its fragility and elusiveness, leads Eisenstein to urge sketches and drawings:

When you are in a good working mood, images swarm through your busy imagination. Keeping up with them and catching them is very much like grappling with a run of herring.

You suddenly see the outline of a whole scene and, rising simultaneously before this same inner eye, a close-up in full detail: a head nesting on a great white ruff. . . . Before this mood has finished, you find yourself drawing with your pen and penciling notes for the dialogue—on the sheets of drawings. . . . Whole scenes first take shape as batches of drawings before they take on the clothing of words.

Since many successful scripts are badly written, with impoverished vocabularies, is it expecting too much that the writer also be able to draw? Let him draw stick figures, trace heads with the circle of a silver dollar for close-ups, a quarter for a medium-shot head, a dime for a long-shot head. Experience size and perception, ratio and scale, angle and light. Feel the image by drawing it, sense the movements by drawing the action. Indicate directions with arrows for frame motion, the pans and trucks and tilts and zooms, and for subject motion: arrows that point in the direction of the movement. If the drawing persists in being unintelligible under an untrained hand, then label each object—John, Mary, tree, window—but draw prior to and during composition.

Eisenstein continues:

These are nothing more than attempts to grasp stenographically the features of those images that flash through your mind in thinking about the individual details of your film. These drawings cannot claim to be more than this, nor can they possibly make any claim as drawings!

But neither can they claim less than this! For in them are secured the principal, initial elements of those ideas that will later have to be worked on, developed and realized in the course of the coming weeks and months. . . .

What drawing images can do, above all else, is to expose the writer-director to the choices at his disposal. Does the subject move alone or in conjunction with a frame movement? Move where and how, across or forward? Or would an accelerated action be better? What is being discovered is the proper means for the aim at heart or in the mind.

If means determine ends, can ends select the best means? The laws of aim are infinite, while the outlaw of chance occurs only once. Hundreds of disorders all look disharmonious, while the effective harmony or dissonance appears right. Cinema is characteristically flexible, since so many elements are flowing in it.

The common complaint of editors is that the most grueling, difficult, exhausting, and quarrelsome part of editing is their attempts to solve or correct script deficiencies. Taste and judgment begin with the eliminations affected by the writer-director, what he avoids or omits, and then on what he concentrates. Such taste and judgment are the sum total of the artist in the man, his talent and his training, his sensitivity and intelligence. Italian and French directors are inclined toward accelerated edits more than others; Kurosawa trucks and pans leftward more than Western writer-directors; Bergman moves in and out as though Sweden, interior and exterior, were his private stage. The sum total of a life experience comes to focus on a single choice out of multiple possiblities: to move the actor, to pivot the frame, to move the camera, or to edit. Which one, which combination?

The old terms, time and space, are now replaced by movement and light in a more specific characterization. Visual stimuli in cinema alters in ratio to the rhythms of motion and light. The faces of time not only move but are seen in various light patterns. Design in orchestration of shots relates to the external size of the image (extreme close-up, close-up, long shot, and so on) and also to internal size, the scale of such pictorial elements as line, mass, depth, and angle. All the parts of movements and lights are indeed less than the sum of their whole, since the whole needs to have a cinematic flavor, an essence beyond craft, that is the vision of the writer-director.

Size and angle largely determine perspective. The Battle of Agincourt in *Henry V* is described—the charge of the French knights and the shooting of the English archers—from different and conflicting angles. In describing the dance between Coppelius and the doll in *The Red Shoes* the shot reads: "Angles should emphasise the comedy of the scene." And so on.

All these elements demand attention, and in their selection and elimination lie style and flavor. The interplay between elements exists because none can be separate from another. Not unlike an impressive iceberg, cinema displays above the surface its plastic movements and lights; under the ocean unseen are the dramatic conflicts, the narrative plot and characters, but without which the whole would sink.

Innovations in projection techniques, such as multi-screens at "Expo 67," aim to complicate stimuli, but don't necessarily enhance perception. Actually, such systems, by operating beyond the physical adaptability of the human eye, often seem designed to act as substitutes for perceptional meaning. Stimuli for stimuli's sake is no novel principle, even in a thrill-saturated society. Similarly, Marshall McLuhan, that brilliant provocateur, believes form itself, like a massage, renders overweight bodies thinner without dieting. Intake governs digestion, rather than appetite. Alas, the truth is learned after the heart attack, but Dr. McLuhan is not as concerned, self-admittedly, with the patient as he is with the practice.

Art means freedom for choices, more difficult now that cinema is more fragmented and complex. No longer is the shot of Eisenstein the basic unit, like the atom of the thirties, the pre-bomb period. The atom has been split into protons, neutrons, and electrons. The shot has been fragmented into sections of separate or combined movements, which may be called *the faces of time*. An opening portion might be the face of subject motion, followed by the face of frame motion, and going on as the faces of parallel time. The face, too, may be part of two shots: the end of one and the beginning of another. Thus a shot may have a single or many appearances.

As an empirical tool, the faces of time provide patterns of formation that are capable of syntactic structure. Not the final word, but as a guide, they can serve as syntax in this new language.

Though movement-within-the-frame was the theatrical inheritance that dominated the style of the early creators, cinema today is predominantly fluid through its varied faces that concentrate with interruptions on the continuous present. Because of them our pulse-beat, respiration, and psychic rhythms are stimulated. These multiple faces of time and their combinations give cinema its stylistic power, the richest in potential of all contemporary arts. They are pictorial and psychic gestalts, operating individually and through interactions. The cinema artist is part psychologist and philosopher.

When creator and viewer are in harmony, so powerful is the visual that it robs verbalization for many moments afterward. A presence has possessed us.

For all its complexities and with all its persuasion, the visual sense offers continuity in a jangled world, connections in unrelated separations, and design in a patternless landscape. In the hands of propagandists or salesmen our corruptions can be exploited; in the fingers of artists we could have a perpetual Renaissance.

APPENDIX A

Bibliography

1. AESTHETICS

Alton, John. *Painting with Light*. New York, Macmillan, 1962.

Arnheim, Rudolf. *Art and Visual Perception*. Berkeley, Calif., University of California Press, 1954.

———. *Film as Art*. Berkeley, Calif., University of California Press, 1958.

Bazin, André. *Qu-est-ce que le Cinéma?* Volumes 1–4, Paris, Éditions du Cerf, 1958–62.

———. *What Is Cinema?* Ed. by Hugh Gray. Berkeley, Calif., University of California Press, 1967.

Balázs, Béla. *Theory of the Film*. New York, Roy, 1953.

Benoît-Lévy, Jean. *The Art of the Motion Picture*. New York, Coward-McCann, 1946.

Cocteau, Jean. *On the Film*. Chester Springs, Pa., Dufour, 1954.

Cornwell-Clyne, Adrian. *Color Films*. London, Focal, 1963.

Deren, Maya. *An Anagram of Ideas on Art, Form, and Film*. Yonkers, N.Y., Alicat Book Shop, 1946.

Duca, Lo. *L'Erotisme au Cinéma*. Paris, Jean-Jacques Pauvert, 1962.

Durgnat, Raymond. *Eros in the Cinema*. London, Calder and Boyars, 1966.

Eisenstein, Sergei. *Film Form and Film Sense*. Cleveland, Ohio, World Pub. Co. (Meridian), 1949.

Feldman, Joseph and Harry. *Dynamics of the Film*. New York, Hermitage House, 1952.

Fischer, Edward. *Screen Arts*. New York, Sheed and Ward, 1960.

Gregor, Ulrich, and Enno Patalas. *Geschichte des Films*. Gütersloh, Germany, Sigbert Mohn, 1962.

Halas, John, and Roger Manvell. *Design in Motion.* New York, Hastings House, 1962.

Kepes, Gyorgy. *Language of Vision.* Chicago, Paul Theobold, 1945.

———. *The Nature and Art of Motion.* New York, Braziller, 1964.

Kracauer, Siegfried. *Theory of Film.* New York, Oxford University Press, 1960.

Kyrou, Ado. *Le Surréalisme au Cinéma.* Paris, Arcanes, 1953.

Lawson, John. *Film: The Creative Process.* New York, Hill and Wang, 1964.

L'Herminier, Pierre, ed. *L'Art du Cinéma.* Paris, Éditions Seghers, 1960.

Lindgren, Ernest. *The Art of the Film.* New York, Macmillan, 1962.

Martin, Marcel. *Le Language Cinématographique.* Paris, Éditions du Cerf, 1962.

Morin, Edgar. *Le Cinéma ou L'Homme Imaginaire.* Paris, Éditions de Minuit, 1956.

Nilssen, Vladimir. *The Cinema as Graphic Art.* New York, Hill and Wang, 1959.

Rhode, Eric. *Speculations on the Cinema.* London, Weidenfeld and Nicolson, 1967.

Spottiswoode, Raymond. *Grammar of the Film.* Berkeley, Calif., University of California Press, 1959.

Thomson, David. *Movie Man.* New York, Stein and Day, 1967.

Tyler, Parker. *Rashomon as Modern Art.* New York, Cinema 16, Pamphlet #1, 1952.

———. *The Three Faces of the Film.* New York, Thomas Yoseloff, 1960.

Warshow, Robert. *Immediate Experience.* Garden City, N.Y., Doubleday, 1962.

2. DIRECTORS

Amengual, Barthelemy. *René Clair.* Paris, Éditions Seghers, Cinéma d'Aujourd'hui, #17.

———. *S. M. Eisenstein.* Lyon, Serdoc, Premier Plan Series.

Barry, Iris. *D. W. Griffith: American Film Master.* New York, Museum of Modern Art, 1965.

Bellour, Raymond. *Alexandre Astruc.* Paris, Éditions Seghers, Cinéma d'Aujourd'hui, #10.

Bessy, Maurice. *Orson Welles.* Paris, Éditions Seghers, Cinéma d'Aujourd'hui #6.

Beylie, Claude. *Max Ophuls.* Paris, Éditions Seghers, Cinéma d'Aujourd'hui, #16.

Bounoure, Gaston. *Alain Resnais.* Paris, Éditions Seghers, Cinéma d'Aujourd'hui, #5.

Briot, René. *Robert Bresson*. Paris, Éditions du Cerf, 1957.

Buache, Freddy, *Luis Buñuel*. Lyon, Serdoc, Premier Plan #13, 1960.

———, ed. *Jean Vigo*. Lausanne, Switzerland, Cinémathèque Suisse, 1962.

Cauliez, Armand. *Jacques Tati*. Paris, Éditions Seghers, Cinéma d'Aujourd'hui, #7.

Chapier, Henry. *Louis Malle*. Paris, Éditions Seghers, Cinéma d'Aujourd'hui, #24.

Chaplin, Charlie. *My Autobiography*. New York, Simon and Schuster, 1964.

Collet, Jean. *Jean-Luc Godard*. Paris, Éditions Seghers, Cinéma d'Aujourd'hui, #18.

Coursodon, Jean Pierre. *Keaton et Cie*. Paris, Éditions Seghers, Cinéma d'Aujourd'hui, #25.

Cowie, Peter. *Antonioni, Bergman, Resnais*. New York, Thomas Yoseloff, 1964.

———. *The Cinema of Orson Welles*, New York, Barnes, 1965.

De Mille, Cecil B. *Autobiography*. Ed. by Donald Harper. Englewood Cliffs, N.J., Prentice Hall, 1959.

Donner, Jorn. *The Personal Vision of Ingmar Bergman*. Bloomington, Ind., Indiana University Press, 1964.

Eisenstein, Sergei. *Notes of a Film Director*. London, Lawrence and Wishart, 1959.

Esteve, Michel. *Robert Bresson*. Paris, Éditions Seghers, Cinéma d'Aujourd'hui, #8.

Ferrara, Giuseppe. *Luchino Visconti*. Paris, Éditions Seghers, Cinéma d'Aujourd'hui, #21.

Flaherty, Frances H. *The Odyssey of a Filmmaker, Robert Flaherty's Story*. Urbana, Ill., University of Illinois Press, 1960.

Frydland, Maurice. *Roger Vadim*. Paris, Éditions Seghers, Cinéma d'Aujourd'hui, #12.

Guyon, François. *Ingmar Bergman*. Lyon, Serdoc, Premier Plan #3, 1959.

———. *Jean Renoir*. Lyon, Serdoc, Premier Plan #22, 23, 24.

Jeanne, René, and Charles Ford. *Abel Gance*. Paris, Éditions Seghers, Cinéma d'Aujourd'hui, #14.

Kyrou, Ado. *Luis Buñuel*. New York, Simon and Schuster, 1963.

Lacassin, Francis. *Louis Feuillade*. Paris, Éditions Seghers, Cinéma d'Aujourd'hui, #22.

Leprohon, Pierre. *Michelangelo Antonioni*. New York, Simon and Schuster, 1963.

Ledieu, Christian. *Joseph Losey*. Paris, Éditions Seghers, Cinéma d'Aujourd'hui, #11.

Moullet, Luc. *Fritz Lang*. Paris, Éditions Seghers, Cinéma d'Aujourd'hui, #9.

Moussinac, Léon. *Sergei Eisenstein*. Paris, Éditions Seghers, Cinéma d'Aujourd'hui, #23.

Mussman, Toby, ed. *Jean-Luc Godard: A Critical Anthology*. New York, Dutton Paperbacks, 1968.

Neergaard, Ebbe. *Carl Dreyer: A Film Director's Work*. London, British Film Institute, 1950.

Nizhny, Vladimir. *Lessons with Eisenstein*. New York, Hill and Wang, 1962.

Perry, George, S. *Films of Alfred Hitchcock*. New York and London, Dutton/Vista Picturebacks, 1965.

Pingaud, Bernard. *Alain Resnais*. Lyon, Serdoc, Premier Plan #18, 1961.

Queval, Jean. *Jacques Becker*. Paris, Éditions Seghers, Cinéma d'Aujourd'hui, #3.

Renzi, Renzo. *Federico Fellini*. Lyon, Serdoc, Premier Plan #12, 1960.

Richie, Donald. *The Films of Akira Kurosawa*. Berkeley, Calif., University of California Press, 1966.

Sadoul, Georges. *Georges Méliès*. Paris, Éditions Seghers, Cinéma d'Aujourd'hui, #1.

Salachas, Gilbert. *Federico Fellini*. Paris, Éditions Seghers, Cinéma d'Aujourd'hui, #13.

Seton, Marie. *Sergei M. Eisenstein*. New York, Grove Press, 1960.

Simon, John. *Acid Test*. (Including four essays on Antonioni, Bergman, Dassin, Wilder.) New York, Stein and Day, 1963.

Solmi, Angelo. *Storia di Federico Fellini*. Milano, Rizzoli, 1962.

Thirard, Paul-Louis. *Michelangelo Antonioni*. Lyon, Serdoc, Premier Plan #15, 1960.

Truffaut, François. With the collaboration of Helen G. Scott. *Hitchcock*. New York, Simon and Schuster, 1967.

Verdone, Mario. *Roberto Rossellini*. Paris, Éditions Seghers, Cinéma d'Aujourd'hui, #15.

Weinberg, Herman G. *Ernst Lubitsch*. New York, Dutton Paperbacks, 1968.

———. *Josef von Sternberg*. Paris, Éditions Seghers, Cinéma d'Aujourd'hui, #45, 1966; New York, Dutton Paperbacks, 1967.

Wood, Robin. *Hitchcock's Films*. New York, Barnes, 1965.

Zalzman, A. *Joris Ivens*. Paris. Éditions Seghers, Cinéma d'Aujourd'hui, #19.

3. GENERAL

Agee, James. *Agee on Film: Reviews and Comments*. Boston, Mass., Beacon Press, 1964.

Alpert, Hollis. *The Dreams and the Dreamers*. New York, Macmillan, 1962.

Anstey, Edgar, *et. al. Shots in the Dark*. London, Allan Wingate, 1952.

Battcock, Gregory. *The New American Cinema*. New York, Dutton Paperbacks, 1967.

Barnouw, Erik, and S. Krishnaswamy. *Indian Film*. New York, Columbia University Press, 1963.

Barry, Iris. *Film Notes: The Silent Film*. New York, Museum of Modern Art, 1949.

Béranger, Jean. *La Grande Aventure du Cinéma Suedois*. Paris, Le Terrain Vague, 1960.

Bessy, Maurice et Jean-Louis Chardans. *Dictionnaire du Cinéma et de la Télévision*. Paris, Jean-Jacques Pauvert, Vol. I, 1965; Vol. II, 1966; Vol. III, 1966.

Callenbach, Ernest. *Our Modern Art: The Movies*. Chicago, Ill., Center for the Study of Liberal Education for Adults, 1955.

Cameron's Encyclopedia of Sound Motion Pictures. Coral Gables, Fla., Cameron, 1959.

Clason, W. E. *Dictionary of Cinema, Sound, and Music*. New York, Van Nostrand, 1956.

Contemporary Polish Cinema. New York, Heinman Imported Books, 1962.

Cook, Olive. *Movement in Two Dimensions*. London, Hutchinson, 1963.

Cowie, Peter, ed. *International Film Guide*. Two volumes. New York, Barnes, 1965, 1966.

Dictionnaire Illustré du Cinéma. Paris Éditions Seghers, 1962.

Farber, Manny. *Manny Farber's America*. New York, Chelsea House, 1965.

Getlein, Frank, and H. C. Gardiner. *Movies, Morals, and Art*. New York, Sheed and Ward, 1961.

Graham, Peter. *Dictionary of the Cinema*. New York, Barnes, n.d.

Hardy, Forsyth. *Grierson on Documentary*. New York, Harcourt, Brace, 1947.

Huaco, George A. *Sociology of Film Art*. New York, Basic Books, 1965.

Hughes, Robert. *Film Book 1 and 2*. New York, Grove Press, 1959, 1962.

Jacobs, Lewis. *Introduction to the Art of the Movies*. New York, Farrar, Straus, and Giroux, 1960.

Kael, Pauline. *I Lost It at the Movies*. Boston, Little, Brown, 1965; New York, Bantam, 1965.

Lapierre, Marcel. *Les Cent Visages du Cinéma*. Paris, Éditions Bernard Grasset, 1948.

Lejeune, C. A. *Chestnuts in Her Lap*. London, Phoenix, 1947.

Leonard, Harold. *The Film Index: Volume I, The Film as Art*. New York, Museum of Modern Art, 1941.

Leyda, Jay. *Films Beget Films*. New York, Hill and Wang, 1964.

Lindgren, Ernest. *The Cinema*. New York, Macmillan, 1960.

MacCann, Richard D. *Film and Society*. New York, Scribner, 1964.

———. *Film: A Montage of Theories.* New York, Dutton Paperbacks, 1966.

Manvell, Roger. *Experiment in the Film.* London, Grey Walls Press, 1949.

———. *Film.* Baltimore, Md., Penguin Books, 1950.

———. *The Living Screen.* London, Harrap, 1961.

———. *What Is a Film?* London, MacDonald, 1965.

———. *New Cinema in Europe.* New York and London, Dutton/Vista Picturebacks, 1966.

———. *New Cinema in the USA.* New York and London, Dutton/Vista Picturebacks, 1968.

Mayer, Michael F. *Foreign Films on American Screens.* New York, Arco, 1965.

Montagu, Ivor. *Film World.* Baltimore, Md., Penguin Books, 1960.

Morin, Edgar. *Stars.* Tr. by Richard Howard. New York, Grove Press, 1960.

Nicoll, Allardyce. *Film and Theatre.* London, Harrap, 1936.

Powdermaker, Hortense. *Hollywood. The Dream Factory.* Boston, Mass., Little, Brown, 1950.

Renan, Sheldon. *An Introduction to the American Underground Film.* New York, Dutton Paperbacks, 1967.

Robinson, W. R., editor, with assistance from George Garrett. *Man and the Movies.* Baton Rouge, La., Louisiana State University Press, 1961.

Ross, Lillian. *Picture.* Garden City, N.Y., Doubleday, 1962.

———. *The Player: A Profile of an Art.* New York, Simon and Schuster, 1962.

Rotha, Paul. *Documentary Film.* New York, Hastings House, 1964.

Schary, Dore. *Case History of a Movie.* New York, Random House, 1950.

Schumach, Murray. *Face on the Cutting Room Floor.* New York, William Morrow, 1964.

Seldes, Gilbert. *Public Arts.* New York, Simon and Schuster, 1957.

———. *Seven Lively Arts.* New York, Barnes, 1962.

Shinde, M. K. *Dictionary of Cine Art and Film.* Bombay, Bhatkal, 1963.

Simon, John. *Private Screenings.* New York, Macmillan, 1967.

Sontag, Susan. *Against Interpretation.* New York, Farrar, Straus, and Giroux, 1966.

Stephenson, Ralph, and J. R. Debrix. *The Cinema as Art.* Baltimore Md., Penguin Books, 1965.

Talbot, Daniel. *Film: An Anthology.* New York, Simon and Schuster, 1959.

Telberg, Val G., comp. *Russian-English Dictionary of Science, Technology, and the Art of Cinematography.* 2nd ed. rev. New York, Telberg Book, 1964.

Vassal, J., *et. al. Cinéma Univers de l'Absence*. Philadelphia, Pa., Chilton, 1960.

Von Sternberg, Joseph. *Fun in a Chinese Laundry*. New York, Macmillan, 1965.

Weegee, and Melvin Harris. *Naked Hollywood*. New York, Farrar, Straus, and Giroux, 1953.

Wolfenstein, Martha. *Movies*. New York, Macmillan (Free Press), 1950.

Zinser, William K. *Seen Any Movies Lately?* Garden City, N.Y., Doubleday, 1958.

4. HISTORY

Agel, Henri, *et. al. Sept Ans de Cinéma Français: 1945–52*. Paris, Éditions du Cerf, 1953.

Anderson, Joseph L., and Donald Richie. *Japanese Film: Art and Industry*. New York, Grove Press, 1960.

Bardeche, Maurice, and Robert Brasillach. *History of Motion Pictures*. New York, Norton, 1938.

Borde, Raymond, and André Bouissy. *Nouveau Cinéma Italien*. Lyon, Serdoc, Premier Plan #30, 1963.

Crowther, Bosley. *Lion's Share: The Story of an Entertainment Empire*. New York, Dutton, 1957.

————. *Hollywood Rajah*. New York, Holt, Rinehart, and Winston, 1960.

————. *The Great Films: Fifty Golden Years of Motion Pictures*. New York, G. P. Putnam's Sons, 1967.

Cuenca, Carlos Fernández. *Historia del Cine*. 3 volumes. Madrid, Afrodisio, 1950.

Dickinson, Thorold. *Soviet Cinema*. London, Falcon Press, 1948.

Durgnat, Raymond. *Nouvelle Vague: The First Decade*. Essex, Loughton, 1963.

Eisner, Lotte H. *L'Écran Démoniaque*. Paris, Le Terrain Vague, 1967.

Everson, William K. *The American Movie*. New York, Atheneum, 1963.

Fenin, George N., and William K. Everson. *Western: From Silents to Cinema*. New York, Grossman, 1962.

Fulton, Albert R. *Motion Pictures*. Norman, Okla., University of Oklahoma Press, 1960.

Goodman, Ezra. *Fifty Year Decline and Fall of Hollywood*. New York, Simon and Schuster, 1961.

Haudiquet, Phillippe. *Nouveaux Cinéastes Polonais*. Lyon, Serdoc, Premier Plan #27, 1963.

Hendricks, Gordon. *The Edison Motion Picture Myth*. Berkeley, Calif., University of California Press, 1961.

Houston, Penelope. *Contemporary Cinema*. Baltimore, Md., Penguin Books, 1964.

Hovald, Patrice G. *Le Néo-Réalisme Italien et ses Créateurs*. Paris, Éditions du Cerf, 1959.

Jacobs, Lewis. *Rise of the American Film*. New York, Harcourt, Brace, 1939.

Knight, Arthur. *Liveliest Art*. New York, New American Library of World Literature, 1959.

Kracauer, Siegfried. *From Caligari to Hitler*. New York, Noonday, 1959.

Lauritzen, Einar. *Swedish Film*. New York, Doubleday (Museum of Modern Art), 1962.

Leprohon, Pierre. *Histoire du Cinéma*. Paris, Éditions du Cerf, 1961.

Leyda, Jay. *Kino: History of the Russian and Soviet Film*. New York, Macmillan, 1960.

Lindgren, Ernest. *Picture History of the Cinema*. Chester Springs, Pa., Dufour, n.d.

Low, Rachel, and Roger Manvell. *History of the British Film*. 3 volumes: Vol. I, 1896–1906; Vol. II, 1906–1914; Vol. III, 1914–1918. London, Allen & Unwin, 1948, 1949, 1950.

Malerba, Luigi, and Carmine Siniscalco, eds. *Fifty Years of Italian Cinema*. Rome, Carlo Besteti, 1954.

Marek, K. W. *Archeology of the Cinema*. New York, Harcourt, Brace, 1965.

Niver, Kemp R. *Motion Pictures from the Library of Congress Paper Print Collection, 1894–1912*. Berkeley, Calif., University of California Press, 1967.

Ramsaye, Terry. *A Million and One Nights in Hollywood*. New York, Simon and Schuster, 1964.

Richie, Donald. *Japanese Movies*. Rutland, Vt., Japan Pub. Trading Co., 1961.

———. *Illustrated History of Japanese Movies*. Rutland, Vt., Japan Pub. Trading Co., 1965.

Rondi, Gian. *Italian Cinema Today*. New York, Hill and Wang, 1965.

Rotha, Paul. *Rotha on the Film*. London, Faber and Faber, 1958.

———, and Richard Griffith. *Film Till Now*. New York, Twayne, 1960.

Sadoul, Georges. *Histoire Générale du Cinéma*. 5 volumes. Paris, Éditions Denoël, 1946–54.

———. *Histoire du Cinéma Français, 1890–1962*. Paris, Paris Club des Éditeurs, 1962.

———. *Histoire d'un art; Le cinéma des origines à nos jours*. Paris, Flammarion, 1949.

Siclier, Jacques. *Nouvelle Vague?* Paris, Éditions du Cerf, 1961.

Spinazzola, Vittorio, ed. *Film 1962*. Milano, Feltrinelli Editore, 1962.

Taylor, John Russell. *Cinema Eye, Cinema Ear*. New York, Hill and Wang, 1964.

Tyler, Parker. *Classics of the Foreign Film: A Pictorial Treasury*. New York, Citadel, 1962.

Wagenknecht, Edward. *Movies in the Age of Innocence*. Norman, Okla., University of Oklahoma Press, 1962.

5.   PRODUCTION

American Cinematographers Manual. Los Angeles, Calif., American Society of Cinematographers, 1960.

Anderson, Lindsay. *Making a Film*. London, Allen & Unwin, 1952.

Babitsky, Paul, and John Rimberg. *Soviet Film Industry*. New York, Praeger, 1955.

Baddeley, Hugh. *Technique of Documentary Film Production*. New York, Hastings House, 1963.

Clarke, Arthur. *Professional Cinematography*. Los Angeles, Calif., American Society of Cinematographers, 1964.

Conant, Michael. *Antitrust in the Motion Picture Industry*. Berkeley, Calif., University of California Press, 1960.

Duca, Lo. *Cinema Technique*. New York, Walker, 1965.

Eisler, Hans. *Composing for the Films*. New York, Oxford University Press, 1947.

Evans, Ralph. *Eye, Film, and Camera in Color Photography*. New York, John Wiley, 1959.

Feild, Robert D. *The Art of Walt Disney*. New York, Macmillan, 1943.

Gaskill, Arthur L., and David A. Englander. *How to Shoot a Movie Story: The Technique of Pictorial Continuity*. 2nd ed., rev. Hastings-on-Hudson, N.Y., Morgan and Morgan, 1961.

Halas, John, and Roger Manvell. *Technique of Film Animation*. New York, Hastings House, 1959.

Hitchcock, Alfred. "Film Production Technique" in *British Kinematography*, Vol. 14, #1, 1949.

Lean, David. "Film Director" in *Working for the Films*, ed. by Blakestone. London, Focal Press, 1947.

Levitan, Eli. *Animation Techniques and Commercial Film Production*. New York, Reinhold, 1962.

London, Kurt. *Film Music*. London, Faber and Faber, 1936.

Manvell, Roger, and John Huntley. *Technique of Film Music*. New York, Hastings House, 1957.

Nisbett, Alex. *Technique of the Sound Studio*. New York, Hastings House, 1962.

Nurnberg, Walter. *Lighting for Photography*. New York, Hastings House, 1956.

Offenhauser, William H. *Sound Motion Pictures*. New York, Wiley (Interscience), 1949.

Poncet, Marie Thérèse. *Dessin Animé: Art Mondiale*. Paris, Le Cercle du Livre, 1956.

Pudovkin, V. I. *Film Technique*. London, George Newnes, 1933.

————. *Film Technique and Film Acting*. London, Vision Press, 1959.

Riesz, Karel. *Technique of Film Editing*. New York, Hastings House, 1959.

Skilbeck, Oswald. *ABC of Film and TV Working Terms*. New York, Hastings House, 1960.

Skinner, Frank. *Underscore: Music*. Hackensack, N.J., Wehman Bros., 1960.

Spottiswoode, Raymond. *Film and Its Technique*. Berkeley, Calif., University of California Press, 1957.

Spraos, John. *The Decline of the Cinema: An Economist's Report*. London, Allen & Unwin, 1962.

Stork, Leopold. *Industrial and Business Films*. London, Phoenix House, 1962.

6. Scripts

Agee, James. *Agee on Film: Five Film Scripts*. Boston, Mass., Beacon Press, 1964.

Antonioni, Michelangelo. *Screenplays by Michelangelo Antonioni*. New York, Orion, 1963.

Bergman, Ingmar. *Four Screenplays of Ingmar Bergman*. New York, Simon and Schuster, 1965.

————. *Wie in einem Spiegel* (scenario of *Through a Glass Darkly*). Hamburg, Marion von Schroeder, #1 in Cinemathek Series, 1960.

Bluestone, George. *Novels into Film*. Berkeley, Calif., University of California Press, 1961.

Boyer, Deena. *200 Days of 8½*. New York, Macmillan, 1964.

Clair, René. *Schweigen ist Geld* (scenario of *Silence Is Gold*). Hamburg, Marion von Schroeder, #2 in Cinemathek Series, 1960.

Cocteau, Jean. *The Blood of a Poet*. Tr. by Lily Pons. New York, Bodley Press, 1949.

8½ by Fellini. Bologna, Capelli, Dal Soggetto al Film, #27, 1963.

Gassner, John, and Dudley Nichols. *Great Film Plays*. New York, Crown, 1959.

Il Grido by Antonioni. Bologna, Capelli, Dal Soggetto al Film, #8, 1957.

La Dolce Vita by Fellini. New York, Ballantine, 1961.

L'Avventura by Antonioni. Bologna Capelli, Dal Soggetto al Film, #15, 1960.

Lawson, John Howard. *Theory and Technique of Playwriting.* New York, Hill and Wang, 1960.

L'Éclisse by Antonioni. Bologna, Capelli, Dal Soggetto al Film, #23, 1962.

Marshall, Herbert, and Ivor Montagu. *S. M. Eisenstein's Screenplay: Ivan the Terrible.* New York, Simon and Schuster, 1962.

Resnais, Alain. *Hiroshima Mon Amour.* Text by Marguerite Duras. New York, Grove Press, 1961.

Robbe-Grillet, Alain. *Last Year at Marienbad* (film by Alain Resnais). New York, Grove Press, 1962.

Vadim, Roger. *Les Liaisons Dangereuses* (scenario from the novel by Choderlos de Laclos). Paris, Julliard, 1960.

The Virgin Spring by Ingmar Bergman. New York, Ballantine, 1960.

7. Periodicals

Cahiers du Cinéma (English edition)
635 Madison Ave., New York, N.Y.

Catholic Film Newsletter
National Legion of Decency, 453 Madison Ave., New York, N.Y.

Cinema
9641 Santa Monica Blvd., Beverly Hills, Calif.

Film: The Magazine of the Federation of Film Societies
81 Dean St., London, W. 1, England

Film Comment
11 St. Luke's Place, New York, N.Y.

Film Culture
G.P.O. Box 1499, New York, N.Y.

Film Facts
P.O. Box 53, Village Station, 150 Christopher St., New York, N.Y.

Film Heritage
Box 42, University of Dayton, Dayton, Ohio

Film News
250 West 57th St., New York, N.Y.

Film Quarterly
University of California Press, Berkeley, Calif.

Film Society Review
144 Bleecker St., New York, N.Y.

Films in Review
31 Union Square, New York, N.Y.
Green Sheet
522 Fifth Ave., New York, N.Y.
Motion Picture Herald
1270 Ave. of the Americas, New York, N.Y.
New York Film Bulletin
116 East 60th St. New York, N.Y.
Screen Education
Society for Education in Film and Television in the U.S., c/o School of Public Relations and Communications, Boston University, Boston, Mass.
Sight and Sound
Quarterly of the British Film Institute, 81 Dean St., London, W. 1, England
Variety
154 West 46th St., New York, N.Y.

APPENDIX B ⚬⚬

Glossary

Accelerated subject motion. A version of accelerated time achieved through the slowing down of camera speed so that, upon projection, the characters or objects appear to move at faster than normal speeds.

Accelerated time. An edited motion that contrives, via the juxtaposition of images, to compress less than sixty seconds to the minute so that action and place leap forward beyond normal expectation. *See* Jump-cut.

Animation. The arrangement of static drawings or objects so that when photographed they produce the illusion of movement.

Aperture. The orifice through which light is admitted to a lens. The diameter of the aperture in relation to the focal length and transmission of the lens determines its effective speed.

Aspect ratio. The proportion between the width and height of a projected picture and the screen that it fills. Thus the aspect ratio of a square picture would be 1:1, of a standard sound film 1.37:1, of Cinemascope 2.34:1, etc.

Background music. Subdued music accompanying speech, dialogue, sound effects, or other recorded music.

Boom. A crane-like device suspending a microphone in mid-air.

Camera angle. Angle of view subtended at the lens by the portion of the subject included within the picture area; designated "high angle," "medium angle," or "low angle"; also "wide angle."

Cinemascope. A proprietary system of wide-screen projection involving the use of anamorphic lenses. *See* Wide screen.

Cinerama. A proprietary development of cinematography that, by the use of three films simultaneously running through three projectors, makes possible the projection of a moving picture so wide that it extends in a broad arc from the extreme right of the spectator's field of vision.

Close-up (CU). Shot taken with the camera very close to subject, revealing a detail only, e.g., the head of a person. *See* Evaluation chart.

Continuous time. An edited motion in which the action alters in size and light but the pulsebeat is familiar; that is, the flow is normal and the temporal structure is familiar.

Crane shot. Moving shot taken by the camera on a specially constructed crane (traveling shot: horizontal, vertical, or diagonal).

Crosscut. An editing method to create parallel time and space, the juxtaposition of which permits the viewer to be in two or more times and places at once.

Cut. 1 (noun), The instant there occurs the joining of two shots for narrative, descriptive, or expository purposes. 2 (verb), To trim length of shots; to terminate a shot as the end of a camera operation.

Decelerated subject motion. A version of decelerated time achieved through the speeding up of camera speed so that, upon projection, the characters or objects appear to move at slower than normal speeds. (Slow motion is the opposite of accelerated time.)

Decelerated time. An edited motion that interrupts continuous time by slowing familiar temporal structures to 70, 80, 90 seconds per minute, thus stretching the moment, by repeating the ends of previous shots.

Dissolve. Gradual merging of the end of one shot into the beginning of the next, produced by the superimposition of a fade-out onto a fade-in of equal length.

Documentary. A fact film in contrast to a fictional film, utilizing material, actual or reconstructed, taken from real life.

Dolly. A vehicle on which camera and cameraman can be wheeled about during the taking of a traveling shot.

Dub. To re-record the sound track of a film by substituting, for the speech of the language originally used, a spoken translation in some other language.

Edit. 1 (noun), A cut, the juxtaposition of two shots. 2 (verb), To assemble a complete film from its various component shots and sound tracks.

Emulsion. Gelatin, containing silver bromide or silver chloride in suspension, with which cinematograph film is coated in order to make it sensitive to the action of light.

Evaluation chart. A method of identifying, analyzing, and evaluating all the components in a shot and/or an edit. *See* Appendix D.

Extreme close-up (XCU). Shot taken with the camera extremely close to the subject, revealing a minute detail, e.g., an eye of a person.

Fade-in. Beginning of a shot that starts in darkness and gradually lightens to full brightness.

Fade-out. Opposite of fade-in.

Flashback. Sequence in a film that takes the action of the story into the past. *See* Past time.

Frame. A single composition within a shot wherein space has been sharpened, and motion is implied or present.

Freeze frame. The ultimate in decelerated time wherein the flow of images is held on one frame that freezes all action.

Full shot (FS). Shot in which an object or figure is completely visible within the frame. *See* Evaluation chart.

Jump-cut. An edit that breaks continuity of time by jumping forward from one part of an action to another obviously separated from the first by an interval of time. *See* Accelerated time.

Kinescope. A proprietary form of telerecording; a cinematograph film record of a television program made by photographing directly from the cathode-ray tube of a television receiver.

Library shot. Existing shot from past film material available for use in another production.

Lighting contrast. The ratio of key light to filler light. Key light is designated by high key, medium key, or low key.

Long shot (LS). Shot covering a setting or landscape or large interior. *See* Evaluation chart.

Medium shot (MS). In general, a shot taken with the camera nearer the subject than for a long shot, but not so near as for a close-up. *See* Evaluation chart.

Montage. A type of accelerated time. A quick-cut assembly and/or superimposition of shots or sounds made to convey an impression, e.g., the passing of time.

Multiple exposure. Two or more exposures made on the same series of film frames.

Nontheatrical. Pertaining to film shows (especially on substandard film) that are not presented for public entertainment in ordinary cinemas.

Opticals. Dissolves, superimpositions, and such film devices made in the laboratory with an optical printer, such as a fade, dissolve, wipe, or special effects.

Pan. To rotate the camera horizontally in taking a shot from a fixed position.

Parallel time. Edited motion that enables the viewer to be in two or more places concurrently and also at two or more different times simultaneously. *See* Crosscut.

Past time. Edited motion which alters the flow of continuous time by cutting to a previous place and time. *See* Flashback.

Persistence of vision. Tendency of a visual impression to remain on the retina of the eye for a brief space of time (approximately one-tenth of a second) after the actual light stimulus is removed.

Phase. A unit of film space composed of several sequences unified by a period in time or history or by a place, such as a country.

Primary colors. In color cinematography, the so-called primaries are blue, green, and red, in which series the records are made on film by different layers of appropriately sensitive emulsions.

Print. A positive copy made from negative or master film.

Processing. Developing, fixing, washing, etc., of film, carried out in the labs.

Reel. Roll of film, or the amount of film, that can be wound on a standard-size spool. A 2,000-foot spool is the commercial projection size. The 16 mm equivalent of the 1,000-foot reel is 400 feet.

Running time. Length of time a film will run when projected at its correct speed.

Scenario. Film story cast in the form of sequences and scenes. *See* Shooting script.

Scene. A unit of film time and space composed of shots so arranged as to express a minor dramatic climax or an expository statement.

Score. Music specially composed for a film.

Sequence. A unit of film composition composed of scenes that constitute a major dramatic climax or a major expository statement, and as such corresponds to an act in the theater.

Set. An erected formation of scenery; interior or exterior.

Setup. The position of camera, mike, lights, artists, etc., at any given moment; generally applied to the positions at the start of a shot.

Shooting script. Written content of an entire film in precise detail and separated into serially numbered shots.

Shot. A unit of film expression composed of "frames," the result of a single camera operation, its final length determined by editing.

Slow motion. A method of shooting with camera running over normal speed so that, in projection, the action will appear slowed down. *See* Decelerated time.

Special effects. Usually, trick camera work, such as stop motion; often involving models, miniatures, etc.

Spot lighting. Light sources that project a beam, the angle of which is variable, enabling the lighting to be focused. The majority of lamps in a studio are "spots."

Still (noun). Photograph of a scene from a film or frame from a shot.

Superimposition. Two or more shots photographed or printed on one piece of film.

Synopsis. A very brief form of treatment giving a bare outline of plot or other content of a film.

Take. One complete photographing of a shot.

Technicolor. A proprietary color process using three separate negatives within a special camera, registering the blue, green, and red elements respectively, although the projection point is a single position.

Telephoto. A very long focus lens assembly, permitting relatively close shots to be photographed at considerable distance from the camera.

Tempo. Impression of speed that a film makes, either by the rate of movement or the rhythm of the sound.

Tilt. To swing the camera in the vertical plane up or down.

Title. Lettering on the screen, of an introductory or explanatory nature, not being an insert.

Tracking shot. Shot taken with the camera moving sideways, forward, or backward.

Treatment. Main content of a film written in nontechnical, literary form, but usually with sequences indicated.

Truck. A form of traveling shot, usually toward, away from, or in movement often parallel with, the object being photographed.

Two-shot (noun). Close shot of two persons filling the frame.

Wild shooting. Shooting the picture of a sound film without at the same time recording the sound of the action.

Wipe. Form of transition from one shot to another in which a line appears to travel across the screen, removing, as it travels, one shot and revealing another.

Zoom. A filmic device by which an object seems to close in upon the audience. Can be achieved by variable focus lens or in the optical printer.

APPENDIX C ✻

Fifteen Tests for Plastic Sensitivity, Visual Memory, and Visual Intelligence

NOTE: These tests are devised to discover the degree to which cinema is a visual language as well as to examine one's own affinity for the language. They should be repeated periodically, just as with chest X-rays.

TESTS FOR PLASTIC SENSITIVITY

1. Look at the room you are now seated in. Draw with pencil the corner before you, the two walls, the ceiling, and the floor. Include objects. You are to reduce the portion of the room as you see it from your perspective. Finally, enclose your drawing in a frame.
2. Now do a second version in color, using ordinary crayons.
3. Draw a human figure, head to feet, nude or dressed, male or female. Enclose in a frame.
4. Draw a face, profile or full, male or female. Enclose in a frame.
5. Draw a three-dimensional geometric pattern of any design.

TESTS FOR VISUAL MEMORY

6. Recall a scene from any recent film you have seen, and draw a single shot within that scene that impressed you the most. A single shot, being determined by a single camera operation, may have a beginning that differs from its middle or its end. Such are the cases in traveling shots—trucks, pans, and zooms. Identify the portion of the shot you chose: the beginning, middle, or end. Enclose in a frame.

7. Recall a scene from any recent TV program you have seen, and do the same. Enclose the shot in a frame.

8. Recall from either a film or TV a single edit, that is, the joining of two shots. You are more likely to recall a surprise cut, an image you hadn't expected to follow its immediate predecessor. Draw these two shots at the cut, which would be the end of one and the beginning of the other, and try to keep them in their original perspectives.

9. Draw a composition from any film or TV in which movement of any kind conveyed the major impact. Identify the type of movement: that is, Was a character moving, which is called "subject motion"; or was the scene itself moving either in a panoramic sense or increasing/decreasing in size, all of which are "frame motions"; or was it a combination of both "subject motion" and one or several "frame motions"?

10. Draw a composition from any film or TV in which light and shadow conveyed the major impact.

TESTS FOR VISUAL INTELLIGENCE

11. Identify and explain the *idea* (concept or purpose) behind your shot in Question 6.

12. Identify and explain the *idea* behind the TV shot in Question 7.

13. Taking your edit example in Question 8, identify the two *ideas* in the two shots. What made their juxtaposition so memorable? In a way, you will be explaining why you recalled the cut.

14. Explain how the major or dominant motion in your example in Question 9 relates to the *idea* behind the image. How or why did motion make the *idea* so effective you can recall it later?

15. Do the same for Question 10, using light and shadow instead of motion.

APPENDIX D ❧

Evaluation Chart

NOTE: This chart is a means of acquiring shot-consciousness, the basis for achieving an academic discipline or a professional point of view. It may be used in conjunction with classroom screening instructions, whereby students might recognize the cinematic inseparability of form and content.

FRAME, SHOT, EDIT (A & B) ANALYSIS

INSTRUCTIONS: Circle appropriate word and symbol. For edit example check the shots in juxtaposition as A & B and use different colors.

REACTION:

A. Total predisposition: favorable, unfavorable, indifferent.
B. General viewing conditions: comfortable, uncomfortable, distracted.
C. Shot or edit residue: pleasant, unpleasant, indifferent.
D. Shot or edit judgment: plus (+), minus (−), zero (o).

IDENTIFICATION:

A. *Spatial:*
    1. Size: XCU (eye), CU (head), MCU (shoulders), MS (waist), LMS (¾ shot), FS (feet), LS (setting), XLS (far).
    2. Light: HK (high key), MK (medium key), LK (low key).
    3. Angle: LA (low) ∨ , NA (normal, eye level) −·− , HA (high) ∧ .

B. *Temporal:*
   1. Subject motion (SM) : Accelerated, Normal, Decelerated.
Describe the action within the frame in one sentence:
   2. Frame motion (FM) :
     Pan is a contraction of the word "panorama." Traveling shots are executed by trucks, autos, cranes, helicopters. Zoom refers to the lens.

HORIZONTAL		VERTICAL	
PL (pan left)	←	PU (pan up)	↑
TL (travel left)	←	TU (travel up)	↑
PR (pan right)	→	PD (pan down)	↓
TR (travel right)	→	TD (travel down)	↓

DIAGONAL		IN—OUT	
TLU (travel left up)	↖	TI (travel in)	
TRU (travel right up)	↗	ZI (zoom in)	
TLD (travel left down)	↙	TO (travel out)	
TRD (travel right down)	↘	ZO (zoom out)	

   3. Edited motion (X) :
     1. Continuous time. 2. Parallel time (crosscut) . 3. Accelerated time (jump-cut) . 4. Decelerated time. 5. Previous time (flash-back) .

C. *Sound:* Balance or Imbalance.
   1. Dialogue. 2. Music. 3. Sound effects.

D. *Miscellaneous:*
   1. Camera movement: . . . . . 3. Overlap dissolve: ✕ 5. Fade-in: <
   2. Actor movement: ——— 4. Superimposition: ⊡ 6. Fade-out: >

REASONS FOR JUDGMENT (several sentences) —use other side.

APPENDIX E ✗✗

Sources for Film Rentals

For the convenience of those wishing to screen the films mentioned in this book, and which are available on 16 mm, a list is presented. Following each title an abbreviation refers to the distributor of that film. If there is no 16-mm distributor, the abbreviation N.D. is noted. Since the rights to films and their distributors may change, the periodical supplements issued by the Educational Film Library Association, 250 West Fifty-seventh Street, New York, N.Y. 10019, should be consulted. The distributors' list was compiled from *Feature Films on 16*, edited by James L. Limbacher, distributed by the EFLA.

LIST OF DISTRIBUTORS

Association Films, Inc. (AF)
347 Madison Avenue
New York, N.Y.   10017

Audio Film Classics (AU)
10 Fiske Place
Mount Vernon, N.Y.

Brandon Films (BR)
221 West Fifty-seventh Street
New York, N.Y.   10019

Carousel Films (CA)
1501 Broadway
New York, N.Y.   10036

Cinema 16 (CS)
80 University Place
New York, N.Y.

Consort-Orion Films (CN)
116 East Sixtieth Street
New York, N.Y.   10022

Contemporary Films (CF)
Mc Graw Hill Book Co.
330 West Forty-second Street
New York, N.Y.   10036

Continental 16 (CO)
241 East Thirty-fourth Street
New York, N.Y.   10016

Creative Film Society (CR)
14558 Valerio Street
Van Nuys, California   91405

Embassy Films (EM)
1301 Avenue of the Americas
New York, N.Y.   10019

EmGee Film Library (MG)
Glenn Photo Supply
3246 Veteran Avenue
Los Angeles, California   90034

Entertainment Films (EF)
850 Seventh Avenue
New York, N.Y.   10019

Film Classic Exchange (FC)
1926 S. Vermont Avenue
Los Angeles, California   90007

Film-Maker's Cooperative (FM)
175 Lexington Avenue
New York, N.Y.   10016

Films Incorporated (FI)
1150 Wilmette Avenue
Wilmette, Illinois   60091

Films of India
109 S. Edinburgh Avenue
Hollywood, California   90048

GO Pictures (GO)
37 W. Fifty-seventh Street
New York, N.Y.   10019

Harrison Pictures (HA)
1501 Broadway
New York, N.Y.   10036

Hoffberg Productions (HO)
261 West Forty-fourth Street
New York, N.Y.   10018

Ideal Pictures (IP)
1010 Church Street
Evanston, Illinois   60201

Institutional Cinema Service (IC)
29 East Tenth Street
New York, N.Y.   10003

International Films Bureau (IF)
332 S. Michigan Avenue
Chicago, Illinois   60604

Irving Lesser Enterprises (IL)
527 Madison Avenue
New York, N.Y.   10022

Janus Film Library (JF)
24 West Fifty-eighth Street
New York, N.Y.

Modern Sound Pictures (MP)
1410 Howard Street
Omaha, Nebraska   68102

Museum of Modern Art Film Library (MA)
11 West Fifty-third Street
New York, N.Y.   10019

Pictura Films (PI)
41 Union Square West
New York, N.Y.   10003

Royal 16 Films International (RF)
711 Fifth Avenue
New York, N.Y.   10022

Standard Film Service (SF)
21702 Grand River
Detroit, Michigan   48219

Sterling Educational Films (ST)
241 East Thirty-fourth Street
New York, N.Y.   10016

Swank Motion Pictures, Inc. (SW)
621 N. Skinker Boulevard
St. Louis, Missouri   63130

Trans-World Films (TW)
332 S. Michigan Avenue
Chicago, Illinois   60604

Twelvetrees, Inc. (TT)
125 S. Atherton Street
State College, Pennsylvania   16801

Twyman Films, Inc. (TF)
329 Salem Avenue
Dayton, Ohio   45401
United World Films (UW)
221 Park Avenue South
New York, N.Y.   10003

FILMS

Abe Lincoln in Illinois N.D.
The Adventures of Tom Sawyer CR
Alexander Nevsky BR
Alice in Wonderland CF, UW
All About Eve FI
All Quiet on the Western Front CF, CR, TT, UW
All That Money Can Buy (See *The Devil and Daniel Webster*)
Anna Christie BR, FI
Anna Karénina FI
Beat the Devil RF
Becket FI
Becky Sharp FC, IC
The Big Sleep BR, CF, TW
Birth of a Nation AU, MA, TW
Blood and Sand FI
The Bridge on the River Kwai AU, BR, IP, TW
The Bridge of San Luis Rey CF, FC, UW
Caesar and Cleopatra TT, UW
The Caine Mutiny AU, BR, CF, IC, MP, PI, SW, TF, TW
The Cat and the Canary MA
The Champion AF, AU, BR, CR, IC, IP, MP, PI, TF, TW
Un Chien Andalou MA
Citizen Kane BR, CF, FI, JF, MP, TW
Crime in the Streets CR, IP
The Devil and Daniel Webster AU, BR, IC, PI
Dial "M" for Murder N.D.
La Dolce Vita AU
Double Indemnity CF, TT, UW
8½ EM
The Emperor Jones N.D.
The End of the Affair N.D.
Executive Suite FI
Fahrenheit 451 N.D.

For Whom the Bell Tolls TT, UW
From Here to Eternity AU, BR, CR, IC, IP, MP, PI, TF, TW
Golden Boy BR, CR, IC, IP, PI
Great Expectations CF, CR, TT, UW
Greed BR
Il Grido CF
Hamlet CF, CR, TT, UW
Hamlet (USSR) N.D.
A Hard Day's Night N.D.
The Heiress CF, TT, UW
Henry the Fifth CF, TT, UW
High Sierra BR, CF
Hiroshima Mon Amour AU
How Green Was My Valley BR, FI
The Importance of Being Earnest CR, JF, TT, UW
The Informer BR, CF, FI, JF
Intermezzo BR, CF, SF, TF, TW
Intolerance MA
Ivan the Terrible BR, JF
Judgment at Nuremburg N.D.
Jules and Jim JF
Juliet of the Spirits EM
Kitty Foyle BR
The Knack N.D.
Lady in the Lake FI
Last Year at Marienbad AU
The Lavender Hill Mob CF, CR, TF, TT, UW
Les Liaisons Dangereuses AU
The Loneliness of the Long Distance Runner CO
Long Day's Journey into Night EM
Lord of the Flies CO
Lost Horizon BR, CF, CR, IC, IP, MP, PI, TF, TW
Madam Bovary FI
The Magician JF
Man of Aran BR, CF, JF
The Married Woman RF
Marty N.D.
A Midsummer Night's Dream BR, CF, FI, IC, IP, PI, SF, TF
Mildred Pierce BR, CF, MP
Moana of the South Seas MA
Moby Dick SF
Murder in the Cathedral N.D.
My Fair Lady N.D.
Nanook of the North AU, BR, CF

The Night of the Iguana FI
Nobody Waved Goodbye N.D.
Nothing But a Man N.D.
An Occurrence at Owl Creek Bridge CF
Odd Man Out CF, CR, TT, UW, JF
Of Mice and Men BR, CF, FC, TW
One Potato, Two Potato N.D.
Open City BR, CF
Ossessione N.D.
Othello CF, IL
The Oxbow Incident BR, FI
The Pawnbroker N.D.
A Place in the Sun FI
The Postman Always Rings Twice N.D.
Potemkin BR, CF, JF
The Private Life of Henry VIII BR, MP
Pygmalion N.D.
Quantrill's Raiders IP
Que Viva Mexico N.D.
Rashomon AU, JF
The Red Badge of Courage BR, FI
Red Desert AU
The Red Shoes CF, UW
The River (1936) CF, FI
Romeo and Juliet (1936) CF, FI; (1954) CF, TT, UW
Ruggles of Red Gap CF, MA, TT, UW
San Francisco FI
The Seventh Seal JF
Ship of Fools N.D.
The Silence JF
Soft Skin N.D.
The Spanish Earth BR
Splendor in the Grass N.D.
Stairway to Heaven CF, CR
A Streetcar Named Desire N.D.
Sunset Boulevard BR, FI
A Tale of Two Cities (1935) FI; (1958) TF, TT, UW
Things to Come IC, PI
Through a Glass Darkly JF
Tom Jones N.D.
Wuthering Heights FI

Index

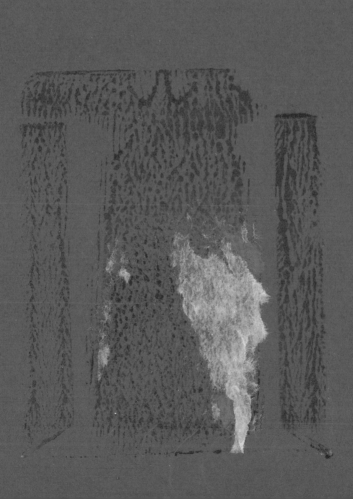